Using Spanish

This is a guide to Spanish usage for those who have already acquired
the basics of the language and wish to extend their knowledge. Unlike
conventional grammars, it focuses on those areas of vocabulary and
grammar which cause most difficulty to English speakers. It fully
illustrates the differences between the Spanish of Spain and Latin
America, and looks in detail at register variation. Complete with a full
word index, this clear and easy-to-consult text guides students through
the richness and diversity of this major world language.

   This new edition has been extensively revised and updated to take a
fuller account of Latin-American usage. The vocabulary sections have
been significantly expanded, and now include examples which
contextualize each word or expression. The presentation of many
sections has been improved to make reference even easier than before,
and some completely new material has been added on semi-technical
vocabulary and Anglicisms.

RONALD E. BATCHELOR has now retired from the University of
Nottingham, where he taught French and Spanish for forty years. He
has also held teaching posts at the universities of Besançon, France, and
Valencia, Spain. He has published ten books, including in this series
Using Spanish Synonyms, *Using Spanish Vocabulary*, *Using French* and
Using French Synonyms. He is currently working on *A Student Grammar
of Spanish*, also to be published by Cambridge University Press
(forthcoming 2005).

CHRISTOPHER J. POUNTAIN is Professor of Spanish Linguistics at
Queen Mary, University of London. He has held previous
appointments at the University of Nottingham and the University of
Cambridge, where he is a Life Fellow of Queens' College. He has a
long experience of teaching Spanish at various levels, and his previous
books include *Modern Spanish Grammar: A Practical Guide*, *Practising
Spanish Grammar*, *A Comprehensive Spanish Grammar*, *A History of the
Spanish Language through Texts* and *Exploring the Spanish Language*.

Companion titles to *Using Spanish*

Using French (third edition)
A guide to contemporary usage
R. E. BATCHELOR AND M. H. OFFORD
ISBN 0 521 64177 2 hardback
ISBN 0 521 64593 X paperback

Using Spanish (second edition)
A guide to contemporary usage
R. E. BATCHELOR AND C. J. POUNTAIN
ISBN 0 521 00481 0 paperback

Using German (second edition)
A guide to contemporary usage
MARTIN DURRELL
ISBN 0 521 53000 8 paperback

Using Russian (second edition)
A guide to contemporary usage
DEREK OFFORD AND
NATALIA GOGLITSYNA
ISBN 0 521 54761 X paperback

Using Italian
A guide to contemporary usage
J. J. KINDER AND V. M. SAVINI
ISBN 0 521 48556 8 paperback

Using Japanese
A guide to contemporary usage
WILLIAM MCLURE
ISBN 0 521 64155 1 hardback
ISBN 0 521 64614 6 paperback

Using Portuguese
A guide to contemporary usage
ANA SOFIA GANHO
AND TIMOTHY MCGOVERN
ISBN 0 521 79663 6 paperback

Using Arabic
A guide to contemporary usage
MAHDI ALOSH
ISBN 0 521 64832 7 paperback

Using Spanish Synonyms
R. E. BATCHELOR
ISBN 0 521 44160 9 hardback
ISBN 0 521 44694 5 paperback

Using German Synonyms
MARTIN DURRELL
ISBN 0 521 46552 4 hardback
ISBN 0 521 46954 6 paperback

Using Italian Synonyms
HOWARD MOSS AND VANNA MOTTA
ISBN 0 521 47506 6 hardback
ISBN 0 521 47573 2 paperback

Using French Synonyms
R. E. BATCHELOR AND M. H. OFFORD
ISBN 0 521 37277 1 hardback
ISBN 0 521 37878 8 paperback

Using Russian Synonyms
TERENCE WADE AND NIJOLE WHITE
ISBN 0 521 79405 6 paperback

Using French Vocabulary
JEAN H. DUFFY
ISBN 0 521 57040 9 hardback
ISBN 0 521 57851 5 paperback

Using German Vocabulary
SARAH FAGAN
ISBN 0 521 79700 4 paperback

Using Italian Vocabulary
MARCEL DANESI
ISBN 0 521 52425 3 paperback

Using Spanish Vocabulary
R. E. BATCHELOR
AND MIGUEL A. SAN JOSÉ
ISBN 0 521 00862 X paperback

Further titles in preparation

Using Spanish

A guide to contemporary usage

Second edition

RON BATCHELOR
Formerly of the University of Nottingham

CHRISTOPHER POUNTAIN
Queen Mary, University of London

CAMBRIDGE
UNIVERSITY PRESS

CAMBRIDGE UNIVERSITY PRESS
Cambridge, New York, Melbourne, Madrid, Cape Town, Singapore, São Paulo, Delhi

Cambridge University Press
The Edinburgh Building, Cambridge CB2 8RU, UK

Published in the United States of America by Cambridge University Press, New York

www.cambridge.org
Information on this title: www.cambridge.org/9780521004817

First edition published 1992. Reprinted 1994, 1995, 1997, 1999, 2002.
Second edition published 2005
Reprinted 2008

Printed in the United Kingdom at the University Press, Cambridge

A catalogue record for this publication is available from the British Library

Library of Congress Cataloguing in Publication data

Batchelor, R. E. (Ronald Ernest)
Using Spanish: a guide to contemporary usage / Ron Batchelor, Christopher
Pountain. – 2nd edn.
   p. cm.
Includes bibliographical references and index.
ISBN 0-521-00481-0 (paperback)
1. Spanish language – Textbooks for foreign speakers – English.
2. Spanish language – Grammar. I. Pountain, Christopher J. II. Title
PC4129.E5B32 2005
468.2′421 – dc22 2005046962

ISBN 978 0 521 00481 7 paperback

Contents

Authors' acknowledgements   *page* xviii
Preface to the second edition   xix
List of abbreviations and symbols   xx
Glossary   xxii

1   Introduction   1

1.1   The Spanish language today   1
1.2   Local variety and standard   1
1.3   Peninsular and American Spanish   2
1.4   Register   2
    1.4.1   R1   2
    1.4.2   R2   3
    1.4.3   R3   3
1.5   'Correctness'   3

2   Passages illustrating register and local variety   4

2.1   Example of R1* (Peninsular Spanish): *Un encuentro en la calle*   4
2.2   Example of R1 (Mexican Spanish): *¡Pélate! Que vamos al cine*   6
2.3   Example of R1 (Peninsular Spanish): *Cosas de críos*   7
2.4   Example of R1 (Argentine Spanish): from *Don Segundo Sombra*, by R. Güiraldes   8
2.5   Example of R2 (Peninsular Spanish): *Una agencia de viajes*   10
2.6   Example of R2 (Latin-American Spanish): from *Resumen*, Caracas, 12 August 1984   12
2.7   Example of R2–3 (Peninsular Spanish): *Intercambio de casas*   13
2.8   Example of R2–3 (Peninsular Spanish): from *San Manuel Bueno, mártir*, by M. de Unamuno   15
2.9   Example of R2–3 (Latin-American Spanish): *Viajando a través de la ciudad de México* by Jorge Larracilla   16
2.10   Example of R3 (Latin-American Spanish): from *El Comercio*, Quito, 2 October 1985   17

Contents

Part I   Vocabulary

3   Misleading similarities between Spanish and English   23

3.1   Similar form – different meaning   23
3.2   Similar form – partly similar meaning   33
3.3   Differences in register between Spanish words and their English cognates   48
3.4   Adjectives and nouns in Spanish   52
       3.4.1   Adjectives used as nouns   52
       3.4.2   Spanish past participles used as nouns   52

4   Similarities between Spanish words   55

4.1   Similar form – similar meaning   55
4.2   Similar form – different meaning   80
4.3   Similar verb stem   89
4.4   Words distinguished by gender   94
       4.4.1   Different gender – similar meaning   94
       4.4.2   Different gender – different meaning   102

5   Fields of meaning – vocabulary extension   108

       abrigo   108
       accidente   109
       acordar   110
       agujero   110
       lo alto   111
       amable   111
       anillo   112
       aparecer   113
       apariencia   113
       apoderarse de   113
       apresurarse   114
       arma (de fuego)   114
       avisar   115
       ayudar   115
       barco   116
       barrio   116
       basto   117
       borde   117
       botella   118
       brillar   118
       cara   119
       charco   120
       chirriar   121
       coger   121
       colina   122
       competición   122

contento   123
convertirse   124
cortar   125
crecer   125
cuarto   126
cuerda   127
culo   128
dar   128
decir   129
dejar   129
delgado   130
delito   131
derrotar   131
destruir   132
dibujo   133
diente   133
dinero   134
disparar   134
disputa   135
divertirse   136
empezar   136
encontrar   137
enfadarse   138
enfrentarse (a)   138
engañar   139
engaño   139
enseñar   140
enviar   141
espalda(s)   141
estropear   141
estupendo   142
fila   142
fuego   143
fuerte   143
gafas   144
golpear   144
gordo   145
gracioso   146
grupo   146
hermoso   147
intentar   147
investigar   148
jefe   149
lado   150
lengua   150
letrero   151
levantar   151
listo   151

lleno   152
llevar   153
malgastar   154
malhechor   154
mejora   155
modelo   155
molestar   156
muchacho/a   157
nativo   157
nombre   158
ocurrir   158
orgulloso   159
palo   160
pared   160
pedir   161
pelo   161
pelota   162
pensar   162
perezoso   163
piedra   164
pobre   164
poner   165
profesor   165
rebelarse   166
regalo   166
rico   167
rincón   167
robar   168
rodaja   168
romper   169
saber   169
salvaje   170
sonidos emitidos por los animales   170
subir   171
sucio   172
sueldo   173
suerte   174
talón   174
terco   175
tienda   175
tirar   176
tirarse   176
tonto   177
tormenta   177
trabajo   178
triste   178
vacaciones   179

valiente   180
vaso   180
ventana   181
ver   181
viaje   182
vidrio   182
viejo   183
viento   183

6   Complex verbal expressions   184

6.1   A complex expression in Spanish corresponding to a single verb in English   184
6.2   A single verb in Spanish corresponding to a complex expression in English   185
6.3   Common complex expressions in Spanish corresponding to complex expressions in English   188
6.4   Spanish verbs which take an infinitive as their subject   189
6.5   Reflexive verbs + **la** or **las**   190

7   Affective suffixes   192

8   Idioms, similes and proverbs   195

8.1   Idioms   195
8.2   Some idioms based on colour   201
8.3   Some idioms based on numbers   202
8.4   Similes based on adjectives   203
8.5   Similes based on verbs   204
8.6   Proverbs and proverbial expressions   204

9   Proper names   207

9.1   Names of people   207
    9.1.1   The Ancient Greek world   207
    9.1.2   The Ancient Roman world   208
    9.1.3   The Bible: Old Testment   208
    9.1.4   The Bible: New Testament   209
    9.1.5   People in the medieval and Renaisance world   209
9.2   Names of places   209
    9.2.1   Europe   209
    9.2.2   Asia   211
    9.2.3   Africa   211
    9.2.4   North America   211
    9.2.5   South America   212
9.3   Names of rivers   212
9.4   Names of mountains and volcanoes   212

Contents

10   Adjectives pertaining to countries and towns   213

10.1   España   213
        10.1.1 Regions   213
        10.1.2 Towns   214
        10.1.3 Islands   214
10.2   América Latina / Latinoamérica   214
10.3   Europa   216
10.4   África   217
10.5   Asia y Australia   218
10.6   Oriente Medio   219
10.7   América del Norte   219

11   Abbreviations   220

11.1   Abbreviations of titles and common words   220
11.2   Abbreviations of weights and measures   222
11.3   Abbreviations of major national and international
        organizations   223
11.4   Other abbreviations from Spanish-speaking countries   224
11.5   Truncated words   226

12   Latin expressions   227

13   Anglicisms   229

14   Grammatical terms   233

15   Interjections   235

16   Fillers   237

17   Transition words   239

18   Numerals   241

19   Measurements   242

19.1   Length   242
19.2   Weight   243
19.3   Area   244
19.4   Volume   244
19.5   Temperature   245
19.6   Time   245
19.7   Currencies   246
19.8   Traditional measurements   246

20   Semi-technical vocabulary   247

20.1   Banking   247
        20.1.1   Buildings, people and things   247
        20.1.2   Opening an account   248
        20.1.3   Accounts: types of account   248

20.1.4   Accounts: cheques (Brit), checks (US), etc   248
20.1.5   Accounts: management   249
20.1.6   Saving   249
20.1.7   Cash   249
20.1.8   Changing money   250
20.1.9   Loans   250
20.1.10   Investment   251
20.2   The Stock Exchange   251
20.2.1   Buildings, people and activities   251
20.2.2   Stocks and shares   252
20.2.3   Market activity   252
20.2.4   Speculation   253
20.2.5   Takeovers   253
20.3   Commerce   253
20.3.1   General   253
20.3.2   Production and distribution   253
20.3.3   Marketing   254
20.3.4   Prices   254
20.3.5   Finance   255
20.3.5.1   General   255
20.3.5.2   Bills and payment   255
20.3.5.3   Debt   256
20.3.5.4   Money   256
20.3.5.5   Credit   256
20.3.5.6   Interest   256
20.3.5.7   Profit and loss   256
20.3.5.8   Exchange   257
20.3.6   Salaries   257
20.3.7   Competition   257
20.3.8   The economy   257
20.4   Insurance (general)   258
20.4.1   General   258
20.4.2   Taking out an insurance policy   259
20.4.3   Terms   259
20.4.4   Claims   260
20.4.5   Different kinds of insurance   261
20.4.6   Home insurance policy   261
20.4.7   Financial planning and pensions   262
20.5   Tax   262
20.5.1   General   262
20.5.2   Types of tax   263
20.5.3   Filling in a tax return   264
20.5.4   Assessment   265
20.5.5   Taxation policy   266
20.6   Social Security   267
20.6.1   General   267
20.6.2   People   267

        20.6.3   Benefits   267
        20.6.4   Assessment   268
        20.6.5   Policy   269
        20.6.6   Charitable work   269
 20.7   Justice   270
        20.7.1   General   270
        20.7.2   People   270
        20.7.3   Crimes   271
        20.7.4   Investigation and apprehension   271
        20.7.5   Courts   272
        20.7.6   Proceedings   273
        20.7.7   Verdict and sentencing   274
        20.7.8   Punishments   275
        20.7.9   Policy   276
 20.8   Computing   276
        20.8.1   General   276
        20.8.2   System   277
        20.8.3   Hardware and peripherals   277
        20.8.4   Display, keyboard and mouse   278
        20.8.5   Files   279
        20.8.6   Programs   279
        20.8.7   Internet   279
        20.8.8   Word processing   280
        20.8.9   Graphics and fax   280
        20.8.10   E-mail   280

Part II   Grammar

 21   Gender   283

 21.1   Gender and sex   283
 21.2   Gender associated with types of noun   284
 21.3   Gender associated with noun ending   284
 21.4   Gender of compound nouns   286
 21.5   Adjectives as nouns   286
 21.6   Words of varying gender   287
 21.7   Names of towns   288
 21.8   Formation of masculine/feminine pairs   288
 21.9   Family relations and titles   289
 21.10   The neuter   290
 21.11   Homonyms distinguished by gender   290
 21.12   Problem genders   292

 22   Number   296

 22.1   Formation of plurals   296
 22.2   Some Spanish plurals which correspond to English singulars   298

22.3   Some Spanish singulars which correspond to English plurals   299
22.4   Number concord   300

23   Word order   301

23.1   Subject and verb   301
23.2   Subject, verb and object   302
23.3   Verb, objects and adverb   303
23.4   Noun and adjective   303
    23.4.1   One adjective   303
23.5   Numerals, quantifiers and **otro**   307
23.6   Fixed order expressions   307

24   Prepositions   308

24.1   **a**   308
    24.1.1   Basic meanings   308
    24.1.2   **a** in time expressions   308
    24.1.3   **a** expressing rate   309
    24.1.4   **a** expressing manner   310
    24.1.5   Adverbial idioms with **a**   310
    24.1.6   **a** expressing position   312
    24.1.7   **a** expressing instrument   313
    24.1.8   Complex prepositional expressions with **a**   313
    24.1.9   'Personal' **a**   313
24.2   **ante**, **delante de**, **antes de**, **antes que**   316
24.3   **bajo**, **debajo de**   316
24.4   **con**   317
    24.4.1   Basic meanings   317
    24.4.2   **con** in complex prepositional expressions   317
    24.4.3   **con** expressing manner   317
24.5   **contra**, **en contra de**   318
24.6   **de**   318
    24.6.1   Basic meanings   318
    24.6.2   **de** in adverbial expressions of time   320
    24.6.3   **de** in adverbial expressions of position   320
    24.6.4   **de** in expressions of price and measurement   320
    24.6.5   **de** with professions   321
    24.6.6   **de** in adverbial expressions of manner   321
    24.6.7   Common idioms and expressions involving **de**   321
    24.6.8   **de** expressing direction to or from   322
    24.6.9   'Grammatical' uses of **de**   322
    24.6.10   Complex prepositions with **de**   323
24.7   **desde**   323
24.8   **en**   324
    24.8.1   Basic meanings   324
    24.8.2   **en** in expressions of measurement   325
    24.8.3   **en** indicating material   325

24.8.4 **en**, corresponding to English *from*, with nouns indicating receptacles 326

24.8.5 Common idioms and expressions involving **en** 326

24.9 **encima de** 327

24.10 **enfrente de**, **frente a** 327

24.11 **hacia** 328

24.12 **hasta** 328

24.13 **para** and **por** 329

24.13.1 Basic meanings 329

24.13.2 **para** and **por** in time expressions 330

24.13.3 Other uses of **para** 331

24.13.4 **por** expressing rate 331

24.13.5 **por** expressing agent 331

24.13.6 **por** in expressions of manner and means 331

24.13.7 **por** in adverbial idioms of manner 331

24.13.8 **por** with other prepositions 332

24.13.9 Complex prepositions with **por** 332

24.14 **sin** 332

24.15 **sobre** 333

24.16 **tras**, **detrás de**, **después de**, **después que** 333

24.17 **a través de** 334

24.18 Accumulation of prepositions 335

25 Prepositional constructions with verbs, nouns and adjectives 336

25.1 Verbs with no preposition before an infinitive 336

25.1.1 Infinitive as subject of the verb 336

25.1.2 Infinitive as direct object 337

25.1.3 Verbs of ordering 339

25.1.4 Verbs of perception 339

25.1.5 Verbs of saying 339

25.1.6 Other verbs 340

25.2 **a** before an infinitive 340

25.2.1 Attainment and figurative motion 340

25.2.2 Verbs of beginning 341

25.2.3 Agreement 341

25.2.4 Encouragement, help or other influence 341

25.2.5 With verbs of motion 343

25.2.6 **a** for **para** and **por** 343

25.2.7 **a** + infinitive as imperative 343

25.3 **a** before a noun 343

25.3.1 Indirect object **a** rendered by a preposition other than *to* in English 343

25.3.2 Noun + **a** + noun 344

25.3.3 With verbs of smell and taste 346

25.4 **de** before an infinitive or noun 346

25.4.1 Cessation 346

25.4.2   'Negative' idea   346
25.4.3   Causation   347
25.4.4   'Advantage'   348
25.4.5   'Instrument'   348
25.4.6   With verbs of change   349
25.4.7   Other uses of **de**   349
25.5   **por** before an infinitive or noun   349
    25.5.1   **por** = *on account of*   349
    25.5.2   **por** = *by*   350
    25.5.3   **por** = *in favour of*   350
    25.5.4   With verbs and nouns of 'effort'   350
25.6   **para** before an infinitive or noun   351
    25.6.1   Ability and inability   351
    25.6.2   Sufficiency   352
    25.6.3   Persuasion   352
25.7   **en** before an infinitive or noun   352
    25.7.1   **en** corresponding to English *in, into, on*   352
    25.7.2   With verbs of 'persistence'   353
    25.7.3   With verbs of 'hesitation'   353
    25.7.4   With verbs of 'noticing'   353
25.8   Verbs followed by the gerund   354
25.9   Varying prepositions   354
    25.9.1   No preposition in Spanish: preposition in English   363
    25.9.2   Preposition in Spanish: no preposition in English   364
    25.9.3   Some prepositions which do not correspond in Spanish and English   366

26   Constructions with verbs of movement   368

27   Negation   370

27.1   General   370
27.2   Negation of adjectives   371
27.3   Negative pronouns, adjectives and adverbs   371
27.4   Expressions which require **no** before the verb   372
27.5   Other negative contexts   372

28   Use of tenses   373

28.1   Present tense (**hago**, etc)   373
    28.1.1   Present and Perfect   374
28.2   Future tense (**haré**, etc)   375
28.3   Future Perfect tense (**habré hecho**, etc)   375
28.4   Conditional tense (**haría**, etc)   375
28.5   Conditional Perfect tense (**habría hecho**, etc)   376
28.6   Imperfect and Preterite (**hacía**, etc; **hice**, etc)   376
    28.6.1   Imperfect tense: other uses   377
    28.6.2   Preterite tense: other uses   377

28.7   Perfect tense (**he hecho**, etc)   377

     28.7.1   Perfect and Preterite   378

28.8   Pluperfect tense (**había hecho**, etc)   378

28.9   Past Anterior tense (**hube hecho**, etc)   378

28.10   -**ra** tense (**hiciera**, etc)   379

29   Periphrastic verb forms   380

29.1   **ir a** + infinitive   380

29.2   **acabar de** + infinitive   380

29.3   **estar** + gerund   381

29.4   **ir** + gerund   381

29.5   **venir** + gerund   381

29.6   **llevar** + gerund   382

29.7   **tener** + past participle   382

29.8   **llevar** + past participle   382

29.9   **ir** + past participle   383

30   Modal auxiliaries   384

30.1   Obligation   385

30.2   Ability   386

30.3   Inference   387

30.4   Possibility   388

31   The Subjunctive   389

31.1   Sequence of tenses in Subjunctive constructions   390

31.2   Commands and related structures   390

     31.2.1   Direct commands   390

     31.2.2   Indirect command, request, necessity   392

     31.2.3   Suggestion   396

     31.2.4   Permission and prohibition   397

     31.2.5   Conjunctions expressing purpose or intention   398

     31.2.6   Other expressions of influence   399

31.3   Expressions of emotion   400

31.4   Expressions involving a negative idea   403

     31.4.1   Verbs and verbal expressions of denial and doubt   403

     31.4.2   'Negative' conjunctions   404

31.5   Expressions of opinion and thought   404

     31.5.1   Apparent negation   405

     31.5.2   Doubt or hesitation   405

     31.5.3   Emotional overtone   405

31.6   Expressions of possibility and probability   406

31.7   Hypothetical expressions   407

     31.7.1   Verbs and expressions of imagining and wishing   407

31.7.2   Conjunctions of supposition, provision and concession   408

31.7.3   Conditional sentences   410

31.8   Temporal clauses   411

31.9   Relative clauses   413

31.9.1   Superlative antecedent   413

31.10   Noun clauses   414

32   ser and estar   415

32.1   With nouns, pronouns, infinitives and clauses   415

32.2   With adverbs of place   416

32.3   With other adverbs   416

32.4   With a gerund   416

32.5   With a past participle   417

32.6   With an adjective   419

32.7   With a prepositional phrase   421

32.8   In isolation   421

32.9   Idioms with prepositions, etc   422

33   Personal pronouns   423

33.1   Order   423

33.2   Pronouns and verb   424

33.3   'Redundant' pronouns   425

33.4   Second-person pronouns   426

33.5   Third-person (including usted, ustedes) object pronouns   428

33.6   Personal pronouns expressing possession   429

34   The reflexive   430

34.1   Genuine reflexives   430

34.2   Inherent reflexives   431

34.3   The reflexive as a marker of the intransitive   431

34.4   The reflexive as an intensifier   433

34.5   The impersonal reflexive   435

34.6   Further notes on se   436

34.7   The reflexive and the passive   436

35   Comparison   439

35.1   Comparison of inequality   439

35.2   mayor / más grande, menor / menos grande   440

35.3   Comparison of equality   440

35.4   Comparison of clauses   441

36   Usage with names of countries   442

Index   443

Authors' acknowledgements

Second edition

We are deeply indebted to the following Spanish speakers for the endless hours they have given so indefatigably to us in our efforts to provide as accurate a picture as possible of the present state of the Spanish language:

Armando Lechuga Arribas

José Luis Ayesa Lacosta

Dr Jorge Larracilla

The perfection of the text would not have been attained without the keen and expert support of our copy-editor, Leigh Mueller. We would also like to thanks Mary Leighton and Helen Barton at Cambridge University Press.

First edition

Information for this book has all been collected from, or checked with, native speakers, and we are particularly indebted to the following for their generous giving of time and effort in this respect: José-Luis Caramés Lage, Teresa de Carlos, Carmen Melbourne, María Amparo Ortolá Pallás, Gaspar Pérez Martínez, Alfonso Ruiz, and innumerable students from the University of Valencia.

Richard King and Sara Palmer read the entire manuscript with an eye, respectively, to US English usage and Latin-American Spanish usage, and made many additions and amendments.

We would also like to thank Annie Cave, Peter Ducker, Julia Harding and Ann Mason of Cambridge University Press for their care, thoughtfulness and imaginativeness in bringing this material to the printed page.

Preface to the second edition

Since the appearance of the first edition of this book, the range of Spanish-language reference material has been transformed by a significant number of welcome additions and developments. Larger and more comprehensive Spanish/English bilingual dictionaries, based on huge electronic corpora and incorporating much information on register usage, have been published by Collins, Oxford University Press and Larousse; the *CLAVE Diccionario del uso del español* (Madrid: Ediciones SM) has brought the illustration of word meaning through contextual example to a fine art; substantial on-line corpora have been made available by the Real Academia Española (www.rae.es) and by Professor Mark Davies (www.corpusdelespanol.org), and the presence of Spanish on the Internet provides a wealth of linguistic information. We enthusiastically commend such rich resources. However, the purpose of this book remains what it was, that of providing a selective guide to areas of Spanish usage which we know through years of teaching experience pose problems for English-speaking learners, and we hope that, as such, it will be clear, easy to use and not too daunting. We have therefore retained the style and the bulk of the material of the original project whilst taking the opportunity to make some changes, additions and updatings. Some of the chapters on vocabulary have been completely rewritten and extended, and there are new chapters on anglicisms and on semi-technical vocabulary. We have continued to focus on vocabulary and grammar, and there is no systematic treatment of pronunciation or of essentially morphological features such as verb forms. However, the pronunciation of anglicisms is indicated in Chapter 13 using the standard characters of the International Phonetic Alphabet, and the gender of all nouns not ending in *-o* or *-a* is indicated in the vocabulary section of the book where it is not obvious from the context.

We gratefully acknowledge the many comments made on the first edition and look forward to receiving views on the second.

REB
CJP

Abbreviations and symbols

Note. Spanish alphabetical order is followed in lists of Spanish words and expressions.

ADJ	adjective
Am	Latin-American Spanish
Arg	Argentine Spanish
Brit	British English
Eng	English
esp	especially
f	feminine
fig	figurative(ly)
gen	general
ger	gerund (eg Spanish **hablando**)
indic	Indicative
inf	infinitive (eg Spanish **hablar**)
intr	intransitive
IO	indirect object (**a**^{IO} introduces the indirect object)
lit	literal(ly)
m	masculine
Mex	Mexican Spanish
N	noun
pej	pejorative
Pen	Peninsular Spanish
PERS	personal (**a**^{PERS} denotes the Spanish personal **a**)
pl	plural
PP	past participle
PREP	preposition
R1*, R1, R2, R3	markers of register (see pp 4–19)
refl	reflexive
sb	somebody
sg	singular
sth	something
subj	Subjunctive

tr	transitive
US	US English
usu	usual(ly)

= is used in Chapter 25 to indicate that the subject of the main verb in a sentence is the same as that of the dependent infinitive.

$\boxed{!}$ is used to indicate forms which are in regular use but which might be considered 'incorrect' in an examination.

---

† indicates that more information about the word or expression is to be found in another section. Look up the word or expression in the Spanish word index at the end of the book.

Glossary

The page number in brackets indicates where the term is first used.

adjectival complement (p 415) 'Copular' verbs, such as English *be*, Spanish *ser* and *estar*, are usually considered to take **complements** rather than objects. When these verbs are followed by an adjective, this may be termed an adjectival complement.

affective suffix (p 192) Spanish suffixes (eg *-ito, -illo, -ón*, etc) which have an emotive or ironic overtone.

agent (p 319) The performer of a verbal action: in an active sentence, the agent is typically the subject of the sentence; in a passive sentence, the agent (the subject of the corresponding active sentence) is usually introduced by *by* in English and by *por* in Spanish.

anteriority (p 375) An earlier stage.

aspect/aspectual (p 374) Relating to the way in which an action or state is viewed: continuous, repeated, within fixed limits, etc. The difference between the Imperfect and the Preterite in Spanish is usually thought of as an aspectual difference, though several other verb forms, and especially the **periphrastic** (see below) verb forms, have aspectual values.

cognate (p 23) English and Spanish have many words which are very similar in form, often because they are derived from the same Latin or Greek word (eg *sinfonía/symphony*). Such matching words are known as cognates. Although they are very often essentially the same or similar in meaning, they are sometimes different in meaning **(deceptive cognates)**. Deceptive cognates thus present hidden difficulties for the learner, and are traditionally known as 'false friends' *(falsos amigos)*.

complement (p 336) See **adjectival complement**. The term 'complement' is also used in this book to denote a sentence, infinitive or gerund which acts as the object or subject of a verb.

deceptive cognate (p 23) See **cognate**.

demonstrative (p 52) A pronoun or adjective which expresses proximity to or remoteness from the speaker (eg English *this, that*, Spanish *este, ese, aquel*).

diminutive (p 7) A form which indicates smallness (eg Spanish *-ito*).

disjunctive pronoun (p 423) A (personal) pronoun which is free-standing or the object of a preposition (eg Spanish *yo, mí, usted*). (In English all personal pronouns are effectively disjunctive.)

ellipsis (p 2) Partial expression of an idea.

falso amigo (p 23) See **cognate**.

gerund (p 19) In this book, the term is used to refer to the English verb form in *-ing* and the Spanish verb-form in *-ndo*.

homonyms (p 94) Words that sound the same although spelt differently, eg English *bow* and *bough*. Standard Peninsular Spanish has relatively few homonyms, but Latin-American Spanish has a number as a result of the absence of a *c/s* contrast, eg *cima/sima*.

impersonal verb (p 393) A verb which does not normally take a subject which refers to a person or thing. Impersonal verbs may have an infinitive or a clause beginning with *que* as their subject, eg *Te conviene contestar, No es de extrañar que se haya marchado*.

implied subject (p 336) A subject which is not explicitly stated by a noun, pronoun or the verb ending, but which is necessarily understood (eg in *Prometí hacerlo*, 'I promised to do it', *yo*, 'I', is not only the expressed subject – through the verb ending – of *prometer* but also the implied subject *of hacer*).

instrument (p 348) The thing employed to carry out an action: eg *hammer* is the instrument in *I hit the nail with the hammer*.

interference (p 23) The influence of one's native language on the foreign language one is learning.

metaphorical (p 290) Relating to metaphor, a figure of speech in which a thing, person or action is referred to as something else which it resembles in some way (eg *a pain in the neck* = 'a (person who is a) nuisance'). The boundary between 'literal' and 'metaphorical' meaning is sometimes difficult to determine because words often change or extend their meaning metaphorically (eg *a shark* = 'a rogue').

mood/modal (p 374) Relating to the attitude which certain verb forms express (eg *Serán las diez*, 'It must be ten o'clock', expresses supposition; *Me da un kilo de patatas*, 'Can I have a kilo of potatoes', expresses a kind of command). Traditionally, forms such as the Indicative, Subjunctive, etc, have been distinguished on the basis of mood, but it is clear that modal meanings can be expressed by most verb forms.

paronym (p 55) A word similar in form to another (in the same language).

periphrastic (p 380) Relating to paraphrase, and used here of structures in which a number of words are involved (eg *voy a ir* is described as a periphrastic future by comparison with the simple future *iré*).

pleonastic (p 412) Redundant, not strictly necessary (from the point of view of meaning).

positive imperative (p 424) An imperative which is not negated (eg English *Do it!*, Spanish *¡Hazlo!*).

topic (p 301) The element in a sentence which is currently being talked about.

truncation (p 2) Shortening or curtailing (of a sentence or word).

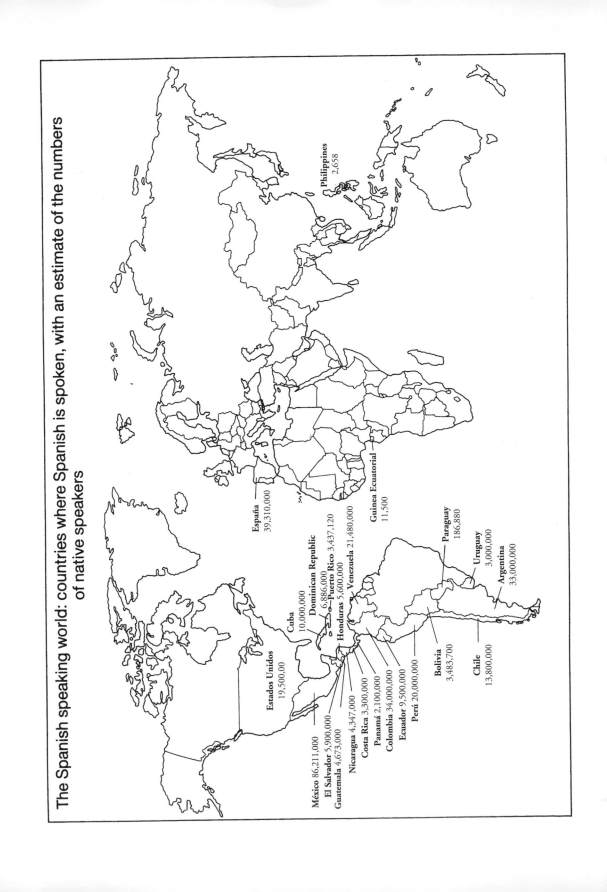

The Spanish speaking world: countries where Spanish is spoken, with an estimate of the numbers of native speakers

Philippines 2,658

España 39,310,000

Guinea Ecuatorial 11,500

Cuba 10,000,000

Dominican Republic 6,886,000

Puerto Rico 3,437,120

Honduras 5,600,000

Venezuela 21,480,000

Paraguay 186,880

Uruguay 3,000,000

Argentina 33,000,000

Estados Unidos 19,500,00

México 86,211,000

El Salvador 5,900,000

Guatemala 4,673,000

Nicaragua 4,347,000

Costa Rica 3,300,000

Panamá 2,100,000

Colombia 34,000,000

Ecuador 9,500,000

Perú 20,000,000

Bolivia 3,483,700

Chile 13,800,000

1 Introduction

1.1 The Spanish language today

There are currently about as many native speakers of Spanish as of English (around 350 million), and, with Spanish-speaking populations continuing to grow, it is anticipated it will remain the third most widely spoken language in the world after Chinese and English for the first half of the twenty-first century. It is the official language (or the principal official language) of some twenty nations, and is also widely spoken in the USA, where the rapidly growing Hispanic population is now the largest 'ethnic' group. The areas of Central and South America over which Spanish is spoken are enormous: for example, Mexico City is as far from Buenos Aires as Beijing is from London. It can quickly be appreciated, therefore, that the task of providing a guide to contemporary Spanish usage is a daunting one. The linguistic consequence of the diffusion of Spanish in the New World has been the appearance of many local differences in speech; and within Spain itself there are also considerable differences from region to region. At the same time, speakers from different areas are generally mutually intelligible, and the written language, while sometimes reflecting differences in speech, maintains a remarkable degree of uniformity which, because of the wide acceptance of a commonly agreed norm amongst the national Academias (see **1.5**), seems likely to last.

1.2 Local variety and standard

The Spanish standard is generally taken to be the speech of Old Castile. Yet it is immediately apparent that, if that is the case, more than 95 per cent of Spanish speakers do not speak 'standard' Spanish! In practice, the speech of any national capital or important regional centre tends to create its own 'standard'. An Andalusian or a Latin-American speaker would only under rather unusual circumstances adapt his or her speech and usage to that of the Castilian 'standard'. It is important to realize that in the Spanish-speaking world there is no stigma attached to speaking a local variety of the language. This can be rather difficult for

English (as distinct from British) people to appreciate, since standard English is not identifiable with any local variety, but is rather the variety of a particular socio-economic class; furthermore, speakers of the English standard tend to look down on speakers of local varieties of English (or dialects, as they are often categorized).

1.3 Peninsular and American Spanish

A major distinction is often drawn in reference works between Peninsular and American Spanish, and it is one which will be used in this book. However, it is in some ways misleading. First, although 'American Spanish' does have a number of general features, it is not really a homogeneous variety of Spanish: there are many differences in pronunciation and usage from region to region, even within the same country. Secondly, so-called 'American' features are often shared with local varieties of Peninsular Spanish, particularly with Andalusian.

Forms marked 'Am' (American) in this book are in fairly wide use in Spanish-speaking Latin America. Only the most striking of more localized usages (eg Arg, Mex) are given, and are marked accordingly. Forms marked 'Pen' (Peninsular) are not used commonly in Latin America. It is beyond the scope of this book to reflect finer details of local usage.

1.4 Register

Speakers employ a number of styles of language depending upon the situation in which they find themselves; even a single individual may regularly oscillate between a number of such styles, or registers. A formal letter to an unknown person, a chat in a bar, a scientific report – all call for quite different words and constructions, even pronunciations. Three basic registers, described below, are distinguished in this book.

1.4.1 R1

Informal, colloquial usage, characterized by slang expressions, vulgarisms, restricted range of general vocabulary and 'loose' syntax involving repetition, ellipsis and truncation. Vocabulary used is often ephemeral, since fashions in slang words come and go. R1 would probably be used in a conversation between family or friends. A special sub-register of R1 would be adults talking to children.

Within R1 we also distinguish R1*. R1* words and expressions are those generally considered indecent or 'taboo'; they often sound odd on a foreigner's lips, and a foreigner should in any case be very circumspect about using them. We make no apology for including such terms – they are among the most frequent in colloquial Spanish, and must be understood!

1.4.2 R2

The 'neutral' register: careful, educated speech, characterized by the absence of slang and vulgarisms, and by the use of full sentences. This is also the informal written language register. R2 would probably be used by a teacher and pupils in a classroom, in a radio or TV news bulletin, in a letter to a penfriend.

1.4.3 R3

Formal written language, characterized by 'officialese', archaic expressions, rarer vocabulary and often very convoluted syntax. There are many identifiable sub-registers, such as those used in journalistic writing, financial reports, legal documents, business letters, formal lectures and addresses, etc.

This division between the three registers is rough and ready, but it seems unnecessarily complicated to refine it more. In any case, a piece of Spanish and its constituent elements rarely fall into one register exclusively; and the vast majority of words and constructions (unmarked for register in this book) can be used in all registers.

1.5 'Correctness'

There are two senses in which Spanish can be 'correct'. The first relates to a foreigner's command of the language – if what is said is unacceptable to a native speaker in any variety or register, then it is 'incorrect'. The second relates to the native speaker's attitude to his own language, and is a more complex matter. In both the popular and educated mind, there is a close association between 'correctness' and the 'standard' language: features of local varieties and registers which differ from the 'standard' are deemed in this way 'incorrect' even though they are regularly used by native speakers. The Real Academia Española has traditionally been recognized, even outside Spain, as the guardian of 'correctness' in Spanish. The Academia has generally been sensitive to changes in the language, although inevitably many judgements on 'correctness' are essentially arbitrary.

The problem in presenting contemporary Spanish usage is that sometimes actual usage does not conform to the accepted view of what is 'correct' in this second sense. This is a book with a primarily pedagogical purpose, to be used by learners who will take examinations, and since the assessment of what is 'correct' is sometimes stricter in examinations than it is among Spanish speakers, we indicate such 'incorrectness' by the sign $\boxed{!}$. Forms and structures marked in this way exist and are in regular use, but are not to be copied by foreign learners.

2 Passages illustrating register and local variety

2.1 Example of R1* (Peninsular Spanish): *Un encuentro en la calle*

Pepe:	¡Eh! ¡macho!
Paco:	¡Joder! No te había visto.
Pepe:	¿Qué hay? ¿Cómo te va?
Paco:	Psa, tirando . . . ¿y tú?
Pepe:	Yo, me voy tirao tirao.
Paco:	Joder, ya será menos.
Pepe:	Quita, tío, quita, que estoy de una mala leche.
Paco:	Bueno, a ver qué coño te pasa ahora.
Pepe:	Que me se ha escacharrao el coche.
Paco:	No, ¿otra vez?
Pepe:	Otra vez, joder, otra vez.
Paco:	Mucha pasta.
Pepe:	Coño, no sé . . . jo, pero como sea mucha lo tiene claro porque hasta que yo no cobre el mecánico no ve un duro.
Paco:	Va, tío, olvídate. Esta noche me voy al cine con unas tías. ¿Te vienes?
Pepe:	Hum, no sé. Tengo faena.
Paco:	Pero que coño vas a tener tú faena. Pero, macho, de que vas. Si es esta noche.
Pepe:	Es que . . . no sé, joder, no sé.
Paco:	Pero coño, tío, si es un rato. No me seas cabrón.
Pepe:	Jo, tío, que plomo eres, pero ¿no te he dicho que no lo sé?
Paco:	¿Que tienes plan?
Pepe:	Te pego un telefonazo.
Paco:	Bueno, bien . . . Pero . . . jo, es que esta noche no ceno en casa. Mira, yo te llamo y te digo lo que hay.
Pepe:	Hecho.
Paco:	Sobre las nueve.
Pepe:	Muy bien, tío, nos vemos.

The R1* forms are: the expletives †**¡joder!** and its shortened form
†**¡jo!** (= *damn*, lit = *fuck*) and **(qué)** †**coño** (= *shit*, lit = *cunt*); the
nouns **tías** (familiarly=*girls*, though also=*whores or prostitutes*) and
†**cabrón** (lit=*billygoat*, but familiarly=*bastard*), and the expression **de
una mala leche** (=*in a foul mood*).

Apart from these R1* forms, the conversation has many features
which are typical of R1.

Pronunciation is not systematically represented here, but the
dropping of **-d-** in the **-ado** ending is widespread in speech, and is
often shown in the representation of R1, as here, in the spelling of
spoken forms (**tirao, escacharrao**).

Vocabulary and idioms

¿qué hay?/te digo lo que hay	*how are things? / I'll tell you what's happening*
(voy) †tirando / me voy †tirao	*I'm OK / things have got me down*
escacharrarse	*to break down*
†pasta	*money*
ser (un) plomo	*to be a bore*
tener †plan	*to have a girlfriend, have sth arranged (with sexual connotations)*
pegar un telefonazo	*to give a call*

Forms of address

- †**macho**, **tío**, used between men (= *mate, man*).

Syntax

- **me voy tirao / ¿te vienes?** In R1 the reflexive form of verbs of
  motion is frequently used. The reflexive has an 'intensive' value by
  comparison with the non-reflexive form (see **34.4**).
- **a ver** A very common imperative form (see p. 343).
- **me se** [!] **ha escacharrao** In standard Spanish, **se** is always the first
  pronoun in a sequence (see **33.1**).
- †**como sea mucha** = **si es mucha**
- †**hasta que yo no** [!] **cobre** NOTE: the meaning is *until I'm paid*; the
  no has no literal negative value. It is not used in standard Spanish.
- **pero / (de) que / es que / si** are all used in R1 as connectives.
- †**bueno** is an R1–2 connective which often introduces the answer to a
  question.
- **te llamo y te digo** The Present tense is used instead of a Future (**te
  voy a llamar, te llamaré**). See **28.1**.
- Note the elliptical nature of many of the remarks, eg **mucha pasta** =
  eso te va a costar . . .

2.2 Example of R1 (Mexican Spanish): *¡Pélate! Que vamos al cine*

Mario:	Ahorita vengo.
Teresa:	¿Adónde vas?
Mario:	A la farmacia. Necesito unas hojas de afeitar y un rastrillo nuevo. ¿Se te ofrece algo?
Teresa:	No, gracias. Ah, sí, se me pasaba: unas curitas y un paquete de algodón.
Mario:	¿Es todo?
Teresa:	Creo que sí. No te tardes, gordo. ¿Ya viste la hora? La película empieza al cuarto para las seis.
Mario:	¿Al cuarto? Tenemos que salir en diez minutos.
Teresa:	Ya lo sé. ¡Pélale!
Mario:	¿Y Susana? ¿No iba a lanzarse con nosotros?
Teresa:	Sí, dijo que se caería por aquí como a eso de las cinco.
Mario:	Tu cuatita es la impuntualidad con patas. Dale un fonazo a su chamba para ver si ya salió.
Teresa:	Bueno, pero ¡vuélale! Ya sabes que a esta hora el tráfico se pone de la cachetada.
Mario:	Sí, y para acabarla de amolar está lloviendo. ¡Qué lata! ¡Vuelvo!

It is in R1 that specifically regional forms of Spanish are most frequent and apparent.

Vocabulary and idioms

curitas	*plasters* (*Pen* parches, esparadrapo, tiritas)
rastrillo	*razor* (*Pen* maquinilla de afeitar; *Pen* rastrillo = *rake*)
¿se te ofrece algo?	*do you want sth?*
al cuarto para las seis	*at a quarter to six* (**Pen** a las seis menos cuarto)
¡pélale!/¡vuélale!	*get a move on!*
†lanzarse	*to go, come*
se †caería por aquí	*she would come here*
cuatita (*diminutive of* cuata)	*friend*
impuntualidad (*f*) con patas	*lateness personified*
fonazo (**see Chapter 7**)	*phone call*
chamba	*job, work*
se pone de la cachetada	*it's getting hopeless*
para acabarla de amolar	*and for good measure*

Form of address

- †**gordo**, used between men. (Women would consider **gorda** an insult: they use **flaca**.)

Syntax

- †**ahorita/cuatita** Diminutives which are widespread in R1 but especially common in American Spanish. In the very common **ahorita** the diminutive is attached to an adverb rather than to a noun.
- **no te** †**tardes** Reflexive corresponding to Peninsular non-reflexive. See **34.3**.
- **viste la hora?** The Preterite is used extensively in Mexican Spanish where a Perfect would be expected in the standard language.
- **en diez minutos** = Pen **dentro de diez minutos**

2.3 Example of R1 (Peninsular Spanish): *Cosas de críos*

Carmen:	¡María! ¡Chissst! ¡María!
María:	Huy, ¡hola! ¿Qué tal? ¿Cómo estáis?
Carmen:	Bien, estupendamente, ¿y vosotros?
María:	Regular, tengo a la nena pachucha.
Carmen:	Sí, chica, ¿qué le pasa?
María:	No, nada, que está muy costipada.
Carmen:	¡Vaya, mujer!
María:	Vino ayer el médico y le dio un jarabe porque se ha pasado toda la santa noche tosiendo.
Carmen:	No te preocupes, cosas de críos.
María:	Oye, pero es que me asusté un poco. Bueno, y tú ¿qué me cuentas?
Carmen:	Pues me voy al cole a hablar con el tutor de Carlos.
María:	Sí, pero ¿es que tenéis algún problema?
Carmen:	Mira, no sé. Dice que el niño no atiende, que está en la higuera. Vamos, que pasa de las clases, y oye, con siete años es un poco pronto para empezar a pasar de nada, ¿no te parece?
María:	Y él ¿qué te dice?
Carmen:	¿Carlos? Bueno, según él, pues que se cansa, que se aburre, que le duele la cabeza.
María:	¿Habéis mirado si tiene algo en la vista?
Carmen:	Ya lo creo. Mira, pasó las revisiones médicas en el colegio y yo lo llevé además al oculista y el niño ve perfectamente.
María:	Se le pasará.
Carmen:	Eso espero porque ya me tiene frita.
María:	Huy, mira la hora que es. Me voy, que se me ha hecho tardísimo.
Carmen:	Me he alegrado mucho de verte.
María:	Yo también. A ver si pasáis un rato a tomar café, o mejor aún veniros a cenar.
Carmen:	Venga, a ver si encuentro un rato y nos vemos tranquilamente. Yo te llamo.
María:	Muy bien. ¡Que no se te olvide! Recuerdos a tu marido.
Carmen:	Gracias, igualmente.

The R1 features covered in 'Un encuentro en la calle', and also found here, are not dealt with a second time.

7

Pronunciation

- **Costipada** $\boxed{!}$ reflects a common R1 pronunciation of standard †**constipada**.

Vocabulary and idioms

estupendamente	*fine*
†nena	*little girl* (= niña)
pachucha	*sick*
toda la santa noche	santa *is an expletive* (= *all the blessed night*)
críos	*kids*
¿qué me cuentas?	*what's your news?*
el cole	*Abbreviation for* el colegio. *Such shortenings are typical of R1.*
está en la higuera	*he's in a world of his own*
†pasa de las clases	*he's not interested in the classes*
¡ya lo †creo!	*I should say so!*
me tiene frita	*I'm sick and tired of him*

Forms of address

- **chica**, **mujer**, used to women by women or men.

Interjections

- This exchange has many interjections (Chapter **15**): **¡chissst!**, **¡huy!**, **¡vaya!** (invariable for person), **¡oye!**, **¡mira!**, **¡venga!** (invariable for person).

Syntax

- Note the 'highlighting' of the pronoun (see **23.2**) in **tú ¿qué me cuentas?** and **él ¿qué te dice?**

2.4 Example of R1 (Argentine Spanish): from *Don Segundo Sombra*, by R. Güiraldes

Y yo admiraba más que nadie la habilidad de mi padrino que, siempre, antes de empezar un relato, sabía maniobrar de modo que la atención se concentrara en su persona.

– Cuento no sé nenguno – empezó –, pero sé de algunos casos que han sucedido y, si prestan atención, voy a relatarles la historia de un paisanito enamorao y de las diferencias que tuvo con un hijo'el diablo.

– ¡Cuente, pues! – interrumpió un impaciente.

"– Dice el caso que a orillas del Paraná donde hay más remansos que cuevas en una vizcachera, trabajaba un paisanito llamao Dolores.

"No era un hombre ni grande ni juerte, pero sí era corajudo, lo que vale más."

Don Segundo miró a su auditorio, como para asegurar con una imposición aquel axioma. Las miradas esperaron asintiendo.

"– A más de corajudo, este mozo era medio aficionao a las polleras, de suerte que al caer la tarde, cuando dejaba su trabajo, solía arrimarse a un lugar del río ande las muchachas venían a bañarse. Esto podía haberle costao una rebenqueada, pero él sabía esconderse de modo que naides maliciara de su picardía.

"Una tarde, como iba en dirición a un sombra'e toro, que era su guarida, vido llegar una moza de linda y fresca que parecía una madrugada. Sintió que el corazón le corcoviaba en el pecho como zorro entrampao y la dejó pasar pa seguirla."

– A un pantano cayó un ciego creyendo subir a un cerro – observó Perico.

– Conocí un pialador que de apurao se enredaba en la presilla – comentó Don Segundo – y el mozo de mi cuento tal vez juera'e la familia.

"– Ya ciego con la vista'e la prenda, siguió nuestro hombre pa'l río y en llegando la vido que andaba nadando cerquita'e la orilla.

"Cuando malició que ella iba a salir del agua, abrió los ojos a lo lechuza porque no quería perder ni un pedacito."

– Había sido como mosca pa'l tasajo – gritó Pedro.

– ¡Cáyate, barraco! – dije, metiéndole un puñetazo por las costillas.

In this very famous novel of gaucho life, Güiraldes is concerned to reproduce the everyday language of the gauchos, and although written as long ago as 1926 it is still a convenient text with which to illustrate features of rural Argentine speech.

Pronunciation

- The **-d-** of the **-ado** ending is regularly lost: **enamorao, llamao, aficionao, costao, entrampao, apurao**.
- **d-** is also lost from **de** following a vowel: **hijo'el diablo, sombra'e toro, juera'e, vista'e, cerquita'e**.
- **f-** is pronounced very lightly, almost like English *h*, and is represented by **j-**: **juerte, juera**.
- **-ll-** is pronounced as **-y-**: **cáyate**.
- **i** and **e**, especially when unstressed, may be switched by comparison with the standard language: **nenguno (ninguno), dirición (dirección), corcoviaba (corcoveaba), perdir (perder)**.
- **para** is **pa**; in **pa'l** the **e** of the article is also lost.

Vocabulary

- There are many Americanisms:

†paisano	*peasant (= compatriot; civilian in Pen)*
polleras	*skirts, and hence women (= chicken coop; petticoat in Pen)*
rebenqueada	*whipping* (rebenque = *whip*)
maliciar	*suspect*
barraco	*pig (here a term of abuse)*

- Some words denote local things:

vizcachera	*burrow of a vizcacha (type of rodent)*
toro	*a cabin made of branches*
zorro	*not fox here, as in Pen, but skunk*
pialador (*m*)	*a gaucho skilled in using a lasso; the action is* pialar
tasajo	*jerked meat (ie meat left to dry in the sun)*

Syntax

- Diminutives are widespread here, not only with nouns (**paisanito, pedacito**) but also with other parts of speech (**cerquita**).
- **en llegando** This has only an R3 value in Pen (=*on doing sth*). NOTE ALSO **naides (nadie)** and **vido (vio)**, which are found archaically in Pen, and **ande (donde)**, which is found dialectally.

2.5 Example of R2 (Peninsular Spanish): *Una agencia de viajes*

Señora:	Buenos días.
Señor:	Buenos días. Un segundo, si es tan amable, y en seguida le atiendo.
	. . .
	Sí, dígame.
Señora:	Me gustaría que me diera información sobre los vuelos de fin de semana a Londres.
Señor:	¿Para qué fecha tiene prevista la salida?
Señora:	Bueno, pues lo más pronto que fuera posible.
Señor:	Vamos a ver, ahora lo consulto con el ordenador . . . Me temo que no va a ser posible para este fin de semana. Está todo completo.
Señora:	¿Y en el siguiente?
Señor:	Sí, aquí sí que hay asientos libres. ¿Cuántos?
Señora:	Cuatro, por favor.
Señor:	Muy bien, hasta aquí de acuerdo. Vamos con los horarios. El avión sale el jueves a las trece veinte y tiene la llegada prevista a las catorce treinta a Heathrow.
Señora:	¿El traslado al hotel corre por nuestra cuenta?
Señor:	No, habrá un autobús de la agencia esperándoles a su llegada para llevarles al hotel y les volverá a recoger el domingo para trasladarles al aeropuerto.
Señora:	¿Y el horario de la vuelta?

Señor: Salida a las catorce diez, llegada a las diecisiete veinte, hora local. ¿Ha estado ya en Inglaterra?

Señora: No, es la primera vez.

Señor: Ya sabe que tiene que personarse en los mostradores de Iberia con hora y media de antelación al horario de salida. Puede facturar hasta veinte kilos sin recargo por equipaje.

Señora: ¿Cuánto alcohol puedo llevar?

Señor: ¿Sin tenerlo que declarar se refiere?

Señora: Sí, claro.

Señor: Son dos litros de vino o uno de coñac o whisky y puede pasar hasta doscientos cigarrillos.

Señora: Bueno, pues yo creo que ya está todo, muchísimas gracias.

Señor: A usted, señora, y buen viaje.

This exchange contains some of the connectives which, as we have already seen, are typical of conversation in R1 (†**pues**, †**bueno**). But the speech of the people in this more formal situation is free of expletives and interjections, and is less prone to ellipsis. The need to be polite requires polite formulae, circumlocution, and vocabulary which is sometimes shared with R3.

Polite formulae

- **si es tan amable, me gustaría que** + Past Subjunctive, **me temo que** (see **31.3**), **por favor** (used much more infrequently than Eng *please*), **muy bien**, **muchísimas gracias**, **a usted**.

Circumlocution

- **¿Para qué fecha tiene prevista la salida?** = **¿Cuándo piensa salir?**; **¿corre por nuestra cuenta?** = **¿tendremos que pagarlo nosotros?** Such expressions 'soften the blow' of more direct expressions in making enquiries and giving information. Note how often expressions involving nouns rather than the corresponding verbs are used: **salida**, **horario**, **llegada**, **traslado**, **recargo**.

Vocabulary shared with R3 and 'officialese' in tone

- †**atiendo**, **personarse**, **facturar**, **se refiere**.

Form of address

- **Usted** is used here (but see **33.4**), and the formal **señora**.

2.6   Example of R2 (Latin-American Spanish): from *Resumen*, Caracas, 12 August 1984

Resumen:

Ha sorprendido mucho a la opinión, que un miembro de una organización que aparece ante la opinión pública como anticastrista, viaje a La Habana, y además los comunicados de la ODC (Organización Diego Cisneros) dicen que los ataques que ellos dicen recibir, son porque ellos son anti-comunistas. Luce como contradictorio que por una parte están furibundos, y por otra parte una persona que no vea nada de malo ir a Cuba con sus ejecutivos en su avión.

Oswaldo Cisneros:

Todos mis viajes han tenido un carácter familiar. Para nadie es un secreto que mi padre y la familia de mi padre eran cubanos y que yo tengo familiares allá a los que he tenido la oportunidad de ayudar en alguna forma cada vez que he ido. Cualquier otra interpretación es maliciosa y además en cierta forma risible. Ya aclaré con bastante amplitud en mi rueda de prensa del jueves, lo relativo a estos viajes. Sin embargo, como parece que a pesar de ello todavía flota en su mente alguna duda, déjeme aclarar que todos los días, por así decirlo, viajan a Cuba personajes de todo plumaje y color, sin que hasta el momento se haya tratado de estigmatizar a nadie por ello. Yo soy venezolano, demócrata y hombre de negocios, además que estoy convencido que únicamente se puede prosperar en un clima de libertades que definitivamente no existen en Cuba. Me fui a La Habana en mi último viaje y realicé allí una de mis habituales reuniones con mis ejecutivos, muchos de los cuales también tenían familiares allá. Sin embargo, el principal motivo de esta reunión en La Habana no fue la visita que cada quien hizo a miembros de su familia, sino mi interés más personal de que estos hombres, que manejan miles de trabajadores en sus operaciones diarias pudieran ver con sus propios ojos las proporciones del paraíso soviético-castrista. Lo demás es pura especulación.

The participants in this interview express themselves carefully: there is little difference between this style of speech and informal written style. Conversational connectives are few (we may note the emphatic **déjeme aclarar que** and the explanatory **por así decirlo**).

Vocabulary

- A minority of words used are perhaps more typical of R3 than R2:

†luce como contradictorio	*it seems contradictory*
furibundos	*furious*
con bastante amplitud (f)	*at sufficient length*
†realicé una reunión	*I held a meeting*

Form of address

- **Usted** is used; but notice how the interviewer refers indirectly to Cisneros (**un miembro de una organización, una persona**).

Syntax

- Complete sentences are used; there is no ellipsis. While some of the sentences are quite long, their structure is not unduly complex.
- **una persona que no vea nada de malo . . .** Movement of the 'topic' **una persona** (which properly belongs to the **que** clause) to the front of the sentence is typical of conversational style (see **23.2**).
- **estoy convencido que** Omission of **de** is frequent in Am R2.

Style

- Cisneros uses a metaphor (**flota en su mente alguna duda**) and his description of Cuba as **el paraíso soviético-castrista** is ironical.

2.7 Example of R2–3 (Peninsular Spanish): *Intercambio de casas*

Albacete, 7 de febrero de 1986
Distinguido Sr:

Me es muy grato dirigirme a Vd. en relación con el posible cambio de uso de mi casa de Lo Pagán, con otra de Nottingham de un colega suyo.

Mi propuesta consiste en brindarle el alojamiento durante un mes completo, cualquier mes del año, aunque junio, julio, agosto o septiembre son preferibles por hacer mejor tiempo. Junio y septiembre son más tranquilos, mientras que julio y agosto son más animados en el lugar.

A cambio, su amigo me solucionaría mi alojamiento familiar en Nottingham para 15 días de julio o agosto, pero para una familia de un matrimonio con ocho hijos.

Lo Pagán es un pequeño pueblo situado en la costa del Mar Menor que es un pequeño mar comunicado con el

Mediterráneo. Hay playas muy tranquilas en el mismo pueblo (a menos de 150 m. de la casa).

La casa tiene 4 dormitorios, un cuarto de estar espacioso, una cocina de buen tamaño, donde se puede comer, un cuarto de baño, un aseo, una terraza amplia a la calle y un tendedero interior. Está amueblada sin lujo, pero con comodidad suficiente para uso vacacional. Son utilizables hasta 11 camas, una de matrimonio. Su situación es muy buena para mi gusto, en el centro del pueblo viejo, junto a la iglesia, un cine al aire libre, con comercio muy próximo de todas clases. Hay aeropuerto (el de Murcia-Cartagena) a menos de 5 km.

Le envío alguna documentación gráfica de la situación del piso y de la propia finca.

Quedo a su disposición para aclararle cualquier detalle, espero sus noticias sobre el respecto y le saludo muy atentamente.

Formal letters, even from one private individual to another, as on this occasion, tend to include many R3 features.

The form of address used on paper is **usted**, since the correspondents do not know each other, even though it is likely that they would soon be using the **tú** form in conversation on meeting.

Letter-writing formulae

Distinguido Sr	*Dear Sir*
dirigirme a Vd.	*to write to you*
espero sus noticias	*I look forward to hearing from you*
le saludo (muy) atentamente	*yours sincerely*

Other polite formulae

me es muy grato	*I am pleased to*
quedo a su disposición (f) para	*I would be glad to*

Other R3 vocabulary and expressions

mi propuesta consiste en	*this is my proposal*
†brindar	*to offer*
solucionar	*to solve (lit); here, to provide*
mi alojamiento familiar	*accommodation for my family*
uso vacacional	*holiday use*
documentación gráfica	*here, a map or diagram*
sobre el respecto	*concerning it*

Notice how the register lowers to R2 as the owner describes the village and house in a style which he might well use in careful speech.

2.8 Example of R2–3 (Peninsular Spanish): from *San Manuel Bueno, mártir*, by M. de Unamuno

Ahora que el obispo de la diócesis de Renada, a la que pertenece esta mi querida aldea de Valverde de Lucerna, anda, a lo que se dice, promoviendo el proceso para la beatificación de nuestro don Manuel, o, mejor, san Manuel Bueno, que fue en ésta párroco, quiero dejar aquí consignado, a modo de confesión y sólo Dios sabe, que no yo, con qué destino, todo lo que sé y recuerdo de aquel varón matriarcal que llenó toda la más entrañada vida de mi alma, que fue mi verdadero padre espiritual, el padre de mi espíritu, del mío, el de Ángela Carballino.

De nuestro don Manuel me acuerdo como si fuese de cosa de ayer, siendo yo niña, a mis diez años, antes de que me llevaran al colegio de religiosas de la ciudad catedralicia de Renada. Tendría él, nuestro santo, entonces unos treinta y siete años. Era alto, delgado, erguido, llevaba la cabeza como nuestra Peña del Buitre lleva su cresta, y había en sus ojos toda la hondura azul de nuestro lago. Se llevaba las miradas de todos, y tras ellas los corazones, y él al mirarnos parecía, traspasando la carne como un cristal, mirarnos al corazón. Todos le queríamos, pero sobre todo los niños. ¡Qué cosas nos decía! Eran cosas, no palabras. Empezaba el pueblo a olerle la santidad; se sentía lleno y embriagado de su aroma.

Creative writers often manipulate register for stylistic purposes. In this passage, for instance, there is a striking oscillation of R3 and R2. To R3 belong the 'legalistic' resonances of the first paragraph, consistent with the deposition-like nature of its content: **esta mi querida aldea**, **que fue en ésta (aldea) párroco**, **quiero dejar consignado**. To R2 belong the parenthetical insertions of the fictitious authoress, which lessen the formal tone: **a lo que se dice, o, mejor . . . a modo de confesión, y sólo Dios sabe, que no yo**.

Other stylistic devices which belong to literary R3

- Imagery: **llevaba la cabeza como nuestra Peña del Buitre lleva su cresta**; **había en sus ojos toda la hondura azul de nuestro lago**; **traspasando la carne como un cristal**; the village began to **olerle la santidad**, and was **embriagado de su aroma**.
- In the first paragraph, mention of the writer's name, Ángela Carballino, is deliberately delayed so that it appears in the position of maximum stress, and hence of maximum surprise to the reader. **Mi** and **mío** are used in successive phrases which build expectations until the 'key' is given.
- The deliberately unexpected juxtaposition of **varón** and **matriarcal**.

2.9 Example of R2–3 (Latin-American Spanish): *Viajando a través de la ciudad de México* by Jorge Larracilla

La ciudad de México es una de las más grandes del mundo, y como en toda gran ciudad, el transporte es muy diverso y ofrece muchas opciones para viajar de un lugar a otro. Se puede viajar en automóvil, taxi, colectivo, camión, bicicleta, trolebús, moto, metro y tren ligero. La mayoría de la población hace uso del transporte público como el metro y los colectivos. Los vehículos más utilizados de manera privada son los automóviles y los taxis.

Caminar es una opción poco utilizada porque la gente normalmente requiere viajar grandes distancias. Sin embargo existen lugares que se disfrutan más cuando se viaja a pie, como Chapultepec, Coyoacán y el Centro Histórico entre otros. En esos mismos lugares se pueden usar bicicletas o patines dado que el acceso de vehículos motorizados está prohibido. Muy recientemente, en los lugares donde hay gran cantidad de tráfico, se han introducido los 'bici-taxis' que son pequeños carruajes para dos pasajeros, jalados por una bicicleta, al estilo oriental.

Es importante reconocer que desplazarse dentro de la ciudad de México usando bicicleta o motocicleta son opciones muy arriesgadas. El tráfico es muy intenso, no hay carriles específicos para estos vehículos y la gente no está acostumbrada a dejar los espacios necesarios para los mismos.

La forma más rápida y económica es el metro. Con un solo boleto se puede viajar de un extremo al otro de la ciudad. El precio es el mismo independientemente a la distancia que se recorra; pero eso sí, hay que evitar las horas pico si uno quiere evitar los empujones y los apachurrones.

Los colectivos se conocen comúnmente como peseros o peseras; son una alternativa complementaria al metro y de gran uso por la población de la ciudad de México. Existen múltiples rutas, circulan muy frecuentemente y son mucho más económicos que el taxi. Lo único difícil para los visitantes es conocer las rutas porque no existen mapas de las mismas; cuando uno quiere usar las peseras hay que preguntarle a un ciudadano o al chofer si esa ruta pasa por el destino que uno quiere visitar. Al igual que el metro, hay que evitar los horarios pico porque se tiene tumultos y empujones que pudieran ser desagradables para el viajero.

Los camiones y los trolebuses son los menos utilizados porque son más lentos y no pasan muy frecuentemente. Cuando se lleva prisa lo más conveniente es el taxi; siempre hay que buscar taxis de sitio.

Spelling

México is spelt with an **x**, though it is pronounced [ˈmexiko] as is the Pen spelling **Méjico**. The use of **x** in words of Amerindian origin (eg **Oaxaca**, **nixtamal** = cooked maize) has been adopted as standard in Mexico.

Vocabulary

There are a number of Americanisms in the field of meaning of transport:

automóvil (m)	*car (Pen* coche *(m))*
colectivo	*no real Pen equivalent: normally a minibus or car which has a standard fare*
camión (m)	*bus (Pen* autobús *or* autocar*)*
tren ligero	*suburban light railway*
bici–taxi *(m)* BUT NOTE bici *(f)*	*rickshaw-type taxi*
jalado	*drawn (the Pen form of this verb is* halar*, which is used predominantly in a nautical context; in Am* jalar *is much more widely used and corresponds here to Pen* tirar*)*
boleto	*ticket (Pen* billete*)*
horas/horario pico	*rush/commute hour (Pen* hora punta*)*
apachurrones	*pushing and shoving*
pesero/a	*minibus*
chofer	*driver (Pen* chófer *– note difference in stress)*
taxis *(m pl)* de sitio	*taxis available at stand/rank*

The vocabulary used is for the most part R2, although there are some items which verge on R3: **requiere** (**necesita** in R2), **desplazarse dentro de la ciudad** (rather than, amongst other possibilities, **recorrer la ciudad** in R2).

Syntax

There is nothing in the syntax of this passage that distinguishes it as originating from Mexico, reflecting again the homogeneity of Spanish at the formal cultured level. An R3 feature is the use of **los mismos / las mismas** to refer back to a noun already introduced, eg **no existen mapas de las mismas** (= **rutas**). On the other hand, the formula **pero eso sí** is more typical of colloquial R1 register.

2.10   Example of R3 (Latin-American Spanish): from *El Comercio*, Quito, 2 October 1985

Plausible desde todo punto de vista que la política agropecuaria implantada por el Gobierno tenga como metas específicas la producción de alimentos básicos para satisfacer la demanda interna y la diversificación y mejoramiento de los productos de exportación. Con lo primero se solucionará el problema de la escasez y el déficit de varios alimentos que inciden en la malnutrición de los ecuatorianos. Con lo segundo, el país obtendrá nuevos ingresos por concepto de la venta al exterior de frutos y materias primas que tengan acogida foránea por su calidad.

En ambos casos se estará contribuyendo positivamente a incrementar e incentivar la actividad agrícola que se vio afectada por varias circunstancias. Era necesario otorgarle toda la importancia que el campo ha tenido siempre en nuestro desarrollo y en el autoabastecimiento. Por desgracia, el Ecuador tuvo que convertirse en importador de productos que hasta poco tiempo atrás exportaba, con grave detrimento para la economía nacional.

Con satisfacción se ha venido anunciando que varios países se hallan interesados en adquirir flores, frutas frescas, hortalizas, varios elaborados, fibras y otros elementos utilizados en la agroindustria. Continuamente se suscriben convenios que tienen como fundamento estas transacciones e, igualmente, se buscan mercados para ampliar la venta de los mismos. Es así como ya se ha emprendido en la diversificación de cultivos cuya adquisición se ha asegurado. En este sentido, el trabajo rural conseguirá su justa recompensa que ha sido uno de los factores que venían desalentándolo.

As expected in a higher register passage, there is little in this text that is specifically Latin-American, with the exception of the expression **hasta poco tiempo atrás** (= Pen **hasta hace poco tiempo**).

Vocabulary

- The subject matter of the editorial necessitates a good deal of specialized R3 vocabulary from the field of economics (see **20.2** and **20.3**):

agropecuaria	*agricultural*
demanda	*demand*
de exportación (*f*)	*for export*
déficit (*m*)	*deficit*
ingresos	*income*
actividad agrícola	*farming*
desarrollo	*development*
autoabastecimiento	*self-sufficiency*
importador (*m*)	*importer*
elaborados	*produce*
agroindustria	*agricultural industry*
convenios	*agreements*
transacciones (*f pl*)	*transactions*
mercados	*markets*

- More general R3 vocabulary:

implantada	*introduced*
mejoramiento	*improvement*
†incidir en	*to affect*
por concepto de	*by means of*
foránea	*foreign (*= en el extranjero*)*
incentivar	*a neologism: to give incentive to*
†otorgar	*to grant*
detrimento	*detriment*
†se hallan	*(they) are (find themselves (lit))*
ampliar	*to widen*
†emprender en	*to embark upon*

Syntax

- Sentences are of medium length, though they contain many relative clauses. Many sentences are introduced by an adverbial phrase: **en ambos casos**, **por desgracia**, **con satisfacción**, **continuamente**, **en este sentido**.
- The first sentence has no main verb: **(Es) plausible . . . que . . .** , an R3 affectation.
- Journalistic and academic writing in Spanish is making increasing use of verbal paraphrases. Here **venir** + gerund (=*to keep doing sth*, see **29.5**) is used: **se ha venido anunciando**, **venían desalentándolo**. Use of this aspect makes the meaning of the verb more immediate and hence more distinctive.

Part I Vocabulary

3 Misleading similarities between Spanish and English

3.1 Similar form – different meaning

There are many pairs of Spanish and English words which are very similar in form but which are different in meaning. Such pairs are often known informally as **falsos amigos**.

Interference from one language to another is likely in these cases, and it is worthwhile giving special attention to them.

'Falso amigo'	English equivalent	English cognate	Spanish equivalent
actual	present	actual	**verdadero, auténtico,** †**real**
La situación actual es grave = The present situation is serious			
†**adjudicar algo a uno**	to award sth to sb	to adjudicate	†**juzgar, decidir**
El comité le adjudicó el premio = The committee awarded him the prize			
†**agenda** (f)	diary, appointment book	agenda	**orden** (m) **del día** (although **agenda**, an anglicism, is sometimes used)
Tengo que consultar mi agenda = I must look at my diary			
agonía	death pangs	agony (gen)	**dolor** (m) **intenso, angustia**
Sufría mucho durante la agonía = He suffered greatly in his death throes			
agonizar	to be in the death throes	to agonize (over sth)	**ponderar (algo) mucho, sufrir un suplicio (por algo)**
Estaba agonizando cuando llegaron = He was in his last moments when they arrived Nuestra civilización agoniza (R3) = Our civilization is crumbling			

'Falso amigo'	English equivalent	English cognate	Spanish equivalent
artífice (m/f)	creator, crafts(wo)man	artifice	**artificio,** [†]**estratagema** (m)

Fue el artífice de la victoria / del proyecto (R3) = He was the architect of the victory / the project

[†]**atender a**[PERS] **uno**	to attend to sb, to pay attention to sb	to attend sth	[†]**asistir a algo**

Me atendía la dependienta = The shop assistant served me

barraca	hut, cabin	barracks	**cuartel** (m)

El pobre vivía en una barraca = The poor fellow lived in a hut

[†]**bizarro**	gallant, generous	bizarre	[†]**extraño, estrafalario**

un bizarro soldado (R3) = a gallant soldier

bordar	to embroider	to board sth (transport)	**embarcarse en algo,** [†]**subir a algo**
		to board (= to give board and lodging to) (tr)	**hospedar**
		to board (to take board and lodging)	**hospedarse**
		to border on sth	[†]**lindar con algo**

un mantel bordado = an embroidered table cloth

NOTE: The PP is also used metaphorically in the sense of 'perfect; excellent': **Le salió un partido bordado** = He had a brilliant match; **Escribió un artículo bordado** = She wrote an excellent article.

cafetería	café	cafeteria	**autoservicio**

En la cafetería, el camarero nos trajo el menú = In the café, the waiter brought us the menu

carpeta	file, folder	carpet	**alfombra**

Guarda todos los apuntes en una carpeta = Put all the notes in a file

castigar	to punish	to castigate	**censurar, criticar**

castigar a un niño = to punish a child

casual(mente)	fortuitous(ly), accidental(ly)	casual(ly)	**despreocupado (de manera despreocupada)**

un hecho casual = a coincidence, a chance happening

caución (f) (R3)	guarantee of surety for sth	caution	**cautela, prudencia**

un seguro de caución = a surety

cava (f)	wine cellar	cave	**cueva, caverna**
cava (m)	sparkling wine		

Tiene muy buen vino en la cava = He has very good wine in his cellar
Es un cava seco = It's a dry sparkling wine

24

'Falso amigo'	English equivalent	English cognate	Spanish equivalent
†**cavilar**	to ponder	to cavil	**objetar, poner peros a** (R1)

Cavilaban sobre los problemas actuales = They pondered the present problems

collar (m)	necklace	collar	**cuello**

Lucía un hermoso collar = She was wearing a beautiful necklace

comando	commando group; terrorist group	commando	**integrante, miembro de un comando**
	(military) command (Am)	command (gen)	†**orden** (f), **mando**
	three-quarter-length coat		

Los soldados formaban un comando eficaz = The soldiers formed an effective commando group
un comando suicida = a suicide squad
El comando le protegía del frío = The coat protected him from the cold

comediante/a	actor, actress fraud	comedian	†**cómico**

Es una comediante nata = She's a born actress

comodidad (f)	comfort, BUT in Am = commodity	commodity	**artículo de consumo, mercancía**

Su situación económica le permitía vivir con comodidad = Her economic situation allowed her to live comfortably

compás (m)	beat, rhythm	compass (indicating direction)	**brújula**
		compass (for drawing a circle)	

Bailaban al compás de la música = They were dancing to the beat of the music
Con el compás tracé un círculo = I drew a circle with the compass

concreto	concrete (ADJ), BUT in Am = concrete (N)	concrete (N)	**hormigón** (m) (Pen)

en términos concretos = in concrete terms

conductor(a)	driver	conductor (on bus, Brit)	**cobrador(a)**
	conductor (of heat, electricity, etc)	conductor (on train, US)	**revisor(a)**
		conductor (of an orchestra)	**director(a)**
		lightning conductor	**pararrayos**

El conductor no vio acercarse la furgoneta = The driver did not see the van approaching
El oro es buen conductor = Gold is a good conductor

25

'Falso amigo'	English equivalent	English cognate	Spanish equivalent
†**confidencia**	confidential remark	confidence, trust (abstract)	†**confianza**
Te haré una confidencia = I'll tell you a secret			
congelar	to freeze	to congeal	**coagular**
congelar el agua (f) / **los sueldos** = to freeze water / salaries			
consistente	solid, thick (of sauce, etc):	to be consistent with	**estar de †acuerdo con, ser consecuente con**
salsa consistente, lona consistente		to be consistent	**ser coherente**
NOTE ALSO used metaphorically in the sense of 'solid, weighty, logical': **Fue un argumento consistente** = It was a solid argument.			
estar †constipado	to have a cold	to be constipated	**estar estreñido**
†**contestar**	to answer	to contest	†**negar, poner en tela de juicio**
No contesté a su pregunta = I didn't answer her question			
corpulento	tall, strong	corpulent	**gordo**
dato	piece of information (**datos** (pl) = data)	date	**fecha** (day) **dátil** (m) (fruit)
resumir todos los datos = to summarize all the data			
decepción (f)	disappointment	deception	†**engaño**
La derrota del equipo causó decepción = The team's defeat caused disappointment			
†**departir** (R3)	to converse	to depart	†**salir,** †**marcharse**
Los escritores departieron sobre el tema = The writers conversed about the subject			
desgracia	misfortune	disgrace	**vergüenza, escándalo** (event); **deshonra** (moral state); BUT fall into disgrace = **caer en (la) desgracia**
Tuvo la desgracia de caerse = She had the misfortune to fall down			
deshonesto	dishonest; BUT ALSO indecent, lewd	dishonest	**falso, tramposo**
un político deshonesto = a dishonest politician			
un acto deshonesto = an indecent act			
desmayo	fainting fit, faltering	dismay	**consternación** (f)
Con el golpe sufrió un desmayo = He fainted as a result of the blow			
destitución (f)	dismissal	destitution	**indigencia,** †**miseria**
la destitución de un obrero / del ministro = the dismissal of a worker / of the minister			

'Falso amigo'	English equivalent	English cognate	Spanish equivalent
dilapidado	squandered	dilapidated	**destartalado, desvencijado**
Ha dilapidado toda su fortuna = He's squandered all his money			
disgustado	upset, annoyed	disgusted	**enfurecido, repugnado, avergonzado**
Estoy disgustado conmigo mismo = I'm annoyed with myself			
disgustar	to displease, upset	to disgust	**repugnar, dar asco a**
Me disgustó la reseña = The review upset me			
disgusto	displeasure	disgust	**aversión, asco**
La noticia me produjo un disgusto muy grande = The news gave me great displeasure			
disponer de	to have at one's disposal	to dispose of	**deshacerse de, vender**
Disponemos de poco dinero = We don't have much money			
†**divisar**	to catch sight of	to devise	†**inventar**
Desde la cumbre se divisaba todo el río = From the summit we could see the whole river			
editar	to publish	to edit	**redactar (un articulo); corregir**
Editó su octavo libro = She published her eighth book			
editor(a)	publisher	editor	**redactor(a);** †**jefe/a,** †**director(a)** (head of paper)
El editor le pidió el manuscrito = The publisher asked her for the manucript			
embarazada (ADJ f)	pregnant	embarrassed	**confuso**
Estaba embarazada de tres meses = She's three months pregnant			
embarazar/ embarazarse	to make pregnant / get pregnant	to embarrass	**desconcertar, turbar**
Se embarazó antes de casarse = She was pregnant before she was married			
encuesta	enquiry, survey	inquest	**encuesta judicial**
Hicieron una encuesta sobre la calidad de vida del barrio = They carried out a survey on the quality of life in the area			
engrosar	to swell (tr); (refl) to increase in quantity or size	to engross (tr)	**absorber**
La venta de acciones engrosó su capital = Selling shares increased his capital			
La clase media se ha engrosado = The middle class has grown			
NOTE: **engrosar** can also be used intransitively, though the reflexive is more common. It is not normally used of people or animals: **engordecer** (intr) is used in this context.			
ermita	hermitage, ALSO chapel	hermit	**ermitaño/a**
Un ermitaño vive en una ermita = A hermit lives in a hermitage			

'Falso amigo'	English equivalent	English cognate	Spanish equivalent
escuálido	weak, skinny	squalid	†sucio, †asqueroso

Don Quijote tenía un aspecto escuálido = Don Quixote had a skinny appearance

eventual	possible; temporary, casual (of a job, etc)	eventual	†final

Hay que estar preparado para un eventual desastre = We must be prepared for a possible disaster
Mi contrato es eventual = My contract is temporary

†éxito	success	exit	salida

El libro fue un éxito = The book was a success

extenuar	to weaken	to extenuate	atenuar, disminuir

El calor la dejó extenuada = The heat made her weak

fábrica	factory	fabric (cloth)	tela, tejido

Todos los días voy a la fábrica = I go to the factory every day

fastidioso	annoying	fastidious	puntilloso, quisquilloso

Ese ruido es fastidioso = That noise is annoying

fracaso	failure	fracas	†riña, gresca

el fracaso escolar = failure at school

gala	full, best dress; elegance; variety show	gala	†fiesta, verbena (celebration); †competición, †certamen (m) (contest)

vestido de gala = dressed formally

genial	full of genius, inspired	genial	afable, cordial

Einstein fue genial = Einstein was a genius

guerrilla	guerrilla warfare; guerrilla band	guerrilla (fighter)	guerrillero

La guerrilla se enfrentó al ejército = The guerrilla group confronted the army

†hábil	skilful, clever; fit	able	capaz

un futbolista muy hábil = a very skilful footballer

hostal (m)	simple hotel	hostel	residencia (for students), albergue (m) juvenil (= youth hostel)

El hostal no tiene restaurante = The boarding house doesn't have a restaurant

incidencia	repercussion, consequence; BUT = incidence in a technical sense, eg **ángulo de incidencia**	incidence	frecuencia, ritmo

Sus palabras tuvieron mucha incidencia en la política exterior = His words had a great impact on foreign policy

'Falso amigo'	English equivalent	English cognate	Spanish equivalent
ingenuidad (f)	naivety	ingenuity	**ingeniosidad** (f)
Creer en los políticos es una ingenuidad = To believe in politicians is naive			
injuria	insult, outrage	injury	**herida**, **†lesión**
Lo que me dijo es una injuria = What she said to me is insulting			
†injuriar	to insult	to injure	**†herir, lesionar**
Las dos pandillas se injuriaron a gritos = The two gangs yelled insults at one another			
instancia(s)	legal process	instance	**†ejemplo**
La ley establece instancias muy claras = The law establishes very clear processes			
intoxicar	to poison	to intoxicate	**embriagar**
La comida estaba intoxicada = The food was poisoned			
†jubilación (f)	retirement, pension	jubilation	**júbilo**
Se discute mucho la edad de la jubilación obligatoria = The compulsory retirement age is much discussed			
largo	long	large	**†grande, extenso, amplio**
un camino largo = a long path			
lectura	reading	lecture	**†conferencia** (formal), **clase** (f) (gen in university, etc)
Procedió a la lectura del acta = He proceeded to read the minutes			
librería	bookshop	library	**biblioteca**
Compró el libro en la librería = She bought the book in the bookshop			
librero	bookseller	librarian	**bibliotecario/a**
Los libreros venden a los bibliotecarios = Booksellers sell to librarians			
lívido	pale	livid	**furioso, amoratado**
Tenía el rostro lívido = Her face was pale			
maniático	peculiar, cranky, neurotic	maniac	**loco, demente, maníaco**
Es un maniático de la puntualidad = He's neurotic about punctuality			
marrón	brown; unpleasant (R1)	maroon	**carmín**
Los troncos de los árboles son marrones = Tree trunks are brown			
†miseria	poverty, squalor	misery	**sufrimiento, pena, aflicción**
Vivían en la absoluta miseria = They lived in absolute squalor			
†molestar	to trouble, to annoy	to molest	**importunar**
El ruido me molesta = The noise is annoying me			
moroso	slow to pay; slow, sluggish	morose	**hosco, malhumorado**
Era un cliente moroso = He was a customer who was slow to pay			

'Falso amigo'	English equivalent	English cognate	Spanish equivalent
motorista (m/f)	motorcyclist	motorist	**conductor(a) (de coche)**

¡Ay, los motoristas que adelantan por la derecha! = These motorcyclists who overtake on the right!

muslo	thigh	muscle	**músculo**

El muslo es el músculo más grande = The thigh is the largest muscle

notorio	well-known	notorious	**de mala fama**

Era un actor notorio = He was a well-known actor

obsequioso (R3)	obliging, helpful	obsequious	**servil**

Es muy obsequiosa la conserje; siempre está dispuesta a ayudarme = The caretaker is very obliging; she's always willing to help me

†**paisano/a**	fellow countryman; civilian; BUT in Arg = peasant, farm worker	peasant	**campesino/a**

Carlos es un paisano mío: nacimos en la misma ciudad = Carlos is from the same area as me: we were born in the same town

El militar asistió a la fiesta vestido de paisano = The solider attended the party dressed as a civilian

parangón (m) (R3)	comparison, similarity	paragon	†**dechado**

No tiene parangón = She is beyond compare

pariente/a	relation, relative	parent	**padre** or **madre** (must be specified)
		parents	**padres**

Todos los parientes están invitados a la boda = All the relatives are invited to the wedding

parsimonioso (R3)	slow, calm	parsimonious	**mezquino, tacaño**

Mi abuela es muy parsimoniosa haciendo las cosas = My grandmother is very slow in doing things

patético	moving, pitiful (pathetic (lit))	pathetic (in pejorative sense)	**horrible, malísimo**

Después de la carrera tenía una pinta patética, tan cansado estaba = After the race he looked pitiful, he was so tired

pavimento	ground, road surface	pavement	**acera**

un pavimento con baches = a road surface with potholes

petróleo	petroleum oil; paraffin, kerosene	petrol (Brit) petrol (US)	**gasolina, nafta**

De los pozos se saca petróleo = Oil comes from wells

petulancia (R3)	arrogance, haughtiness, smugness	petulance	**malhumor** (m), **displicencia**

Se expresaba con mucha petulancia = He expressed himself very arrogantly

'Falso amigo'	English equivalent	English cognate	Spanish equivalent
pinta	look; stain; pint	paint	**pintura**
Tenía pinta de sucio = It looked dirty			
pope (m)	Orthodox priest, pope	Pope (Catholic)	**Papa**
predicamento	prestige	predicament	**apuro**, **situación difícil**
un cirujano con mucho predicamento = a very prestigious surgeon			
preservativo	contraceptive	preservative	**conservante** (m)
†**pretender que . . . ;** **pretender hacer algo**	to claim that . . . ; to try to do sth	to pretend	†**fingir**, †**aparentar**
En esta ponencia pretendo analizar las causas de la calvicie = In this paper I will attempt to analyse the causes of baldness			
prevaricar (R3)	to be guilty of corrupt practices	to prevaricate	**recurrir a evasivas**
Al juez se le acusó de prevaricar = The magistrate was accused of corrupt practice			
†**pupilo/a**	lodger; ward (legal)	pupil	**alumno/a**
los pupilos de la residencia = the lodgers at the hostel			
†**querella**	complaint, charge; dispute	quarrel	†**riña**, †**disputa**
Presentó una querella contra la empresa por negligencia = He charged the company with negligence			
Hubo una querella entre los vecinos = There was a dispute between the neighbours			
†**quitar**	to take away; to take off	to quit	†**dejar**, **salir de**
Se quitó la ropa mojada = He took off his wet clothes			
El ladrón me quitó la cartera = The thief took my wallet			
†**realizar**	to put into effect	to realize	**darse cuenta de**
realizar una colecta / una encuesta = to take a collection / carry out a survey			
recluso/a	prisoner	recluse	**ermitaño/a**
Los reclusos se amotinaron = The prisoners rioted			
recolección (f)	act of harvesting, gathering	recollection	**recuerdo**
la recolección del trigo = the wheat harvest			
reconvenir (R3)	to reprimand	to reconvene	**convocar de nuevo**
Conviene reconvenir a los que obran mal = Those who do evil should be reprimanded			
refrán (m)	proverb, saying	refrain	**estribillo**
un refrán chino = a Chinese proverb			

'Falso amigo'	English equivalent	English cognate	Spanish equivalent
reino	kingdom	reign	**reinado**
El reino abarcaba toda la península = The kingdom stretched over the whole peninsula			
relevancia	importance	relevance	**pertinencia**
un asunto de mucha relevancia = a subject of great importance			
relevante	outstanding; important	relevant	**pertinente,** **relacionado con**
una relevante personalidad / aportación = an outstanding personality / contribution			
[†]**renta**	(unearned) income	rent	**alquiler** (m)
la declaración sobre la renta = income tax return			
resumir	to sum up, to summarize, to abridge	to resume	**reanudar**
Resumió el libro en tres páginas = She summarized the book in three pages			
ruin (R3)	despicable, mean	ruin	**ruina**
cometer un acto ruin = to commit a despicable act			
[†]**sensible**	sensitive	sensible	[†]**sensato**
Tiene la piel sensible = He has sensitive skin			
simpático	nice	sympathetic	**compasivo;** [†]**comprensivo**
Es un chico simpático que se entiende con todo el mundo = He is a nice guy who gets on with everyone			
suburbios (pl)	poor district of town, slum	suburb	[†]**barrio** (exterior), [†]**afueras** (pl)
Los pobres viven en los suburbios en chabolas = The poor live in shacks in the slum areas			
suceso	event; accident, crime	success	[†]**éxito**
un suceso trágico/curioso = a tragic/curious event			
[†]**tabla**	plank, board	table	**mesa**
una tabla de windsurf = a windsurf board			
tópico	cliché, hackneyed expression	topic	**tema**
Utiliza muchos tópicos al hablar = He uses a lot of clichés when he speaks			
transpirar (R2–3)	to sweat	to transpire	[†]**ocurrir,** [†]**suceder**
El atleta transpiraba abundantemente = The athlete was sweating profusely			
truculento (R3)	macabre	truculent	**agresivo,** **malhumorado**
imágenes truculentas = macabre images			
visionar	to view (critically)	to envision (US)	**prever**
Los censores visionan las nuevas películas antes de que las vea el público = Censors view new films before the general public sees them			

3.2   Similar form – partly similar meaning

Sometimes the meaning of Spanish and English cognates does
correspond in part, but either the Spanish or English word has
additional meanings.

Spanish	English look–alike	Notes
†**abandonar**	to abandon	ALSO = to leave in a more general sense **abandonado** = sloppy, scruffy **Abandonó la casa a las ocho** = He left the house at eight **Parece abandonado, no se peina, se viste mal** = He looks scruffy, he doesn't comb his hair, he dresses badly
†**abusar** **abusar de la comida / de las mujeres** = to eat too much / to abuse women	to abuse (to take advantage of)	BUT to abuse (to insult) = **insultar,** †**injuriar**
†**acusar**	to accuse	ALSO = to reveal, to show **acusado** (R3) = marked, pronounced **El futbolista acusaba cansancio** = The footballer showed signs of tiredness **Tiene un acusado sentido de humor / Tiene rasgos acusados** = He has a pronounced sense of humour / He has pronounced features
alterar	to alter, to change	ALSO = to upset **El niño chilla tanto que me altera los nervios** = The child screams so much that it upsets my nerves
amasar **amasar una fortuna** = to amass a fortune	to amass (fig)	(i) BUT to amass (lit) = **amontonar** (ii) ALSO = to knead **El panadero amasó la masa** = The baker kneaded the dough
aplicación (f)	application (diligence; putting into practice)	BUT application (for a job) = †**solicitud** (f)
†**apostar** **Aposto al mayordomo en la puerta** = I am positioning the butler at the door	to post, to station	BUT **apostar** = to bet **Yo apuesto por el otro equipo** = I'm betting on the other team

NOTE: **apostar** 'to bet' is a radical-changing verb (**apuesto**, etc); **apostar** 'to post' is not
  radical-changiing (**aposto**, etc)

Spanish	English look-alike	Notes
†**aprobar**	to approve	ALSO = to pass (an exam) **Aprobó en matemáticas** = She passed in math(s)
argüir **Este artículo arguye en contra de la eutanasia** = This article argues against euthanasia	to argue (to present a case)	BUT to argue (quarrel) = **discutir, reñir**
argumento	argument (plot of book, etc; line of reasoning)	BUT argument (quarrel) = †**debate** (m), **discusión, triña**
armar **armar a los soldados** = to arm the soldiers	to arm	ALSO = to cause (quarrel, scandal, noise) (Rl); to assemble **armar un escándalo** = to kick up a fuss **armar muebles prefabricados** = to assemble ready-made furniture
asesor(a) **la nueva asesora del presidente** = the president's new adviser	assessor (adviser)	BUT assessor (valuer) = **tasador(a), persona que valora, que aconseja**
†**asistir a**[PERS] **uno** **asistir a un enfermo** = to help a sick person **dirección asistida** = power-assisted steering	to assist sb (R2–3)	ALSO **asistir a also** = to be present at sth **No asistimos a la reunión** = We didn't attend the meeting
atestar **La mujer atestó en el juicio** = The woman testified at the trial	to attest	ALSO = to pack, cram **La sala estaba atestada** = The room was packed
audición (f) **dar una audición** = to have an audition **hacer una audición a uno** = to audition sb NOTE: **prueba** is also used in this sense.	audition	ALSO = sense of hearing **He perdido la audición** = I've lost my sense of hearing
audiencia *La audiencia opina* = *What listeners think* (title of a radio programme) **Los Reyes fueron recibidos en audiencia por el Papa** = The King and Queen were received in audience by the Pope	audience (esp radio or TV) (R3); audience (eg with Pope)	BUT in R2, audience (in theatre, etc) = **público, espectadores** (pl) ALSO = lawcourt **El abogado entró en la Audiencia** = The lawyer went into the lawcourt

Spanish	English look-alike	Notes
banco	bank	ALSO = bench
Saqué dinero del banco = I withdrew money from the bank		**Me senté en el banco** = I sat down on the bench
†**bárbaro**	barbarous	ALSO = tremendous (Rl)
cometer un acto bárbaro = to commit a barbarous act		**una fiesta bárbara** = a wonderful party
bomba	bomb	ALSO = pump
†**cámara** (f)	camera	ALSO = room, chamber (R3); inner tube (tyre)
cámara (m/f)	cameraman/woman	
una cámara de vídeo = a video camera		**Entraron en la cámara nupcial** = They went into the bridal chamber
		tener la cámara pinchada = to have a flat tyre
†**camping** (m)	camping	ALSO = campsite
hacer camping = to camp		**El camping dispone de todos los servicios** = The campsite has every facility
canciller(a)	chancellor	(i) BUT chancellor of a university = **rector(a)**, Chancellor of the Exchequer = **Ministro/a de Hacienda**
		(ii) BUT in Am = Foreign Minister
		(iii) ALSO = member of diplomatic staff
†**carácter** (m)	character (characteristics; letter, etc)	BUT character (in play, etc) = **personaje**
los caracteres de la escritura griega = the characters of the Greek alphabet		**Interpreté el personaje de Hamlet** = I played the part of Hamlet
el carácter de una persona = a person's character		
caramelo	caramel	ALSO = sweet (hard, ie one made out of caramelized sugar)
		El niño desenvolvió el caramelo = The child unwrapped the sweet
carta	card (playing card)	ALSO = letter
jugar a las cartas = to play cards		**escribir una carta** = to write a letter
NOTE: **naipe** is also used in this sense.		

Spanish	English look-alike	Notes
†**cartel** (m)	cartel (commercial)	ALSO = poster
carrera	career	ALSO = race; course (education) **Terminó tercero en la carrera de los cien metros** = He finished third in the 100 metres race **Estudió la carrera de medicina** = He studied medicine
†**celebrar** **Juan acaba de celebrar su cincuenta cumpleaños** = Juan has just celebrated his fiftieth birthday	to celebrate	ALSO = to hold (meeting, etc) **celebrar una reunión** = to hold a meeting
colegio	college	ALSO = school; association **Los niños van cada día al colegio** = The children go to school every day **el Ilustre Colegio de Abogados de Madrid** = the Madrid Lawyers' Association
colonia	colony (gen)	ALSO = estate (of houses); eau-de-cologne **la colonia donde vive mi hermano** = the estate where my brother lives **Se echó colonia** = She put on some eau-de-cologne
†**competencia** **Resolvió el problema con competencia** = She solved the problem competently	competence	ALSO = competition; competitiveness **Hubo competencia por el primer puesto** = There was competition for the first place
†**competición** (f) **una competición de tiro con arco** = an archery competition **hacer competición a otra empresa** = to compete with another firm	competition (sport, business)	BUT gen sense of competitiveness = **rivalidad** (f), †**competencia**
compromiso **llegar a un compromiso** = to reach an agreement	compromise	ALSO = engagement (gen commitment, and agreement to marriage); awkward situation **No puedo ir esta noche: tengo otro compromiso** = I can't go tonight: I've got another engagement **Adela y Jaime acaban de hacer público su compromiso matrimonial** = Adela and Jaime have just announced their engagement **Se puso en un compromiso** = She placed herself in an awkward situation

Spanish	English look-alike	Notes
concentración (f)	concentration	ALSO = gathering and preparation of a team before a match; rally
Le falta concentración a la niña = The child lacks concentration		**La selección francesa ha iniciado su concentración** = The French team have begun their pre-match training **una concentración de motos** = a motorcycle rally
†**conferencia**	conference (meeting)	ALSO = lecture; long-distance call
la Conferencia de Versalles = the Versailles Conference NOTE: **congreso** is more generally used in this sense.		**Dio una conferencia en el Aula** (f) **Magna** = She gave a lecture in the Great Hall **una conferencia internacional** = an international call
controlar	to control	ALSO = to check, to verify
controlar la circulación = to control the traffic		**velocidad controlada por radar** = radar speed check
copia	copy (of paper, etc)	BUT copy (of book) = **ejemplar** (m)
Te mando una copia de la carta = I'm sending you a copy of the letter		
coraje (m)	courage	ALSO = anger
Tuvo el coraje de criticar al dictador = He had the courage to criticize the dictator		**Me dio coraje que empezase a llover** = It made me angry that it was beginning to rain
†**corresponder**	to correspond	ALSO = **corresponder a uno** = to be someone's turn, task; to return (a favour, etc)
Estos dos formularios no se corresponden = These two forms don't correspond		**Hoy te corresponde fregar** = Today it's your turn to do the washing up **Me hizo un favor y le correspondí con otro** = She did me a favour and I reciprocated with another
criatura	creature	ALSO = baby
curso	course	ALSO = year of school, university
El río siguió su curso por el valle = The river followed its course along the valley		**Es alumna de segundo curso** = She's a second-year student
defectivo	defective (grammar)	BUT defective (gen) = **defectuoso**
un verbo defectivo = a defective verb		
†**demandar**	to demand (R3 only)	BUT to demand (R2) = **exigir** ALSO = to sue
La sociedad demanda médicos = Society needs doctors		**Le demandé judicialmente** = I sued him

Spanish	English look-alike	Notes
departamento	department	ALSO = compartment (train) ALSO in Am = flat, apartment
el departamento de física = the physics department		**Tengo un departamento en una zona céntrica** (Am) = I have a centrally located flat
dependencia	dependence	ALSO = outbuilding
la dependencia de la droga = dependence on drugs		**una dependencia de la granja** = a farm outbuilding
derivar(se)	to derive	ALSO **derivar** = to drift, to deviate
Esta palabra (se) deriva del latín = This word derives from Latin		**El barco estaba derivando peligrosamente** = The boat was drifting dangerously **La conversación derivó hacia la política** = The conversation turned to politics
descubrir	to discover	ALSO **descubrirse** = to take one's hat off
descubrir un país = to discover a country		**Se descubrió al entrar en la iglesia** = He took off his hat when he went into the church
†**destino**	destiny	ALSO = destination
Cada hombre tiene su destino = Every man has his destiny		**Salió con destino a México** = She left for Mexico
diario	diary (journal)	BUT diary (appointment book) = †**agenda** (f) ALSO = daily paper
Describió sus sentimientos en el diario = She described her feelings in the diary		**En el diario de hoy, dicen que . . .** = In today's paper it says that . . .
diligencia	diligence	ALSO = (i) piece of business; pl = formalities, enquiries; (ii) stagecoach
Hizo el trabajo con mucha diligencia = She did the work very diligently		**El juez instruyó las diligencias para . . .** = The magistrate instituted proceedings for . . . **Los bandidos atacaron la diligencia** = The bandits attacked the stagecoach
diplomático/a	diplomatic (ADJ)	ALSO = diplomat (N)
el cuerpo diplomático = the diplomatic corps **una enfermedad diplomática** = a diplomatic illness		**Es diplomático en las Naciones Unidas** = He is a diplomat at the United Nations
dirección (f)	direction	ALSO = address; management (of firm)
Voy en dirección norte = I'm going in a northerly direction		**Dame la dirección de tu amigo** = Give me the address of your friend **La dirección dio un incremento salarial a todos los empleados** = The management gave all the employees a salary increase

Spanish	English look-alike	Notes
discutir	to discuss	A L S O = to argue
El parlamento discutió sobre / de la economía = Parliament discussed the economy		**Se les oyó discutiendo en el patio** = You could hear them arguing in the yard
dormitorio	dormitory	A L S O = bedroom (in house; in hotel only **habitación** is used)
Los internos duermen en un dormitorio = The boarders sleep in a dormitory		**Esta casa tiene tres dormitorios** = This house has three bedrooms
duelo	duel	A L S O = grief
efectivamente	effectively	A L S O = indeed, sure enough
Realizó el trabajo efectivamente = She carried out the work effectively		**Dijo que volvería y, efectivamente, volvió** = He said he would come back, and, sure enough, he did
emoción	emotion	A L S O = excitement
		¡Qué emoción! = How exciting!
†**equipo**	equipment	A L S O = team (sport)
El escalador se pertrechó con todo el equipo necesario = The climber equipped himself with all the necessary equipment		**El equipo juega fuera** = The team is playing away
escenario	scenario (but considered an anglicism)	A L S O = scene, setting (gen); stage (theatre)
		el escenario del crimen = the scene of the crime
		La actriz salió al escenario = The actress came on stage
escolar (m/f)	pupil, student	B U T scholar (researcher, learned person) = **estudioso**
†**espacio**	space	A L S O = programme (on TV, radio)
		un espacio informativo = a news broadcast
espectro	spectre	A L S O = spectrum
El espectro me aterró = The ghost terrified me		**el espectro de colores** = the colour spectrum
estación (f)	station	A L S O = season (of year)
Me bajo en la próxima estación = I'm getting off at the next station		**La primavera es la estación más bella del año** = Spring is the most beautiful season of the year
Las catorce Estaciones de la Cruz = The fourteen Stations of the Cross		

Spanish	English look-alike	Notes
estadio **un estadio de cien mil espectadores** = a stadium holding 100,000 spectators	stadium	ALSO = phase **el último estadio de una enfermedad** = the last phase of an illness
estudio	study (act of studying, written or composed study); studio	BUT study (room) = **despacho**, †**oficina**
evolucionar **Ha evolucionado la política agraria** = Agrarian policy has developed	to evolve, to develop	ALSO = to move around (fish in pool, cars on track, dancers in hall, etc) **La bailarina evolucionó graciosamente** = The ballerina moved gracefully
NOTE: **evolucionar** is increasingly used transitively, though it is condemned by purists: [!] **Los técnicos han evolucionado un model más avanzado** = The technicians have developed a more advanced model			
experimentar **Experimentaban sobre los genes** = They were experimenting on genes	to experiment with, to try out, to test	ALSO = to experience, to undergo **Experimentaron una sensación de vértigo** = They experienced a feeling of vertigo
explotar a^PERS **explotar a una persona** = to exploit a person	to exploit	ALSO = to explode **La bomba explotó** = The bomb exploded
NOTE: **explotar** is increasingly used transitively in the sense of 'cause to explode', though it is condemned by purists: [!] **El ejército explotó la bomba** = The army exploded the bomb.			
†**facilitar** **Su ayuda me facilitó la solución** = Her help made the solution easier for me	to facilitate	ALSO = to provide **Esta empresa facilita ropa al ejército** = This company provides clothing for the army
†**falta** **cometer una falta** = to make a mistake	fault, error	ALSO = lack, need **la falta de comida** = the lack of food
fallo **Juan tiene sus fallos** = Juan has his weaknesses	failure, weakness	ALSO = judgement, sentence **El juez emitió su fallo** = The judge passed sentence
familiar **Esta calle me es familiar** = This street is familiar to me	familiar	ALSO = pertaining to the family **El entorno familiar es agradable** = The family environment is pleasant
firma	firm, small business	ALSO = signature
fiscal	fiscal (ADJ)	ALSO as N = prosecutor, attorney
†**forma** **Tiene una forma ovalada** = It has an oval shape	form, shape	ALSO = manner, way (of doing sth) **No me convence su forma de trabajar** = I'm not convinced by his way of working

Spanish	English look–alike	Notes

formación (f)   formation
Los aviones volaban en formación =
  The planes were flying in formation
		ALSO = training, education
		Tiene una formación muy sólida = He has a
		  very solid training

formal   formal, serious
**Es una chica muy formal: estudia
  mucho** = She is a very serious girl: she
  studies hard
		ALSO = reliable, earnest
		Puedes confiar en él: es muy formal = You
		  can trust him: he's very reliable

fotografía photography **Se dedica a la fotografía** = She devotes herself to photography		ALSO = photograph **una fotografía preciosa** = a lovely photograph
†**frase** (f) phrase (restricted) **una frase hecha** = a set phrase		(i) ALSO = sentence (ii) BUT phrase (gen) = **locución**, **expresión** **una frase compleja** = a complex sentence

gracia   grace
Soy español por la gracia de Dios =
  I'm Spanish, by the grace of God
		ALSO = wit; thanks (pl)
		Cuenta los chistes con mucha gracia = He
		  tells jokes very wittily
		Sobrevivió gracias a la medicina = She
		  survived thanks to medicine

gracioso   funny
un chiste muy gracioso = a very funny
  joke
		ALSO gracious
		una graciosa contribución = a gracious
		  contribution

†**historia** history		ALSO = story (lit and in sense of 'lie') **la historia de mi vida** = the story of my life **¡Son historias!** = (Untrue) tales!
honesto honest **un comerciante honesto** = an honest dealer		decent, modest (in sexual sense) **un beso honesto** = a chaste kiss

ignorar   to ignore
Ignoraba mi presencia y me fastidió =
  She ignored the fact that I was there and
  it annoyed me
		ALSO = not to know
		Ignoraban su paradero = They did not know
		  his whereabouts

ilusión (f) illusion		ALSO = hope; excitement, thrill
		Mi mayor ilusión es poder verte = My
		  greatest hope is to be able to see you
		**Me hace mucha ilusión que vengas a
		  visitarnos** = I'm thrilled you're coming to
		  visit us
		NOTE ALSO **ilusionar** = to excite
		Su visita nos ilusionó = Her visit excited us

Spanish	English look-alike	Notes
ilustración (f)	illustration	A L S O = enlightenment
la ilustración de una teoría = the illustration of a theory		**la primera enciclopedia de la Ilustración** = the first encyclopaedia of the Enlightenment
†**importante**	important	A L S O = considerable (sum, loss)
		una cantidad importante = a considerable sum
inconsciente	unconscious	A L S O = thoughtless, careless
El golpe la dejó inconsciente = The blow left her unconscious		**comportamiento inconsciente** = thoughtless behaviour
†**inquirir**	to enquire (to enquire into)	B U T to enquire (gen) = †**preguntar**
El científico inquirió sobre las causas del cáncer = The scientist enquired into the causes of the cancer		
instruir	to instruct	A L S O = to inform; to investigate (legal)
instruir a un alumno = to instruct a pupil		**instruir una causa** = to investigate a case
integrar	to integrate	A L S O = to form, to make up
integrar a los inmigrantes en la sociedad = to integrate immigrants into society		**Seis miembros integraban el equipo** = The team was made up of six members
†**intervenir**	to intervene	A L S O = to take part; to operate on (medical); to confiscate, freeze (assets)
intervenir en un asunto = to intervene in a matter		**El ministro quiere intervenir en el debate** = The mninister wants to take part in the debate
		El torero fue intervenido quirúrgicamente = The bullfighter was operated on
		A los presuntos traficantes de droga les fue intervenida una maleta = A suitcase was confiscated from the presumed drug traffickers
†**invertir**	to invert	A L S O = to invest
invertir la dirección de rotación = to change the direction of rotation		**invertir su capital en acciones** = to invest capital in shares
irracional	irrational	A L S O = incapable of reasoning (eg animals)
un acto irracional = an irrational act		**Los animales son irracionales** = Animals are irrational beings
laguna	lagoon, lake	A L S O = gap, lacuna (in knowledge, etc)
		No saber nada de aquella época es una gran laguna = Not to know anything about that period is a big gap
licencia	licence, permission, permit	A L S O = leave (military)

Spanish	English look-alike	Notes
lima	lime (fruit); lime tree	(i) ALSO = file (tool) (ii) BUT (quick)lime = †**cal** (f)
localidad (f) **una localidad triste** = a sad place	locality, location	ALSO = seat, ticket (eg theatre, sport) **Los espectadores ocuparon su localidad** = The spectators took their seats
malicia **hablar con malicia** = to speak maliciously	malice (R3)	mischief **Para su edad Pepita tiene mucha malicia** = Pepita is very mischievous for her age
manifestación (f) **una manifestación de alegría** = a display of joy	manifestation	ALSO = demonstration (eg political) **una manifestación callejera** = a street demonstration
marcha **marcha nocturna** = night march **Lo decidimos sobre la marcha** = We decide as we go along	march (military); trend, course of events	ALSO = speed (of vehicle); gear (mechanical) **Este coche tiene cinco marchas** = This car has five gears
†**metálico**	metallic (ADJ)	ALSO as N = cash **pagar en metálico** = to pay cash
†**monte** (m)	mountain	ALSO = woodland **Me puse a la sombra de un árbol del monte** = I lay down in the shade of a woodland tree
natural **un talento natural** = a natural talent	natural	ALSO = native (of) **Es natural de Burgos** = He's a native of Burgos
†**ocupar**	to occupy	ALSO = to confiscate (police, customs) **La policía le ocupó una navaja** = The police confiscated a knife from him
óleo	oil painting; ecclesiastical	BUT oil (for cooking, machinery) = **aceite** (m)
†**oposición** (f)	opposition	ALSO in pl = competitive examination undergone by candidates for public appointments **Se presentó a las oposiciones**
particular **un caso particular** = a particular case	particular	ALSO = private (secretary, house, etc) **una casa particular** = a private house
†**partir** **El pelotón partió a las diez** = The squad left at ten	to depart (R3)	ALSO = to split, to divide, to break **Partió el pan en trozos** = She broke the bread into pieces

Spanish	English look–alike	Notes
pensión (f)	pension, allowance	ALSO = accommodation with meals
Percibía una pensión muy gorda = She was getting a very good pension		**No era muy cara la pensión** = The boarding house wasn't very expensive
†**percibir**	to perceive, to notice	ALSO = to earn, to receive (money) SEE **pensión**
petición (f)	petition	ALSO = request (gen) **a petición suya** = at his request
pico	peak	ALSO = beak
el pico del monte = the mountain peak		**el pico de un pájaro** = a bird's beak
pieza	piece (cloth, chess, music, etc)	ALSO = part (mechanical) (eg **pieza de recambio** = spare part); room (R2–3); play (theatre)
componer una pieza musical = to compose a musical piece		
plausible	plausible	ALSO = praiseworthy
†**precioso**	precious	ALSO = pretty, lovely (esp Rl)
una piedra preciosa = a precious stone		**una niña preciosa** = a lovely little girl
piedad (f)	piety	ALSO = pity
piedad religiosa = religious piety		**Ten piedad de mí** = Have pity on me
precoz	precocious	ALSO = early
un niño precoz = a precocious child		**un diagnóstico precoz** = an early diagnosis
primitivo	primitive, uncivilized	ALSO = original (test, state)
un hombre muy primitivo = a very uncivilized man		**su estado primitivo** = its original state
proceso	process	ALSO = lawsuit, trial
el proceso de fabricación = the manufacturing process		**un proceso legal** = a trial (in law)
†**procurar**	to procure, to get hold of	ALSO = to try
Me procuré el libro = I got hold of the book		**Procura adoptar una actitud más seria** = Try and adopt a more serious attitude
promoción (f)	promotion (commercial)	ALSO = class, year BUT promotion (advancement in rank) = **ascenso**
El supermercado hace la promoción de una nueva línea = The supermarket is promoting a new line		**un compañero de mi promoción** = a friend from my year (at school, university)

Spanish	English look-alike	Notes
propaganda **propaganda electoral** = electoral propaganda	propaganda	A L S O = advertising **La empresa hace propaganda de su producto** = The firm is advertising its product
puntual **Nunca tienes que esperar, es muy puntual** = You never have to wait, she's very punctual	punctual	A L S O = relevant, precise **hacer una observación puntual** = to make a relevant remark **presentar datos puntuales** = to present precise data
rancio **queso rancio** = rancid cheese	rancid	A L S O = long-established **de rancio abolengo** = of long-established ancestry
reactor (m) **un reactor nuclear** = a nuclear reactor	reactor	A L S O = jet (plane or engine) **Los reactores han sustituido a los aviones con turbopropulsor** = Jets have replaced turboprop aircraft
†**real** **la vida real** = real life	real, authentic	A L S O = royal **una boda real** = a royal wedding
recuperarse **Tardó dos meses en recuperarse de la enfermedad** = She took two months to recuperate/recover from the illness	to recuperate, recover (intr)	A L S O **recuperar** = to regain, recover (tr) **recuperar energía / popularidad / su dinero perdido** = to recover one's energy / popularity / lost money
referirse a algo a uno **Se refirió a su madre** = She referred to her mother	to refer to sth sb	A L S O = **referir** to tell, relate (a story) (R3) **Refirió los hechos / lo ocurrido** = He related the facts / what had happened
†**registrar** **El secretario registró los datos** = The secretary recorded the data	to register, to record	A L S O = to search, to inspect **La policía registró el equipaje** = The police searched the luggage
regular **el ritmo regular del corazón** = the regular beat of the heart	regular, normal	A L S O = OK, all right (Rl) **– ¿Qué tal? – Regular**. = 'How are you?' 'OK.'
relaciones (f pl)	relations (links)	B U T relations (relatives) = **parientes, familiares, allegados** (R3)
resistencia **la resistencia al enemigo** = resistance to the enemy	resistance	A L S O = (electrical) element **La resistencia de la estufa está oxidada** = The heater element is rusty

Spanish	English look-alike	Notes
†**restar**	as intr = to remain, to be left (R3)	ALSO as tr = to take away, to deduct
Le restan diez euros = He's got ten euros left		**Resta seis de diez y te quedan cuatro** = Take six away from ten and you have four left
revisar	to revise (a document)	ALSO = to check
		BUT to revise (Brit = look at again, US to review) = **repasar**
una edición revisada = a revised edition		**Hay que revisar el coche antes de ir de vacaciones** = We must check the car before going on holiday
rico	rich	nice, good, splendid
un banquero rico = a rich banker		**una comida rica** = a delicious meal
		El mar está rico = The sea is beautiful
†**rudo**	rude (rough)	BUT rude (uncouth, obscene) = †**grosero**, **obsceno**
salvar	to save, to rescue	ALSO = to cross, to get over, to overcome
Los bomberos salvaron a la niña = The firemen saved the little girl		**salvar un obstáculo / una barrera** = to overcome an obstacle / a barrier
semáforo	semaphore	ALSO = traffic light
		saltarse un semáforo = to jump a red light
sentencia	sentence (legal)	BUT sentence (language) = †**frase** (f)
La jueza dictó la sentencia = The judge pronounced sentence		**una frase compleja** = a complex sentence
†**solicitud**	solicitude, care, concern	ALSO = request, application (for post)
con gran solicitud = with great concern		**atender una solicitud** = to deal with a request
		una solicitud de trabajo = a job application
solvente	solvent, free of debt	ALSO = reliable (of source)
una economía solvente = a solvent economy		**noticias de origen solvente** = news from a reliable source
†**suceder**	to succeed (to follow)	(i) ALSO = to happen
		(ii) BUT to succeed (to be successful) = **tener éxito**
La reina Isabel sucedió a su padre = Queen Elizabeth succeeded her father		**Sucedió algo extraordinario** = Something extraordinary happened
sujeto	subject (grammar)	BUT (school) subject = **asignatura**; subject (of country) = **súbdito**
		ALSO = bloke, guy, chap (R1)
superioridad (f)	superiority	ALSO = (higher) authority (R3)
		órdenes de la superioridad = orders from the authorities

Spanish	English look–alike	Notes
†**susceptible**	susceptible, capable (of)	A L S O = sensitive, touchy
El contrato es susceptible de prórroga = The contract can be extended		**Es una persona muy susceptible** = He's a very touchy person
suspender	to suspend, to hang	A L S O = to fail (a candidate); (intr) to fail (an exam) (Rl)
Suspendieron el cuadro para exhibirlo = They hung the picture to exhibit it		**suspender a un candidato** = to fail a candidate – **¿Qué tal el examen? – Suspendí.** = 'How was the examination?' 'I failed.'
técnico	technical (ADJ), technician (N)	A L S O = (football) manager
un técnico de la televisión = a television technician		**El técnico les enseñó tácticas** = The manager taught them tactics
†**temporal**	temporal (ADJ)	A L S O = temporary A L S O as N (m) = storm, rainy weather
el poder temporal = temporal power		**una decisión temporal** = a temporary decision **Un fuerte temporal provocó el hundimiento** = Heavy rain caused subsidence
tensión (f)	tension	A L S O = pressure
tensión política = political tension		**tensión arterial** = blood pressure
término	terminus	A L S O = term (language); boundary (of land) **un término lingüístico** = a linguistic term **un término municipal** = a municipal boundary
tra(n)scendencia **Note**: similarly **tra(n)scendente** and **tra(n)scendental**	transcendence	A L S O = importance, significance
		un acontecimiento de mucha transcendencia = an event of great importance
tronco	trunk (of tree; of body)	B U T trunk (of car) = **maletero**; trunk (for packing) = **baúl** (m); trunk (of elephant) = **trompa**
turismo	tourism	A L S O = (saloon, sedan) car
hacer turismo = to tour		**un accidente entre dos turismos** = an accident involving two cars

Spanish	English look-alike	Notes
único **un ejemplo único** = a unique example	unique	ALSO = only; extraordinary **Es el único reloj que tengo** = It's the only watch I have **un hijo único** = an only child **¡Es único!** = It's extraordinary!
†**vago** **una idea vaga sin sentido** = a vague, senseless idea	vague	ALSO = lazy, slack (of person) (R1–2) **un chico vago que no hace nada** = a lazy boy who does nothing
verificar	to verify	ALSO = to check **verificar la presión de los neumáticos** = to check the tyre pressure
violento	violent	ALSO = awkward, embarrassing (of situation), embarrassed (of people) **Me siento violento en su presencia** = I feel awkward in her presence

3.3   Differences in register between Spanish words and their English cognates

R2 Spanish often has near equivalents of R3 English words. As a result, English speakers often feel that such words are inappropriate in register and hesitate to use them. Typically, the Spanish word is wider in meaning than the English and includes the R3 meaning as well. The Spanish R2 meanings are exemplified in the following list.

Spanish (R2)	English near equivalent	Wider meaning in Spanish
acceder **acceder al jardín** = to have access to the garden	accede	to have access
amplio **una casa amplia** = a big house **un estudio amplio** = a comprehensive study	ample	big, full, comprehensive
anfitrión (m) **un anfitrión generoso** = a generous host	(Amphytrion, a name)	host
anterior **la semana anterior** = last week	anterior	last, previous
antológico **una actuación antológica** = a marvellous performance	anthological	marvellous, brilliant

Spanish (R2)	English near equivalent	Wider meaning in Spanish
†**anular**	annul	to cancel

anular una cita = to cancel a date

asesinar	assassinate	to murder

Jack el destripador asesinó a muchas mujeres = Jack the Ripper murdered many women

asesino	assassin	murderer

un asesino acusado de numerosas muertes = a murderer accused of many killings

auscultar	auscultate	to sound (eg opinion); to listen to, to sound (med)

auscultar la opinión pública = to sound out public opinion
El médico le auscultó el pecho = The doctor sounded his chest

auténtico	authentic	real; great (R1)

Fue un auténtico escándalo = It was a real scandal
un gol auténtico = a great goal

autóctono	autochthonous	native, indigenous

una costumbre/tribu/lengua autóctona = a native custom / tribe / an indigenous
  language
los autóctonos del país = the natives of the country

autonomía	autonomy	range

Este coche tiene una autonomía de seiscientos kilómetros = This car has a range of
  600 kms

comentar	comment	to say (make a comment), discuss
		NOTE: **comentar algo** = to comment on sth

Le comenté que no me gustaba = I told him I didn't like it
Voy a comentarlo con mi esposa = I'll discuss it with my wife
La clase comentó la obra = The class commented on the work

conceder	concede	to give

La actriz nos concedió una entrevista = The actress gave us an interview

consumir	consume	to drink

Consumimos mucho vino aquel día = We drank a lot of wine that day
Estaba consumido por los celos = He was consumed with jealousy

convertir	convert	to change

Jesús convirtió el agua en vino = Jesus turned the water into wine
convertir euros en dólares = to change euros into dollars

convocar	convoke	to call, to summon

convocar una junta / una elección / un paro = to call a meeting / an election / a strike

cutis (m)	cutis	skin

El sol perjudica el cutis = Sunlight damages the skin

Spanish (R2)	English near equivalent	Wider meaning in Spanish
denunciar	denounce	to report

denunciar un robo = to report a robbery
El líder de la oposición denunció al presidente = The leader of the opposition
  denounced the president

disminuir	diminish	to make/get smaller

Disminuye la diferencia = It lessens the difference

elaborar	elaborate	to make, put together, construct, produce

elaborar un manifiesto / una traducción / una teoría = to put together a manifesto /
  produce a translation / construct a theory
Este producto se elabora en condiciones higiénicas = This product is made in hygenic
  conditions

elegir	elect	to choose

elegir un libro = to choose a book

elevado	elevated	high, lofty

una montaña/temperatura elevada = a high mountain/temperature
un tono elevado = a lofty tone

emitir	emit	to give (out); emit

Los críticos emitieron su opinión = The critics gave their opinion

fisonomía	physiognomy	appearance

la fisonomía de una persona / de una ciudad = a person's / town's appearance

fomentar	foment	to promote, encourage; stir up

fomentar el turismo = to encourage tourism

indemnizar	indemnify	to compensate

indemnizar a los damnificados = to compensate the victims

infantil	infantile	pertaining to children

un libro / una enfermedad / un juego infantil = a children's book / illness / game

inferior	inferior	lower

en la foto inferior = in the lower photo
Vive en el piso inferior = She lives in the flat/apartment below

iniciar	initiate	to begin

iniciar una reforma = to begin a reform

interlocutor	interlocutor	person you are speaking to

Mi interlocutor me dijo que . . . = The person I was speaking to told me that . . .

†**lamentar**	lament	to be sorry (for), to regret

Lamento informarle que . . . = I'm sorry to tell you that . . .
Lamento el resultado = I regret the result

†**lesión**	lesion	injury

El futbolista sufrió una lesión muscular = The footballer suffered a muscular injury

Spanish (R2)	English near equivalent	Wider meaning in Spanish
luminoso	luminous	bright
una idea luminosa = a brilliant idea		
mantener	maintain	to keep
Manténgase en lugar frío = To be kept in a cold place		
motivo	motive	reason, motive
el motivo de su interés/viaje = the reason for her interest/visit		
norma	norm	rule; norm
las normas de conducta = rules of the road, highway code		
observar las normas = to keep the rules		
núcleo	nucleus	group
un núcleo familiar/rural = a family group / a rural centre		
†**opinar**	opine	to think
Opino que . . . = I think that . . .		
patrimonio	patrimony	heritage
el patrimonio nacional = the national heritage		
preocupar	preoccupy	to worry
		NOTE: **preocuparse por algo/uno** = to be worried about sth/sb
Me preocupa mucho este chico = I'm very worried about this boy		
Me preocupo por ella = I'm worried about her		
†**pronóstico**	prognosis	forecast
el pronóstico del tiempo = the weather forecast		
propicio	propitious	favourable
Aprovechó el momento propicio para . . . = She took advantage of a favourable moment to . . .		
†**realizar**	realize	to do, carry out
realizar un acto/viaje = to carry out an action / to make a journey		
recuperar	recuperate	to get back, to recover
recuperar fuerzas = to get one's strength back		
La policía recuperó los artículos robados = The police recovered the stolen articles		
sibarita	sybaritic	gourmet
Es un sibarita comiendo = He likes to eat well		
†**solicitar**	solicit	to request
solicitar ayuda/permiso = to request help/permission		
superior	superior	upper
en la foto superior = in the upper photo		
Vive en el piso superior = She lives in the flat/apartment above		

Spanish (R2)	English near equivalent	Wider meaning in Spanish
tema (m)	theme	subject
Este artículo trata el tema del desempleo = This article deals with the subject of unemployment		
terminar	terminate	to end, finish
terminar un trabajo = to finish a piece of work		
tránsito	transit	passing through
el tránsito de camiones = lorries passing through		
valiente	valiant	brave
El Cid era muy valiente = El Cid was very brave		
zona	zone	area
una zona urbana = an urban area		

3.4 Adjectives and nouns in Spanish

3.4.1 Adjectives used as nouns

Spanish does not have such a clearcut distinction as English between nouns and adjectives, and almost any adjective can also function as a noun. Although this can happen in English too, it is much more restricted. In many cases, an English adjective can only denote a plural as a noun, e.g. *the young* = **los jóvenes**, while **el joven** = *the young person*. The English construction is frequently higher in register, eg *the accused* (R2–3). Translation of such Spanish adjectival nouns into English is often difficult and cumbersome: two strategies often involved are the use of a general noun (**un gracioso** = *a funny man*) or a demonstrative pronoun (**los afectados** = *those affected*).

3.4.2 Spanish past participles used as nouns

The English equivalent is often a completely different word or has to be translated by a paraphrase. A few words correspond to English words ending in -*ee*, eg **detenido** = *detainee*.

abonado	subscriber
accidentado	sb who has been injured, casualty
acusado	defendant, accused
afectado	sb/sth who has been affected
• **Este sector es uno de los más afectados por la crisis**	• This sector is one of the worst affected by the crisis
afiliado	member
aprobado	sb who has passed an exam

• **Se publicó la lista de los aprobados y los suspensos**	• The list of those who had passed and those who had failed was published
arrepentido	sb who has repented
arrestado	sb who has been arrested, detainee
atendido	sb who has been treated, patient
• **La mayoría de los atendidos presentaban síntomas alarmantes**	• The majority of patients had alarming symptoms
concentrado	concentrate; (pl) people who have gathered, usu at a demonstration
congregado	(pl) people who have met, usu for a political purpose
consultado	sb who has been consulted
contagiado	sb infected by a contagious disease
• **los contagiados del SIDA**	• people infected with AIDS
damnificado	victim, esp of a natural disaster
desaparecido	sb who has disappeared
descartado	a player who has been dropped from a team; a reject
• **Vamos a ver quiénes serán los descartados de la selección nacional**	• Let's see who will be dropped from the national team
detenido	sb who has been arrested, detainee
encapuchado	sb wearing a hood or mask, esp a criminal
• **El banco fue atracado por cuatro encapuchados**	• The bank was raided by four masked men
encarcelado	prisoner
encargado	sb responsible for or in charge of sth, often = manager or director
• **Yo soy el encargado de organizar la sesión de clausura**	• I'm responsible for organizing the closing session
• **el encargado de prensa**	• the press officer
encuestado	sb polled (in an opinion poll)
• **La mayoría de los encuestados estaban de acuerdo con la política del gobierno**	• The majority of those polled agreed with government policy
evadido	fugitive
excluido	sb excluded from society, social outcast

● **Buscamos un futuro para los excluídos del sistema**	● We are seeking a future for those who are outside the system
exiliado	exile
herido	sb who has been wounded
implicado	sb who is involved in sth
● **los implicados en el escándalo**	● those involved in the scandal
imputado	sb who is blamed for sth
● **Los imputados fueron condenados a veinte años de prisión**	● The guilty were sentenced to twenty years in prison

NOTE: This use of **imputado**, though common in the press, is condemned by purists.

infectado	sb who has been infected
infiltrado	infiltrator
inscrito	sb who has entered, registered
interesado	interested party
● **Se invita a todos los interesados a participar en el congreso**	● All those interested are invited to take part in the conference
invitado	guest
jubilado	sb who has retired, pensioner
licenciado	graduate
marginado	sb who is marginalized, outside society, down-and-out
nacionalizado	sb who has been naturalized
● **Los nacionalizados en la UE no requieren visado**	● Naturalized EU citizens do not require a visa
naufragado	sb who has been shipwrecked
necesitado	sb who is in need
olvidado	sb who has been forgotten
parado	unemployed person
perjudicado	sb who has suffered loss or damage
● **Los pobres son los más perjudicados por la situación económica**	● The poor are those worst affected by the economic situation
privilegiado	sb who is privileged
procesado	defendant
querellado	defendant
rescatado	sb who has been rescued
rezagado	straggler, sb who has fallen behind
secuestrado	sb who has been kidnapped
sondeado	sb whose opinion has been canvassed
sublevado	rebel

4 Similarities between Spanish words

4.1 Similar form – similar meaning

Pairs or sets of words in a language may be easily confused because they are similar in form. Such pairs or sets are known as paronyms. Sometimes these similar words are related in meaning and sometimes they are quite unrelated. The following sets of words are related in meaning or are formed from the same root.

abertura	apertura	obertura
hole, gap, orifice	act of opening, opening in the sense of inauguration (eg theatre, **las Cortes**)	overture (music)
una abertura en el muro = a hole in the wall	**la apertura del congreso** = the opening of the conference	**la obertura de Guillermo Tell** = the William Tell overture

abrevar	abreviar
to water; to drink	to abbreviate
Hay que abrevar las ovejas = We must water the sheep	**Abrevió la tesis** = She shortened the thesis
Las vacas abrevan en el río = The cows drink from the river	

acatar	catar
to obey, respect, comply with	to taste (in order to evaluate, esp wine)
acatar la ley = to comply with the law	**catar el vino** = to taste the wine

accesible	†asequible
accessible (place), approachable (person)	obtainable, reasonable (price), feasible. Also widely used in the sense of approachable (person), though purists insist that only **accesible** has this meaning.
persona / sitio accesible = accessible person / place	**un precio asequible** = a reasonable price

acepción (f)
sense, meaning
en esta acepción del vocablo = in this
meaning of the word

aceptación (f)
acceptance, approval
la aceptación de una invitación =
acceptance of an invitation

---

aclarar
to clarify, to shed light on; ALSO to rinse
(clothes), to dilute (liquid)
aclarar una duda = to clear up a query
**La lavadora primero remoja, después
aclara** = The washing machine first of all
soaks, then rinses

esclarecer (R3)
to clarify

esclarecer los hechos = to clarify the facts
esclarecer un delito = to clear up a crime

---

acompañante (m/f)
sb who accompanies (escort or musician)

El pianista hizo de acompañante =
The pianist acted as accompanist

compañero/a
companion, often in general sense of friend;
comrade (political)
un policía y su compañero = a policeman
and his comrade

---

acondicionar
to equip, fit out
acondicionar una casa = to equip a
house
aire acondicionado = air-conditioned

condicionar
to condition, determine
**El clima condiciona nuestra forma de
vivir** = Climate conditions our lifestyle
Los estudios condicionan nuestro futuro
= Studying determines our future

---

aderezar
to prepare, to embellish
Aderezó la ensalada = She dressed the salad

enderezar
to straighten, to set upright
Esta verja hay que enderezarla = This
railing must be straightened

---

afrentar
to affront, to insult

No soporto que me afrentes así = I can't
tolerate your insulting me in this way

†afrontar
to place (two things or persons) face to face; to
confront (danger, difficulties)
afrontar un peligro / una dificultad = to
face up to a danger / difficulty

---

†agrupación (f)
association, gathering (political, religious,
etc)
una agrupación política/religiosa = a
political/religious group

†grupo
group (gen)

un grupo de chicos = a group of young
people

---

agüero
omen, augury
un pájaro de mal agüero (**agüero** used
much more than **augurio** in such a
context) = a bird of bad omen

augurio
omen, augury; ALSO wishes
con mis mejores augurios = with my best
wishes

alimentario
pertaining to food (more abstract than
  alimenticio)
la industria alimentaria = the food
  industry

alimenticio
pertaining to food, nutritious

un producto alimenticio = a food product
Los plátanos son muy alimenticios =
  Bananas are very nutritious

N O T E : **alimentario** and **alimenticio** appear to be interchangeable in many contexts, though
some purists insist that **alimenticio** should only be used in the sense of 'nutritious'.

---

ambiente (m)
atmosphere, milieu, environment
un ambiente muy agradable = a very
  pleasant atmosphere

ámbito
compass, field, range
Esto pertenece al ámbito de la psicología
  = This belongs to the realm of psychology

---

ametralladora
machine gun

metralleta
sub–machine gun

---

amor (m)
love
Tiene mucho amor a su esposa = He
  loves his wife very much

amorío(s) (usu pl)
love affair
El joven tuvo muchos amoríos = The
  young man had a lot of affairs

---

amortiguar
to deaden noise, to cushion blow, to absorb
  shock (**amortiguador** = shock absorber)
amortiguar el ruido = to deaden the noise

amortizar
to pay off (debt, loan, mortgage)

amortizar una deuda = to pay off a debt

---

animado
lively, merry, anything with life or movement
Con vino se pone animado = He gets
  animated with wine
El local éste está animado = This bar is
  very lively

†**animoso**
courageous, energetic
un hombre animoso que no tiene miedo
  = a courageous man who is not afraid

---

apaciguar
to pacify, calm down (gen)
La música suave apacigua mi tristeza =
  Gentle music calms my sadness

pacificar
to pacify (after a war or conflict)
Los cascos azules pacificaron el territorio
  = The blue helmets [UN troops] pacified the
  area

---

aparición (f)
act of appearing, eg publication of book,
  apparition
fecha de aparición = date of publication
una aparición de la Virgen = an
  appearance of the Virgin

†**apariencia**
outer appearance, impression

juzgar por las apariencias = to judge by
  appearances

---

atracción (f)
act of attracting (physical and psychological);
  entertainment
un parque de atracciones = a theme park

la atracción de un imán = the attraction
  of a magnet

atractivo
attractive quality, appeal

Su atractivo despertó interés en los demás
  = Its appeal awoke interest in the others

---

autobús (m)
local bus serving town
El autobús va al centro = The bus is
  going to the (town) centre

autocar (m)
coach, long-distance bus
**El autocar hace el recorrido Barcelona–
  Valencia** = The coach runs between
  Barcelona and Valencia

---

autónomo
autonomous (gen)
**En muchas cosas los gobiernos locales
  son autónomos** = Local governments are
  autonomous in a lot of things

autonómico
relating to regional autonomy in Spain
el gobierno autonómico de Galicia = the
  autonomous government of Galicia

---

†**avance** (m)
advance (military, financial, etc); résumé of
  news on TV
un avance técnico = a technical advance
Te hago un avance ahora = I'll make you
  an advance now
avance informativo = advance news
  summary

avanzada
advance party

La avanzada salió una hora antes = The
  advance party left an hour beforehand

---

†**baja**
drop, fall (esp in price,
  temperature, economic
  activity); casualty (military)
una baja de temperatura = a
  fall in temperature
El ejército sufrió bajas = The
  army suffered casualties

bajada
act of lowering; slope, descent

la bajada del telón = the
  lowering of the curtain
**una bajada prolongada en
  carretera** = a long
  downward slope on the road

†**rebaja**
reduction (in sale)

las rebajas de enero =
  the January sales

---

balance (m)
balance sheet; hesitation

un balance positivo = a credit
  balance (also used more gen to
  mean a positive outcome, eg
  for negotiations)

balanza
weighing scales; ALSO in
  phrases **balanza de
  comercio** = balance of
  trade, **balanza de pagos** =
  balance of payments
**Se mete la harina en la
  balanza** = Put the flour on
  the scales

balanceo
rocking, swaying

**el balanceo del barco /
  de los árboles** = the
  rocking of the boat /
  the swaying of the trees

---

†**barba** beard; chin	**barbilla** chin (exclusively, and more common than **barba**)

beneficioso beneficial **un clima beneficioso para la salud** = a climate which is beneficial to health	**benéfico** beneficial; for benefit, charity **La práctica de un deporte es benéfica para el cuerpo** = Practising a sport is beneficial to the whole body **una función benéfica** = a charity event

bocado mouthful (gen); bite (to eat); bit (horse) ALSO **el bocado de Adán** = Adam's apple **Nos vamos a tomar un bocado antes de ir al cine** = We'll have a bite to eat before going to the cinema	**bocanada** mouthful in sense of contents of mouth being swallowed or ejected, esp a puff of smoke (from mouth) **Me echó una bocanada de humo a la cara** = He blew a puff of smoke in my face	**boqueada** gasp, esp in phrase **dar sus últimas boqueadas** = to breathe one's last	**bocadillo** baguette-type sandwich (ALSO **bocata** (m) in R1)

†**bravío** wild, abandoned (of persons or countryside) **un paisaje bravío** = a wild countryside **El joven era bravío** = The young man was wild	†**bravo** brave, tough **un toro bravo** = a brave bull

busca used in the phrase **en busca de** = in search of; search, sometimes pejorative	**búsqueda** search (gen) **una búsqueda de los archivos** = a search of the records

calidad (f) quality (abstract and gen) **un vino de calidad** = a quality wine **la calidad del chocolate** = the quality of the chocolate	**cualidad** (f) individual quality **Tiene buenas cualidades** = She has good qualities

cálido hot (climate); warm (colour) **Un clima/color cálido**	**caliente** hot, warm (drink, food) **una bebida/comida caliente**	**caluroso** warm (welcome, day) **un día caluroso / una acogida calurosa**

†**cambiar**	**canjear** (R3)
to change, to exchange, to swap	to exchange
cambiar ideas = to exchange ideas	**canjear notas diplomáticas / prisioneros**
cambiar de ropa = to change clothes	**de guerra** = to exchange diplomatic
Voy a cambiarme = I'm going to get	notes / prisoners of war
changed	

campamento	†**camping** (m)	**campo**
camp (military, or for organized group)	campsite	camp (esp in set phrases such as **campo de concentración, campo de refugiados**); camp (side); many other gen meanings, eg field, countryside
un campamento militar = a military camp	**Pasamos las vacaciones en un camping de tres estrellas** = We spent the holidays on a three-star campsite	**Pasó al campo enemigo** = He went over to the enemy camp **Prefiero vivir en el campo** = I prefer to live in the countryside

canción (f)	†**cantar** (m)	**cante** (m)	†**canto**
song	ballad	singing (Andalusia)	song of a bird; art of singing; edge or border of a place; rock, piece of stone
una canción popular = a popular song	**el Cantar de Mío Cid** **el Cantar de los Cantares** = the Song of Songs	**cante flamenco** **cante jondo**	**el canto del gallo** = cock-crow **el canto gregoriano** = Gregorian chant **el canto de una moneda / de una piedra** = the edge of a coin / a stone

captar	**capturar**	**cautivar**
to attract (attention, esteem, interest, etc); to grasp, to catch (understand); to collect (eg water from a spring); to receive (eg radio programme)	to capture, to apprehend	to attract, to captivate
captar la atención = to capture the attention **captar agua en el campo** = to collect water in the field **captar un programa musical** = to receive a music programme	**Los soldados capturaron a los terroristas** = The soldiers captured the terrorists	**Le cautiva la música de Beethoven** = She is captivated by Beethoven's music

carreta	**carrete** (m)	**carretilla**
long, low cart with two wheels	spool, reel (photography, fishing, sewing) (but in Am this is **carretel**, **carretón**)	wheelbarrow; jaw (Am)
Los bueyes tiraban de la carreta = The oxen drew the cart	**un carrete de película** = a reel of film	**la carretilla del albañil** = the builder's wheelbarrow

carro	**carrito**	**carromato**
cart, tank; trolley (supermarket, airport); in Am = car	shopping trolley (domestic, smaller than supermarket trolley)	covered wagon
un carro de combate = a tank	**Cuando salgo de compras llevo el carrito conmigo** = When I go shopping I take the trolley with me	**el carromato de un gitano** = a gipsy's wagon
Llenó el carro de comida = She filled the trolley with food		**Los vaqueros hicieron un corro con los carromatos** = The cowboys made a circle with the wagons
¿Vamos en carro o en tren? (Am) = Are we going by car or by train?		

†**caza**	**cacería**
act of hunting; animals which are the object of hunting, game	hunting party; total of animals killed in hunt
Me gusta la caza = I like hunting	**Salían de cacería cada domingo** = They went out hunting every Sunday
La caza en este restaurante es muy rica = The game in this restaurant is delicious	

celeste	**celestial**
pertaining to the sky, eg colour	heavenly (with spiritual connotations)
azul celeste = light blue, sky blue	**una música celestial** = a heavenly music

cemento	**cimiento**
cement	foundation of building; premise, principle or idea
El albañil preparó cemento = The builder prepared the cement	**los cimientos de un edificio** = the foundations of a building

central (ADJ)	**céntrico**
central, main	in or near the centre of a town
la calefacción central = the central heating	**La biblioteca es céntrica** = The library is centrally placed

[†]**cerco**	**circo**	[†]**círculo**
enclosure; rim; siege	circus	circle
Construyeron un cerco = They built an enclosure	**Le gustaba ir al circo con los niños =** She liked going to the circus with the children	**trazar un círculo =** to draw a circle
el cerco de Numancia = the siege of Numancia		

chapotear	**chapucear** (R1)	**chapuzar**
to splash (about)	to do a botched or unprofessional job	to duck; to dive into water (refl)
La niña chapoteaba en la bañera = The little girl splashed about in the bathtub	**Está chapuceando en el televisor para ver si lo arregla =** He's fiddling with the TV set to see if he can fix it	**Me meto en el agua pero no me chapuzo =** I'll go in the water but I'm not going completely under

NOTE: The corresponding nouns are **chapoteo**, **chapuceo** or **chapuza** and **chapuzón**.

cintura (SEE ALSO **cinta**, **cinto** on p. 96)	**cinturón** (m)
waist	belt, safety belt, girdle
una cintura de avispa = wasp waist	**un cinturón de seguridad =** a safety belt
	apretarse el cinturón = to tighten one's belt

color (m)	**colorido**	**colorado** (ADJ)
colour	colouring, degree of intensity of colour; colourful atmosphere	red
Me gusta el color de tu top = I like the colour of your top	**colorido desvaído =** faded colouring	**una tierra colorada =** a red soil
	el colorido de Andalucía = the colourful atmosphere of Andalusia	

comerciar	**comercializar**
to trade (in)	to put on the market
comerciar en antigüedades = to deal in antiques	**Esta fábrica comercializa yogures =** This factory produces yoghurt

competer (a uno) (R3)	**competir**
to be within the competence, to be under the jurisdiction of sb	to compete
No me competía pronunciarme sobre el asunto = It was not within my competence to pronounce on the matter	**Compitieron con afán =** They competed eagerly

complementar	**cumplimentar**	†**cumplir** (ALSO with **con**)
to complement, to complete	to pay one's respects to, to congratulate	to fulfil, to comply with; **cumplir x años** = to reach the age of x, to have one's xth birthday
La corbata complementa la chaqueta = The tie complements the jacket	**El primer ministro cumplimentó a la embajadora** = The prime minister congratulated the ambassador	**cumplir con sus obligaciones** = to fulfil one's obligations

comprensible	†**comprensivo**
understandable	understanding (of person)
Es comprensible que no le guste criticar a su amigo = It's understandable that he doesn't like criticizing his friend	**Hay que ser más comprensivo con los hijos** = One has to be more understanding with one's children

concejo; **concejal** (m)	**consejo**; **consejero**
council; councillor	counsel, advice; adviser, consultant, counsellor
un concejo / concejal municipal = a town council / councillor	**Te doy un consejo** = I'll give you a piece of advice
	Hay que consultar a un consejero = You should see a counsellor

conciliar	**reconciliar, reconciliarse con**
to reconcile (gen)	to reconcile (esp of people), to be reconciled with
conciliar dos ideas = to reconcile two ideas	**Ella consiguió reconciliar a sus padres** = She managed to reconcile her parents
conciliar a los vecinos = to reconcile the neighbours	**Se reconcilió con su hermano** = She was reconciled with her brother
conciliar el sueño (R3) = to get to sleep	

†**confianza en uno**	†**confidencia**
confidence, trust in sb	secret, item of confidence
Tengo confianza en ti = I have confidence in you	**Me hizo una confidencia** = She confided in me

consumar; consumación (f)	**consumir; consumición** (f)
to consummate; to complete, carry out (of crime) (R3); consummation	to consume, to eat, to use up, to burn (fuel); meal or drink in a bar, restaurant
consumar el matrimonio = to consummate one's marriage	**consumir toda la gasolina** = to use up all the petrol
Se consumó el atentado el día cinco = The attack was carried out on the fifth	**¿Quién paga las consumiciones?** = Who's paying for the drinks?
la consumación de los siglos (R3) = the end of the world	

costo	coste (m)	costa
cost of a large project	cost, price (gen)	cost in set expressions: **a costa de** at the expense of, **a toda costa** at all costs; pl = legal costs; coast

NOTE: A distinction between **costo** and **coste** is drawn by purists; but for practical purposes the two are synonymous.

costos de funcionamiento = operating costs	**el coste de un vestido** = the cost of a dress	**costas legales** = legal costs **la costa sur** = the south coast

dedicación (f)	dedicatoria
act of dedicating (eg church); devotion (to subject, etc)	(written) dedication (in book, etc)
su dedicación al trabajo = her dedication to work	**En la portada escribió una dedicatoria** = He wrote a dedication on the front page

desértico	desierto (ADJ)
pertaining to a desert; hardly frequented by anyone	deserted (of area, building, road, etc)
un clima desértico = a desert climate	**una calle desierta** = a deserted street ALSO **La subasta quedó desierta** = No buyer was found at the auction

desfiladero	†desfile (m)
pass, gorge	procession, (military) parade

doble (m/f)	doblete (m)	doblez (f)
double (ADJ and N)	double (sport)	fold; cunning, deceitfulness
doble vidriera = double glazing	**Hicieron doblete, ganaron copa y liga** = They won the double, the cup and the league	**Alargó la falda para quitar la doblez** = She stretched her skirt to get rid of the crease
tres doble = double three (dominoes)		
Es la doble de Marilyn Monroe = She's Marilyn Monroe's double		**Actúa con doblez** = He's acting deceitfully

dolor (m)	dolencia
pain	illness
Tengo un dolor en la espalda = I've got a pain in my back	**Su dolencia fue muy larga** = She had a long illness

efectivo	eficaz (R2)	eficiente (R3)
effective (eg remedy); real (cf **en efecto** = in fact); (N) cash	effective (more gen than **efectivo**); efficient	efficient (preferred for people)
un remedio efectivo = an effective remedy	**una medida eficaz** = an effective measure	**una persona eficiente** = an efficient person
pagar en efectivo = to pay cash		

ejercer
to exercise, exert (influence), practise (a career, profession)
ejercer el poder = to exercise power
ejercer influencia = to exert influence
ejercer su profesión = to practise one's profession

ejercitar
to exercise (a member of the body, skills)
Me ejercito bailando = I exercise by dancing
Le gusta ejercitar sus cualidades de orador = He likes to exercise his skills as a speaker

---

emocionante
exciting, thrilling
un partido emocionante = a thrilling match

emotivo
emotional, related to emotions
Votó al candidato por razones emotivas = He voted for the candidate for emotional reasons

---

encajar
to fit (one thing into another); to let in (a goal); to dish out or to receive (a blow) (R1)
Esta chaveta encaja en la ranura = This pin fits in the slot
El cuadro encaja en el ambiente = The picture fits in with the atmosphere

encajonar
to put and keep in a box (eg for transport); to squeeze into a tight place
encajonar a los animales para su transporte = to squeeze animals (into a truck) for transport

---

energético
related to fuel, energy
fuentes energéticas sostenibles = sustainable sources of energy

enérgico
energetic
un director de orquesta muy enérgico = a very energetic conductor

---

enjuiciar
to pass judgement on, assess
La jueza enjuició a los responsables del delito = The judge passed judgement on those responsible for the crime

juzgar
to judge (legal and gen), consider
El juzgado lo está juzgando = The court is considering it
Tú en seguida juzgas a la gente = You judge people instantly

---

equipar
to equip
equipar el equipo de botas nuevas = to equip the team with new boots

equiparar
to equate
Equipara su trabajo al que hace el director = He equates his work with what is done by the director

---

escena
scene (as constituent of act in play)
Vamos a ensayar la primera escena = Let's rehearse the first scene

escenario
stage; scene (gen)
El alcalde subió al escenario para hacer un discurso = The mayor went up on stage to make a speech
Esta plaza fue escenario de muchas atrocidades = This square was the scene of many atrocities

---

especia
spice
aromatizado con especias = flavoured with
   spices

especie (f)
species, kind, sort
una especie de mariposa = a kind of
   butterfly

---

expectación (f)
expectancy, anticipation, excitement (emotion
   involved)
El partido levantó mucha expectación =
   The match created a great sense of
   expectancy
**Esperaron los resultados con mucha
   expectación** = They waited excitedly for
   their results

expectativa
expectation, expectancy (act of expecting)

**Las expectativas de venta de este
   producto son buenas** = The expectations
   for sales of this product are good
estar a la expectativa = to be expectant
expectativas de vida = life expectancy

---

felicidad (f)
happiness, good fortune; pl = congratulations
   (R3)
Su rostro expresaba felicidad = Her face
   expressed happiness
¡Felicidades por tu aprobado! =
   Congratulations on passing

felicitación (f)
congratulation, pl = congratulations

Le di mis felicitaciones = I congratulated
   her

---

fundación (f)
act of founding; foundation in sense of
   organization
la fundación de Roma = the foundation of
   Rome
la Fundación March = the March
   Foundation

fundamento
basis on which sth is built, both concrete and
   abstract
Esta teoría no tiene fundamento = This
   theory has no basis

---

gestar
to gestate, prepare
Se estaba gestando la revolución = The
   revolution was brewing

gestionar
to negotiate, administer, manage
gestionar un negocio = to manage a
   business

---

gobernador(a)
governor, usu in official capacity
el gobernador de una provincia = the
   governor of a province

gobernante (m/f)
anyone who governs, ruler
**No sé por qué nos fiamos de nuestros
   gobernantes** = I don't know why we trust
   those who govern us

---

guarda (m/f)
watchman (of factory, building
   site, etc), security guard

el/la guarda de la fábrica
   = the factory security guard
(NOTE ALSO **un(a)
   guardabosque** =
   gamekeeper)

†**guardia** (m/f)
guard, police officer, f =
   guard, police as a group;
   custody, care

un(a) guardia de tráfico
   = a traffic police officer

guardián (m) / **guardiana** (f)
custodian, keeper (in museum,
   etc)

**el guardián / la guardiana
   del museo** = the custodian
   of the museum

---

†hilo	†hilera	hilandero/a	fila
thread	line, row	person who spins (cotton)	line, row
Cosía con un hilo azul = She was sewing with a blue thread	una hilera de árboles = a row of trees	*Las Hilanderas* de Velázquez	una fila de coches = a row of cars aparcarse en doble fila = to double park Los niños se pusieron en fila = The children formed a line

†historia	historial (m)	historieta
story, history	record, survey of performance (of business, club, etc)	anecdote; comic strip
Cuéntame una historia = Tell me a story la historia de México = the history of Mexico	un historial criminal = a criminal record	Las historietas de los tebeos son divertidas = Comic strips are amusing

†honesto	†honrado	honroso	honorable
decent, decorous, modest, chaste (often related to sexual morality)	honest, upright (often related to money)	respectable, highly esteemed	honourable
una relación honesta = a chaste relationship	un hombre honrado que no defraudaba = an honest man who did not cheat	un puesto honroso = a respectable position	Es honorable, te puedes fiar de su palabra = He's honourable, you can trust his word

honor (m)	honra	honradez (f)
honour (gen)	personal honour, self-esteem, reputation	honesty, integrity
mi palabra de honor = my word of honour	¡Soy española a mucha honra! = I'm Spanish and proud of it!	La honradez es una cualidad básica del hombre = Honesty is a basic quality of man

incluido	inclusive	incluso
included	inclusive	even
El desayuno está incluido = Breakfast is included	hasta el día dieciocho inclusive = until the eighteenth inclusive	todo el mundo puede ir, incluso los menores de edad = Everyone can go, even minors

información (f)
information

¿Tiene más información sobre la crisis? = Do you have any more information about the crisis?

informe (m)
report (on sth that has happened)

Redactaron un informe sobre la situación económica = They drew up a report on the economic situation

informática
information science, computing

Muchos jóvenes cursan estudios de informática = Many youngsters take computing courses

---

interrogación (f)
question
punto de interrogación = question mark

†**interrogatorio**
interrogation, questioning in court
Lo sometieron a un interrogatorio = He was submitted to questioning

---

invento
invention, invented thing

La rueda fue el principal invento de la humanidad = The wheel was mankind's chief invention

invención (f)
invention (R3); imagination, inventiveness (R2)

Son invenciones de una mente instable = They are figments of an unstable mind

---

invertir
to invest; to invert, reverse
invertir fondos = to invest money
invertir tiempo en un trabajo = to invest time in a job
Invirtieron la dirección de la marcha = They reversed the direction of travel

investir
to invest (to swear in)
Se le invistió al presidente = The president was invested

revestir
to cover; to assume
revestir las paredes con corcho = to cover the walls with cork
Sus comentarios no revisten importancia = Her comments assume no importance

verter
to pour
Virtió aceite en la sartén = He poured oil into the frying pan

vestir(se)
to clothe (tr; ALSO intr in R3); to dress (oneself) (refl)
La maestra vistió a los niños más pequeños = The teacher dressed the smallest children
Siempre (se) viste de verde = She always dresses in green
Se vistió con elegancia = He dressed elegantly

---

judicial
pertaining to justice
El presunto asesino pasó a disposición judicial = The suspected murderer was charged (in the Spanish system, is sent to appear before a *juez*)

jurídico
pertaining to law
fuentes jurídicas = legal sources

liberar
to free from physical restraint; to free from obligation
Los secuestradores liberaron a los rehenes = The kidnappers freed the hostages
Me libré de mis obligaciones = I freed myself from my obligations

libertar (R3)
to free from physical restraint
Libertaron a los presos = The prisoners were freed

librar
to free from obligation; to rescue from danger
Me libré del chaparrón por los pelos = I only just escaped the downpour

---

lucido
splendid, brilliant
una interpretación lucida = a brilliant performance

†**lúcido**
lucid, clear (person, mind)
una mente lúcida = a clear mind

---

lujo, lujoso
luxury, luxurious
Viven en el lujo = They live in luxury

lujuria, lujurioso
lust, lustful
La lujuria es un pecado capital = Lust is a cardinal sin

---

llama
flame, blaze, passion; llama (animal)

las llamas del fuego = the flames of a fire
la llama del amor (R3) = the flames of love

llamada
call, knock on door

Oí una llamada a la puerta = I heard a knock at the door

llamamiento
call (eg to arms, to strike)

un llamamiento a las armas = a call to arms

llamarada
sudden, short-lived blaze; sudden flush to face

La casa ardió con grandes llamaradas = The house burned in a great blaze

---

mantenimiento
maintenance (for conservation)
el mantenimiento de un avión = maintenance of an aircraft

manutención (f)
maintenance (keeping alive with food, etc)
El sueldo casi no nos alcanza para la manutención = Our wages scarcely cover our upkeep

---

materia
matter; material(s) (abstract); subject
El mundo físico está formado por materia y energía = The physical world is made up of matter and energy
Hay materia para la reflexión = There's food for thought
Es experta en materia de derechos humanos = She's an expert in human rights matters

material (m)
material (lit or fig)
recoger material para un libro = to collect material for a book
Este material es impermeable = This material is waterproof

media	promedio	medio
mean (maths); mid-field players (soccer); stocking	average	middle; medium; means
La media actual de vida es de ochenta años = The present average lifespan is eighty years	**Como promedio, voy al cine dos veces al mes** = On average, I go to the cinema twice a month	**en medio de la carretera** = in the middle of the road
La media no juega bien = The mid-fielder does not play well	**Los obreros cobran un promedio de €1.400 al mes** = The workers earn an average of €1,400 a month	**los medios informativos** = the (information) media
Hoy en día se suele usar medias hasta la cintura = Today people wear stockings up to the waist		**por todos los medios** = by all means

medicamento	medicina	medicación
medicine (drug)	study of medicine; cure in abstract sense	medication
La médico le recetó un medicamento = The doctor prescribed a medicine	**estudiar medicina** = to study medicine	**tomar su medicación** = to take one's medication
	tomar medicinas para el corazón = to take medicines for one's heart	
	una medicina amarga = a bitter pill to swallow	

NOTE: **medicamento**, **medicina** and **medicación** are all used after **tomar**.

montañés (ADJ)	montañero (N)	montañoso (ADJ)
native of **la Montaña** in Cantabria	mountaineer	mountainous
	Es la ambición de todos los montañeros subir al Everest = Every mountaineer's ambition is to climb Everest	**una región montañosa** = a mountainous region
montés (ADJ)	**montaraz** (ADJ) (R3)	
mountain-dweller, wild (of animal)	wild	
una cabra montés = a mountain goat	**Su aspecto montaraz asustaba** = His wild look frightened people	
un gato montés = a wild cat		

†**monte** (m)
mountain (lower than **montaña** but also used in
    many proper names of mountains); woodland
**Se puede subir a la cumbre del monte en
    media hora** = You can get to the top of the hill
    in half an hour
el monte Sinaí = Mount Sinai
Los bandidos se refugiaron en el monte =
    The outlaws hid in the woodland

montaña
mountain, mountainous area

escalar una montaña = to climb a
    mountain

---

†**moral** (f)
morality, ethics; drive, push, energy; morale
estudiar la moral = to study ethics
Tiene mucha moral = She has a lot of drive
Tiene la moral por los suelos = His morale is at
    rock bottom

moraleja
moral (of a story, etc)
la moraleja de este cuento = the
    moral of this tale

---

movedizo	**movible**	**móvil**	**conmovedor**
restless; unstable, loose; inconstant (fig)	movable	mobile	moving (in psychological sense), poignant
arenas movedizas = quicksands	**una silla movible** = a movable chair	**teléfono móvil** = a mobile phone	**La ceremonia era muy conmovedora** = The ceremony was very moving

---

nombrar
to appoint
La nombraron presidenta = She was
    appointed president

nominar
to nominate
nominar para un Óscar = to nominate
    for an Oscar

---

nuevo
new
Es nuevo en esta vecindad = He's new in
    the neighbourhood
Me he comprado un coche nuevo = I've
    bought a new car

novedoso
novel
un coche con adelantos novedosos = a
    car with new (technical) advances

---

oferta	**ofrecimiento**	†**ofrenda**
offer in a shop, gift, bargain; supply (commercial)	offer to do sth	offering (in religious sense)
Artículos de limpieza están de oferta = Cleaning materials are on offer	**Acepté su ofrecimiento para ir** = I accepted her offer to go	**Hizo una ofrenda a sus dioses** = He made an offering to his gods
una oferta de trabajo = a job offer		
la oferta y la demanda = supply and demand		

oficial
official (ADJ); official, officer (N)
Lo sé de forma oficial = I know from
  official sources
**El oficial dio la orden de lanzar el
  ataque** = The officer gave the order to
  launch the attack

oficioso
unconfirmed (not official)
fuentes oficiosas = unofficial,
  off-the-record sources

oficio
trade, profession
Es fontanero de oficio = He's a plumber by
  trade

†**oficina**
office (room, agency)
¿Dónde está la oficina de turismo? =
  Where's the tourist office?

---

ola
wave
Se dejó llevar por una ola
  = He let himself be carried
  by a wave

oleaje (m)
swell
**No nos pudimos bañar
  porque había demasiado
  oleaje** = We couldn't bathe
  because there was too much
  swell

oleada
wave (fig)
**El ejército atacó en
  oleadas** = The army
  attacked in waves
**Una oleada de pánico
  recorrió la ciudad** = A
  wave of panic spread
  through the town

---

papa (m)
Pope
El Papa vive en el Vaticano = The Pope
  lives in the Vatican

papá (m)
Daddy
¡Hola, papá! = Hi, Dad!

---

parada
stop (eg bus stop); parade
  (military)
dos minutos de parada =
  two minutes' stop
una parada militar = a
  military parade

parador (m)
hotel run by state agency
  (Pen)
**El Hostal de los Reyes
  Católicos se convirtió
  en parador**

paradero
whereabouts; in Am = bus
  stop; train station
de paradero desconocido
  = of unknown
  whereabouts
**Bajamos en el próximo
  paradero** (Am) = We'll
  get off at the next stop

paro
unemployment; standstill

Está en paro = He's unemployed
paro cardíaco = cardiac arrest

parado
unemployed (ADJ and N);
  stationary (ADJ)
**El número de parados va
  en aumento** = The
  number of unemployed is
  rising
El ascensor está parado =
  The lift is stationary

párroco
parish priest

El párroco dio una homilía sobre la envidia = The parish priest gave a homily on jealousy

parroquiano
parishioner; regular customer

Hay que atender primero a nuestros parroquianos = We must attend to our customers first

parroquia
parish, parish church; clientele

Se casaron en la parroquia = They got married in the parish church
Esta carnicería tiene una parroquia extensiva = This butcher's has an extensive clientele

---

†**parte** (m)
message, report
el parte meteorológico = weather forecast

†**parte** (f)
part, share
Me comí una parte del pastel = I ate a part of the cake

parto
childbirth
un parto prematuro = a premature delivery

---

perjuicio
damage, harm
La avería de la caldera produjo perjuicios en el piso de abajo = The fault in the boiler caused damage to the flat below

prejuicio
prejudice
Estás lleno de prejuicios = You're full of prejudice

---

pesca
fishing
ir a la pesca = to go fishing

pescado
fish when caught
Este pescado huele mal = This fish smells bad

†**pez** (m)
fish when alive
Hay muchos peces en el río = There are a lot of fish in the river

---

†**pisar**
to walk on; to walk off with (sth that sb else was hoping to have) (R1)
Perdón, te he pisado el pie = I'm sorry, I trod on your foot
Me ha pisado lo que tenía pensado = She's already said what I had thought

†**pisotear**
to trample on, to stamp on

Después de tirarlo al suelo lo pisotearon = After throwing it to the ground they trampled on it

---

†**plan** (m) (SEE ALSO **plana**, **plano** on p. 101)
plan, scheme; basis, arrangement

†**plano**
plane, level; plan, map (of city)

El plan de urbanización se refleja en el plano de la ciudad = The development plan is reflected in the map of the town

planear
to plan (more abstr and less precise than **planificar**); to hover, glide, soar
Estoy planeando mi futuro = I'm planning my future
El águila (f) **planeaba en el cielo** = The eagle soared in the sky

planificar
to plan
planificar la economía = to plan the economy

NOTE: The nouns **planeamiento** and **planificación** are similarly discriminated; **planificación** is used in such contexts as **planificación familiar**, **planificación urbana**.

---

plantar
to plant; to throw out (R1); to curb (R1)
plantar árboles = to plant trees

plantear
to pose (problem)
Planteó el problema y lo resolvió = He posed the problem and solved it

---

†**plato** (n)
plate
Dame el plato = Give me the plate

plató
set (cinema)
Vamos al plató a rodar la escena = Let's go on set to film the scene

---

población (f)
population; village
La población de esta ciudad es de doscientos mil = The population of this town is 200,000
Hay una población en el centro del valle = There is a village in the centre of the valley

poblado
settlement
un poblado de África Central = a Central African settlement

pueblo
people; village or small town
el pueblo español = the Spanish people
un pueblo de mil habitantes = a town of 1,000 inhabitants

---

poder
power, authority; physical strength (R3)
el poder del estado = the power of the state

poderío
dominion, supremacy; physical strength (R3)
el poderío del ejército = the might of the army

potencia
of motor, machine
la potencia de la moto = the power of the motorbike
Estados Unidos es una gran potencia = The USA is a great power

---

poema (m)
long or epic poem
El Poema de Mío Cid

poesía
shorter poem; poetry in general
Le leyó una poesía a la niña = She read the little girl a poem
Prefiero la novela a la poesía = I prefer novels to poetry

---

policíaco	**policial**
related to the police (but used in a restricted number of contexts)	related to the police (gen)
novela policíaca = thriller (novel)	**medidas policiales** = police measures
expediente policíaco = police file	
investigación policíaca = police investigation	

polvo	**pólvora**	**polvera**	**polvareda, polvero (Am)**
dust, powder	gunpowder	powder compact	cloud of dust
Los muebles están cubiertos de polvo = The furniture is covered in dust	**como un reguero de pólvora** = like wildfire	**Metió la polvera en el bolso** = She put the powder compact in her handbag	**Se levantó una polvoreda/polvero tras la explosión** = A cloud of dust rose after the explosion

preparación (f)	†**preparativos** (pl)
act of preparing; preparedness	preparations, preliminaries
un atleta de gran preparación = a well-prepared athlete	**Estoy haciendo los preparativos para el viaje** = I'm making preparations for the journey

†**presenciar**	†**presentar**
to be present at, to witness	to present (gen), to introduce sb
presenciar un accidente = to witness an accident	**presentar los papeles** = to present one's papers
	Me presentó a su amiga = She introduced me to her friend

prodigio	**pródigo**
prodigy	prodigal, lavish
un niño prodigio = a child prodigy	**la parábola del Hijo Pródigo** = the parable of the Prodigal Son

programa (m)	**programación** (f)
individual program(me) (radio, TV, theatre, computer, etc)	collection of individual programmes; development of a programme
Cómprame un programa, por favor = Buy me a program(me), please	**La programación de esta semana es malísima** = The programmes this week are dreadful
Con este nuevo programa es posible hacer dibujos animados = With this new program you can make cartoons	**Al comienzo del año se realiza la programación de las actividades del año** = At the beginning of the year we do the programme of activities for the year

proposición (f)
proposition, proposal
Mi proposición es que esperemos un poco antes de decidir = My proposal is that we wait a bit before deciding

propósito
aim, purpose
Tengo el propósito de adelgazar = My aim is to lose weight

---

rebasar
to exceed, go beyond

El tema me rebasa el entendimiento = The matter goes beyond my understanding
La pelota rebasó la raya = The ball went over the line

repasar
to revise (BrEng), review (Am); to iron, mend (clothes)
Los alumnos repasaron la lección = The pupils revised/reviewed the lesson
La madre repasó las camisas de su hijo = The mother mended her son's shirts

---

recepción (f)
act of receiving; reception as ceremony; desk in hotel, etc

En el mostrador de recepción había una chica = There was a girl at the reception desk
Ofreció una recepción a los embajadores = He held a reception for the ambassadors

recibimiento
reception in moral sense, welcome

El recibimiento fue apoteósico = The reception was tremendous

recibo
receipt (written)

Dame un recibo, por favor = Please give me a receipt

---

respecto
respect (relation)
con respecto a = with respect to
en este respecto = in this respect

respeto
respect, deference
Hay que mostrar más respeto a los ancianos = You should show more respect for old folk

---

retiro
retirement; quiet spot; retreat (religious)
Hizo más en el retiro que cuando trabajaba = He did more in retirement than when he was at work
un retiro espiritual = a spiritual retreat

retirada
retreat (military)
la retirada de Moscú = the retreat from Moscow

---

rodar
to roll, to travel; to shoot (film)
Rodó la piedra hacia abajo = She rolled the stone down
rodar una película = to shoot a film

rodear
to surround
Los soldados se encontraron rodeados = The soliders found themselves surrounded

---

romántico	**romance**	**románico**
related to Romanticism; sentimental; generous	N = Romance (language); Castilian; verse form comparable with ballad ADJ = Romance (of languages)	Romanesque, Norman (architecture); Romance (of languages)
romano	**rumano**	**romanista**
Roman	Rumanian	versed in Roman law or Romance languages

---

rotura	**ruptura**
breaking, smashing, tearing	breaking off
la rotura de un jarro / del tobillo = the breaking of a jug / of one's ankle	**la ruptura de relaciones diplomáticas / las conversaciones** = the breaking off of diplomatic relations / conversations
La rotura de vaqueros está de moda = Torn jeans are in fashion	

---

seco	**reseco**
dry	very dry; thin and wizened
Llovió anoche pero ahora todo está seco = It rained last night but now everything is dry	**el aspecto reseco de la anciana** = the wizened appearance of the old woman

---

secretaria	**secretaría**
female secretary	secretariat

---

semilla	**semillero**
seed, pip	nursery, seedbed (for plants); den, hotbed, breeding ground (of vice)
la semilla de una flor / de una fruta	**Sacaron las plantas del semillero para transplantarlas** = They took the plants out of the seedbed to transplant them
	un semillero de talentos = a nursery for talent
	un semillero de delincuencia = a breeding ground for crime

[†]**sensato**	[†]**sensible**
sensible	sensitive; noticeable (change, increase, etc)
Dejemos al niño con su prima: es una chica muy sensata = Let's leave the boy with his cousin: she's a very sensible girl	**Los rubios tienen la piel muy sensible al sol** = Fair people's skin is very sensitive to the sun
	un sensible cambio en las temperaturas = a noticeable change in temperature

seña
sign; address (pl); distinguishing features (pl)
Le hice una seña = I signalled to him
Mis señas son . . . = My address is . . .
Con las señas que me has dado me es difícil saber de qué se trata = From the features you've given me it's difficult to know what it's about

señal (f)
sign, signal, mark
El golpe le dejó una señal en la frente = The blow left a mark on his forehead
La debilidad es una señal de anemia = Weakness is a sign of anaemia

---

significado
meaning (usu in verbal sense)
¿Cuál es el significado de esta palabra? = What is the meaning of this word?

significación (R3)
meaning; significance, importance
La significación verdadera de sus palabras sólo se reveló después = The true meaning of her words was only revealed later
un discurso de gran significación = a speech of great significance

---

solo (ADJ)
alone
Está triste porque se encuentra sola = She is sad because she's alone

sólo, solamente (ADV)
only
Queda sólo / solamente un pastel = There's only one pastry left

---

†**sostener**
to maintain, to hold, support (lit and fig)
sostener a una familia = to support a family

Puso el palo para sostener la tabla = He positioned a stick to hold up the plank
sostener un argumento / una teoría = to support an argument / theory

sustentar (R3)
to maintain support; to sustain (opinion, etc)
sustentar a la familia = to support the family

sustentar una idea = to sustain an idea

NOTE: **sostener** and **sustentar** appear to be largely interchangeable, but **sostener** is much more frequent, and is preferred with **que . . . Sustentar** is mainly used in abstract contexts.

---

sueño
dream, sleep
Tengo sueño, voy a la cama = I'm tired, I'm going to bed
Anoche tuve un sueño horrible = Last night I had a horrible dream

ensueño
fantasy
una casa de ensueño = a dream house

---

sugerencia
suggestion (gen), idea, invitation
Mi sugerencia es que vayamos al cine = My suggestion is that we go to the cinema

sugestión
act of suggesting
las sugestiones del diablo = the devil's suggestions
la sugestión hipnótica = hypnotic suggestion

†**tabla**	**tablero**	**tablado**
plank, board (large); table (in mathematics, etc)	plank (small), slat; board (for chess, etc)	plank floor, esp stage
una tabla de madera = a wooden plank	**un tablero de ajedrez** = a chessboard	**Los artistas bailaban sobre el tablado** = The artistes were dancing on the stage
la tabla de multiplicar = the multiplication table	**el tablero de la mesa** = the table top	

tapar	**tapiar**
to cover up, seal, obscure (view)	to wall up
Tápate bien, hace frío = Wrap up well, it's cold	**Hay que tapiar las ventanas de la vieja fábrica** = The windows of the old factory must be boarded up
Tapó la botella con un tapón = She closed the bottle with a stopper	
El nuevo edificio tapa la vista = The new building obscures the view	

tarta	**torta**	**tortilla**
tart, often as dessert and elaborate	pie, anything that has been kneaded, and has a round, thin shape	omelette (Pen); maize/corn pancake (Mex)
De postre prefiero tarta = I prefer tart for dessert	**una torta de aceite** (a thin, aniseed-flavoured wafer)	**una tortilla de patatas** = a potato omelette

†**tempestad** (f)	**temporada**	†**temporal** (m)
storm (lit and fig)	season, period, spell	spell of rough weather, usu at sea
La tempestad hizo zozobrar el barco = The storm made the boat capsize	**la temporada futbolística** = the football season	**El temporal obligó a amarrar la flota pesquera** = The rough weather compelled the fishing fleet to moor

N O T E : **tempestad** and **temporal** are to a considerable extent interchangeable.

terreno	**terruño**	**tierra**
piece of land, field; terrain	native soil, homeland	earth; land (as opposed to sea), soil, country
Se compró un terreno en el campo = He bought a plot of land in the countryside	**su amor al terruño** = his love for his homeland	**La Tierra es redonda** = The Earth is round
		Los marineros habían perdido las esperanzas de ver tierra = The sailors had lost hope of seeing land
		Tenía las botas llenas de tierra = He had his boots full of soil
		Me gusta mi tierra = I like my country

tratamiento (SEE ALSO trata, trato on p. 102)	†trato	tratado
treatment (medical, chemical, etc); style of address	relationship between people; behaviour	treaty; treatise
un tratamiento médico = a medical treatment	Tengo mucho trato con mis vecinos = I have a lot to do with my neighbours	firmar un tratado = to sign a treaty
tratamiento de tú = addressing someone as *tú*		

válido	valioso	†valeroso
valid; strong	valuable; powerful	brave, valiant
Este certificado no es válido = This certificate is not valid	una pulsera muy valiosa = a very valuable bracelet	El Cid era valeroso = The Cid was valiant
valiente	valido (R3)	
courageous	favourite	
un chico muy valiente que no se acobarda por nada = a very courageous boy who is not scared by anything	el valido de la reina = the queen's favourite	

votación (f)	voto
act of voting; number of votes cast	vote (political); vow (religious); pl = wishes (R3)
La votación tuvo lugar el domingo pasado = Voting took place last Sunday	depositar el voto en la urna = to place one's ballot paper in the box
La votación ha dicho mayoritariamente sí = There has been a majority 'yes' vote	ejercer el derecho al voto = to exercise the right to vote
	un voto de castidad = a vow of chastity
	Hacemos votos por su pronta recuperación = We send our best wishes for her full recovery

4.2 Similar form – different meaning

The following sets of paronyms are similar in form but unrelated in meaning.

abrasar	abrazar
to burn up, to scorch, to parch (ALSO fig)	to embrace (sb, a cause); to seize (opportunity)
El incendio abrasó completamente el palacio = The fire completely burned down the palace	Al llegar a la estación se abrazaron = They embraced when they arrived at the station
Nos abrasábamos en el coche = We were sweltering in the car	El político abrazó la causa de los pacifistas = The politician embraced the pacifists' cause
Me abrasaba la curiosidad = I was consumed by curiosity	

acantilado	alcantarilla	cantera	cántaro
cliff	sewer	quarry	pitcher

acunar	acuñar
to rock (of baby)	to coin
La madre acunaba al niño = The mother rocked the child	**acuñar monedas** = to mint coins
	acuñar una expresión = to coin an expression

†**adjudicar (algo a uno)**	**ajusticiar**
to award (sth to sb)	to execute, to put to death
El comité le adjudicó el premio = The committee awarded him the prize	**El verdugo ajustició al reo** = The executioner executed the convict

alcaide (m)	**alcalde** (m)
prison governor	mayor

alegar	**allegar**
to allege, to plead	to gather, to bring together; to add, to state in addition
El acusado alegó su inocencia = The accused pleaded his innocence	**allegar los datos** = to gather data

legar	**ligar**	**liar(se)**
to bequeath	to bind; to court, to pick up (R1); to make thicker (cooking)	to tie, to wrap, to roll; to die (R1); to get into a muddle (refl)
El padre legó la casa a su hija = The father bequeathed the house to his daughter	**Las cuerdas le ligaron los brazos** = The ropes bound his arms	**Lió los periódicos para tirarlos** = She tied up the newspapers in order to throw them out
	El chico se ligó a / ligó con una chica = The boy picked up a girl	
	ligar la salsa = to thicken the sauce	

amagar	**amargar(se)**
to threaten	to make bitter (lit and fig); to become bitter (refl)
Me amagó con una navaja = He threatened me with a knife	**Estas hierbas amargarán demasiado la sopa** = These herbs will make the soup too bitter
Amaga con llover = It's threatening to rain	**Me amargó su actitud** = Her attitude made me bitter
	Se ha amargado recordando su pérdida = He has become bitter in remembering his loss

aparejar
to get ready (tr)
Estaba aparejado el buque para zarpar = The ship was ready to sail

aparear
to mate (tr and refl)
La vaca y el toro se estaban apareando = The cow and the bull were mating

†aparecer
to appear, to come into sight
La muchacha apareció detrás de los cristales = The girl appeared outside the window

---

apuntalar
to prop up

Apuntalaron la casa que amenazaba ruina = They propped up the house which was threatening to fall down

apuntar
to aim, to point (gun); to point out, to point at; to note down; to prompt (theatre)
Apuntó con su escopeta = He took aim with the gun
Se apuntó a la lista de espera = She put her name on the waiting list

---

asentamiento
settlement, emplacement
Colocaron los cañones en su asentamiento = The cannons were mounted in their emplacement
un asentamiento de los colonos = a colonists' settlement

asentimiento
assent, consent
Los padres dieron su asentimiento a la boda = The parents gave their consent to the wedding

---

aterrar
to frighten

Los monstruos aterran a los niños = Monsters frighten children

aterrizar
to land (only on land: to land on the sea = **amar(iz)ar**, to land on the moon = **alunizar**)
El avión aterrizó suavemente = The plane landed gently

---

atracar
to hold up (eg bank); to moor, to bring alongside; to stuff, to cram with food
atracar un banco = to rob a bank
El barco atracó en el muelle = The boat moored at the quay

atrancar
to bar (eg door); to clog (eg pipe), to jam

atrancar la puerta = to bar the door

---

aun
even
Aun los más torpes lo acertaron = Even the dimmest people got it right
Aun con los ojos vendados te reconocería = I'd recognize you even with my eyes blindfolded

aún
still, yet
Aún vive tu madre = Your mother is still alive
Aún no ha contestado = She still hasn't replied

NOTE: Purists insist that these words are stressed differently, but many speakers pronounce them the same.

averiguar	**averiarse**
to find out (address, time of train, etc)	to break down
Tengo que averiguar su domicilio = I must find out her address	**Se me averió el coche** = My car has broken down

avisar	**avistar**
to inform, let know	to descry, see far off
Te aviso mañana si puedo ir = I'll tell you tomorrow if I can go	**Los tripulantes avistaron un barco a la deriva** = The crew espied a drifting boat

baca	**vaca**
roofrack	cow

bandeja	**bandera**
tray	flag

barreno	**barreño**
shot hole, (large) drill	washbowl
Volaron la piedra con barrenos = The rock was blown up with shot holes	**Se lavaron en el barreño** = They washed in the bowl
Para hundir los barcos Cortés empleó barrenos = To sink the ships Cortés used drills	

bronco	**ronco**
rough (surface), gruff (voice), rude (manner)	hoarse
modales broncos = rude manners	**una voz ronca** = a hoarse voice

cacharro	**cachorro**	**cachondo** (ADJ)
earthenware pot; useless object, old car (R1)	puppy	sexy
un cacharro de cocina = a cooking pot	**La perra tiene cachorros** = The bitch is having puppies	**Se puso cachondo al ver la película** = He got turned on by the film
Tengo la casa llena de cacharros = My house is full of useless objects		

calar	**colar**	†**callar**
to soak, to drench, to permeate	to filter, to strain off (eg water from vegetables); to slip sth through (eg customs) (more frequently refl)	to be quiet
Me caló la lluvia = The rain drenched me	**colar el café** = to strain the coffee	**¡Cállate, tío!** = Shut up!
	Se coló en el estadio = He slipped into the stadium	
	NOTE ALSO the R1 expression **no cuela** = it doesn't hold water (I don't believe your story)	

campana	**campaña**	**campiña**
bell	countryside (esp Am); campaign (gen)	open country, flat stretch of farmland
Por quien doblan las campanas = *For whom the bell tolls*	**una casa en la campaña** = a house in the countryside **lanzar una campaña militar** = to launch a military campaign	**la verde campiña holandesa** = the green Dutch countryside

†**cana**	†**caña**	
white, grey hair (usu pl)	reed, stalk, cane (of sugar); rod (for fishing); tall wine-glass, beer-glass (for draught beer)	
Me están saliendo canas = I'm beginning to get grey hair	**caña de azúcar** = sugarcane **una caña de pescar** = a fishing rod **¿Me pagas una caña?** = Will you buy me a beer?	

canon (m) (R3)	†**cañón** (m)	**canónigo**
canon (music, law, etc); official, regular payment	tube, pipe, barrel (gun), canyon (as ADV) wonderful (R1)	canon (religious)
La Iglesia marca cánones de conducta = The Church lays down canons of conduct **Aboné el canon anual de mi plaza de garaje** = I paid the annual rental for my parking space	**Un rifle de dos cañones** = a double-barrelled rifle **el Gran Cañón** = the Grand Canyon **Lo pasamos cañón** (R1) = We had a great time	**Es canónigo de la catedral de Toledo** = He's a canon of Toledo cathedral

capo	**capó** (m)
boss, chief	bonnet/hood of car
los capos de la droga = the drug barons	**Levantó el capó para revisar el motor** = She raised the bonnet to check the engine

casa	**caza**
house, company	hunting
una casa adosada = a terraced house	**la caza del zorro** = fox hunting
una casa de perfume = a perfume company	

celda	**célula**
cell (prison)	cell (biological; political)
Metieron al preso en la celda = The prisoner was put in the cell	**las células del cuerpo humano** = the cells of the human body **una célula comunista** = a communist cell

cigarra	**cigala**
cicada	crayfish
Las cigarras cantaban alegremente = The cicadas sang merrily	**La cigala es un marisco** = Crayfish is a kind of seafood

NOTE: There is much confusion between these two terms.

†**cima**	**sima**
peak	abyss

ciudad (f)	**cuidado**
city, town	care

coro	**corro**
chorus, choir	ring, circle (of people)
Un coro de niños cantaba en el coro de la iglesia = A children's choir was singing in the choir of the church	**Formaron un corro** = They formed a circle

crear	†**creer**	**criar**
to create	to believe, to think	to produce (eg of the earth); to nurture, to raise, to bring up, to educate, to rear
Dios creó el mundo = God created the world	**Se cree inteligente** = She thinks herself intelligent	**criar caballos** = to rear horses
		Al huérfano le criaron los tíos = The orphan was brought up by his aunt and uncle

crepitar	**increpar**
to crackle (R3)	to shout angrily at
El fuego crepitaba en el hogar = The fire crackled in the hearth	**El peatón increpó al conductor por saltarse el semáforo** = The pedestrian shouted angrily at the driver because he had jumped the traffic-light

cuna	**cuña**
cradle (lit and fig)	wedge; influence, influential person (R1)
la cuna de la civilización = the cradle of civilization	**Pon cuñas bajo las ruedas del camión** = Put wedges under the wheels of the lorry

derrocar	†**derrochar**	†**derrotar**
to throw down; to demolish (building); to overthrow (government)	to squander (money)	to defeat, to rout (army)
Los rebeldes derrocaron al rey = The rebels overthrew the king	**Derrocharon su fortuna** = They squandered their money	**derrotar al enemigo** = to defeat the enemy

dividir to divide **dividir en porciones** = to divide into portions **Divide diez entre cinco** = Divide ten by five	†**divisar** to make out, to descry **Divisó el barco en el horizonte** = He made out the ship on the horizon
enjugar to wipe **Se enjugó las lágrimas** = He wiped his tears	**enjuagar** to rinse **Hay que enjuagar la ropa después de enjabonarla** = You must rinse the clothes after soaping them
expresar to express (words, actions, etc) **Expresamos nuestro agradecimiento** = We expressed our thanks NOTE: French *exprimer* = to express	**exprimir** to squeeze out, to wring; to exploit **exprimir un limón** = to squeeze a lemon **Exprimió sus ropas mojadas** = She wrung out her wet clothes **Esta empresa exprime a sus trabajadores** = This firm exploits its workers
feraz (R3) fertile (only with **tierra**) **una tierra feraz** = fertile land	†**feroz** fierce **un animal feroz** = a fierce animal **Tengo un hambre feroz** = I'm starving

fundar to found	†**fundir(se)** to fuse, to melt	**hundir** to sink (tr) (to sink (intr) = **hundirse**); the PP **hundido** = demoralized, crestfallen	†**hender** to cleave, to make one's way through (a crowd)
fundar una asociación = to found an association	**El metal se fundió** = The metal melted **Se fundieron en un abrazo** (fig) = They melted in an embrace	**hundir un barco** = to sink a ship **La noticia la dejó hundida** = The news left her downcast	**El portaaviones hendía las aguas** (R3) = The aircraft-carrier cut through the waters

grabadora tape-recorder	**grapadora** stapler
†**jugar** to play (game)	†**juzgar** to judge

mentar	†mentalizarse	mentir
to mention (refer to, usu pejoratively); to mention (gen) = **mencionar**	to prepare oneself mentally, make up one's mind	to lie
En la discusión mentó a mi madre = In the argument he insulted my mother	**Se mentalizó para ganar** = He made up his mind to win	**¡Mientes como un bellaco!** = You lie like a rogue!

†negar	anegar (R2–3)
to deny	to flood
Niega haber cometido el delito = He denies having committed the crime	**El agua anegó el local** = The water flooded the premises

pana	paño
corduroy	cloth (gen); duster, rag
un pantalón de pana = a pair of corduroy trousers	**un paño de cocina** = a dishcloth

panal (m)	pañal (m)
honeycomb	nappy, diaper

†pelo	piel (f)
hair	skin, peel, fur, leather
Tiene el pelo rubio = She has fair hair	**Tengo la piel sensible** = I have sensitive skin
	un bolso de piel = a leather handbag

pena	peña
sadness, pity, shame	crag, rock, circle (of people)
Es una pena que no pueda venir = It's a pity she can't come	**escalar la peña principal** = to scale the main summit
Da pena verla tan abatida = It's sad to see her so depressed	**una peña ciclista** = a cycling club

picar	pinchar	pellizcar
to sting (of insect), to bite (of fish); to itch (of eyes, skin, etc); to burn (of sun); to punch (holes in paper); to believe (R1)	to prick, to puncture (tyre); to eat **pinchos** (= snacks); to inject (drugs) (refl)	to pinch (with fingers)
Pican los insectos = The insects are biting	**El clavo me pinchó el neumático** = The nail punctured the tyre	**Me pellizcó en el brazo** = She pinched my arm
El pez picaba el anzuelo = The fish bit on the hook	**¿Quieres pinchar?** = Do you want to have some *pinchos*?	
Me pican los ojos = My eyes itch		
Pica el sol = The sun is burning		
El revisor picaba los billetes = The inspector punched the tickets	**Se pincha para combatir el dolor** = She injects drugs to combat the pain	
Le dije una mentira y picó (R1) = I told him a lie and he believed it		

rallar	**rayar**
to grate	to scratch, to make a line on, to cross (out); to border on
queso rallado = grated cheese	**Esta mesa está rayada** = This table is scratched
	Raya en lo fantástico = It borders on the fantastic
	Raya en los cincuenta (años) = She's almost fifty

remedar	**remediar**	**remendar**
to copy, to imitate, to be like	to remedy, to make good	to mend (usu clothes), to repair
La casa remeda un palacio = The house looks like a palace	**Hay que remediar la situación** = We must remedy the situation	**remendar un calcetín** = to mend a sock

sabana	**sábana**
savannah	sheet (on bed)

sauce (m)	**saúco**
willow	elder

semanario	**seminario**
weekly (paper)	seminary, seminar

soliviantar	**solventar** (R3)
to incite, stir up	to pay, settle, resolve
El cacique soliviantó a la población = The local boss stirred up the populace	**He solventado mis deudas** = I've paid off my debts
	Hemos solventado nuestras diferencias = We have settled our differences
	solventar una avería / un problema = to rectify a fault / resolve a problem

sotana	**sótano**
cassock	basement, (bank) vault

talante (m)	**talento**
mood, willingness	talent
estar de buen/mal talante = to be in a good/bad mood	**Tiene talento para la música** = She has a talent for music
hacer las cosas de mal talante = to do things grudgingly	

tina	**tiña**
vat, bathtub; echo	ringworm; filth
Arquímedes salió gritando de la tina = Archimedes got out of the bathtub shouting	**Está enferma de tiña** = She's got ringworm
	Tienen la casa llena de tiña = Their house is filthy

tope (m)
limit; collision; snag; buffer
fecha tope = deadline
Frenó a cinco centímetros del tope = He
  braked five centimetres away from the buffer

topo
mole (animal), ALSO = spy (fig)
El topo tiene fama de ser ciego = Moles
  have a reputation for being blind
Había un topo infiltrado en la banda = A
  mole had infiltrated the group

valla
fence, barrier, hurdle (athletics)

valle (m)
valley

4.3 Similar verb stem

The sets of words in this section each have the same or a similar verb
stem. Such sets are especially liable to confusion.

alumbrar
to light up, to shed light on (lit
  and fig); to give birth to (R3)
Esta bombilla alumbra poco
  = This bulb gives out little
  light
**El municipio decidió
  alumbrar el parque** = The
  town decided to illuminate
  the park
**Los periodistas alumbraron
  el escándalo** = The reporters
  brought the scandal to light
**La Virgen alumbró al Niño
  Jesús** = The Virgin gave birth
  to the Child Jesus

†deslumbrar
to dazzle (lit and fig)

Me deslumbraba el sol =
  The sun dazzled me
**Quedé deslumbrado con
  su belleza** = I was
  dazzled by its beauty

vislumbrar
to catch a glimpse of (lit and
  fig)
**vislumbrar la solución al
  problema** = to glimpse a
  solution to the problem

avalar
to support, to endorse, to
  guarantee

**Me avaló mi padre para la
  compra** = My father
  guaranteed the purchase for
  me

evaluar (R2–3)
to assess, evaluate (to estimate
  a value for)

**El professor evalúa los
  exámenes** = The teacher
  assesses the exams
**Las pérdidas se evaluaban
  en cien millones de
  euros** = The losses were
  estimated at 100 million
  euros

valorar
to value, to price (to place a
  value on, in a positive
  sense) (**valorizar** and
  valuar are also used in
  these senses)
**En esta casa se valora
  mucho la puntualidad**
  = In this house
  punctuality is highly
  valued

†**caer**	**decaer**	**recaer**
to fall (gen); **caer en algo** (R1) = to understand sth	to decay, to decline (health, fortune), to flag (effort)	to fall again; to have a relapse (health), to backslide (criminal); often fig as in responsibility or advantage falling to sb
Se cayó al suelo = She fell to the ground **caer en la tentación** = to fall into temptation	**El imperio romano decayó lentamente** = The Roman empire decayed slowly **Su moral estaba decaída** = His morale was flagging **Decaía su salud** = Her health was declining	**El enfermo recayó** = The sick person had a relapse **El premio recayó en mi colega** = The prize fell to my colleague

†**coger**	**acoger**	†**escoger**	**recoger**
to take hold of, to catch, to seize, to pick (fruit)	to welcome; avail oneself of (refl)	to choose	to gather, to pick up (sth fallen), to collect (things and people, eg from station); to put in order
coger fruta / el tren / un catarro / al niño = to pick fruit / to catch the train / to catch a cold / to pick up the child	**Se acogieron calurosamente** = They welcomed each other warmly **Se acogió a su derecho** = He claimed his rights	**Escoge el libro que quieres** = Choose the book you want	**Se cayó y la recogí** = It fell and I picked it up **Te recojo a las cinco en la estación** = I'll pick you up at five at the station **El cuarto estaba desordenado y lo recogí** = The room was untidy and I tidied it up

†**correr**	**descorrer**	†**recorrer**
(intr) to run (of water, person), to pass quickly (of time); to travel quickly (of car) (tr); to cover (distance); to draw (bolt, curtain)	to pull back (eg bolt, curtain)	to travel through (a place, country)
El río corría mansamente = The river flowed peacefully **Corre el tiempo** = Time is passing quickly **Este coche corre mucho** = This car goes very fast **correr el cerrojo** = to draw the bolt	**descorrer el cerrojo / la cortina** = to pull back the bolt / the curtain	**Recorrió todo el país / la ciudad** = She travelled the whole country / through the town

†**cortar**
to cut (gen)

acortar
to shorten length or duration of

recortar
to cut away excess, to cut back; to cut out (eg from newspaper)

cortar el pan / la conversación = to cut the bread / to interrupt the conversation

acortar una falda / la estancia = to shorten a skirt / one's stay

El gobierno recortó el presupuesto = The government cut the budget

Recorté el artículo en el periódico = I cut the article out of the paper

---

gastar
to spend (money, time), to waste; to wear out (clothes)

desgastar
to wear out, to wear away, to waste

†**malgastar**
to waste, to squander

engastar
to set (eg stone in ring)

Gastamos mucho dinero = We spent a lot of money
gastarse la ropa = to wear out one's clothes

Mi hijo desgasta los zapatos muy de prisa = My son wears shoes out very quickly

malgastar una fortuna = to squander a fortune

El joyero engastó los diamantes = The jeweller set the diamonds

---

†**llevar**
to carry, to transport, to take; to wear; to spend (time) (SEE **25.8** and **29.6**)

conllevar
to entail; to bear, to suffer (with patience), to put up with (sb who is difficult)

sobrellevar
to put up with

Te llevo a la estación = I'll take you to the station
Llevaba una falda = She was wearing a skirt
Llevábamos mucho tiempo esperándola = We had spent a long time waiting for her

Este puesto conlleva viajar mucho = This job entails a lot of travelling
Conlleva su enfermedad con optimismo = He bears his illness optimistically

Sobrellevó su enfermedad durante diez años = He put up with his illness for ten years

---

mantener
to maintain (gen of a conversation, interview, etc); to hold up

†**sostener**
to sustain; to hold up (lit): more frequent in this sense than **mantener**

Mantuvo una entrevista con el ministro = He held a conversation with the minister
Le costó mucho mantenerse en pie = He found it difficult to keep standing
Mantén la cuerda mientras la anudo = Hold the string while I tie a knot in it
Mantuvo su promesa = He kept his promise

sostener una conversación = to sustain a conversation
Sostuvo el cuadro que caía = She held up the picture that was falling down

---

matar
to kill (person, time)

rematar
to finish off; to polish off (work, etc)

---

†mover	conmover	conmocionar	remover
to move (tr) (physical)	to move (tr) (emotional)	to shock, to upset, to trouble	to stir
mover una cosa de sitio = to move something from its place	**Me conmovió su actitud/ sufrimiento** = His attitude/suffering moved me	**Quedó conmocionada por el golpe** = She was shocked by the blow	**Hay que remover la leche** = You must stir the milk

NOTE: to move (intr) = **moverse**

†negar (algo a uno)	denegar (algo a uno)	†renegar (de algo)
to deny (sb sth)	to refuse, to reject, to turn down; to deny (sb sth)	to renounce, to deny sth
Los ateos niegan la existencia de Dios = Atheists deny the existence of God	**Le denegaron el permiso** = They refused him permission	**Los mártires no renegaron de su fe** = The martyrs did not renounce their faith
Me han negado mis derechos = I've been denied my rights		

NOTE: **negarse a hacer algo** = to refuse to do sth

†poner	componer	descomponer	recomponer
to put; to lay (table, egg); to plant (bomb); (refl) to put on (clothes, play, etc)	to compose; to fix,	to decompose (tr); to upset (order, tranquillity)	to fix, to repair
Puso un libro en el estante = She put a book on the shelf	**componer una melodía / una poesía** = to compose a tune / a poem	**El cuerpo se descompone** = The body is decomposing	**Se rompió el reloj y lo recompuso** = The watch broke and he repaired it
poner la mesa = to lay the table		**El prisma descompone la luz** = The prism separates the light	
La gallina no puso muchos huevos hoy = The hen didn't lay many eggs today			
Los terroristas pusieron una bomba en el almacén = The terrorists planted a bomb in the store			
Se puso la ropa = He put on his clothes			

†probar	†aprobar	comprobar	reprobar
to prove, to test, to taste, to try (food), to try on	to approve of; to pass (exam)	to check, to verify	to reproach, to blame, to condemn
¿Has probado este vino? = Have you tried this wine?	aprobar un examen / las cuentas = to pass an exam / to approve the accounts	comprobar el estado de los neumáticos = to check the state of the tyres	El padre reprobó al hijo = The father reproached his son
Se probó el vestido = She tried on the dress			

reglar	regir	arreglar
to rule (line); to make rules for; to regulate, to adjust	to rule (country), to run (business, college); to govern (grammar)	to arrange, sort out; to repair; to tidy up; to set up, organize
reglar el sistema bancario = to regulate the banking system	regir un país con una mano férrea = to rule a country with an iron hand	Me voy a arreglar el pelo = I'm going to arrange my hair
Regló la alineación de los faros de su coche = He adjusted the alignment of his car's headlights	Rigió la empresa con prudencia = He ran the business prudently	No puedo arreglar este interruptor = I can't fix this switch
		Arreglé la entrevista = I arranged the interview

reglamentar	regular
to make rules for	to regulate
La vida está demasiado reglamentada = Life has too many rules	La calefacción se regula con el termostato = The heating is regulated with a thermostat

†seguir	†conseguir	perseguir	proseguir
to follow, to carry on	to get, to obtain; conseguir + inf = to succeed	to chase, to hunt, to persecute	to carry on, to continue (R3)
El detective siguió al sospechoso = The detective followed the suspect	conseguir un puesto = to get a job	El tigre perseguía la presa = The tiger was hunting its prey	El peregrino prosiguió su camino = The pilgrim pursued his journey
	No conseguí verla = I didn't manage to see her	Nerón persiguió a los cristianos = Nero persecuted the Christians	

†volver	revolver	devolver
(tr) to turn round, to turn over; to give back (R1); to turn, to make (intr) to return; **volver a +** inf = to do again	to stir, to mess up, to disturb	to give back; to vomit
Se volvió para mirar = She turned round to look **Estas moscas me vuelven loca** = These flies are driving me mad **La volví a encontrar** = I met her again	**Revolvió el café** = He stirred the coffee **Las niñas revolvieron la habitación** = The children messed up the bedroom	**Te lo devuelvo mañana** = I'll give it you back tomorrow **La comida le sentó mal y la devolvió** = The meal disagreed with him and he was sick

4.4   Words distinguished by gender

Because of its distinctive gender endings, Spanish does not have many words with the same form but different meanings (true homonyms). However, there are many pairs of words distinguished only by the **-o** and **-a** (and sometimes also **-e**) endings which are easily confused. These are known as gender paronyms.

4.4.1   Different gender – similar meaning

SEE ALSO **21.11**.

acta	acto
minutes, record (of proceedings), often pl	action, deed, act (in play)
El notario levantó acta de los hechos = The lawyer took a record of the proceedings	**Fue un acto cruel** = It was a cruel act NOTE ALSO **en el acto** = immediately

ánima	ánimo
soul, spirit (as religious concept)	energy, courage, spirit (as quality)
las ánimas del Purgatorio = the souls in Purgatory	**¡Ánimo!** = Courage! **Trabajaban con ánimo** = They were working with spirit

banca	banco
banking (as system); bank (in a game of chance)	bank (as individual establishment); bench
servicios de banca = banking services **Gana la banca** = The bank wins (in a casino)	**¿Hay un banco en esta calle?** = Is there a bank in this street? **un banco de datos / de sangre** = a data/blood bank **Me senté en un banco para esperar a mi novia** = I sat down on a bench to wait for my girlfriend

†**banda**
band, gang; band (music); strip, ribbon
una banda de jóvenes = a gang of
   youngsters
la banda sonora = the soundtrack
Le impusieron la banda de la orden de
   San Antonio = They conferred on him
   the ribbon of the order of St Anthony

†**bando**
faction, party, side; edict
el bando opuesto = the opposite side
publicar un bando = to publish an edict

---

†**barca**
small boat (rowing, fishing, etc)
una barca de remos = a rowing boat

†**barco**
boat (gen), ship, vessel
El barco se encontraba en alta mar =
   The ship was on the high seas

---

bolsa
bag (gen); purse; stock exchange
una bolsa de plástico = a plastic bag
invertir fondos en la Bolsa = to invest
   money in the stock exchange
NOTE ALSO: **bolsillo** = pocket

bolso
handbag, bag (more stylish than **bolsa**)
un bolso de mujer = a woman's handbag

---

calzada
roadway
La calzada no es para los peatones = The
   road is not for pedestrians
una calzada romana = a Roman road

calzado
footwear
una tienda de calzado = a shoe shop

---

†**caña**
reed, stalk, cane (of sugar), rod (for fishing);
   tall wine-glass, beer-glass (for draught beer)

caño
pipe, jet

el caño está oxidado = the pipe has rusted

---

carga
load to be carried; duty; charge (military and
   explosive)

una carga pesada (lit and fig) = a heavy
   burden
una carga explosiva = an explosive charge

cargo
burden (fig), responsibility

Desempeña el cargo de contramaestre =
   He carries the responsibility of being the
   boatswain
El trabajo corre a cargo del albañil =
   The work is the responsibility of the builder

NOTE ALSO: **cargamento** = act of loading; shipment, cargo

---

cerca
hedge, fence

una cerca de madera = a wooden fence

†**cerco**
hedge, fence, enclosure (more gen than
   cerca); ring, hoop, rim; siege
Saltó el cerco del jardín = He jumped over
   the garden fence
Alrededor del malabarista había un cerco
   de curiosos = There was a circle of
   curious spectators around the juggler
El ejército puso cerco a la ciudad = The
   army laid siege to the city

cesta
basket (for shopping, waste paper)
una cesta de la compra = a shopping basket
(set phrase, both literal and in sense of
weekly shopping)

cesto
basket, usu larger than **cesta**
Recogió cuatro cestos de fresas = She
picked four baskets of strawberries

---

charca
pond
la charca del pueblecito = the village pond

charco
puddle
Ha llovido, cuidado con los charcos =
It's been raining, be careful of the puddles
BUT **cruzar el charco** = to cross the pond
(the Atlantic)

---

cinta
band, strip, ribbon; tape (magnetic); (conveyor)
belt
Siempre llevaba una cinta en el pelo = She
always wore a ribbon in her hair
¿Tienes una cinta de vídeo vacía? = Do
you have a blank videotape?
una cinta transportadora = conveyor belt

cinto
belt (around waist)
Llevaba el llavero colgado del cinto = She
carried the keyring hanging from her belt
NOTE: **cinto** is only used for a belt that is
worn. Compare **cinturón de seguridad**
= safety belt (and see **cinta** opposite).

---

conducta
conduct, behaviour
un chico de muy buena conducta = a very
well-behaved boy

conducto
conduit
El conducto de agua estaba atascado =
The water conduit was blocked

---

cuba
cask, barrel
La cuba estaba llena de ron = The barrel
was full of rum

cubo
cube; bucket, bin (for rubbish)
un cubo de hielo = an ice cube
La niña llenaba el cubo de arena = The
little girl filled the bucket with sand
el cubo de la basura = the dustbin (US
trashcan)

---

cuchilla
blade; big, heavy knife, kitchen knife, butcher's
knife
una cuchilla de afeitar = a razor blade
**El carnicero partía las chuletas con una
cuchilla** = The butcher split the chops with
a cleaver

cuchillo
knife (gen)

un cuchillo afilado = a sharp knife

---

cuenca
basin (geographical)
la cuenca del río = the river basin

cuenco
earthenware bowl
Bebía leche del cuenco = She drank milk
from the bowl

---

†**cuenta**
account, bill, calculation; report (of event)

Llevo las cuentas en el ordenador = I do
my accounts on the computer

cuento
story, tale; pl = troubles, upsets, tales, silly
things (R1)
contar un cuento = to tell a story
¡Son cuentos lo que dices! = You're telling
me tales!

---

derecha
right hand, right side, right wing (political)
a la derecha = on the right
un partido de derechas = a right-wing party

derecho
right (rightful claim), justice, law
estudiar el derecho = to study law
Estoy en mi derecho = I'm within my
rights
el derecho divino de los reyes = the
divine right of kings

---

directiva
board (of directors), guideline
la directiva de la empresa = the company
directors
**Le dio a la empleada directivas para
vender los productos** = He gave the
employee guidelines for selling the products

directivo
manager, executive
el directivo de la compañía = the director
of the company

---

emisora
radio station
**La emisora retransmitía el partido de
fútbol** = The radio station was broadcasting
the football match

emisor (m)
transmitter
**El emisor de ondas cortas estaba en el
sótano** = The shortwave transmitter was in
the basement

---

escala
scale; stop (on air journey)

Hicimos escala en Buenos Aires = We had
a stopover in Buenos Aires
**un terremoto de cinco grados en la escala
Richter** = an earthquake measuring five
degrees on the Richter scale
El plano está a escala 1:1000 = The map is
on a scale of 1:1000

escalo
common only in the phrase **robo con escalo**
= breaking and entering

---

espina
thorn; bone in fish
Me he pinchado con las espinas del rosal
= I've pricked myself on the thorns of the
rosebush

espino
hawthorn
El espino tiene flores blancas y olorosas
= Hawthorn has white, scented flowers

falla	fallo
fault	verdict; weakness, drawback
una falla del terreno = a fault in the ground	**el fallo del jurado** = the jury's verdict
	Este argumento tiene sus fallos = This argument has its drawbacks

NOTE ALSO: **las fallas valencianas** = annual festivity in Valencia (Spain) in which satirical cardboard figures are burnt

fosa	foso
grave; depression in sea or on land	pit, hole, ditch, moat
Metieron el féretro en la fosa = They placed the coffin in the grave	**el foso del castillo** = the castle moat
la fosa de Java = the Java trench	

fruta	fruto
fruit (what is eaten, on the table), ALSO fig	fruit (gen of trees and plants, and fig)
Me gusta la fruta ésta = I like this fruit	**los frutos de la tierra** = the fruits of the earth
fruta seca = dried fruit like prunes, raisins, apricots	**el fruto de su labor** = the fruit(s) of her labour
	NOTE: **frutos secos** = nuts

gesta	gesto
exploit	gesture
las gestas de los conquistadores = the exploits of the conquistadors	**Hizo un gesto con la mano** = She made a gesture with her hand

gimnasia	gimnasio
gymnastics	gymnasium
Practico la gimnasia en el gimnasio = I practise gymnastics in the gymnasium	

†gira	giro
tour, trip (eg theatrical)	gyration, turn; trend (in events)
La artista hizo una gira en Cuba = The artist went on a tour in Cuba	**el giro de las hélices** = the turning of the propellors
	el giro de los acontecimientos = the turn of events
	Le mandé un giro postal = I sent him a postal order

gorra	gorro
cap with peak	tight-fitting cap with no peak (eg swimming)
Se quitó la gorra para saludar al capitán = He took off his cap to salute the captain	**un gorro de natación** = a swimming cap
	un gorro de cocinero = a chef's hat
	un gorro de lana = a woolly hat

grada
step, stair
Subió las gradas del estadio = He went up the stadium steps

grado
degree, rank
Las temperaturas bajaron hasta los cero grados = The temperature dropped to zero
Este militar tiene grado de general = This soldier has the rank of general

---

grana
cochineal, deep red

El torero iba vestido de oro y grana = The bullfighter was dressed in gold and red

grano
grain (cereals); particle (eg sand); pimple (on face)
un grano de arena = a grain of sand
Tienes un grano en la mejilla = You've got a pimple on your cheek

---

helada
frost
una fuerte helada = a sharp frost

helado
ice-cream
Tomo un helado vainilla = I'll have a vanilla ice cream

---

huerta
(large) garden, typically for cultivation of fruit and vegetables
una extensa huerta = a vast garden
la huerta valenciana = the area of irrigated land around Valencia (Spain)

huerto
(small, private) garden

Tengo un huerto cerca de la casa = I have a garden near my house
Estos tomates son del huerto = These tomatoes are from the garden

---

labia (R1)
talkativeness
Tiene mucha labia = He has a lot of lip (is very talkative)

labio
lip (lit)
Tenía un cigarrillo entre los labios = He had a cigarette between his lips

---

leña
wood, firewood
Echaba leña a la lumbre = She threw wood on the fire
La policía dio mucha leña = The police struck out at people

leño
log
El leño duró un par de horas = The log burned for a couple of hours

---

madera
wood, plank
Este mueble es de madera = This piece of furniture is made of wood

madero
piece of wood, timber
Fabrican maderos en la serrería = They make timber in the sawmill

---

manta
blanket, large shawl
una manta eléctrica = an electric blanket

manto
cloak, gown; mantle (R3)
Don Juan llevaba un manto negro = Don Juan wore a black cloak
La hierba se cubría de un manto de nieve = The grass was covered with a mantle of snow

marea tide	**mareo** travel sickness
moda fashion, style **Esta falda está de moda** = This skirt is in fashion	**modo** way, method; mood (grammar) **El modo de escribir es éste** = This is the way to write **en modo subjuntivo** = in the subjunctive mood
muñeca wrist; female doll, tailor's dummy **En la muñeca llevaba un reloj de oro** = On her wrist she was wearing a gold watch **La niña jugaba con sus muñecas** = The little girl was playing with her dolls	**muñeco** male doll **un muñeco de nieve** = a snowman
negativa negative (act of negating) **Contestó con la negativa** = He answered in the negative	**negativo** negative (photography)
paga pay, instalment, pocket money **Mi padre me daba la paga cada domingo** = My father used to give me my pocket money every Sunday	**pago** (single) payment **El pago lo hizo en metálico** = She paid in cash
papelera container for rubbish, waste-paper basket; desk; paper mill **Tira los papeles a la papelera** = Throw the papers in the waste-paper basket	**papelero** stationer, paper manufacturer **El papelero me vendió un cuaderno** = The stationer sold me an exercise book
†**partida** departure (R3); register, certificate; game (chess, cards); party (eg hunting) **El embajador anunció su partida** (R3) = The ambassador announced his departure **una partida de nacimiento** = a birth certificate **una partida de ajedrez** = a game of chess **una partida de caza** = a hunting party	**partido** party (political); game, match; advantage **un partido político** = a political party **un partido de fútbol** = a football match **sacar partido (de algo)** = to benefit (from sth)
pesa weight (physical object placed on scales or pendulum of clock) **Pon la pesa en el peso** = Put the weight on the scales	**peso** weight (measurement and gen); weighing scales **peso pesado** = heavyweight (boxing) **Se me ha quitado un peso de encima** = That's a weight off my mind **un argumento de peso** = a weighty argument

pimienta	**pimiento**
pepper for seasoning	sweet pepper (vegetable)

plana	†**plano**
sheet (of paper)	plane, level; map (usu showing streets)
Le hice escribir toda la plana = I made him write on the whole sheet of paper	**un plano de la ciudad** = a map of the city
la plana mayor de la empresa = the top people in the firm	

punta	†**punto**
point, sharp end; touch, tinge	dot, speck; point in scoring or in discussion or in time or place; full stop; stitch (sewing)
la punta de una espada = the point of a sword	**La ciudad está representada como un punto en el mapa** = The town is shown as a dot on the map
sacarle punta a un lápiz = to sharpen a pencil	**Puso el punto final a la carta** = She put the final full stop to the letter
	el punto principal = the main point
	conseguir noventa puntos = to get ninety marks
	hacer punto = to knit

rama	**ramo**
branch, bough (from trunk) (lit and fig)	(small) branch (from another branch); bunch (of flowers); area (of science or industry)
El roble tenía gran cantidad de ramas = The oak tree had a great number of boughs	**Les extendí un ramo de olivo** = I held out an olive branch to them
La sintaxis es una rama de la lingüística = Syntax is a branch of linguistics	**Domingo de Ramos** = Palm Sunday
	un ramo de flores = a bunch of flowers
	Tiene una amplia experiencia en el ramo de la higiene = He has wide experience in the area of hygiene

resta	†**resto**
subtraction (in arithmetic)	remains, remainder
La resta es una operación aritmética = Subtraction is an arithmetical operation	**Come lo que quieras y el resto lo tiramos** = Eat what you like and we'll throw the rest away

ría	**río**
estuary (north-west coast of Spain)	river

suela	**suelo**
sole (of shoe): **la suela del zapato**	ground, surface, floor(ing) (of house)
	Se cayó al suelo = She fell to the ground
	Tiene la moral por los suelos = His morale is at rock bottom

†**tormenta**	**tormento**
storm (with thunder and lightning) (lit and fig)	torment, anguish

trata trade (esp slaves, etc)	**†trato** relationship between people, behaviour; pact, deal
la trata de blancas = the white slave trade	**Tienen un trato muy cordial** = They have a very cordial relationship **Hicimos un trato ventajoso para todo el mundo** = We struck a good deal for everyone

4.4.2   Different gender – different meaning

acera pavement, sidewalk	**acero** steel
ara altar: **el ara** (f) **de la iglesia** = the church altar NOTE: **en aras de** (R3) = in the interests of	**aro** children's hoop
arca chest, box **las arcas del estado** = the state coffers NOTE: **el arca** (f) **de Noé** = Noah's ark, **el Arca** (f) **de la Alianza** = the Ark of the Covenant	**arco** arch(way); bow (violin, archery); spectrum **el arco de un violín** **el Arco de Triunfo** = the Arc de Triomphe **un arco iris** = a rainbow **Abarca todo el arco de posibilidades** = It includes the whole range of possibilities
†barra bar, rail; parallel bars (gymnastics); toolbar (computing) **la barra de la cortina** = the curtain rail **La gimnasta hizo ejercicios en la barra** = The gymnast did exercises on the parallel bars **Este botón muestra o oculta la barra de herramientas** = This button shows or hides the toolbar	**barro** mud; clay, earthenware **Se cayó en el barro** = He fell in the mud **una vasija de barro** = an earthenware vessel
baza trick (at cards); ace, trump card (fig) **ganar una baza** = to win a trick **jugar su última baza** = to play one's trump card NOTE: **bazo/a** as ADJ = fawn, brownish	**bazo** spleen
†bola ball, often solid, as in bowls or billiards **una bola de billar**	**bolo** skittle

bomba
bomb; pump
Explosionaron la bomba = They exploded the bomb
Utilizó la bomba para hinchar la rueda = He used the pump to inflate the tyre

bombo
bass drum; exaggerated praise (R1)
Se anunció a bombo y platillo = It was announced amid a great song and dance

---

braza
breast stroke, style (swimming)
nadar a braza = to swim the breaststroke

brazo
arm (of person or chair)

---

caca (R1)
pooh (US poop)
El bebé hizo caca en el pañal = The baby did a pooh/poop in its nappy/diaper (US)

caco (R1)
thief
El caco entró por la ventana = The thief entered by the window

---

casa
house, home, business, firm

caso
case, instance; case (grammar); notice
NOTE: **hacer caso a** = to notice

---

casca
bark (used in tanning); grape skins (after being trampled)

casco
helmet (soldier, motorcyclist); area of city

el casco antiguo = the old quarter

---

caza (m and f)
(f) hunting; (m) fighter
ir a la caza = to go hunting
Dos cazas fueron abatidos = Two fighters were shot down

cazo
small saucepan; ladle
echar agua al cazo = to put water in the saucepan
Serví la sopa con el cazo = I served the soup with the ladle

---

cepa
plant (of vine), stock
Las cepas no suelen ser muy altas en España = Vines are not usually very tall in Spain
de pura cepa = born and bred

cepo
wheel clamp; trap (for catching game)
No dejes el coche allí, te ponen un cepo = Don't park there, they'll clamp you
El conejo cayó en el cepo = The rabbit fell into the trap

---

cigarra
cicada

cigarro
cigarette, cigar

---

†**copa**
glass, goblet, cup, trophy; top (esp of tree)

una copa de coñac = a glass of brandy
ganar la copa = to win the cup
la copa del árbol = the treetop
un sombrero de copa = a top hat

copo
flake (snowflake: **copo de nieve**, cornflake: **copo de maíz**); small bundle of wool, etc, ready to be woven

cota	**coto**
contour, level; coat (of mail): **una cota de malla**	reserve (game, fishing); goitre (Am)
La inflación ha alcanzado cotas alarmantes = Inflation has reached worrying levels	**un coto de caza** = a game reserve
†**cuadra**	**cuadro**
stable (for all animals); block (of flats, houses) (Am)	any shape made with right angles; pane (of glass); frame, picture; (garden) patch
Vive a dos cuadras de aquí (Am) = She lives two blocks away	**un cuadro de Velázquez** = a picture by Velázquez
	En el cuadro plantaba todo tipo de flores = He planted all kinds of flowers in the bed
cuña	**cuño**
wedge	die, die stamp for coining
	un noble de nuevo cuño = a recently created nobleman
deuda	**deudos** (only pl) (R3)
debt	members of a family
Tenía una deuda de quinientos euros = He had a € 500 debt	**Dé el pésame a los deudos** = Give my condolences to the family
foca	**foco**
seal (animal)	focus, focal point; headlight, spotlight
	ser un foco de atención = to be a focus of attention
	Los focos del coche me cegaron = I was blinded by the car headlights
fonda	†**fondo**
tavern, small restaurant	bottom, background; fund
gama	**gamo**
hind (female deer); scale, range	buck (male deer)
toda la gama de colores = the whole colour range	
grupa	†**grupo**
rump (of horse)	group (gen)
libra	**libro**
pound (weight, money)	book
libreta	**libreto**
savings book, pass book	libretto
la libreta de la caja de ahorros	**el libreto de una ópera**
†**loma**	†**lomo**
small hill	back (of animal)

llanta	**llanto**
metal rim of wheel	weeping, crying
El golpe rompió la llanta de la rueda = The bump broke the wheel rim	**Se oyó un llanto desconsolado** = Inconsolable weeping could be heard
manga	**mango**
sleeve (coat, shirt)	handle; mango
	el mango de un cazo
marca	**marco**
brand, trademark; record (sport); sign, mark, line	frame, framework
una marca comercial = a trade mark	**el marco del cuadro** = the picture frame
Estableció una nueva marca mundial = She established a new world record	**dentro del marco de la teoría** = within the framework of the theory
una marca de agua = a watermark	
pala	**†palo**
shovel, spade	stick, post, mast
palma	**palmo**
palm (of hand: **la palma de la mano**; or of palm tree: **la palma de una palmera**)	any short length or distance
	Su casa está a dos palmos de aquí = His house is two steps from here
	El chico está creciendo a palmos = The boy is growing bit by bit
pasa	**paso**
raisin	passage, way through; (mountain) pass; footstep; rate
	el paso del tiempo = the passage of time
	Ceda el paso = Give way (on Spanish roads)
	Seguí en sus pasos = I followed in his footsteps
	A este paso, nunca vamos a llegar = At this rate, we'll never get there
pasta	**pasto**
pasta; paste, pastry, pulp; cash (R1)	pasture
¿Te gusta la pasta italiana? = Do you like Italian pasta?	
pasta de anchoa = anchovy paste	
estirar la pasta = to roll out the pastry	
tener mucha pasta = to have a lot of money	
pata	**†pato**
foot, paw (of animal); leg (of animal, furniture); leg (of human) (R1)	duck
El perro tenía una espina en la pata = The dog had a thorn in its paw	
meter la pata = to put one's foot in it	

pelas (pl) (R1)	**pelo**
cash: originally referred to pesetas but is still used with this general meaning in Spain	hair
Tiene muchas pelas = She has lots of cash	**Tiene el pelo rubio** = She has fair hair

†**plata**	†**plato**
silver; money (Am)	plate, dish, course (of meal)

plaza	**plazo**
public square; place (eg in car-park); job; (fortified) town	period of time, time limit; periodic payment
la plaza del mercado = the market place	**dentro de un plazo de diez años** = within a period of ten years
Este aparcamiento dispone de 400 plazas = This car park has 400 spaces	**pagar a plazos** = to pay by instalments
una plaza fuerte = a fortified town	

puerta	**puerto**
door, gate	port; pass (in mountains)

puesta	†**puesto**
pp of **poner**, and used in many of the senses of this verb	place, position; job, post; stall
puesta en marcha = starting (of engine)	**en tercer puesto** = in third place
puesta en escena = staging (of play)	**Busco un puesto de trabajo en el extranjero** = I'm looking for a job abroad
	Había muchos puestos en el mercado = There were many stalls on the market

pulpa	**pulpo**
pulp	octopus; luggage strap

†**pupila**	†**pupilo**
pupil (of eye); ward (legal)	lodger; ward (legal)

†**rata**	**rato**
rat	short time
NOTE ALSO: **ratón** (m) = mouse (also for computer)	

raya	**rayo**
line, streak (on paper, stone, sand, etc); boundary; limit	ray, beam of light; (flash of) lightning; thunderbolt
la raya del pelo = parting (hair)	**los rayos del sol**
la raya del pantalón = crease (in trousers)	
Trazó una raya en la arena = He drew a line in the sand	**Fue fulminado por un rayo** = He was struck by a thunderbolt
pasarse de la raya = to overstep the mark	

rodilla	**rodillo**
knee	roller, rolling pin

rosca	**rosco**
thread (of screw)	bread roll (in ring shape); zero, nothing
la rosca del tornillo	**En el examen me han puesto un rosco =** They gave me zero in the exam
seta	**seto**
mushroom	fence, hedge
sigla	**siglo**
symbol, abbreviation, acronym	century
tira	**tiro**
strip (of paper, cloth, etc)	throw, shot (military, sport); team (of draught animals)
una tira de papel	**disparar un tiro =** to fire a shot
	el tiro al arco = archery
	El tiro de carruaje era de cuatro caballos = There were four horses drawing the carriage
[†]**trama**	**tramo**
woof (weaving); plot (literary); intrigue	section, stretch (eg of road); flight of steps **un tramo de escalera**
la trama de una novela	**Este tramo es muy sinuoso =** This stretch is very winding
traza	**trazo**
layout (architecture) (R3); appearance (of person, often pej): **mala traza**; traces (R2)	line, stroke
Hay trazas de que hay lobos = There are signs of wolves	**escribir con trazos muy firmes =** to write with firm strokes
tuna	[†]**tuno**
student music group	member of a *tuna*; rascal (R1)
vela	**velo**
wakefulness, vigil; candle; sail; pl = snot (R1)	veil
pasar la noche en vela = to spend the night awake	**Las musulmanas suelen llevar velo =** Muslim women usually wear the veil
encender una vela = to light a candle	
Los marineros izaron (las) velas = The sailors set sail	
Este niño siempre lleva las velas colgando = This child always has snot hanging from his nose	

5 Fields of meaning – vocabulary extension

This section looks at the vocabulary of a number of general fields of meaning. Choice of these fields has been motivated partly by the richness of Spanish vocabulary in certain areas of meaning, and partly by the rather different divisions of meaning which Spanish and English often make. The information is presented in tabular form, with the most general Spanish word (if there is one) usually at the top of the diagram. This method of presentation reveals the structure of vocabulary within each field more clearly and more memorably than is possible in a traditional dictionary. The information in this section may be used in order to build up a wider and more finely tuned vocabulary. The material presented here may be approached either via the title of each diagram (arranged for ease of reference in alphabetical order) or via the individual Spanish words, all of which are listed in the Spanish word index at the end of the book. Examples of current usage are given, but are not translated, since English equivalents are not always helpful and it is better to gain familiarity with the kinds of context in which the Spanish words are used.

ABRIGO

jacket, short coat		
chaqueta	jacket	**una chaqueta de cuadros**
americana		**Llevaba una americana cruzada**
chamarra (Mex)		**Ponte la chamarra, hace aire**
saco (Am)	(often of a suit)	**un saco sport / de lana**
cazadora	casual, usu with zip	**Esta cazadora se cierra con cremallera**
campera (Arg)		**Casi todas las camperas llevan cremallera**
chubasquero	windcheater, anorak	**un chubasquero de nailón**
three-quarter-length coat		
tres cuartos (m)		**El soldado llevaba puesto un tres cuartos**
trenca	duffel coat	**Los estudiantes solían llevar una trenca**

full-length coat, overcoat

abrigo	overcoat	Se quitó el abrigo al volver a casa
gabán (m) (R2–3)		Coge el gabán, hace frío
sobretodo (R3)		El caballero se puso el sobretodo
tapado (Am)	winter coat	Con este frío me compro un tapado

waterproof

gabardina	raincoat	Va a llover, toma la gabardina
impermeable (m)		El clima húmedo la obligó a comprarse un impermeable

housecoat, overalls

guardapolvo	for cleaning	El encargado de almacén llevaba un guardapolvo
bata	housecoat; schoolchild's overalls; doctor's white coat; dressing gown	Al levantarse se puso la bata del médico

bathrobe

albornoz (R2–3)	bathrobe	Al salir del baño se puso el albornoz

ACCIDENTE

general

accidente (m)		Ha ocurrido un accidente en carretera

minor

↑ **contratiempo**	(minor) mishap, unforeseen upset	¡Qué contratiempo! He perdido el tren.
percance (m)	(minor) misfortune, more serious than *contratiempo*	He tenido un percance al rozar el coche
siniestro (R3)	(serious) accident, catastrophe (esp natural disaster)	El terremoto originó un siniestro Las compañías de seguro siempre se refieren a siniestros, no a accidentes

↓ *major*

ACORDAR

to accept a suggestion

†acceder a algo / a hacer algo	to agree to sth / to do sth	Accedió a mi petición Accedieron a ir conmigo
†aceptar algo / hacer algo		Aceptó acudir a la cita
†consentir en hacer algo		El padre consintió en la boda
quedar en hacer algo		Quedamos en vernos el domingo
reconocer que . . .		Reconozco que tiene razón

to agree with sb else (one person with another or two or more people together)

estar †de acuerdo (con uno)	to be in agreement (with sb)	Estuvimos de acuerdo con ellos en la causa del accidente
ponerse †de acuerdo (con uno)	to come to an agreement (with sb)	Nos pusimos de acuerdo para salir mañana
†acordarse (con uno) (R3)		Acordé con él una entrevista
avenirse (con uno) / (en algo) / a hacer algo (R3)		Se avinieron en el reparto de la herencia
†acordar algo / hacer algo	to agree on sth / to do sth	Acordamos la hora de la cita
†convenir en algo / en hacer algo		Convenimos en el precio Convinieron en reunirse
†concordar en que . . .		Concordamos en que es un documento importantísimo

to agree, to tally (of things)

†concordar (con algo)	to agree, to tally (with sth)	La realidad concuerda con la teoría
†corresponder (a algo)		Las cifras se corresponden

AGUJERO

agujero	hole through sth; hole in a wall	Hay un agujero en la pared / la puerta
bache (m)	pothole (in the road)	La rueda cogió un bache en carretera
boquete (m)	large, irregular-shaped hole	El disparo hizo un boquete en el muro
brecha	gap (in fence or wall)	Las tropas abrieron una brecha en el muro / en las defensas enemigas

cavidad (f)	cavity	Tengo una cavidad en una muela La pared tiene una cavidad

hoyo	hole in ground	Los jugadores se quejaron porque
		  había hoyos en el campo
		un terreno de golf de dieciocho
		  hoyos

hueco	hollow, gap	Me escondí en el hueco de un árbol

LO ALTO

general

la parte superior	top, upper part	No alcanzo las herramientas, están en la parte superior del armario
la parte de arriba		Los libros están en la parte de arriba de la estantería
lo alto	the high part (eg of stairs)	No me gusta que el bebé esté en lo alto de la escalera

specific

†pico	summit (of hill)	Escaló hasta el pico más alto
cumbre (f)		la cumbre de la montaña / del éxito una conferencia cumbre
†cima		la cima de la montaña / del éxito
cresta	crest (of hill or wave)	la cresta de la colina / ola
†copa	of tree	El niño subió hasta la copa del árbol
remate (m)	of building	el remate de la fachada
principio	of list	el principio de la lista
†final (m)	of street	el final de la calle
†superficie (f)		la superficie del lago / del agua

AMABLE

amable	friendly	Gracias, eres muy amable
amistoso		Jugaron un partido amistoso Mantuvieron una convivencia amistosa

benévolo (R2–3) or
  benevolente
	kind, indulgent (of
	  people)
		El sacerdote era un hombre benévolo

111

benigno	mild, benign	un clima benigno un tumor benigno
cariñoso afectuoso	affectionate	Mi abuela es muy cariñosa un abuelo afectuoso
entrañable	likeable; intimate	amigos entrañables = bosom friends
†bueno bondadoso bonachón (R1)	good-natured	Es buena persona Tiene un carácter bondadoso El San Bernardo es un perro bonachón
bienintencionado	well-meaning	Es bienintencionado, nunca quiere hacer daño a nadie
generoso	generous	Los padres suelen ser generosos con sus hijos
filantrópico (R2–3)		La entidad tenía carácter filantrópico

ANILLO

general
  concrete

anillo	ring (gen)	los anillos de Saturno
aro	(also = hoop)	El niño jugaba con el aro
argolla	usu metal	Ató el burro en la argolla

  abstract

círculo	circle	Trazó un círculo; un círculo de amigos

specific
  for finger

anillo	ring (gen)	un anillo de compromiso
sortija	ring with stones	La sortija tenía un diamante
alianza anillo de boda / matrimonio argolla (Am)	wedding ring	El novio puso la alianza a la novia Llevaba un anillo de boda en el dedo Su esposa perdió su argolla
sello	signet ring	El cardenal lleva un sello en el dedo anular

  other

llavero	keyring	Se compró un llavero como recuerdo
anilla	for curtains; for birds; in gymnastics	las anillas de la cortina La atleta hacía gymnasia en las anillas

servilletero	serviette ring	Metió la servilleta en el servilletero
†pendiente (m) arete (m) aro (Am)	earring	Me regalaron unos pendientes/aretes/ aros (Am) de plata

APARECER

†aparecer	to come into view	Aparecen las estrellas a las siete
†comparecer	to appear in a court (legal)	El gamberro compareció ante la juez
†parecer	to seem	Me parece que no tiene razón
surgir	to arise	Un fantasma surgió ante mí Nos surgieron problemas
brotar	to sprout	Las plantas brotan

APARIENCIA

apariencia	act of coming into view	Su apariencia inesperada me sorprendió
aspecto pinta (R1)	visual impression	La casa tenía un aspecto ruinoso Tiene pinta de pordiosero
porte (m) (R3) aire (m) presencia (R2–3)	bearing	Su porte elegante le daba aires de princesa Se ve allí un aire muy acogedor La presencia del rey dignificó el acto
†semblante (R3) †facha (R1)	face	Tenía un semblante cadavérico una facha desastrosa

APODERARSE DE

general
adueñarse de (R2–3)	to take over, take control of	Entró y se adueño de la situación

†**posesionarse de** (R3)	to take possession of	El embajador se posesionó de su cargo
†**apoderarse**		El ejército se apoderó de la ciudad

specific

†**ocupar** (R3)	to confiscate	La policía ocupó a los traficantes dos kilos de drogas
confiscar		confiscar un camión de contrabando
hacerse con	to get hold of, appropriate	El dictador se hizo con el poder
†**apropiarse de** (R2–3)		Siempre se apropia de lo ajeno
usurpar (R3)	to usurp	usurpar el poder

APRESURARSE

†**apresurarse**	to hurry	Se apresuró a subir al tren
†**darse prisa**		Se dio prisa por / en terminar la redacción
†**apurarse** (Am)		Apúrate o llegaremos tarde
espabilarse (R1)		¡Espabílate!
aligerar (el paso) (R1)		Me dijo que aligerase

ARMA (DE FUEGO)

general

arma (de fuego)	weapon, (fire)arm	Las armas de fuego son peligrosas

specific

revólver (m)	revolver	El vaquero sacó su revólver
pistola	pistol	Los policías llegaron armados con pistolas
fusil (m)	rifle (military)	La compañía llevaba fusiles de asalto
rifle (m)	rifle (smaller, eg for hunting)	El forajido apuntó con el rifle al vaquero
escopeta	shotgun	una escopeta de caza
		Los maleantes atracaron el banco con escopetas recortadas
†**cañón** (m)	large gun	un cañón de artillería
artillería	artillery, guns	el cuerpo de artillería

AVISAR

general		
informar	to inform	El departamento me informó de los resultados

specific		
avisar	to notify	Ya te avisaré
notificar (R3)		El gobierno notificó a la embajada
anunciar	to announce	Los amigos anunciaron su llegada
indicar	to communicate	Le indicaron por dónde tenía que ir
comunicar		Le comuniqué el mensaje
		Me comuniqué con la policía
manifestar (R2–3)		Le manifesté mi disgusto
prevenir	to warn	Les previne de las consecuencias de su actuación
advertir		Le advertí del peligro que corría

AYUDAR

general		
†**ayudar**	to help	La ayudé a fregar
		Me ayudó en mi trabajo

more specific		
auxiliar (R3)	(suggests difficulty or danger)	Llegó la ambulancia para auxiliar a los heridos
socorrer (R3)		socorrer a los damnificados
apoyar	to support	Te apoyaré en tu candidatura
†**asistir**	to assist (R3)	asistir a niños necesitados
	to attend (medical) (R2)	Asistieron a su padre anciano
		Los heridos fueron asistidos en el hospital
echar un cable / †una mano a (R1)	to give a hand to	¡Oye! ¿Me echas un cable / una mano?

BARCO

general

| †**barco** | | Hicimos el viaje en barco |
| | | Los piratas abordaron un barco |

specific

   small

↑ †**barca**	rowing-boat, or small boat with motor	Los dos hicieron un paseo en barca
patera (Pen)	small boat	Los inmigrantes ilegales cruzan el Estrecho en pateras
bote (m)	dinghy	Rescataron al chico en un bote
lancha	inflatable boat with motor	Los marines desembarcaron lanchas
embarcación (f)	craft, small vessel	una embarcación menor/ pesquera/deportiva
nave (f)	vessel, sailing ship	una nave espacial = spaceship
navío	sailing ship, naval ship	un navío de guerra
		un capitán de navío
buque (m)	big ship with engine: merchant ship; warship	un buque de guerra

   large

BARRIO

general

†**barrio**	any area of a town	un barrio viejo
		un barrio en construcción
		En los barrios no hay tanta contaminación como en el centro
arrabal (m)	outer district	Hay muchas chabolas en los arrabales
periferia	suburbs on edge of town or just outside	Los autobuses comunican la periferia con el centro

wider area outside town, including neighbouring towns

†**afueras** (pl)	outskirts	Vivo en las afueras de la ciudad
alrededores (m pl)	surrounding area, vicinity	No vive en la ciudad, vive en los alrededores
cercanías (pl)		un tren de cercanías = a suburban train
inmediaciones (f pl)		Recorrí el castillo y sus inmediaciones
aledaños (m pl) (R2–3)		El avión se estrelló en los aledaños de la sierra

BASTO

general		
basto (R1–2)	coarse (lit or fig)	**un tejido basto**
		una madera basta
		tener modales muy bastos
†**rudo**	rough (lit) (R3); (of people) (R2)	**una tela ruda**
		un utensilio muy rudo
		rudos modales
burdo (R2–3)	coarse, crude	**un paño burdo**
		No me gustan sus burdos modales
more specific		
vulgar	vulgar (= common)	**Tiene gustos muy vulgares**
ordinario		**modales ordinarios**
†**grosero**	vulgar (= indecent)	**Me ofendió con sus palabras groseras**
incivilizado	uncultivated, uncivilized	**Es tan incivilizado es casi analfabeto**
inculto	uncultivated (lit) (R3); (of people) (R2)	**tierras incultas**
		un hombre inculto que no sabe ni leer
zafio (R3)	uncouth	**Tiene modales zafios**

BORDE

general		
borde (m)	edge	**al borde del abismo**
specific		
†**orilla**	bank, shore (of river, sea, etc)	**a orillas del río**
margen (f) (R3)		**las márgenes del río**
límite (m)	boundary (of territory); fullest extent	**Han pintado el límite del nuevo aparcamiento**
		el límite de nuestros conocimientos
†**linde** (m and f) (R3)		**los/las lindes del bosque**
		la linde oficial entre los dos pueblos
†**margen** (m)	area outside (page, society, etc)	**el margen de la página**
		al margen de la sociedad
†**canto**	edge of a coin, book, etc	**el canto de un libro / de una moneda**

| arista | edge of a cube, etc | El mueble tenía unas aristas muy agudas |
| [†]corte (m) filo | sharp edge of knife, etc | el corte de la navaja el filo del cuchillo |

BOTELLA

general
  small

↑	botellín (m)	bottle	Con un botellín fue suficiente
	botella		¡Se bebió toda la botella!
↓	botellón (m)		Un botellón, está bien para cuatro

  large

specific
  for water

botijo	earthenware pitcher (with spout and handle)	Fui a la fuente a llenar el botijo
botija		Bebió agua fresca de la botija una botija de cerámica
cantimplora	canteen	El excursionista llenó la cantimplora

  for wine

| bota | (leather) wineskin | una bota de vino tinto |
| porrón (m) | (glass) jar (with long spout) | Con el porrón se manchó |

  for perfume or medicine, etc

| frasco | flask; also jar | un frasco de perfume! el ¡Mete los insectos en un frasco! |

  for babies' feed

| biberón (m) | | Hay que esterilizar el biberón |
| pezonera (Arg) | | esterilizar la pezonera |

BRILLAR

literal
  constant

brillar	to shine	El sol brilla en el cielo
lucir		Esta bombilla luce poco Las estrellas lucen en la noche
relucir	to shine, blaze	El charol de sus botas relucía
relumbrar		En su mano relumbraba una espada
resplandecer		El metal fundido resplandecía Las estrellas resplandecen en la noche

deslumbrar	to dazzle	Me deslumbraron las luces del coche

intermittent

relucir	to twinkle	Sus ojos relucían
relumbrar (R3)		Las joyas relumbraban
rutilar (R3)	to sparkle	El oro / el diamante rutilaba
centellear	to sparkle, to flash, to twinkle	Una luz centelleaba a lo lejos
refulgir (R3)	to glitter	Las estrellas refulgen
destellar	to flash, to sparkle, to glitter	Los faros del puerto destellaban en la noche
fulgurar (R3)	to shine very brightly, to flash	Las llamas fulguraban en la oscuridad
rielar (R3)	to glimmer, shimmer	Las estrellas rielan; la luna riela en el mar

sudden

centellear		El relámpago centellea

figurative

brillar		El orador brilló por su amenidad
resplandecer (R3)		Su belleza resplandecía entre todas las participantes
sobresalir		María sobresalía por su inteligencia
relucir		María relucía por su inteligencia
lucirse		El torero se lució en la faena

CARA

physical part of body

†cara	face	Tenía la cara sucia
†semblante (m) (R3)		Tenía un semblante serio
†faz (f) (R3)		Su faz reflejaba el pesado paso de los años
rostro (R2–3)		un rostro simpático
jeta (R1)		¡Vaya jeta tiene el tío!

countenance, expression, appearance

†cara		No eres responsable de la cara que tienes, eres responsable de la cara que pones
†semblante (m) (R3)		el semblante que está tomando este asunto

surface

†cara		La moneda cambió de cara
†faz (f) (R3)		la faz de la tierra
†superficie (f)		la superficie del lago

CHARCO

general

  natural

charca	pond	la charca de la aldea

  artificial

estanque (m)	artificial lake or pond	Construyeron un estanque en medio del parque
balsa	pool (usu for irrigation); large puddle	una balsa de regadío Cuando llueve mucho se pueden formar balsas en vez de charcos
pantano	dam, swamp, marsh	Los pantanos abastecen a varias poblaciones Es peligroso andar por la zona de los pantanos

special senses

poza	large puddle; deep pool in river	un terreno lleno de pozas Es peligroso bañarse en este río porque hay muchas pozas
charco	puddle, pool	La lluvia ha dejado charcos en la acera un charco de sangre
piscina pileta (Arg) alberca (Mex)	swimming pool	una piscina/pileta/alberca climatizada

CHIRRIAR

chirriar	to squeak (of locks, hinges, brakes)	**Los frenos chirriaron**
		Le falta grasa a la bisagra y chirria
crujir	to creak, to crunch	**Se oía el crujir de las maderas al pisar**
		Con las pisadas la grava crujía
rechinar	to creak, to grind (of teeth)	**Apreté los dientes hasta que rechinaron**
chillar	to screech, to squeal, to squeak	**Los cerditos chillaban**

COGER

general		
†**coger**	to catch	**Cogí el tren / un catarro coger malas costumbres**
†**agarrar** (Am)		**agarrar el autobús** (Mex/Arg)
†**tomar**	to take	**Toma, es para ti**
atrapar	to catch, to trap	**La policía atrapó al delincuente**
pillar (R1)	to catch	**La policía pilló al ladrón**
		pillar un resfriado
specific		
†**tomar**	to adopt (eg a habit)	**Tomó por costumbre ir a pasear**
†**agarrar(se a)**	to grip, to hold on to (R2–3); to get hold of (R1)	**Le agarré del cuello**
		Para no caer se agarró a la barandilla
†**asir(se de/a)** (R3)	to seize	**La chica asió con fuerza el bolso**
		Se asió a las ramas para no caer
empuñar	to take a firm hold of	**El Cid empuñó su Tizona**
†**echar mano a**	to grab	**El niño echó mano al último pastel**

NOTE: In some parts of Latin America, **coger** = *to screw* (R1*), and is therefore avoided, **agarrar** or **tomar** being used instead.

COLINA

hill as a whole
   large

montaña	mountain	El Mulhacén es una montaña impresionante
†**monte** (m)	lower than **montaña**, with woodland	Tardamos un par de horas en alcanzar la cumbre del monte el monte alto/bajo
cerro	steep hill	Subimos al cerro el Cerro de los Ángeles (the geographical centre of Spain)
colina	hill	Desde la colina se veía el río
†**loma**	hillock	Bajó de la loma al anochecer
altozano		Destacaba el altozano en la llanura
otero	small hill isolated on plain	Desde el otero se dominaba la llanura
collado	ALSO pass	Es un paisaje de collados que se encadenan Pasaron por el collado al otro lado del monte
montículo	small mound	Se veían los montículos de piedras que se habían ido amontonando

   small

slope

cuesta	eg on road	Subimos la cuesta cuesta arriba/abajo
repecho	short, steep slope	El repecho final de la ascensión era duro
bajada	downward slope	Era una bajada muy suave
†**pendiente** (f)		una pendiente muy prolongada
†**vertiente** (f)		El río corría por una vertiente muy inclinada la vertiente norte/sur de la cordillera
†**declive** (m)	ALSO decline	El declive era muy pronunciado El declive del imperio romano
†**ladera**	hillside	Ascendieron por la ladera norte

COMPETICIÓN

general

	competition	una competición deportiva
†**competición** (f)		

concrete

concurso	competition	**un concurso televisivo / hípico / de caza / de belleza** **ganar el concurso** **el concurso para una plaza de médico**
†**certamen** (m) (R2–3)	(of music, literature, art, etc)	**un certamen musical / de dibujo** **convocar un certamen**
†**oposición** (f) (usu pl)	competitive exam for a public job	**Preparó las oposiciones para notario**

abstract

†**competencia**	competition (often commercial); competitiveness	**una competencia desleal** **El comercio libre fomenta la competencia**

CONTENTO

general

feliz	happy	**Con la fiesta hoy estamos felices** **Casi siempre es feliz**
contento	pleased	**Estoy muy contenta con mi nueva casa**

specific

dichoso (R2–3)	happy, fortunate, lucky	**El matrimonio me ha hecho dichoso** **Nos sentimos dichosos de poder ayudarte** **Fue un momento dichoso el día de la graduación**
jovial	cheerful, jovial	**un anciano jovial** **A pesar de su enfermedad es siempre jovial**
alegre	cheerful	**Con vino siempre se pone alegre** **Fue un día alegre** **Está alegre con el buen resultado**
alborozado	overjoyed	**Quedó alborozada al recibir el regalo**
regocijado (R3)	merry, joyous	**La noticia la dejó regocijada**

NOTE: **Contento, alborozado** and **regocijado** are not used with **ser**.

CONVERTIRSE

All the verbs in this table can be used to translate Eng *to become* according to the context.

with noun		
convertirse en	neutral: not as strong as Eng *to be converted into*	**Se convirtió en un asesino**
tornarse en (R3)		**Su duda se tornó en admiración**
transformarse en	stronger than **convertirse en**	**Tomó una poción mágica y se transformó en un monstruo**
metamorfearse en (R3)		**El ogro se metamorfoseó en príncipe**
†**llegar a**	implies progress or achievement	**Llegó a diputado**
with noun or adjective		
volverse	most neutral	**Se volvió loca** **Se ha vuelto más antipático** **El pan se ha vuelto duro** **El sueño se volvió pesadilla**
tornarse (R3)	(more usual with ADJ)	**La protesta se tornó violenta** **El desconocido se tornó una celebridad internacional**
†**hacerse**	implies a neutral or expected development (more usual with N)	**Se hizo ingeniero en tres años** **El financiero se hizo rico**
llegar a ser	implies progress or achievement	**Llegó a ser rey** **Llegó a ser famoso**
†**quedar(se)**	to be left, to begin to be (restricted in use)	**Se quedó viuda / huérfano**
venir a ser	implies casualness: to come to be	**Viene a ser lo mismo**
with adjective		
†**ponerse**	used with adjectives that take **estar**	**Se puso triste/rojo/mareado después de comer**
†**caer**	implies misfortune	**Cayó enfermo**
to become of		
†**ser de**		**¿Qué va a ser / ha sido de ella?**

CORTAR

general		
cortar	to cut	**Cortó el chorizo con un cuchillo**
more specific		
amputar	to amputate, to cut off	**El cirujano le amputó la pierna**
†**hender** (R3) †**partir**	to cleave, to split	**Con el hacha hendió el leño** **Su madre partió el pastel**
podar	to prune	**Pasó toda la tarde podando árboles**
practicar	to cut (a hole)	**Practicó un agujero con el taladro**
reducir	to cut down (fig), to reduce in quantity	**reducir un escrito / los gastos**
seccionar (R3)	to cut into sections; to cut (off), section (medical)	**La nueva avenida secciona en dos la ciudad** **La espada le seccionó el yugular**
suprimir **tachar**	to cut (out), to delete	**Hay que suprimir este párrafo** **Tacha esa palabra, no vale aquí**
recortar	to cut back	**Recortaron el presupuesto**
†**talar** **cercenar**	to cut (down)	**Taló todos los árboles/arbustos** **La máquina le ha cercenado los dedos** **El leñador cercenó el árbol** **El dictador cercenó las libertades democráticas**
†**tallar**	to carve	**Me gustaba tallar la madera / la piedra para crear estatuas**
truncar (R2–3)	to cut (short), to truncate	**Ha truncado la novela, no le gustaba como quedaba**

CRECER

general		
crecer	as natural process, and gen in size	**Ha crecido el niño / la economía / la planta**
more abstract		
acrecentarse (R2–3)*	to increase (in size)	**El número de parados se ha acrecentado estos años**
acrecer (R3)	to accrue, to improve	**Es difícil acrecer los beneficios en estos momentos**

aumentar	to increase (in quantity)	**Los gastos / las temperaturas han aumentado**
incrementarse		**La contaminación se ha incrementado de año en año**

more specific

ampliarse	to expand, to extend	**La población se ha ampliado más de lo que se podía prever**
extenderse		**El panorama se extendía a sus pies**
		El conferenciante se extendió demasiado en la descripción del viaje
engrandecerse (R3)	to get bigger	**Se engrandeció su negocio**
agrandarse		**Se ha agrandado el cráter del volcán**
alargarse	to increase in length	**Los días se alargan**
prolongarse		**La sequía /estancia se prolongó**
†**elevarse**	to increase in height	**El dólar se ha elevado un cinco por ciento**
		El número de accidentes se ha elevado bruscamente este fin de semana

figurative

desarrollarse	to develop	**La economía se ha desarrollado rápidamente**
desenvolverse		**Se desenvuelve bien en situaciones peligrosas**
prosperar	to prosper	**La economía local ha prosperado con las nuevas normas**
		Es una idea que ha prosperado y se adoptará cada vez más
medrar (R3)		**Medró con la ayuda de su compañero**

CUARTO

room in a building

cuarto	gen	**el cuarto para guardar los trastos**
		Juan está metido en su cuarto
sala	large room; public hall	**la sala de actos**
habitación (f)	gen; (bed)room in a hotel, etc	**Esta casa tiene tres habitaciones, salón, comedor, cocina y dos baños**
		El hotel tiene doscientas habitaciones
aposento (R3)	room(s), lodging	**El cortesano entró en los aposentos del rey**

specific rooms

comedor	dining room	**No caben todos los invitados en el comedor**
dormitorio	bedroom	**La casa tiene un salón y dos dormitorios** **Éste es el dormitorio de los niños**
recámara (Mex)		**La recámara es demasiado chica para dos camas**
sala de estar	sitting room	**Me extraña que su salón / sala de estar / living no tenga televisor**
salón (m) (Pen) **living** (m) (Am)		
cocina	kitchen	**Mi madre preparaba la cena en la cocina**
(cuarto de) baño	bathroom (ALSO = lavatory, toilet)	

CUERDA

general
  thick

↑ †**cuerda**	string (gen)	**Ató el paquete con una cuerda** **un instrumento de cuerda**
cordel (m)	cord	**Ata estos paquetes con el cordel**
cordón (m)	cord, shoelace	**Pon los cordones a las zapatillas; el cordón umbilical**
bramante (m)	twine	**Las redes se reparan con bramantes**
↓ †**hilo**	thread	**Cosía con hilo**

  thin

special purposes

sarta		**una sarta de cebollas / de mentiras**
ristra		**una ristra de ajos**

CULO

asentaderas (pl) (R2–3) posaderas (pl) (R2–3)	posterior (euphemistic)	Pon tus asentaderas (= sit down) en una silla Asentó sus posaderas (= sat down) junto a la puerta
nalgas (pl) (R2)	buttocks	El niño se cayó de nalgas
trasero (R2)	behind, backside	Se te ve el trasero por el pantalón roto
culo (R1) pompis (m) (R1)	arse, ass (often ironic)	Se cayó de culo Me dí un golpe en el culo Me he hecho daño en el pompis

DAR

general dar	to give	Mamá, dame un pastel por favor
more specific entregar	to deliver, to hand in, to hand over	Me han entregado este documento para que se lo diera a usted Los romanos entregaban a los cristianos a los leones Hay que entregar los deberes mañana El cartero me entregó la carta
†facilitar proporcionar	to provide	El encargado me facilitó los datos El Ayuntamiento les proporcionó una vivienda digna Me proporcionó las referencias del negocio
abastecer de suministrar	to supply with (eg food, gas, water)	Esta empresa abastece de ropa al ejército La empresa suministraba comida al colegio
donar dotar	to donate to endow	donar dinero/sangre Se dotó el colegio con los mejores equipos electrónicos
regalar conceder (R3)	to give as a present to grant, to bestow (eg prize, honour)	 El alcalde concedió el premio Me concedieron un aumento salarial
†otorgar (R3) deparar (R3)	 to offer, to afford	El rey otorgó el derecho de cazar Se me deparó la oportunidad de ayudarla

DECIR

[†]decir	to say (tr); sometimes = **hablar** (Am)	**Dijo que volvería** **Dices tonterías**
hablar	to speak (a language)	**Hablo castellano / varios idiomas** **Hablaban del tiempo que hacía**
charlar	to chat, to converse	**Los amigos estaban charlando en la calle**
departir (R3)		**Departían amigablemente sobre los hechos**
platicar (R3, Mex R2) conversar		**Los viajeros platicaban animadamente** **Conversamos en el salón**
cotorrear (R1)	to chatter away	**Aquellas mujeres cotorreaban sin parar**
[†]cascar (R1)		**No has parado de cascar toda la tarde**
expresarse	to express oneself	**Siempre se expresaba correctamante**
pronunciarse sobre algo	to make a statement on sth	**No me puedo pronunciar sobre el tema**
pronunciar un discurso	to give a speech	**El presidente pronunció un discurso**
[†]tomar la palabra	to contribute to a meeting	**Y ahora invito a mi colega a tomar la palabra**

DEJAR

transitive		
[†]dejar	to leave	**La dejé en la puerta de la casa** **Dejaron el pueblo a las diez** **Me dejó una nota**
[†]abandonar	(not necessarily as definitive as Eng *to abandon*)	**Abandonó la casa a las ocho** **Las ratas abandonaron el barco** **Su padre les abandonó cuando eran pequeños**

intransitive

†**salir**	to leave, to depart	**Salimos para la India la semana que viene**
		El tren sale a las siete
†**partir**	(usu with idea of destination)	**La expedición partió hacia el Himalaya**
		El viajero partió a primera hora de la mañana
zarpar	(of a ship)	**El barco zarpó rumbo al Caribe**
irse	to go away	**Bueno, me voy**
†**marcharse**	(suggests for a long time, or for ever)	**Se marcharon a las tres**
		Pedro se marchó del país
apartarse de	to wander from, eg a path	**No te apartes del camino**
largarse (R1)	to leave, to clear off	**Se largó sin pagar**
†**pirárse(las)** (R1)		**Son las siete: me las piro**
abrirse (R1)		**Me abro, tengo una cita importante**

DELGADO

general

delgado	thin	**A muchas mujeres les gusta ser delgadas**
flaco		**Estaba flaco como un palo**

more specific

esbelto	slim (suggesting elegance)	**Las modelos suelen ser esbeltas**
huesudo	bony	**Su constitución era huesuda**
descarnado (R3)	emaciated	**Salió del desierto totalmente descarnado**
enjuto (R3)	lean, skinny, gaunt	**Don Quijote era un hombre enjuto**
esquelético	skeletal	**Los prisioneros en Auschwitz estaban esqueléticos**
famélico (R2–3)	skinny, starving	**Los refugiados estaban famélicos, llevaban días sin comer**
enclenque (R3)	skinny, puny, emaciated	**Era un chico enclenque y enfermizo**
esmirriado (R1)		**Este niño es esmirriado y desnutrido**
escuchimizado (R1)		**Es un escuchimizado que no comía nada**

DELITO

†**crimen** (m)	serious crime	**Todos los crímenes son violentos**
†**delito**	(any) crime, offence	**El delito abarca robos y crímenes**
†**infracción** (f)	infringement	**Cometió una infracción de tráfico**
falta	offence; foul (in sport)	**El árbitro pitó una falta**
transgresión (f) (R3)	transgression, sin (moral)	**Dios castiga la transgresión de la ley**
pecado		**El adulterio es un pecado para un creyente**
reincidencia	second offence	**La reincidencia en el delito agrava la condena**

DERROTAR

†**derrotar** **vencer**	to beat (an opponent)	**Derrotaron al enemigo** **Venció la tristeza / a su rival / los problemas**
conquistar	to conquer, to overcome, to win (sb or sth)	**Los Reyes Católicos acabaron por conquistar a los árabes**
triunfar	to triumph over sth/sb	**Nuestro equipo lleva varios años triunfando en la liga**
someter (R2–3)	to conquer, to overcome, to bring under one's control	**Tras conquistar la ciudad las tropas sometieron a los ciudadanos**
subyugar (R3)		**Los invasores subyugaron al país por las armas**
sojuzgar (R3)		**Los conquistadores sojuzgaron a los indios**
dominar		**Hay que dominar la tentación**
†**ganar**	to earn, to win, to gain sth; to win sb over	**El equipo ganó a los campeones**
batir	to beat (= hit); to beat (person, team, record)	**El ejército batió al enemigo** **El atleta batió el récord**

131

DESTRUIR

general		
destruir	to destroy	El juez ordenó destruir las pruebas
		Los gamberros están destruyendo todos los parques
		Te estás destruyendo con el alcohol
specific		
to demolish		
desmantelar	to take down	Pronto se desmantelarán las bases militares
		El abogado desmanteló los argumentos de la testigo
demoler (R2–3)	to pull down	Demolieron un edificio
		Mi profe sabe demoler un argumento
†**tirar**		El municipio ordenó tirar el teatro incendiado
derribar	to knock down, shoot down	Los obreros derribaron el edificio
		El ejército derribó un avión enemigo
		El niño derribó por tierra toda la torre hecha por su padre
derrumbar	to knock down, to fling down	El tornado derrumbó cien casas
derruir	to tear down	una casa derruida
to raze, to lay waste		
devastar	to lay waste	El temporal ha devastado la ciudad
desolar		El terremoto ha desolado toda la zona
		La muerte de su hermana nos ha desolado a todos
talar	to lay waste, to fell (tree)	El enemigo taló todos los campos e incendió la ciudad
		¿Por qué han talado los árboles cerca del río?
arrasar	to raze	El fuego arrasó muchas hectáreas de trigo
asolar		El huracán asoló las tierras de la costa
		Los terroristas asolaron varios pueblos
to smash, to break up		
desbaratar		Has desbaratado la radio y no hay forma de arreglarla
		Desbarató toda su fortuna
destrozar		Los gamberros destrozaron varias cabinas telefónicas
		La tormenta ha destrozado la cosecha

to annihilate		
aniquilar	to annihilate	El boxeador aniquiló al adversario
arrollar	to crush	El ejército arrolló al enemigo
		Tiene una personalidad que arrolla a todo el mundo

to ruin		
arruinar		El granizo arruinó la cosecha
		La droga arruinó a toda la familia

DIBUJO

general		
dibujo	drawing	El niño ha hecho un dibujo de un conejo
specific		
esbozo	sketch, outline	Picasso hizo un esbozo de Guernica en cuatro trazos
		el esbozo de un proyecto
bosquejo		Hizo un bosquejo de la estatuilla
		el bosquejo de un libro / una filosofía
apunte (m)		El aparejador hizo un apunte de la casa
croquis (m)	sketch, plan (often to show where a place is)	Hazme un croquis del camino para que no me pierda
†**diseño**	design (technical); drawing (art)	Aquí tienes el diseño del coche
diagrama (m)	diagram	En este diagrama se representan los sueldos de los empleados
esquema (m)		Éste es el esquema de la instalación eléctrica

DIENTE

diente (m)	tooth (gen), ALSO of saw	El puñetazo le partió los dientes
muela	molar	Las muelas se emplean para triturar la comida
canino	canine tooth	El pastor alemán tiene los caninos muy desarrollados
colmillo	fang, tusk	los colmillos de un tigre / un elefante

DINERO

general		
dinero	money	**Me queda bastante dinero para ir al cine**
†**plata** (Am)		**No tengo plata para comprarlo**

specific		
†**capital** (m)	capital	**El capital de la sociedad era de cien millones de euros**
moneda	coin (individual); coinage; currency	**¿Tienes una moneda para el carrito cambio de moneda**
†**divisas** (pl)	foreign currency	**Voy a buscar divisas para salir al extranjero**
†**metálico**	(hard) cash; coin (collective)	**Pagué en metálico**
pasta (R1)	dosh, cash	**¡Oye, tío! Dame pasta.**
†**fondo(s)**	fund(s)	**Recabar fondos para invertir**
fortuna	fortune, lots of money	**Ganó una gran fortuna jugando a la lotería**
dineral (m)		**He ganado un dineral con este negocio**
caudal (m)		**Tiene muchos caudales**

DISPARAR

to fire (a weapon)		
disparar		**El soldado disparó contra el enemigo**

to shoot (sb)		
herir	to shoot and wound	**Me hirió de un disparo**
matar de un tiro	to shoot and kill	**El maleante la mató de un tiro**
†**tirar a**	to shoot at	**Los soldados recibieron la orden de tirar a matar**
pegar un tiro a		**El cazador pegó un tiro al animal**
fusilar	to execute by shooting	**El pelotón de ejecución le fusiló**

to shoot (game)		
cazar	to go shooting	**Cazaba con rifle**
ir de caza		**El domingo van de caza**

DISPUTA

primarily associated with verbal dispute: 'argument'

†**discusión** (f)	argument	**Se divorciaron tras una discusión muy fuerte**
controversia	controversy	**Los dos políticos se enzarzaron en una controversia**
†**debate** (m)	debate	**No voy a entrar en debates con usted**
†**disputa**	dispute	**Una disputa entre los vecinos**
†**querella**	dispute; lawsuit	**Las dos naciones resolvieron su vieja querella**
		Entabló una querella contra uno de los socios
altercado (R2–3)	argument, altercation	**Oí anoche un altercado en un bar**
rencilla(s)	sg: argument pl: bickering	**Una rencilla entre dos hermanos / dos familias**

primarily associated with physical dispute: 'fight'

contienda (R2–3)	**La dureza de la contienda produjo miles de muertos**
	una contienda familiar
†**riña**	**En la riña sacó una navaja**
†**lucha**	**En la lucha los invasores ganaron mucho territorio**
	Hubo una lucha por el primer ministro
pelea	**Una pelea encarnizada con varios heridos**
reyerta (R3)	**Hubo una reyerta callejera con navajas**
pendencia	**Resultaron lesionados en la pendencia dos jóvenes**
camorra (R1)	**Se armó una camorra**

primarily associated with noise: 'row'

pelotera (R1)	**Cuando su hermano le contradice montan una pelotera de mucho cuidado**
trifulca (R1)	**Montaron una buena trifulca por culpa del coche**
bronca (R1)	**Las hermanas tuvieron una bronca por que no se pusieron de acuerdo sobre las vacaciones**

DIVERTIRSE

general

divertirse		**Me divertí mucho en la fiesta**
		¡Qué te diviertas!
†**disfrutar**		**Disfrutar de la vista**
		Disfrutamos mucho con la cena anoche
†**entretenerse**		**Me entretuve en la conversación con el extranjero**
distraerse		**Se distrae hablando con los vecinos / viendo vídeos**
		Con la conversación me distraje y perdí el tren
†**gozar**		**Gocé leyendo poesía**
		Hay que gozar la vida
		Goza de una buena posición en la empresa

more restricted

†**recrearse** (R3)	(suggests aesthetic pleasure)	**Me recreé leyendo la novela / viendo el panorama**
†**deleitarse** (R3)	(suggests sensual pleasure)	**Se deleitaban escuchando la sinfonía / en la contemplación de las aves**

colloquial expressions

gozarla		**Nosotros la gozamos en cualquier sitio**
pasarlo bien / bomba / en grande (in Mex) **pasarla bien** (etc) **pasarlo de puta madre / cojonudo** (R1*)		**Lo pasamos bien / bomba / en grande / de puta madre / cojonudo en la playa**

EMPEZAR

general

intransitive

†**principiar** (R2–3)	to begin	**La primavera principió con tormentas**

intransitive or transitive

†**empezar**	to begin	**Empiezo hoy mi nuevo trabajo**
		Mi nuevo trabajo empieza hoy
†**comenzar** (R2–3)		**¿Cuándo comenzamos las clases?**
		Las vacaciones comienzan mañana

transitive

†**iniciar** (R2–3)	to begin (sth)	**El Parlamento iniciará su sesión en octubre** BUT NOTE: **La sesión se iniciará**
†**emprender**	to undertake (sth)	**Emprendieron la tarea**

with infinitive

†**empezar a hacer algo**	to begin to do sth	**Empezó a leer**
†**comenzar a hacer algo** (R2–3)		**Comenzaron (a construir) la casa**
†**principiar a hacer algo** (R2–3)		**Principió a escribir la carta**
†**ponerse a hacer algo**		**Se puso a estudiar / leer / pintar**
†**echar(se) a hacer algo**		**Se echó a llorar / correr**

special uses with certain objects

†**entablar**	to start (a conversation, business, lawsuit)	**entablar una conversación / negociaciones / un pleito**
trabar	to start (a friendship, a conversation)	**Trabé amistad con Juan el año pasado**

ENCONTRAR

general

†**encontrar**	to find	**¿Has encontrado el cuchillo?**
hallar (R2–3 Pen, R2 Mex)		**Halló el reloj en el cajón**
		No hallaron la solución

more specific

†**dar con**	to come upon unexpectedly	**Afortunadamente, di con la solución**
		Me fastidia no dar con la palabra correcta
tropezar con		**Tropecé con una piedra**
		Mi proyecto ha tropezado con la oposición del jefe
†**encontrarse**		**Me encontré un billete de cincuenta euros en la calle**
topar con (R3)		**Se topó con su amigo en la calle**
†**descubrir**	to discover	**¿Quién descubrió América?**

ENFADARSE

general

enfadarse (Pen) **enojarse** (LA)	to get angry	**La madre se enfadó/enojó con su hijo por el retraso**

strong, lower register

↑ **cabrearse** (R1*)	to get furious	**Las noticias desagradables hicieron que se cabreara y empezó a berrear**
ponerse hecho una fiera (R1)		**Cuando mi padre le echó la bronca a mi hermano, se puso hecho una fiera**
ponerse negro (R1)		**Me pongo negro cuando la lluvia me impide salir**
irritarse (R2–3)		**Se irritó porque se le averió el coche**
enfurecerse (R2–3)		**Me enfurecí porque no encontraba mis zapatos**
molestarse (R2–3)		**Me molesto cuando los niños chillan tanto**
airarse (R3)		**La negativa hizo que se airase mi padre**
disgustarse (R3)		**Se disgustó al enterarse de los resultados**
↓ **incomodarse** (R3)	to get upset	**Siempre se incomoda con su mal educado vecino**

weak, higher register

ENFRENTARSE (A)

literal

   static

estar enfrente de	to be facing (gen)	**La casa está enfrente de la estación**
†**dar a**	(of room, etc)	**Mi habitación daba al jardín**
mirar a		**El salón mira al sur**

   movement

volver la cara hacia	to turn to face	**Volví la cara hacia el lado izquierdo**
mirar hacia		**Siempre hay que mirar hacia ambos lados**
ponerse de cara a		**Se puso de cara hacia el desconocido**

figurative

†**enfrentar (se a / con)**	to face (up to)	**La distribución de las tierras enfrentó a las dos familias**
		Los dos hermanos se enfrentaron por una tontería
		La policía se enfrentó a los gamberros

encarar(se a)		Siempre encaraba los problemas con buen ánimo
		El periodista encaró a los dos políticos ante el micrófono
		El alcalde se encaró a los manifestantes
arrostrar (R3)		Arrostrar un peligro / un problema / una penalidad
dar la cara a (R1)		¡Dame la cara!
hacer (R2–3) / **plantar** (R2) **cara a**		Si no haces cara al problema no lo vas a solucionar
		Hay que plantar cara a la realidad
†**afrontar**		Hay que afrontar la verdad / el problema / las elecciones con moral de victoria
hacer frente a	to stand up to	Hay que hacer frente a la dificultad
confrontar a uno con algo	to face sb with sth	Confrontar las dos firmas
		Me confrontaron con la necesidad de dimitir

ENGAÑAR

general		
engañar	to deceive	Engañó a su mujer
		Me engañaron en el cambio del dinero
specific		
estafar	to swindle sb out of sth	Estafó un millón de dólares
timar (R1–2)		Me timaron en la compra de zapatos
defraudar	to cheat, swindle sb	No hay que defraudar a Hacienda
engatusar	to inveigle, to coax sb into doing sth	Mi hijo me engatusó para que le comprara una chaqueta muy cara

ENGAÑO

engaño	act of deception	Sufrió un engaño
		Sus promesas son un engaño
truco		El mago hace trucos
treta		Consiguió su empleo a base de tretas

estafa	swindle	El joyero me hizo una estafa y cobró mucho más de lo que debía
trampa ardid (m) estratagema (f) (R2–3)	ruse	No me fío nunca de ella, siempre hace trampas Es capaz de utilizar cualquier ardid para conseguir lo que quiere Empleó un ardid para atraerme los estratagemas de la publicidad
mala pasada faena (R1) jugarreta (R1)	hoax, dirty trick	Me jugó una mala pasada ¡Vaya faena nos han hecho cortando el agua! Espero que esto no sea una jugarreta suya
truco (R1–2) triquiñuela (R1)	knack, skill, trick	Hay un truco para abrir la puerta Empleo esta triquiñuela para volcar la tortilla Inventaba un montón de triquiñuelas para aprobar sin estudiar

ENSEÑAR

general †enseñar	to show; to teach	Mi madre me ha enseñado a conducir ¿Puedes enseñarme tu certificado? Enseñaba idiomas en la universidad
mostrar	to show	Me mostró la foto
more specific señalar	to point out, to indicate	¿Quieres que te enseñe los errores de ortografía? No señales a la gente con el dedo La caída de las hojas señala la llegada del otoño
†indicar		Le indiqué el camino al forastero
demostrar	to demonstrate	Le demostré como se hacía
exponer	to exhibit, to present	Expuse mis cuadros en el museo
exhibir †presentar		Exhibió sus habilidades de mago El embajador presentó sus credenciales El artista presentó su pintura antes de comentarla
ostentar	to show off, to make a show, to flaunt	Ostentaba el grado de general
desplegar	to display (R3); to deploy, to unfold (R2)	Desplegó sus conocimientos desplegar una bandera / las tropas

ENVIAR

general		
†**mandar**	to send	**Mándame un emilio / una carta**
enviar		**Le envié la carta a mi hermana**
more specific		
despachar	to dispatch (goods or people)	**La oficina despachó las mercancías en seguida**
destinar	to post (sb), to assign	**Me destinaron a África del Norte**
expedir (R2–3)	to dispatch (commercial)	**expedir una mercancía**
remitir (R2–3)	to remit, to consign (eg money)	**La empresa me remitió el dinero / el paquete**

ESPALDA(S)

espalda(s)	back of a person	**Me caí y ahora me duele(n) la(s) espalda(s)** **Me criticó a mis espaldas** **Lo hizo a espaldas de mí**
†**lomo**	back of an animal	**el lomo del caballo**
dorso	back of hand, document	**el dorso de la mano / de la tarjeta; ver al dorso**
revés (m)	'wrong' side of fabric	**el revés de una prenda de vestir**
respaldo	back of chair; ALSO (fig) backing, support	**Me apoyé en el respaldo de la silla** **Gracias por tu respaldo**
†**fondo**	back of room, stage	**al fondo de la sala**
parte (f) **posterior**	back of house, etc	**Los carros se descargan por la parte posterior**

ESTROPEAR

†**dañar**	to damage	**La granizada dañó la cosecha**
maltratar	to mistreat	**El esposo maltrató a su mujer**
deteriorar	to damage	**La lluvia deteriora la fachada**

estropear	to spoil	No estropees la mesa con el martillo
		Se han estropeado las vacaciones con el mal tiempo
		La carne está estropeada
†fastidiar	to spoil, to mess up	Tengo el pie fastidiado, no puedo andar
†joder (R1*)	to injure, to do in (Brit)	Tengo la rodilla jodida

ESTUPENDO

†estupendo	splendid	un coche / una película estupendo/a
sorprendente	surprising	un resultado sorprendente
increíble	incredible	¡Tiene una suerte increíble!
admirable	admirable	Fue una actuación admirable
portentoso (R2–3)	prodigious	El boxeador tenía una fuerza portentosa
		una inteligencia portentosa
prodigioso (R2–3)		un récord prodigioso
pasmoso (R2–3)	astonishing	un número de circo pasmoso
		Tienen la habilidad pasmosa de hacer el crucigrama en cinco minutos
cojonudo (R1)	really amazing	un récord / coche / una carrera cojonudo/a
de puta madre (R1*)		una final de puta madre
†bárbaro (R1)	tremendous, super	Tuvimos unas vacaciones bárbaras
tremendo (R1)		La película de James Bond fue tremenda
fabuloso		Beckham metió un gol fabuloso

FILA

general		
fila	row	en fila india
		una fila de coches / sillas / asientos
		Los clientes formaron una fila
		Quedan plazas en la primera fila
†hilera	row, line	Una hilera de árboles/casas/coches

things or people going by		
†**desfile** (m)	procession, march-past	**un desfile militar**
caravana	caravan (of camels); queue (of cars)	**una caravana de coches/camellos**
reata	string (of horses, etc, linked together)	**una reata de mulos/caballos**

abstract		
serie (f)	series	**una serie de números**
retahíla	string (of insults)	**Soltó una retahíla de insultos**
sarta	string (of lies, etc)	**una sarta de perlas/disparates**

FUEGO

fuego	fire to heat or cook; gunfire (ALSO fig)	**Tenía fuego en el corazón** **¿Tienes fuego? Quiero fumar.** **el fuego de la chimenea / de la artillería**
incendio	fire which destroys property	**El incendio arrasó el edificio**
lumbre (f)	fire(light)	**La lumbre ardía en la cocina** **Hicieron lumbre para calentarse**
estufa	heating appliance (electric, gas, etc)	**Pon la estufa, tengo frío**
llama	flame	**Las llamas alcanzaron unos treinta metros**

FUERTE

general		
fuerte	strong	**Una mujer fuerte tiraba del carro**

more specific		
recio (R2–3)	tough, solid	**Los campesinos recios ataban las gavillas**
robusto (R2–3)		**Era una mujer muy robusta capaz de todo trabajo físico**
forzudo	tough, brawny	**El hombre forzudo levantaba pesos de doscientos kilos**
fornido	hefty	**El Cid era un hombre fornido**
vigoroso	vigorous	**Aunque era pequeña era muy vigorosa**

GAFAS

gafas (pl)	spectacles; goggles	**¿Dónde están mis gafas?**
		Es mejor usar gafas para nadar
anteojos (pl) (R2 Arg, R3 Pen)		**Se puso los anteojos**
lentes (m pl) (Mex)		**Para la lectura debo cambiar de lentes**
lente (m or f)	lens	**Esta rayada esta lente**
		Estos lentes de contacto son incómodos
prismáticos (pl)	binoculars, (field)glasses	**El militar ajustó los prismáticos**
gemelos (pl)		**Siempre llevaba los gemelos al teatro**
catalejo	telescope	**Con el catalejo vio el barco a veinte kilómetros**
lupa	magnifying glass	**Sherlock Holmes buscaba huellas con una lupa**

GOLPEAR

to strike with blows		
pegar	to hit, to smack, to slap	**Los dos hombres se pegaron sin cuartel**
golpear	to strike, to punch, to beat	**El boxeador le golpeó en el estómago**
asestar / dar / pegar un golpe a uno	to strike sb a blow	**Le asestó una puñalada al turista y le quitó la cartera**
abofetear	to slap (in the face)	**Me abofeteó en la cara**
apalear	to beat, to thrash	**El muy bruto apaleó a su mujer**
aporrear (R1)	to beat (up)	**Aporreé la puerta para que me dejaran entrar**
azotar	to lash	**Los piratas azotaban a los presos**
sacudir (R1)	to wallop	**Empezaron a discutir y acabaron por sacudirse**
zurrar (R1)		**¡No hagas eso, que te zurro!**

vapulear	to give a beating	**El boxeador vapuleó a su rival**
		Los maleantes vapulearon al pobre hombre
†**cascar** (R1)		**Discutieron y empezaron a cascarse**

other meanings

†**alcanzar**	to hit (of shots)	**El golpe me alcanzó en el brazo**
chocar con/contra	to hit with whole body (of vehicle)	**El camión chocó con/contra el coche / el peatón**

GORDO

general

gordo	fat; large, important	**una cantidad muy gorda**
		Era tan gorda no pasaba ni por la puerta
grueso		**El boxeador grueso pesaba unos cien kilos**

of body

corpulento (R2–3)	hefty, burly, big and strong	**un boxeador corpulento**
		Es un tenista corpulento con un brillante futuro
obeso	obese, stout	**La médico le dijo que estaba un poco obesa**
gordinflón (R1)		**Comía tanto que estaba gordinflón**
tripón (R1)	podgy	**El muy tripón se comió un plato de alubias y tres chuletas**
rollizo	chubby, usu of babies	**Le gustan los bebés rollizos**
rechoncho		**un bebé rechoncho**
regordete		**un niño regordete**
gordezuelo (R1)		**un niño gordezuelo**

more specific

mofletudo	of cheeks	**un bebé con la cara mofletuda**
panzudo (R1)	of belly	**un viejo gordo, panzudo y feo**
ventrudo (R1)		**un hombre ventrudo**

GRACIOSO

†gracioso	amusing, witty	una actriz muy graciosa
		contar chistes graciosos
		Es el gracioso de todas las reuniones
†divertido		un chiste muy divertido
		un divertido grupo de amigos
†cómico	comical	una situación cómica
		Fue una escena muy cómica
chistoso	witty	Estás muy chistosa hoy
		un cuento chistoso
		un accidente chistoso
salado	risqué, spicy, funny, witty	un chiste salado
		una anécdota salada

GRUPO

general

| †grupo | group | un grupo de jóvenes |

more specific

†agrupación (f)	formal association	una agrupación musical / de médicos
camarilla	cronies, clique (pej)	el dictador y su camarilla
†equipo	team	un equipo de baloncesto
conjunto	group (gen or musical)	un conjunto musical
†partida	party (eg hunting)	una partida de caza
†panda	gang	una panda de gamberros
banda	pack, throng	una banda de ladrones
bando	faction, side (suggests two)	el bando de los vencedores
pandilla	gang, clique	una pandilla de amigos/gamberros
corrillo	group of people standing talking	Los antiguos alumnos charlaban en corrillos
cuadrilla	small group; a team of bullfighters	una cuadrilla de amigos
		el matador y su cuadrilla

HERMOSO

general (of people or things)		
hermoso	beautiful	**una mujer hermosa**
		un paisaje hermoso
bello (R2–3)		**una bella actriz**
		un cuadro muy bello

general purpose words		
bonito	nice	**una chica bonita**
		un jardín bonito
lindo (esp Am)		**un lindo país**
		una linda sonrisa
		¡Qué vestido más lindo!
precioso		**¡Qué bebé más precioso!**
		un regalo/jardín
		precioso

more distinctive alternatives (esp R2–3)		
of things		
encantador	charming	**una dama encantadora**
maravilloso	wonderful	**un paisaje maravilloso**
delicioso	delightful	**un postre/helado**
		delicioso

of people only		
guapo	good-looking, elegant, attractive	**un chico / una chica guapo/a**
majo (R1–2)	pretty, attractive, flashy	**Tiene unos amigos muy majos**
		ojos majos
rico	sweet, cute, lovely (of children)	**¡Qué rico es este niño!**

INTENTAR

with noun		
†**intentar hacer algo**	to try to do sth	**Intenté estudiar el chino pero me resultó difícil**
†**tratar de hacer algo**		**Tratamos de escalar la montaña**
†**probar a hacer algo** (R3)		**Probó a cantar la pieza**

†**procurar hacer algo** (R2–3)	to endeavour to do sth	**Procura no mojarte**
†**esforzarse por / en hacer algo**	to strive to do sth	**Siempre me esforzaba por / en ser puntual**
†**esmerarse por / en hacer algo**	to try one's hardest to do sth	**Se esmeró en rematar bien el trabajo**
hacer lo posible por / para hacer algo	to do everything possible to do sth	**Hice lo posible por / para terminar la tarea**

with noun

†**intentar algo**	to attempt sth	**El piloto intentó el aterrizaje pero no le salió bien**
†**probar algo**	to try (on), to taste sth	**Pruébate el pantalón** **Prueba la sopa / el vino** **probar suerte** = to try one's luck
ensayar algo	to test, to try out sth	**ensayar una táctica** **Ensayaron la vacuna antes de ponerla a la venta**
†**esmerarse en algo / con uno**	to go to a lot of trouble over	**El camarero se esmeraba en el servicio de la mesa** **El médico se esmeró con el paciente**

INVESTIGAR

general

examinar	to examine	**El médico examinó al paciente** **El detective examinó las pruebas** **El profesor nos examina de matemáticas** **Examinarse de física**

more specific types of examination

inspeccionar	to inspect	**La policía inspeccionó el lugar del crimen**
†**registrar**	to search	**El aduanero registró las maletas**
escudriñar (R3)	to scrutinize	**La policía escudriñó hasta el último rincón**
escrutar (R3)		**El jurado escrutó la votación**

indagar	to investigate	Hay que indagar la verdad
investigar	to investigate; to research	Los hechos fueron investigados por dos expertos
		El científico investigaba ingeniería genética
†reconocer	to examine (medical); to reconnoitre (military)	La enfermera reconoció al enfermo
		El capitán mandó a dos soldados a reconocer el terreno

JEFE

†jefe (m) / jefa	leader, chief, boss	Se le eligió jefe del partido
		El jefe de la empresa dimitió
		¡Oiga, jefe, cuándo cobramos?
caudillo/a	leader (military)	Se erigió como el caudillo de la tropa
		la caudilla britona Boadicea
cacique (m) / cacica	local boss (who has undue political influence); petty tyrant (used of landowners); chief (of a tribe)	En la España franquista el cacique del pueblo tenía mucho poder
		El gobierno dialogó con los caciques indios
cabecilla (m/f)	leader (pej)	el cabecilla de la revuelta
†líder (m/f)	leader who has a following, as in politics, church	un gran líder político
†patrón (m) / patrona	boss, chief	el patrón de la compañía
		La patrona no deja fumar en las habitaciones

NOTE: **patrono** is also used in the sense of *employer*.

señor(a) dueño/a amo/a	owner, master	el señor de la casa
		Yo quisiera hablar con el dueño del bar
		¿Puedo hablar con el amo de la fábrica/empresa/casa?
†responsable (m/f) †encargado/a	person in charge	Es el responsable de la calidad del proyecto
		¿Puedo hablar con el encargado?

LADO

general		
lado	gen; team in sport	El coche vino por el lado derecho
		Yo sentía un dolor en el lado izquierdo
specific		
costado	side of person; of ship	Me dio un golpe en el costado
		el costado de babor/estribor (port/starboard)
		por los cuatro costados = through and through
ijada	side of animal: flank	El campesino le pegaba al caballo con la fusta en la ijada
†ladera	side of hill	la ladera norte/sur del monte
		Esta ladera es bastante suave/abrupta
		la empinada ladera de la colina
falda		La piedra se deslizaba por la falda del cerro
†cara	of record or tape; face of mountain	La cara de un disco / una moneda
		la cara norte del Eiger

LENGUA

lengua	language (gen)	Mi lengua materna es el chino
		En la torre de Babel se confundieron las lenguas
lenguaje (m)	type of language; faculty of language	el lenguaje de los químicos
		el desarrollo del lenguaje
idioma (m)	individual language (eg Spanish, French, etc)	una academia de idiomas
		El idioma de los informáticos es complejo
habla (f)	speech	Juan tiene un habla dulce (way of speaking)
		el habla de los niños
argot (m)	slang	el argot médico / del barrio
jerga	jargon	la jerga política / estudiantil
jerigonza	gobbledygook, mumbo jumbo (pej)	Hablaba una jerigonza imposible de descifrar

LETRERO

letrero	sign	El letrero decía "Prohibido el paso"
†cartel (m)	poster	No fijar carteles (Stick no bills) un cartel publicitario / de cine
anuncio	advertisement, placard	El muro estaba repleto de anuncios
pancarta	banner, placard (eg at political meetings)	Una pancarta encabezaba la manifestación
†póster (m)	poster (colourful and artistic, as an embellishment)	Los niños coleccionan pósters de sus ídolos
cartelera	publicity board	He visto las carteleras de cine y teatro y no hay nada que me interese

LEVANTAR

†levantar	to raise	levantar la mano
elevar	to raise, to erect (implies to high point)	El globo se elevó a quinientos metros
alzar (R2–3)	to raise, to lift up (eg hand)	Alcé la mano
†subir	to put up (eg blind); to take up (eg suitcases)	subir la persiana / las maletas
izar	to hoist (flag or sail)	Los marineros izaron la bandera / la vela
aupar	to lift up (especially a child)	Aupé a la niña para que viera el desfile

LISTO

general

†listo	clever, intelligent	Es la chica más lista de la clase
inteligente		Una chica muy inteligente que se lleva todos los premios

specific

astuto	shrewd, bright	**El zorro es un animal muy astuto**
		No se deja engañar, es muy astuto
perspicaz (R2–3)		**La policía era muy perspicaz al analizar los hechos**
sagaz (R3)		**Poirot era un detective sagaz**
lúcido (R2–3)	clear-sighted	**Tiene la mente lúcida**
clarividente (R3)		**un adivino clarividente**
despejado	wide-awake, bright	**Tiene una mente muy despejada**
avispado		**Es una chica muy avispada, siempre se las arregla**
despierto		**Es una niña despierta, muy lista para sus años**
(d)espabilado		**Es muy espabilado para las negociaciones**
		Es muy pequeña pero está muy espabilada
agudo	sharp, keen (stresses quality of mind)	**Era muy aguda en sus observaciones**
penetrante		**una mirada penetrante**

LLENO

general

lleno	full	**El depósito está lleno (de gasolina)**
		un plato lleno de sopa
		una sala llena de jóvenes

degrees of fullness

concrete

relleno	full up (stronger than **lleno**)	**El cojín está relleno de plumas**
completo	full to capacity in numbers (eg a bus)	**El camping está completo**
repleto	full to capacity in volume (eg with food)	**Esta maleta está repleta**
		un bar repleto de gente
		No puedo comer más, estoy repleto
†**harto**	full to or beyond sufficiency	**He comido demasiado, estoy harta**
		Estoy harto de trabajar

abstract		
pleno	full	**a plena vista**
completo	finished, complete	**El hotel está completo**
		un estudio completo

specific types of fullness		
abarrotado	packed, crammed	**una sala abarrotada**
atestado	crowded	**La discoteca estaba atestada de jóvenes**
atascado	jammed, clogged up	**una tubería atascada**
atiborrado	stuffed, packed	**Estoy atiborrado de patatas**
colmado (R2–3)	full to brim	**un vaso colmado**
henchido	filled up, swollen	**henchido de orgullo**
rebosante	brimming, overflowing	**rebosante de satisfacción**
ahíto	gorged (with food)	**ahíto de comida**

LLEVAR

†**llevar**	to carry	**Te llevo a la estación**
		Llevaba libros en la mano
†**llevarse**	to take away; to steal	**Se llevó las llaves y ahora las necesito**
conducir	to drive	**La guía nos condujo por la selva**
guiar	to lead, to guide	**Se guió por las estrellas**
transportar	to transport	**transportar mercancías**
trasladar	to transport, to transfer	**Trasladaba los muebles al nuevo domicilio**

NOTE: †**llevar** (= to take from the place the subject is at) and †**traer** (= to bring from the place the subject is at) are rigorously distinguished in Spanish, though in English *bring* is often used in the sense of **llevar**:

Si te quedas allí te lo llevaré

If you stay there I'll bring it to you

A similar rigorous distinction is made in Spanish between †**ir** and †**venir**:

Está llamando alguien a la puerta. ¡Ya voy!

Someone's knocking at the door. I'm coming!

Cuando llegues a Barcelona, dímelo e iré a verte

When you get to Barcelona, tell me and I'll come and see you.

MALGASTAR

†malgastar	to waste	Malgasta todo su dinero en tonterías
		No saldrá adelante, malgasta todo su tiempo
desperdiciar	to waste (food, time)	Ha desperdiciado la comida / oportunidad / su tiempo
perder	to waste (time, opportunity)	No pierdas la oportunidad
despilfarrar	to squander (eg money, resources)	Despilfarra todo lo que gana
†derrochar		derrochar una fortuna / sus recursos
dilapidar		Dilapidó su fortuna en coches
†tirar	to throw away	No tirar basura

MALHECHOR

malhechor/-ora	wicked person	Los malhechores fueron detenidos por la policía
malvado/a		El muy malvado engañaba a todo el mundo
maleante (m/f)		El maleante se dedicaba a robar bancos
delincuente (m/f)	criminal (gen)	Han detenido al delincuente
criminal (m/f)	criminal (serious)	El criminal fue condenado a muerte
gamberro/a	hooligan, juvenile delinquent	Se les acusó a los gamberros de destrozar una cantidad de cabinas telefónicas
enredador/-ora	troublemaker	El muchacho era un enredador que se metía con todo el mundo
canalla (m/f) (R1)	rogue	Este hombre conoce a todos los canallas: ladrones, asesinos, presos peligrosos
NOTE: canalla (f) also = *riffraff*		
bribón (R1–2)		El bribón se marchó con la nómina del mes pasado
sinvergüenza (m/f)	shameless person	El sinvergüenza no hacía más que mentir

pícaro/a	rogue, rascal (gen affectionate)	**Era un pícaro pero caía bien a la gente**
†granuja (m/f) (R1–2)		**¡Granuja! Te has comido todo el pastel.**
tunante (m/f) (R3)		**¡Qué tunante es el tipo ese: siempre consigue los trabajos más fáciles**
†tuno/a		**¡Menudo tuno estás hecho, hijo!**
bellaco (R2–3)		**No te fíes de él, es un bellaco que sólo piensa en sus intereses**
pillo/a		**¡El pillo/pillín me roba golosinas otra vez!**
pillín/-ina		

MEJORA

general		
mejoría	gen, esp state of health (and by extension to economy, performance, etc)	**La economía ha experimentado una mejoría** **Se nota una mejoría en su salud**
mejora	gen, though not normally used of health. May refer to sth concrete (eg home improvement)	**Ha habido una mejora en el nivel de la vida**
specific		
†adelantos (pl)	advances (eg in science)	**los adelantos de la tecnología**
†avances (m pl)		**los avances en física**
†progresos (pl)	progress (in economy, performance, etc)	**los progresos sociales**

MODELO

general		
model		
†modelo (m/f when referring to a person)	model (N and inv ADJ)	**La mujer pasaba como modelo** **una madre modelo** **un modelo de avión** **una granja modelo**
†ejemplo	example	**El estudiante servía de ejemplo a los demás**
†dechado (R3)	perfect model, paragon	**un dechado de perfección/virtudes**

form

†**forma**	form	**Tenía forma de pera**
pauta	guideline(s)	**las pautas a seguir en caso de incendio**

specific

muestra	part, sample of whole	**Mi madre me enseñó una muestra del tejido**
muestrario	collection of samples	**En un muestrario encontré la tela que buscaba**
†**patrón** (m)	pattern for dressmaking	**En la revista viene el patrón para hacer blusas**
plantilla	template, stencil	**una plantilla para dibujar**
†**dibujo**	drawn pattern	**Hizo un dibujo de la que quería**
estampado	pattern printed on cloth	**El estampado de la falda es bonito**
†**diseño**	design (eg pattern on china)	**Me gusta el diseño de este coche**

MOLESTAR

†**fastidiar**	to annoy	**Le fastidia pagar tanto por el taxi por falta de autobuses**
†**molestar**		**La música enlatada** (canned music) **me molesta**

strong, lower register

↑ †**joder** (R1)	to mess around	**¡No me jodas! ¡Déjame tranquilo!**
causar/dar asco (a) (R1)	to annoy intensely	**Da asco ver tanta suciedad** **Los hipócritas me causan asco** **Me dan mucho asco las cucharachas**
crispar (R1–2)		**Su tono de voz me crispa los nervios**
fregar (R1 Am)		**Me friega el cuate ese, es un naco**
meterse (con) (R1)	to provoke, annoy	**¡Jolín! ¡siempre se mete con las chicas!**
dar la lata (R1)	to be a nuisance to, to pester	**Los niños traviesos me dan la lata**
jorobar (R1)		**¡No me jorobes!**
incordiar		**El chico pasa su tiempo incordiando a las niñas**
estorbar	to hinder, to disturb	**¿Estorba esta silla en el pasillo?**
↓ **incomodar**	to inconvenience	**Aquel ruido continuo me incomoda**

weak, higher register

MUCHACHO/A

muchacho/a	boy/girl	Los/las muchachos/as jugaban en la playa
†chico/a		escuela de chicos/as
		Los chicos iban a la piscina todos los días
nene (m) / nena	small baby	Catorce meses tiene el nene / la nena
niño/a	little boy/girl	Mozart era todavía un niño cuando empezó a componer
hijo/a	son/daughter	Mi hijo/a cumple diez años en marzo
chaval (m) / chavala (R1)	boy/girl, young person	El chaval ha crecido, está hecho un mozo
		¡Oye chaval! ¿qué haces allí?
mozo/a		Los mozos no se divierten ahora como nosotros hace treinta años
joven (m/f)		Los jóvenes adolescentes fueron al cine
zagal (m) / zagala (R2–3)	country lad/lass	La zagala vigilaba las ovejas pastando en el prado

NATIVO

of people (N and ADJ)		
nativo	native	Muchas enfermeras son nativas de España
†natural	coming from	Es natural de León
oriundo (R2–3)		Es oriunda de Castilla
indígena (m/f)	usu of cultures and peoples outside Europe	Los indígenas rodearon al explorador
aborigen (m/f)	primitive native (not restricted, as Eng *aborigine*, to Australia)	los aborígenes de Patagonia
of country		
natal		su pueblo natal
of things, cultures, art, etc (ADJ)		
indígena (m/f)		un pueblo indígena
autóctono (R3)		el arte autóctono

of language (ADJ)		
materno		mi lengua materna
nativo		mi lengua nativa

NOMBRE

†nombre (m)	name (gen and first name)	"¿Cuál es tu nombre?" "Miguel López, señor"
nombre (m) de pila	Christian name, first name	Mi nombre de pila es Miguel
apellido	surname	Mi apellido es López
apodo	nickname (often suggests handicap)	El apodo de Francisco es "el cojo"
sobrenombre (m)	nickname (used to distinguish)	Leopoldo Alas tenía el sobrenombre de Clarín
mote (m)	nickname (often insult)	El mote del profesor es "tirano"
seudónimo	pseudonym, nom de plume	Muchos escritores se esconden detrás de un seudónimo
diminutivo	shortened name	Nadie le llama Armando, todo el mundo usa el diminutivo Armandito

OCURRIR

general		
†ocurrir	to happen	¿Cuándo ocurrió el accidente? Se me ha ocurrido una idea
†pasar		Me ha pasado una cosa rara
†suceder		¿Qué ha sucedido con tu hermana?
acontecer (R2–3)		Aconteció algo rarísimo la semana pasada
acaecer (R3)		El accidente acaeció en enero
of event		
tener lugar	to take place	El encuentro tuvo lugar en el parque
celebrarse	(more formal, eg of ceremony, meeting, etc)	La fiesta/reunión se celebró anoche

specific

realizarse	to be fulfilled, accomplished (esp plans, hopes)	**La salida se realizó con puntualidad**
producirse	to come about (esp accident)	**Se produjo un gran silencio tras la revelación** **Se produjo el accidente durante la noche**
surgir	to happen unexpectedly	**Surgió una grave cuestión política cuando murió el rey**
sobrevenir (R3)		**La idea me sobrevino de golpe**

ORGULLOSO

general

orgulloso	proud	**Estaba orgulloso de su apellido / su hijo**

specific and pejorative

arrogante	haughty, arrogant	**Se hacía antipática por ser tan arrogante**
soberbio		**No seas tan soberbio: escucha a los mayores**
altivo (R2–3) **altanero** (R2–3)		**No es simpático, es muy altivo** **Tuvo unos gestos estudiadamente altaneros**
presuntuoso	presumptuous	**Es un presuntuoso, no le aguanto, me cae fatal**
engreído **vanidoso**	vain, conceited	**Presume demasiado, es tan engreída** **Juan es más vanidoso que un pavo real**
fatuo (R2–3)		**Es una persona fatua que no hace caso a las opiniones ajenas**
jactancioso (R3) **presumido**	boastful	**No me gusta su actitud jactanciosa** **¡No seas tan presumido!**
chulo (R1) **fanfarrón** (R1)	cocky loudmouth, show-off	**Presume mucho, es muy chulo** **Los más fanfarrones son los que más deberían callar**
farolero (R1)	boastful, show-off	**Es una farolera, no le creas ni media palabra**

PALO

†**palo**	gen; stick to hold sth with	Me pegó con un palo el palo de la escoba
†**vara**	pole, rod; shaft	Con la vara golpeaba el almendro la vara del carro
bastón (m)	walking stick	El anciano se apoyaba en el bastón
báculo (R3)	staff	un báculo de obispo
porra	truncheon	Disolvieron a los manifestantes con las porras
garrote (m)	cudgel, club	Los primitivos mataban animales con garrotes
tranca	club, metal bar	Echaron la tranca para impedir la entrada Los ladrones le pegaron con una tranca
batuta	baton (music)	la batuta del director de orquesta
varita	wand	la varita mágica del brujo
estaca	stake in ground	Clavó la estaca en la tierra
barra	stick of candy, etc	una barra de hierro/chocolate/pan
astilla(s)	sticks for fire	Recogía astillas para el hogar

PARED

pared (f)	interior wall of building	Colgó el cuadro de la pared
tabique (m)	(thin) partition wall	Las oficinas estaban separadas por tabiques
muro	exterior wall of building; large free-standing wall	el muro del castillo / de una fortaleza El muro del colegio era muy alto
muralla	wall, usu fortified, of city, castle, etc	Una gran muralla rodeaba la ciudad la Gran Muralla de China
barrera	barrier, wall in fig sense	Una barrera me impidió pasar la barrera del idioma
tapia	small, free-standing wall (eg of garden, field)	la tapia del jardín/prado

PEDIR

†**pedir algo a uno / a uno que** + subj	to ask sb for sth / sb to do sth	Pedí más información
		Le he pedido a mi padre que me ayude
†**rogar** (R2–3) (as **pedir**)		Rogó clemencia
		El detenido le rogó al alcalde que atendiera a su petición
requerir (R3) **a uno para que** + subj	to ask sb to do sth	La jueza requirió la presencia del acusado
		Este asunto requiere un análisis detallado
		El médico requirió que el paciente fuese a la clínica
solicitar (as **pedir**)	to request	Mi compañero solicitó mi ayuda
†**suplicar** (R2–3) (as **pedir**)	to beg	El reo suplicó clemencia
		El príncipe le suplicó a su madre que le permitiera casarse con la princesa
†**exigir** (as **pedir**)	to demand	Los obreros exigieron una subida salarial
		Los manifestantes exigieron que el gobierno hiciera caso a su petición
†**reclamar** (as **pedir**)		Los obreros reclamaron aumento de salario
		Reclamo mi herencia
†**demandar** (R3)		El director demandó una explicación

PELO

†**pelo**	hair (gen)	Se lavó el pelo
pelos (pl)	hair (suggests disorder)	¡Vaya pelos tienes!
		Se me pusieron los pelos de punta
cabello(s) (sg/pl) (R3)	head of hair	Este champú es para cabello(s) seco(s)
cabellera	abundant, long hair	La cabellera le llegaba hasta la cintura
pelo	individual hair	Tienes un pelo en tu sopa
cabello		Se arrancó un cabello blanco
cana(s)	white/grey hair	Le salió la primera cana
melena	mane, long hair, bob	la melena del león
		La chica tenía una larga y hermosa melena
vello	body hair, facial hair	Su cuerpo estaba cubierto de vello
		vello facial

PELOTA

general

†**bola**	ball	**La bola rodó cuesta abajo**
esfera (R2–3)	sphere	**la esfera terrestre**
globo	globe; balloon	**el globo terráqueo**
		hinchar un globo
		subir en un globo

for specific purposes

bola	(billiard) ball; (snow)ball; ball bearing; marble; football (R1)	**una bola de billar/nieve** **un cojinete de bolas** (ball bearing)
balón (m)	football	**Colocó el balón en la portería**
pelota	ball	**una pelota de tenis**
		El defensa pasó la pelota al portero
bala	(cannon)ball; bullet	**una bala de cañón/revólver** **disparar una bala**
canica	marble	**Los niños jugaban a las canicas**
ovillo	ball (of wool)	**un ovillo de lana**

PENSAR

to think that . . .

†**pensar** **que . . .**	to think . . .	**Pensaba que podríamos tener problemas**
†**creer** **que . . .**		**Creo que tiene razón** **No creo que venga esta tarde**
†**parecer a** **uno que . . .**		**No me parece que esté lloviendo**
†**figurarse** **que . . .** AND **figurarse a uno que . . .**	to imagine . . .	**Me figuro que ya habrán salido** **Se me figura que está de buen humor**
†**imaginar(se)** **que . . .**		**(Me) imagino que vuelve hoy**

concebir que . . .		No concibo que sea el autor del delito
opinar que . . .	to be of the opinion that . . .	Opinaba que tenía razón

to imagine sth

imaginar	to imagine, to conceive	Imaginó una manera de ganar dinero
idear		idear un plan/proyecto
concebir		concebir una idea/táctica
†inventar		Se dice que Leonardo inventó el submarino

to think (intr and with prep)

reflexionar sobre	to reflect on	Déjame reflexionar sobre el propósito
†cavilar sobre (R3)	to brood over	No caviles más y cómprate el coche
discurrir en/ sobre		Discurría sobre las posibles soluciones
meditar en/sobre (R2–3)	to meditate on	Medito mucho sobre el sentido de la vida

PEREZOSO

general

perezoso	lazy	La tortuga parece un animal perezoso

weaker

↑ indolente (R2–3)	idle	Un estudiante indolente que nunca acude a las clases
ocioso		una vida ociosa
holgazán		Juanito es más holgazán que nunca, pasa todo el día tumbado
haragán (R2–3)		Es un hombre haragán, huye del trabajo como de la peste
†vago		Es tan vago que es capaz de dormir veinticuatro horas
↓ gandul (R1)		Es un chico gandul que pasa todo su tiempo en la cama

stronger

PIEDRA

roca	rock in geological sense; an individual piece of rock *in situ* or collected	**Había una cueva en la roca** **El barco encalló en las rocas**
peña	individual rock *in situ*	**Subió hasta la peña**
piedra	type of rock or individual stone or rock	**un monumento en piedra calija** **Tropecé en la piedra** **Al salir con la tabla de windsurf, cuidado con las piedras**
peñasco	large rock, crag	**En los peñascos anidan las águilas**
canto (rodado)	boulder; pebble	**Cogió un canto rodado en la mano**
guijarro	pebble; cobblestone	**Los guijarros del río suelen ser redondos**
china	pebble	**Se metió una china en el zapato**
grava	gravel	**Construyeron la carretera con grava**

POBRE

needy		
†**pobre**	poor	**Nació en una familia pobre pero se creó una fortuna**
necesitado		**No es cierto que la Iglesia siempre haya auxiliado a los necesitados**
indigente		**Era una familia indigente que carecía de todo**
menesteroso (R2–3)		**La cantidad de gente menesterosa disminuye con la seguridad social**
desvalido (R2–3)		**La Fundación de Ayuda al Desvalido**
unfortunate		
†**pobre**	poor	**El pobre hombre cojeaba**
desgraciado		**El hombre desgraciado se cayó por las escaleras**
desamparado	alone, helpless	**Perdió a sus padres y quedó desamparada**
poor in quality		
malo		**El vestido que se había comprado era malo**

PONER

poner	to put; to lay (eggs); to plant (bomb)	Pon los papeles en la mesa No has puesto las cosas en orden La gallina puso tres huevos Los terroristas pusieron una bomba en la estación
meter	to put in, to insert	Metí la moneda en la ranura / los cubiertos en el cajón
introducir		Introdujo la tarjeta en el cajero; introduje la ficha en la ranura
colocar situar (R2–3)	to place, to situate	Coloca la pila de libros en la mesa El general situó las tropas cerca del río Se situó en la esquina Sitúa Holanda en el mapa
emplazar (R3)		Los soldados emplazaron los cañones en su sitio Han emplazado las oficinas cerca de la alameda
ubicar (R2–3)		¿Dónde se debe ubicar el hotel? La mayoría de las escenas en la novela están ubicadas en Verona
NOTE: **ubicar** is more frequent in Am, where it also means *to find*, *to locate*		Hay que ubicar Cádiz en el mapa de España (Am)
disponer	to lay out, to arrange	Dispusieron las mesas para los invitados
†apostar	to station, to post (eg soldier, policeman)	El centinela se apostó en su garita

PROFESOR

profesor/-ora	gen and more specifically a secondary / high school teacher; teacher in university/college	Es profesora de biología
profe (m/f) (R1)		La profe me ha cateado
enseñante (m/f) (R2–3)	teacher	Han convocado la huelga de los enseñantes

maestro/a	primary/elementary school teacher; also gen in sense of *expert*	**La maestra me enseñó a leer** **Es un maestro en la guitarra**
señorita (R1)	female primary/ elementary school teacher	**¿Qué te ha dicho hoy la señorita?**
†**catedrático/a**	(university) professor; head of department in school	**Es catedrático en la Universidad Complutense** **Acabaron de nombrarla catedrática en el Instituto Luis Vives**
†**director** (m) / **directora**	head teacher, principal	**Es directora de un instituto de mil quinientos alumnos**

REBELARSE

rebelarse	to rebel	**Se rebeló el niño contra sus padres**
alzarse **sublevarse**	to revolt	**Se alzó en armas el ejército** **Se sublevó la marina**
amotinarse	to riot, to mutiny	**Los marineros se amotinaron contra el capitán**

REGALO

present, gift		
regalo	present	**un regalo de Navidad**
†**presente** (m)		**Los Reyes Magos le hicieron presentes al Niño Jesús**
don (m) (R2–3)		**Le entregaron sus dones al príncipe recién nacido**
obsequio (R3)		**Les ofrecemos un obsequio a todos nuestros clientes**
donación (f)	endowment, donation, bequest	**Los creyentes hicieron donaciones para el Tercer Mundo**
donativo		**Dio un donativo al hospital**
†**ofrenda**	offering (in church)	**Los aztecas hacían ofrendas a los dioses**

natural gift		
talento	talent	**Es una chica con mucho talento**
don (m)	gift	**Esta chica tiene el don de imitar otras voces**
†**dote** (f) (often in pl)	gift(s)	**Ese alumno tiene unas dotes extraordinarias para las matemáticas**

RICO

†**rico**	rich	**Nunca serás rico trabajando en los servicios públicos**
†**ricacho** (R1) (pej)	very rich	**Hace gala de sus millones, es un ricacho / un ricachón**
ricachón (R1) (pej)		
acaudalado (R2–3)		**Es un banquero acaudalado**
adinerado (R2–3)		**Se casó con la hija de un industrial adinerado**
acomodado	well-off, well-to-do	**una familia acomodada**
pudiente (R2–3)		**Con un coche Mercedes está claro que es pudiente**

RINCÓN

general		
ángulo	corner	**en el ángulo oscuro del salón**
rincón (m)	inside angle, eg corner of room	**El perro se acurrucó en el rincón**
esquina	outside angle, eg corner of street	**Espérame en la esquina**
specific		
curva	bend, eg in road	**Esta carretera tiene muchas curvas**
†**pico**	sharp corner, eg of a piece of furniture	**Se hizo daño con el pico de la mesa**
rabillo (R1)	corner of the eye	**el rabillo del ojo**
comisura	corner of the mouth	**la comisura de los labios**

ROBAR

†**robar**	to steal (gen)	**El caco me robó la cartera** **Los malvados robaron el banco**
†**hurtar** (R2–3) †**sustraer** (R3)	to steal (implies without violence)	**Los ladrones pasaban su tiempo hurtando en el metro** **La criada sustrajo pequeñas cantidades durante mucho tiempo**
asaltar	to rob (implies with violence)	**El forajido asaltó la diligencia**
afanar (R1) **birlar** (R1) **mangar** (R1)	to pinch, to nick (Brit)	**Se dedicaba a afanar bolsos de mujeres en el mercadillo** **En el colegio me birlaron el estuche** **No dejes la cartera en el bolsillo de atrás, te la mangan en seguida**
limpiar (R1)	to clean out	**Entraron en el piso y lo limpiaron**
sisar (R1)	to diddle, to cheat	**Todos los comerciantes sisan un poquito en el peso** **La criada me sisaba en las cuentas, entonces la despedí**

RODAJA

rodaja	of sausage, salami, lemon: has idea of roundness	**Cortó el salchichón / el salami en rodajas**
rebanada **chusco**	cut slice of bread irregular piece of bread	**una rebanada de pan** **Dame un chusco**
loncha / lonja	slice of ham, etc	**una loncha/lonja de chorizo/jamón/ melón/queso**
tajada	slice of meat, cheese, melon: has idea of cutting	**una buena tajada de carne**
raja	slice of most things except bread, ham and meat in general	**una raja de melón**
trozo	irregular slice or chunk, esp of meat	**un trozo de carne/pan/queso**
cacho	irregular, small piece, esp of bread	**un cacho de pan/queso**

ROMPER

general		
†**romper**	to break, to tear	romper el vaso / la cerradura / la tela / las relaciones

to crack, to split		
quebrantar (R 2–3)	to break, to crack, also fig	La helada ha quebrantado la roca Has quebrantado tu promesa
quebrar (R 2–3 Pen, R 2 Mex)	to break, to crack, to snap	El gamberro quebró la puerta de una patada
†**cascar**	to split, to crack	Has cascado la taza
†**partir**	to divide, to crack	Partió el pan en cuatro trozos
fracturar	to fracture	fracturar una costilla

to break into pieces		
desmenuzar	to crumble, to shred	Desmenuzó el pan con los dedos
hacer pedazos	to crack into pieces	Hizo pedazos la vajilla al dejar caer la bandeja
descuajaringar	to smash to pieces	Tras el choque la bici quedó descuajaringada
hacer añicos	to smash into small pieces	Se me han caído los platos y se han hecho añicos

other		
machacar	to crush	El albañil machacaba los ladrillos con un martillo
rasgar	to tear	Se me rasgó el pantalón al subir al tren

SABER

†**saber**	to have knowledge of sth; to know how to do sth	Sabe chino Sé que Pedro está en casa Que yo sepa, vendrá mañana Sabe tocar el violín
conocer	to be acquainted with	Conozco el país / mis derechos / a Juan

SALVAJE

salvaje	wild (of animals or primitive culture)	un animal/territorio salvaje
silvestre	wild (of plants)	plantas/flores silvestres
†bravo	fierce (of person or animal); rough (of landscape)	el mar / el toro bravo la Costa Brava
†bravío	untamed, wild	un caballo bravío navegar por un mar bravío
agreste	wild of countryside, animal	un paisaje agreste un animal agreste
bruto	brutish, brutal	un hombre bruto que maltrata a su mujer
brutal		Le asestaron una paliza brutal
†feroz	ferocious	un lobo feroz
agresivo	aggressive	Tiene un carácter agresivo La contaminación es muy agresiva para los pulmones

SONIDOS EMITIDOS POR LOS ANIMALES

animal	*verb*	*noun*
burro	rebuznar	rebuzno
caballo	relinchar	relincho
cuervo	graznar	graznido
culebra	sisear	siseo
elefante (m)	barritar	barrito
gallina	cacarear	cacareo
gallo	cantar	canto
gato	maullar	maullido
león (m)	rugir	rugido
mosquito	zumbar	zumbido
oveja	balar	balido

animal	*verb*	*noun*
pájaro	†**cantar**	**canto**
	to sing	song
	trinar	**trino**
	to trill	trilling
	piar	
	to chirp	
pato	**graznar**	**graznido**
perro	**ladrar**	**ladrido**
vaca	**mugir**	**mugido**

N O T E : The verbs may also be used as nouns (**el ladrar**, **el mugir**, etc), but they suggest the sound habitually made by the animal rather than an individual instance: so **el maullar de los gatos** = *cats' miaowing*, **el maullido de un gato** = *a cat's miaow*.

SUBIR

with an object		
†**subir**	to go up, ascend	**subir la escalera / la montaña**
escalar		**Escalaron el Himalaya en tiempo récord**
ascender (R2–3)		**Ascendió rápidamente la escala social**

to mount, to climb on to		
†**subir a**	to mount	**subir al coche / a un caballo**
trepar	to climb	**Los chicos treparon al árbol**
		Trepó por el muro del jardín para robar naranjas
†**encaramarse a/en** (R3)		**Se encaramó al árbol para ver mejor**
encarapitarse (Am) **a**		**encarapitarse a un árbol**

to make sb/sth go up		
†**subir**	to take up	**subir las maletas**
aumentar	to raise	**La empresa ha aumentado los precios**
ascender (R2 in this usage)	to promote	**Ascendieron al capitán a general**

intransitive

†**subir**	to rise	**Ha subido el río tras la tormenta**
		Suben los precios
†**elevarse** (R2–3)		**El humo se elevaba en el cielo**
		El número de accidentes / los precios
		se han elevado
ascender		**Los precios ascienden**
(R2–3)		**La temperatura asciende**
aumentar		**Aumentan los precios**

to go climbing

hacer		**Cada fin de semana hace alpinismo en**
alpinismo		**el Pirineo Aragonés**
(Pen / **hacer**		**Vamos a Bariloche a hacer un poco de**
andinismo (Am)		**andinismo**

SUCIO

general

| †**sucio** | dirty (lit or fig) | **tener las manos sucias / ideas sucias** |

more specific

manchado	stained	**Tenía la camisa manchada**
desaseado (R3)	soiled; messy, untidy	**Llegó al colegio un niño desaseado y**
		poco agradable
mugriento	grimy	**Su ropa estaba mugrienta, llevaba**
		años sin lavarla
		Viven en una casa mugrienta, no
		me atrevo a entrar allí
tiznado		**Tenía la cara tiznada / la nariz**
		tiznada de chocolate

expressing disgust
  higher register

inmundo (R3)		Es como un cerdo inmundo
		un pensamiento inmundo
†asqueroso		una cucaracha asquerosa
		No puedo dormir en una habitación tan
		asquerosa
		La comida allí es asquerosa,
		no la come nadie
sórdido		un ambiente sórdido
		negocios sórdidos
guarro (R1)		El coche está guarro, lávalo
		Estás un poco guarro, ve al baño
cochambroso		Tenía un aspecto cochambroso que me daba
(R1)		asco
cochino (R1*)		Sus ropas estaban cochinas/
marrano (R1*)		marranas/puercas/merdosas
puerco (R1*)		una película cochina/ marrana . . .
merdoso (R1*)		

  lower register

figurative

verde	dirty, of jokes	Se divertía contando chistes verdes

SUELDO

sueldo	salary	Cobro el sueldo a fin de mes
salario	wage, salary	Ha subido mi salario un cinco por
		ciento
paga	pay (usu weekly);	El obrero cobra su paga el viernes
	pocket money	El niño pide su paga el domingo
pago	payment (instalment or	Se realizaba el pago en metálico
	act of paying)	
†honorarios (pl)	(professional) fee,	Los honorarios del dentista/abogado son
	emoluments	muy elevados
jornal (m)	day's pay	El recolector de fruta cobraba su jornal
		cada sábado
nómina	salary, payroll, payslip	Tengo domiciliada mi nómina

SUERTE

general		
suerte (f)	luck	¡Qué suerte! ¡He ganado la lotería!
bad luck		
mala suerte		Tuve la mala suerte de caerme en el barranco
mala ventura		Por mi mala ventura me encuentro sin trabajo
(suerte) negra (R1)		Cuando te toca la negra hay que aceptarlo
mala pata (R1)		Tuve la mala pata de perder todo su dinero
		Siempre tengo mala pata con la lotería
good luck		
buena suerte		Tuve la buena suerte de acertar
(buena) fortuna		Cuando te sonríe la buena fortuna, todo te sale bien
		La fortuna hizo que me tocara el premio gordo
ventura (R3)		Te deseo todo tipo de venturas en tu nueva vida
chance		
azar (m)		Por azar me le encontré en la calle
casualidad (f)		Por casualidad me encontré un billete de cincuenta euros en la plaza
ventura		La ventura quiso que nos encontráramos
fate, destiny		
†**destino**		El destino del hombre es morir
sino (R3)		El héroe luchó contra su sino
hado (R3)		Los hados marcan mi destino
fortuna		No quiso la fortuna que me nombraran

TALÓN

talón (m)	heel (part of foot or part of shoe)	Me he hecho daño en el talón
		el talón de Aquiles
		No me gustan los talones de ese color
tacón (m)	heel (part of shoe; commoner in this meaning than **talón**)	el tacón del zapato
		Llevaba tacones altos

TERCO

terco	stubborn, obstinate	Nunca cambiará de opinión, es muy terca
		Era terca como un mulo
obstinado		Era tan obstinado nunca aceptaba razones
testarudo		No seas testarudo, estás equivocado
persistente	persistent	Produjeron inundaciones las persistentes lluvias
porfiado (R3)		Seguía porfiado en su postura
pertinaz (R3)		Azotaba el campo una sequía pertinaz
tenaz	tenacious	un luchador/atleta tenaz
contumaz (R3)	stubborn in error, incorrigible	Siempre expresa opiniones contumaces
		un interlocutor contumaz que no cambia de opinión
		una actitud contumaz
intransigente (R2–3)	intransigent	un adversario intransigente
cabezón (R1)	pig-headed	Come esta sopa, no seas cabezón

TIENDA

tienda (R2)	shop	Voy a la tienda de la esquina
grandes almacenes (R2)	department store	Hay de todo en los grandes almacenes
negocio (R2)	shop, business	Su padre tiene un negocio de paraguas
comercio (R2)		Los grandes almacenes hunden al pequeño comercio
		un comercio de venta al por mayor/ menor (wholesale/retail)
supermercado (R2)	(small) supermarket	Bajo al supermercado a hacer la compra de hoy
hipermercado (R2)	large supermarket, hypermarket	Fui al hipermercado en las afueras
gran superficie (R2)	shopping centre, shopping mall	Si siguen construyendo grandes superficies en las afueras no quedarán tiendas en la ciudad

TIRAR

†tirar	to throw (gen); to throw away	El chico tiraba piedras a los pájaros ¡Tira la basura!
lanzar	to throw; to launch (suggests aim, precision); to toss	La atleta lanzó la jabalina Se puso tan contenta que lanzó su sombrero al aire El árbitro lanzó la moneda al aire
echar	to kick out; to toss	El patrón me echó a la calle echar una moneda
arrojar	to hurl	Está prohibido arrojar objetos a la vía del tren
proyectar	to project	El sol proyectó su sombra unos diez metros
botar	to launch; to throw out	Botar el barco al agua La botaron del trabajo
disparar	to launch, to fire	Los científicos dispararon un cohete

TIRARSE

to dive (literal or figurative)

tirarse (de cabeza) †echarse (de cabeza) zambullirse (de cabeza)	to dive from bank, etc	El chico se tiró / se echó / se zambulló en la piscina El estudiante se zambulló en la lectura
†echarse	to dive from a height	El muchacho se echó al agua para salvar a la niña
arrojarse		El muchacho valiente se arrojó al río para salvar a la niña Desesperada, se arrojó por la ventana
abalanzarse		El policía se abalanzó sobre el ladrón
lanzarse		Se lanzó al agua desde diez metros
sumergirse	to dive from surface of water (eg submarine, duck)	El submarino se sumergió unos cincuenta metros
saltar	to practise high diving	El nadador saltó de un trampolín de tres metros
bucear	to swim underwater	Me he comprado un equipo de bucear

figurative

†**precipitarse**	to rush	**El coche se precipitó en el vacío**
despeñarse	to throw oneself headlong	**El suicida se despeñó desde lo alto del acantilado**

TONTO

estúpido	stupid	**Tiene que ser estúpido con esas respuestas**
tonto		**Nunca entiende lo que se le dice, es tan tonto**
necio (R2–3)	silly	**Es tan necia que no distingue el bien del mal**
bobo		**José es un poco bobo, no entiende nada de nada**
lerdo	slow of understanding	**Es muy lerda para los estudios**
torpe		**Es torpe para conducir/dibujar**
idiota	idiot, imbecile	**No seas idiota y dime la verdad**
imbécil		**Es un imbécil: se pasa todo el día gastando bromas estúpidas**
cretino		**Son mujeres cretinas que pasan su tiempo chismorreando**
ser un(a) gili(pollas)/ gilí/ jili/jilí(R1*)	to be really stupid	**A ese gili(pollas) no hay quien le aguante**
ser un(a) jilipolla(s) (R1*)		

N O T E : Most of these adjectives are simply insults, and are, to some extent, interchangeable.

TORMENTA

†**tormenta**	thunderstorm (always with heat)	**La tormenta arrasó varios bosques**
		Me dio miedo anoche la tormenta, sobre todo el trueno
borrasca	high wind, squall	**La borrasca hizo zozobrar tres lanchas**
†**temporal** (R2)	storm at sea	**Con el temporal se cerraron las carreteras en la sierra**
†**tempestad**	storm on land or at sea	**La tempestad se desencadenó sin previo aviso**
nevada	snowstorm	**La nevada alcanzó unos treinta centímetros**
granizada	hailstorm	**La granizada hizo estragos en la cosecha**

TRABAJO

trabajo	work (gen)	El trabajo me cansa mucho Tiene un trabajo temporal
empleo †puesto ocupación (f) situación (f) chamba (Mex)	post, position, job	Tengo un empleo en el banco Tiene un puesto de trabajo en París Mi ocupación preferida es la lectura Mi situación en la empresa es buena Dejo la chamba a las siete de la tarde
tarea †faena (R1) labor (f) (R2–3)	task	Desarrolló su tarea a la perfección Se dedica a las faenas del campo Tengo mucha faena en casa hoy El equipo realizó las labores de rescate
tajo (R1) curro (R1)	job and place of work	Adiós, voy al tajo El curro es duro
obra	piece of work	¡Siempre hay obras en esta carretera!
deberes (m pl)	homework	Tenéis que entregar los deberes el lunes

TRISTE

general (of people and things)		
triste	sad	Se puso triste el día de la salida de su amante
of people †descontento	(opposite of **contento**) unhappy, discontented	Estaba muy descontenta con sus notas
pesimista (m/f) tristón (R1)	sad, gloomy (inherent)	Siempre ve las cosas de forma pesimista Hace un día tristón
melancólico (R2–3)	melancholy	La heroína estaba melancólica por la ausencia de su amante
desconsolado (R2–3) afligido (R2–3)	disconsolate, woebegone	Se quedó desconsolado con la muerte de su amigo Se quedó afligida con la noticia de la muerte

abatido	depressed	**Lleva semanas abatida y no hay quien pueda ayudarla**
deprimido		**Se quedó deprimido al saber que un coche había atropellado a su perro**
decaído	in low spirits	**Tiene el ánimo decaído por la pérdida de su gato**
en baja forma (R1)	out of sorts, depressed	**Está en baja forma, tiene la moral por los suelos**
jodido (R1)	down, depressed	**Estoy jodido, no puedo andar y tengo que quedarme en casa**
apenado (R2–3)		**La pérdida de la sortija la dejó apenada**
apesadumbrado (R2–3)		**Su mala suerte la dejó apesadumbrada**

of things

doloroso	painful, distressing	**un acontecimiento doloroso**
lamentable	deplorable	**Estaba en un estado lamentable tras la noticia**

VACACIONES

vacaciones (f pl)	long holiday, usu involving absence	**Todos los trabajadores tienen derecho a vacaciones** **estar de vacaciones**
†**fiesta**	single day (public holiday)	**Ayer fue la fiesta de los Reyes Magos y mañana es la fiesta de mi cumpleaños**
día (m) **festivo**		**Mañana es día festivo**
festividad (f)		**la festividad del primer de mayo**
fiestas (pl)		**Las fiestas de mi pueblo siempre son en agosto**
†**permiso**	(soldier's or prisoner's) leave	**La marina le dio tres días de permiso** **Se le otorgó al preso un permiso de cuatro días**

VALIENTE

general		
†**bravo**	brave	La chica brava ha rescatado a un niño que se ahogaba en el mar
†**valeroso**		El joven valeroso entró en la casa incendiada
valiente		Fue valiente ante el peligro
		Has tomado una valiente decisión

specific		
†**animoso**	lively, spirited	El joven animoso afrontó el peligro sin rechistar
brioso	dashing	un caballo brioso
arriesgado	bold, daring	El chico arriesgado escaló el acantilado para salvar a la niña
atrevido		Hay que ser atrevido para realizar tal gesta
osado (R2–3)		La chica osada escaló la torre sin ayuda
intrépido (R2–3)	fearless, intrepid	Intrépida, se lanzó al mar para rescatar a su hermana
†**bizarro** (R3)	gallant, chivalrous	un jinete bizarro
		un bizarro soldado
caballeroso (R2–3)		El hombre caballeroso le ofreció una rosa a su amada

VASO

vaso	glass (gen)	un vaso de agua
†**copa**	glass with stem; ALSO = drink	¿Vamos a tomar una copa?
		una copa de vino
copita	small (sherry) glass	¿Tomamos una copita?
jarra	jug	una jarra de agua

VENTANA

ventana	window in house	**Abrí las ventanas por que hacía demasiado calor**
†**ventanilla**	window in train, car; office counter	**Es peligroso asomarse por la ventanilla** **Le atenderán en esa ventanilla**
escaparate (m)	shop/store window	**Había dos chicas decorando el escaparate**
vitrina (Am)		**Había joyas en la vitrina**
vidriera	stained-glass window	**La vidriera de la catedral es magnífica**
†**cristal** (m)	pane of glass	**Rompió el cristal con una piedra**

VER

to see		
general		
†**ver**	to see	**Se ve el mar desde el balcón** **Pasa su tiempo viendo televisión**
specific		
observar	to observe	**Se pasa el tiempo observando el vuelo de las aves**
notar		**Se nota la mejoría del tiempo**
descubrir	to spot, to notice	**He descubierto la verdad**
†**percibir**		**Se percibía alguna luz en la oscuridad**
†**reparar en**		**Reparé en la presencia de mi amigo sin darme cuenta que había llegado**
columbrar	to see from a distance	**A lo lejos columbraba a varios caballeros**
vislumbrar		**Entre los árboles, al fondo del jardín, se vislumbraba la casa** **Por muy difícil que fuera, vislumbré la solución**
†**divisar**		**Se divisaba el águila en los peñascos**
atisbar (R2–3)		**Atisbó una figura a lo lejos** **Así atisbo la solución del problema**
†**presenciar**	to witness	**Presencié un accidente ayer**
otear (R2–3)	to scan, to survey	**Oteaba el horizonte con los prismáticos**

to look at
  general

†**mirar**	to look at	**Miraba por la ventana cuando vi un caballo desbocado**

  specific

fijar la vista (en)	to stare at	**No me contestaba y fijaba la vista en el suelo**
echar una mirada/ ojeada/vistazo	to glance	**Eché una mirada / ojeada / un vistazo al periódico**

VIAJE

viaje (m)	journey	**Fue un viaje muy largo**
recorrido **periplo** (R3)	tour, route	**el recorrido del autobús / de la carrera** **El periplo de Cristóbal Colón tuvo como punto de partida un puerto andaluz**
trayecto	short ride (eg on a bus route in town)	**el trayecto del autobús**
excursión (f) †**gira** **vuelta**	trip	**Salimos de excursión a Suiza** **Los cantantes hicieron una gira por el sur** **dar la vuelta al mundo**

VIDRIO

vidrio	glass (gen), the basic raw material	**un envase de vidrio** **El vidrio se puede reciclar**
†**cristal**	pane of glass; covering of glass (eg on watch); type of glass; crystal, quality glass	**Hay que limpiar los cristales** **el cristal de un reloj** **una copa de cristal**

VIEJO

†**viejo**	old (gen)	**una costumbre muy vieja**
anciano	old (of people: more polite than **viejo**)	**Llegó un hombre anciano que cojeaba**
mayor		**una persona mayor**
†**antiguo**	ancient, pertaining to antiquity; antique	**Es una tradición antigua**
vetusto (R3)	ancient (= very old)	**un edificio vetusto**
añejo	old (of wine)	**un vino añejo**
usado	old (of clothes)	**Mi ropa está muy usada**
antiguo	former	**Es mi antiguo profesor**

VIENTO

viento	wind (gen)	**Soplaba el viento del oeste**
ráfaga	gust of wind	**Una ráfaga de aire se llevó todos los papeles**
aire (m)	air, draught, breeze	**Hace falta más aire, el tiempo está bochornoso**
brisa	breeze	**Corría una brisa muy suave**
vendaval (m)	gale	**El vendaval rompió todos los cristales**
huracán (m)	hurricane	**El huracán produjo centenares de muertos**
torbellino **remolino**	whirlwind	**El viento formó un torbellino** **Un remolino de viento le hizo rodar el sombrero por el suelo**
ciclón (m)	cyclone	**Se hundieron varios barcos con el ciclón**
tornado	tornado	**El tornado levantó coches**

6 Complex verbal expressions

It often happens that a simple verb in English has only a 'complex' paraphrase equivalent, with an essentially different syntax, in Spanish, or vice versa. Some very common and useful verbal ideas fall into this category, and a selection of these is given in the following sections.

6.1 A complex expression in Spanish corresponding to a single verb in English

to blame sb	**echar/achacar la culpa a^{IO} uno**
to borrow sth from sb	**†pedir algo prestado a^{IO} uno** (= to ask to borrow)
• I borrowed two books from him	• **Le pedí prestados dos libros** **tomar algo prestado a uno** (= to take sth on loan) NOTE: **prestar** sometimes = to borrow [!] in Am.
to compete with sb	**hacer la competencia a^{IO} uno**
to discharge sb	**dar de alta a^{PERS} uno**
• The doctor discharged us the same day	• **El médico nos dio de alta el mismo día**
to dismiss sb	**dar de baja a^{PERS} uno**
to drop sth	**dejar caer algo**
to ignore sth/sb	**†pasar algo / a^{PERS} uno por alto**
to insist on sth	**hacer hincapié en algo**
to jilt sb	**dejar plantado a^{PERS} uno**

to miss sth/sb	**echar de menos algo / a**[PERS] **uno** (Pen) (= [†]**extrañar** in Am) **echar en falta a**[PERS] **uno**
to notice sth/sb	[†]**hacer caso a/de algo/uno**
to (call into) question sth	**poner algo en entredicho** **poner algo en tela de juicio**
to reprimand, tell off	**pegar/echar la bronca a**[IO] **uno**
to welcome sb	**dar la bienvenida a**[IO] **uno**
to wind up (a watch)	**dar cuerda (a un reloj)**

6.2   A single verb in Spanish corresponding to a complex expression in English

amanecer (R3) • **Cogió el tren en Madrid y amaneció en Córdoba**	to be in a place at daybreak • He caught the train in Madrid and arrived in Córdoba at dawn
ambicionar • **Ambicionaba ser primer ministro**	to have the aim of • He had the aim of becoming Prime Minister
cartearse • **Se cartearon durante un año**	to write letters to each other • They wrote each other letters for a year
[†]**despedirse de uno**	to take one's leave of sb
destacar(se) • **Destacan tres posibilidades** • **Este alumno se destaca de todos los otros / destaca sobre los demás**	to stand out • There are three obvious possibilities • This student stands out from all the others
[†]**no dignarse hacer algo** • **No se dignó contestar**	not so much as to do sth • He didn't even reply
distar de algo • **Mi casa no dista mucho de la tuya** • **Dista mucho de ser inteligente**	to be a long way from sth (lit and fig) • My house isn't far from yours • He's a long way from being bright

†**entrevistarse con uno**	to have an interview, talks with sb
estrenar algo • **Estrenaron sus vestidos para la ópera**	to use sth for the first time • They wore their new clothes for the opera
golear (a^PERS un equipo) (Rl) • **El Real (Madrid) goleó al Barcelona**	to score a lot of goals (against a team) • Real Madrid scored a hatful against Barcelona
guardarse (bien) de hacer algo • **Yo me guardaré bien de salir**	to be (very) careful not to do sth • I'll take good care not to go out
incendiar algo • **El rayo incendió el bosque**	to set fire to sth • The lightning set the wood on fire
incumplir (una promesa)	not to keep / to break (a promise)
independizarse	to become independent
ironizar • **Ironizaba sobre los males del tabaco**	to make fun of • She made fun of the evils of tobacco
limitarse a hacer algo • **Se limitó a decir que . . .**	only to do sth • He just said that . . .
llevar x años a^IO uno • **Mi hermana me lleva dos años**	to be older than sb by x years • My sister is two years older than me
meterse de (eg **peluquero**)	to take on a job as (eg a hairdresser)
†**profundizar en algo**	to go deeply into sth
†**regatear algo**	to haggle over sth, to be stingy with sth
repercutir en algo • **El cambio repercutió en todo el departamento**	to have repercussions on/throughout sth • The change had repercussions throughout the whole department

responsabilizar a^{PERS} **uno de algo**	to lay responsibility for sth on sb
● **El diputado comunista responsabilizó al gobierno del paro**	● The communist deputy laid the responsibility for unemployment on the government
sincerarse con uno	to tell sb the truth
● **Se sinceró conmigo**	● She told me the truth
soler hacer algo	to be accustomed to doing sth, usually to do sth
● **Suelo levantarme a las siete**	● I usually get up at seven
†**tardar (tiempo,** eg **cinco horas) en hacer algo**	to take (time, eg five hours) to do sth
● **El barco tarda cinco horas en llegar**	● It takes the boat five hours to get there (The boat takes five hours to get there)
tratarse de algo	to be a question of sth
†**volver a hacer algo**	to do sth again
● **Volvió a ver la película**	● She saw the film again

In this category are a number of Spanish verbs which correspond to the English notion of 'to make', 'to cause to be':

concienciar a^{PERS} **uno de algo**	to make sb conscious of sth
● **El médico concienció al público de la necesidad de vacunarse**	● The doctor made the public conscious of the need to be vaccinated
dificultar algo	to make sth difficult
● **El barro dificultó el acceso a la finca**	● Mud made access to the farm difficult
entusiasmar a uno	to make sb excited
● **Los goles antológicos entusiasmaron a la afición**	● The series of goals made the fans excited
ilusionar a uno	to make sb excited
● **El regalo me ilusiona vivamente**	● I'm very excited about the present
posibilitar algo	to make sth possible
● **El dinero posibilitó el viaje**	● Money made the journey possible
prestigiar	to make prestigious
● **El fichaje del jugador argentino prestigió al club**	● Signing the Argentine player gave the club prestige

6.3   Common complex expressions in Spanish corresponding to complex expressions in English

sacar adelante	to bring up (eg a child); to produce, to turn out (eg a student); to go on with (eg business)
• **Trabajó mucho para sacar adelante la empresa**	• He worked hard to make the business prosper
salir adelante	to make progress, to get on
tener [†]**afición a algo**	to be enthusiastic about sth
tener a bien hacer algo (R2–3)	to be kind enough to do sth
• **Le pedí que tuviera a bien venir hoy**	• I asked her to be kind enough to come today
dejar constancia de algo	to place sth on record, give evidence of sth
tener algo en cuenta	to take sth into account
traer frito a[PERS] **uno**	to make someone fed up with
• **Sus insultos me traen frita**	• I'm fed up with his insults
llevarse bien/mal con uno	get on well/badly with sb
Ni decir tiene que . . .	It goes without saying that . . .
• **Hacía un sol magnífico, ni decir tiene que la naturaleza se alegraba**	• It was beautifully sunny; it goes without saying that nature was brightening up
ponerse de parte de uno	to take sb's side
• **Me puse de parte de mi amigo**	• I took my friend's side
[†]**pasarse sin algo**	to do without sth
salir al paso a[IO] **uno**	to go and meet sb
• **Me salió al paso**	• He came out to meet me
echarse a perder (intr)	to get ruined/spoiled
• **Se me ha echado a perder la chaqueta**	• My jacket's got ruined
no poder menos de hacer algo	not to be able to avoid doing sth
• **No pudo menos de sonreír**	• He could not help smiling
tener algo presente	to bear sth in mmd
entrar en razón	to see reason

meter/poner/hacer entrar en razón a^{PERS} uno	to make sb see reason
pasar revista a algo/uno	to go through sth; to review sb (eg troops)
● La señorita pasó revista a su guardarropa	● The girl went through her wardrobe
● El primer ministro pasó revista a las tropas	● The Prime Minister reviewed the troops
†dar la vuelta a algo	to go round sth
● Dieron la vuelta a la plaza	● They went round the square

6.4   Spanish verbs which take an infinitive as their subject

The English equivalents of impersonal verbs in Spanish, which sometimes take an infinitive as their subject (see also **25.1.1**), are not always obvious.

†antojarse a^{IO} uno hacer algo	to occur to sb to do sth
● Se le antojó ir al parque	● It occurred to her to go to the park
†bastar	to be sufficient
● Basta (con) decir que sí	● It's enough to say so
● Bastan cinco	● Five's enough
†caber	to be contained
● No cabe aquí	● There's not enough room for it here
● Al ministro le caben dos posibilidades	● The minister has two possibilities
● Cabe recordar que . . .	● It is useful to remember that . . .
escasear (R3)	to be in short supply
● Escasea el azúcar	● Sugar is in short supply
†faltar	to be lacking
● Faltan diez minutos para llegar a Londres	● We'll be arriving in London in ten minutes
● Faltan cinco minutos para que llegue mi tía	● My aunt will be here in five minutes
†importar	to be important, to matter
● Importa saberlo	● It is important to know
● Me importa que vengas	● It's important for me that you come
● ¿Le importa si cierro la ventana?	● Do you mind if I shut the window?

menudear (R3)	to be frequent, numerous
• **Menudean los problemas en esta empresa**	• There are many problems in this firm
†**quedar**	to be remaining
• **Le quedan a ella pocos amigos**	• She has few friends left
†**sobrar**	to be in excess, to be left (over)
• **Me sobran dos kilos de patatas**	• I've got two kilos of potatoes too many
†**urgir** (R3)	to be urgent, imperative
• **Me urge saber la verdad**	• It is imperative I know the truth
valer	to be worth (lit)
• **Su libro le valió un gran premio**	• His book brought him a big prize

6.5   Reflexive verbs + *la* or *las*

There are a number of verbal expressions in Spanish which involve a reflexive verb + **la** or **las**. They have little in common apart from this but the commonest are grouped here together for convenience.

apañárselas	to manage, to get by
• **No te preocupes: me las apañaré**	• Don't worry: I'll manage
arreglárselas	to manage, get by
• **Me las arreglo solo en la cocina**	• I get by on my own in the kitchen
cargársela (R1) (Pen)	to get into trouble
dárselas de (listo)	to give oneself the appearance of being (clever)
echárselas de ADJ/N	to make a show of being ADJ / a(n) N
• **Se las echa de héroe**	• He's playing the hero / He's making a show of being a hero
habérselas con uno (R1)	to deal with, to face sb
• **Se las tendrá que haber con la directora**	• She'll have to face the principal
pegársela a[IO] **uno**	to deceive sb
†**pirárselas** (R1*−1)	to go away, to get out

sabérselas todas (R1)	to be a know–all
traérselas (R1)	to be shocking, difficult (of people)
vérselas con uno	to give an account of oneself to sb
• **Tendrá que vérselas con su padre**	• He'll have to explain it to his father

7 Affective suffixes

One of the characteristic richnesses of Spanish, especially in R1, is its use of suffixes which can express a wide range of affective notions (size, affection, disapproval, irony, etc). Some stems and suffixes are so firmly associated that they form words in their own right, eg **bolita** = *berry*, **telón** = *(theatre) curtain*, **parrilla** = *grill*, **camarín** (m) = *dressing room*, **caballete** (m) = *easel*, **hoyuelo** = *dimple*.

In Mexico, the **–ito** suffix is extremely frequent, and many very common nouns, such as **agüita**, **casita**, **cochecito**, **pancita** and **solito** regularly take the suffix without any implication regarding size.

Affective suffixes are used most often with nouns and adjectives, although the use of **–ito/a** extends to past participles used adjectivally and even to adverbs:

Está completamente dormidito
He's sound asleep
Hay que hablar bajito
You must speak really quietly
Lo haré en seguidita
I'll do it right away
[†]**¡Ahorita!** (used regularly in the sense of Pen **ahora** in Central America)

NOTE: the attachment of some suffixes (the main ones are **–ín**, **–ete**, **–ón** and **–azo**) to noun stems may lead to a change in gender from feminine to masculine, eg **novela** (f), but **novelón** (m).

-ito/a (also *-(e)cito/a*)

This is one of the commonest suffixes, especially in Latin America. Its predominant meaning is diminutive:

Tengo alquilado un cochecito
I've hired a small car
Hernani es un pueblecito en el País Vasco
Hernani is a small village in the Basque Country

It also indicates affection, and is particularly associated with language used to and by children:

Dale un besito a Papá
Give Daddy a kiss
¡Oye, niño, deja al caballito!
Hey, leave the horse alone!
Le duele el dientecito al pequeño
The child's tooth hurts
It can also have an intensifying meaning:
Hace un poco fresquito, ¿no?
It's pretty chilly, isn't it?
Allí tienes un café calentito
There's a nice hot coffee
¡Ay, el pobrecito!
Poor old thing!
Similar to **-ito/a** are **-ico/a** and **-ín**, though by no means as common:
-ico/a is particularly associated with Aragón and with some areas of
Latin America; **-ín** is particularly associated with north-west Spain.

-illo/a (also -(e)cillo/a)

This is a diminutive suffix which often has a pejorative overtone; in
Latin America it is almost exclusively pejorative.
No me gusta este tonillo de superioridad
I don't like this (nasty) superior tone
Había en la tienda un hombrecillo que se quedaba callado
In the shop was a(n insignificant) little man who said nothing
Me parece un poco complicadillo
It seems a bit (unpleasantly) complicated
Es una novela fuertecilla
It's a heavy novel
However, **-illo/a** in 'established' words (see above) is not usually
pejorative: **una †ventanilla** = *a train window*, **un cursillo** = *a short
course*.
NOTE also the non-pejorative use in the following example:
Soplaba un airecillo/vientecillo muy agradable
A very pleasant light breeze was blowing

-uelo/a (also -(e)juelo/a, -(e)zuelo/a and -chuelo/a) and -ete (also -(e)cete)

These are diminutive and pejorative: **plazuela** = *(miserable) little
square*, **riachuelo** = *(trickle of a) stream*, **pequeñuelo** = *little child*;
lugarete = *insignificant little place*.

-ón/-ona

This suffix has a number of values. It may be simply augmentative, as in **hombretón** (m) = *well-built fellow*, **sillón** (m) = *easy chair*. As an augmentative, it most frequently has a pejorative overtone, since largeness or excess is often thought of as being bad, eg **solterón/ona** = *confirmed bachelor/spinster*, †**cabrón** (R1*) (m) = *bastard*, **dulzón** = *over-sweet*. However, where excess could be construed as good, there is no pejorative overtone, eg **fiestón** (m) = *great party*.

-ón can also form pejorative adjectives from nouns **(cabezón =**
  stubborn) and pejorative nouns from verbs **(empollón =**
  hard-working student, swot, **llorón** = *cry-baby*).

-ón also indicates the result of an action, eg **bofetón** (m) = *blow*.

N O T E: in American Spanish, **-ón** often has the meaning/*fairly*, eg
pobretón = *rather poor*.

-azo

This is similar to **-ón**, but is less common, eg **bigotazo** = *big moustache* (neutral), **acentazo** = *bad accent*, but **exitazo** = *great success*; **-azo** also has the meaning of *a blow with*, eg **codazo** = *nudge, blow with the elbow*.

-ote/a

This is augmentative and pejorative, eg **librote** (m) = *dull book*, **palabrota** = *dirty word*, **cabezota** (m or f) = *real bighead*, **brutote** = *rough, clumsy, slow-witted*, **francote** = *very easy-going*.

N O T E, however, **amigote** (m) = *buddy, mate*, which is familiar rather than pejorative.

-ucho/a, -acho/a and -uco/a

These are pejorative:
  Vive en una casucha aislada en el campo
  She lives in an isolated hovel in the country
  un cuartucho asqueroso
  a disgustingly squalid room
  el populacho
  the common herd
  esos capitalistas †ricachos
  those stinking rich capitalists
  un frailuco
  an insignificant little monk
  una mujeruca
  an old woman
N O T E, however, **picachos** = *fierce-looking peaks*.

8 Idioms, similes and proverbs

Language in all registers can be made more lively and interesting by the judicious use of idiomatic expressions. The following expressions are a small selection from the wealth of such material in Spanish. They are all in common use, and may be employed with confidence by learners.

8.1 Idioms

tener (muchas) agallas	to be courageous
hacer su agosto	to make one's pile, to make hay while the sun shines
estar con el agua / la soga al cuello	to be in great difficulties
caerse el alma a los pies	to be down in the dumps
• Se me cayó el alma a los pies	• I was down in the dumps
estar con el alma en un hilo / en vilo	to be in suspense
consultar con la almohada	to sleep on it
tener ángel / mal ángel	to be charming / to lack charm
armarse un ruido / un escándalo / la de Dios / un follón (R1) / una gresca (R1) / la de San Quintín	to cause a row
estar / tener a^{PERS} uno en ascuas	to be / to keep sb on tenterhooks
todo bicho viviente (R1)	every living soul

NOTE: **bicho** is avoided in Caribbean and Chilean Spanish, where it has the meaning of *penis* in R1.

estar / quedarse sin blanca (Pen) / sin un centavo (Am) (R1–2)	not to have a bean

no importar un bledo/comino/pepino (R1)	not to matter two hoots
a pedir de boca	perfectly
hacerse la boca agua a[IO] **uno**	to make sb's mouth water
meterse en la boca del lobo	to enter the lion's den
quedar boquiabierto / quedarse lelo	to be left gaping (in bewilderment)
echar la bronca a[IO] **uno**	to give sb a real dressing down
no caber en sí / su piel	to be beside oneself (with joy, anger); to be presumptuous
caer bien/mal	to be well timed / ill timed
pasar las de Caín (R1)	to have a bad time
dar calabazas a[IO] **uno** (R1)	to jilt; to fail sb (in exam)
meterse en un callejón sin salida	to get into a jam
ponérsele a[IO] **uno la carne de gallina**	to get goose pimples
no saber a qué carta quedarse	to be uncertain
charlar por los codos	to talk incessantly
†**estar en condiciones (de hacer algo)**	to be in good shape, to be able (to do sth)
llevar la contraria	to take an opposite point of view
marchar / nadar / ir contra la corriente	to go against the current, to swim against the tide
ser un cuco	to be cunning
ajustar las cuentas a[IO] **uno** (R1–2)	to settle accounts with sb, to sort sb out
venir a cuento	to be appropriate, fitting
llevarse un chasco	to be disappointed
echar/arrojar/lanzar chispas	to get angry
está chupado (commoner with younger people) / **tirado** (commoner with older people) (R1)	it's a piece of cake
un lío, ruido, etc, de todos los demonios (R1–2)	a hell of a problem, noise, etc
tomar el desquite (de algo) (R3)	to get revenge, to get one's own back (for sth)
todo el santo día (R1–2)	the whole blessed day
mandar a[PERS] **uno al diablo / a paseo** (R1)	to send sb packing
Dios mediante (R3)	God willing
hacer época (R2–3)	to be sensational, to attract much public attention
mandar a[PERS] **uno a freír espárragos** (R1)	to send sb packing
dar el esquinazo a[IO] **uno**	to give sb the slip

tener buena/mala estrella	to be lucky/unlucky
ser la flor y nata	to be the cream
estar fuera de sí	to be beside oneself (emotionally, both positive and negative)
ser la gallina de los huevos de oro (R1–2)	to be the goose that lays the golden eggs
hay gato encerrado	there's sth fishy
dar el golpe de gracia a^{IO} uno	to finish sb off
ir al grano	to go straight to the point
Ni hablar (R1–2)	Nothing doing
hablar en cristiano	to talk plainly, clearly
hacer de las suyas	to be up to one's old tricks
ser harina de otro costal	to be another kettle of fish
estar hecho una fiera	to get furious
estar hecho una pena	to be in a sorry state
estar hecho polvo	to get worn out
estar hecho una sopa	
estar hecho un mar de lágrimas	to get soaked to the skin / to weep floods of tears
estar calado / mojado hasta los huesos	
entrar/poner en juego	to be / to put at stake
tirar (R1) / irse (R2) cada uno por su lado	each to go his/her separate way
dar la lata a^{IO} uno (R1)	to get on sb's nerves
ser una lata (R1)	to be annoying
dormirse en/sobre los laureles	to rest on one's laurels
tener mala leche (R1*) / mal café (R1)	to be a nasty type
levantar la liebre	to spill the beans
tener líos / un lío (R1–2)	to have difficulties
estar loco de atar / de remate (R1–2)	to be completely mad
entre dos luces (R3)	in the evening
estar en la luna	to have one's head in the clouds
salir/sacar a luz	to be published / to publish (eg a book)
dar a luz un niño	to give birth to a child
¡Toca madera!	Touch wood!
estar en mangas de camisa	to be in one's shirt-sleeves
†echar mano a	to take hold of
†echar una mano a^{IO} uno	to give sb a hand
tener buena/mala mano para algo	to be expert/clumsy at sth

un libro de segunda mano	a second-hand book
irse/venir/llegar a las manos / los puños	to come to blows
estar de más / de sobra	to be in excess
sin más ni más	without further hesitation
como el que más	more than anyone
hacer mella en/a[IO] uno	to make an impression on sb
meterse en barullos/berenjenales/líos (R1)	to get into a real mess
meterse en donde no le llaman	to snoop around
hacer (buenas) migas con uno	to hit it off with sb
ser de mírame y no me toques	to be finicky, delicate
ser un mirlo blanco	to be an exceptional thing, an impossible dream
ser moneda corriente (R3)	to be a common occurrence
ser de poca monta	to be of little value
Hay moros en la costa	Careful, people are listening
picarle a[PERS] uno la mosca (R1–2)	to get upset, irritated
desde que el mundo es el mundo	since time began
¡Nada de eso!	Nothing doing!
como si nada/tal	as if nothing had happened
no saber nada de nada	to be totally ignorant
hinchársele a[IO] uno las narices	to lose patience, to get irritated
meter la nariz / las narices en algo (R1)	to snoop around in sth
llamar a las cosas por su nombre	} to call a spade a spade
llamar al pan pan y al vino vino	
estar en las nubes	to be up in the clouds
hacer oídos sordos	to turn a deaf ear
ser todos oídos	to be all ears
tener ojeriza a algo	to take a dislike to sth
¡(Mucho) ojo (con algo)!	Careful (with sth)!
andar con ojo	to go carefully
ser el ojo/ojito derecho de uno	to be sb's pet
no pegar ojo / los ojos en toda la noche	not to sleep a wink all night
en un abrir y cerrar de ojos	in the twinkling of an eye

saltar a los ojos / la vista	to be patently obvious
enseñar la oreja	to show one's true character/intentions, to give oneself away
con las orejas gachas (R1)	depressed
matar dos pájaros de un tiro	to kill two birds with one stone
tener/†tomar la palabra	to have / to take the floor
tener palabra / no tener palabra	to keep one's word / to be unreliable
ser pan comido (R1)	to be as easy as pie
estar/vivir a pan y agua	to live in poverty
perder hasta los pantalones / la camisa	to lose everything
meter la pata	to put one's foot in it
peces gordos	big shots, important people
estar/moverse/sentirse como pez en el agua	to be in one's element
como Pedro por su casa	freely, easily, without obstacle
ser de película	to be magnificent
tomar el pelo a[IO] uno	to pull sb's leg, to kid sb
no vérsele el pelo a[IO] uno	He's made himself scarce
llevarse como el perro y el gato	to be always squabbling
¡A otro perro con ese hueso!	Nonsense!, Tell me another!
caer en picado	to dive (of plane)
cerrar el pico	to shut up, to keep quiet
no dejar piedra por mover remover Roma con Santiago }	to leave no stone unturned
No se tiene de pie	It doesn't hold water (of argument)
dormir a pierna suelta	to sleep soundly
no tener ni pies ni cabeza	to be pointless (of argument), to have no meaning
dorar la píldora	to sugar the pill, to make sth easier to swallow
tragarse la píldora	to swallow the whole story
estar entre Pinto y Valdemoro	to be undecided
irse a pique	to sink (of ship), to be ruined (of family, etc)
pisar fuerte	to show resolve
poner los puntos sobre las íes	to dot the i's and cross the t's
predicar en el desierto	to preach / to talk to deaf ears
no soltar prenda	not to divulge a secret, to keep mum
por el qué dirán	because of what the neighbours will say

sacar de quicio a^{PERS} uno	to get on sb's nerves
andarse por las ramas	to beat about the bush
mantener a raya a^{PERS} uno	to keep sb in check / at bay
dar la razón a^{IO} uno	to say that sb is right
dar rienda suelta a^{IO} uno	to give sb a free rein
costar un riñón (R1)	to cost the earth / an arm and a leg
pegársele a uno las sábanas	to get up later than necessary
sacar en claro / en limpio	to make clear
a lo que salga	come what may, however it turns out
salirse con la suya	to get one's own way
calentársele/encendérsele la sangre a^{IO} uno	to get angry/impatient
no saber a qué santo encomendarse	not to know where to turn
tomar en serio	to take seriously
saltarse los sesos	to blow one's brains out
ir a la suya / a lo suyo	to go one's own way
sobre el terreno	on the job, where the work actually takes place
andando el tiempo	as time goes/went by
ir tirando	to get by
Le salió el tiro por la culata	In the end the joke was on him
faltarle a^{IO} uno un tornillo	to have a screw loose
dar al traste con	to ruin, to spoil (eg plans)
irse al traste	to be ruined
rasgarse la túnica / las vestiduras (R2–3)	to rend one's clothes / to tear one's hair (with frustration, anger)
tomar a^{PERS} uno por cabeza de turco (R2–3)	to use sb as a scapegoat
estar en las últimas (R1)	to be about to die; to be down and out
valer un dineral / un mundo / un ojo de la cara / un Potosí	to be worth a fortune
verlo todo color de rosa	to see life through rose-tinted glasses, to take an unduly cheerful view of things
verlo todo negro/nublado	to be pessimistic
contra viento y marea	against all the odds
hacer(se) (de (Am)) la vista gorda	to turn a blind eye
hacer su santa voluntad	to do just what one likes
volver en sí	to regain consciousness
dar una vuelta	to go for a walk

†dar la vuelta	to go back
dar vueltas a algo	to think sth over
ir/quedar a la zaga (R2–3)	to go/drag behind
ponerle zancadillas a^{IO} uno	to catch sb out

8.2 Some idioms based on colour

blanco

dar carta blanca a uno	to give sb a free hand, carte blanche
pasar la noche en blanco	to have a sleepless night
estar sin blanca	without a bean
ir de punta en blanco	to be elegantly dressed

colorado

| Más vale ponerse una vez colorado que ciento amarillo | It may be difficult now but you'll be sorry if you don't do it |

morado

| ponerse morado de comer | to stuff yourself |
| pasarlas moradas | to be in a difficult/compromising situation |

negro

tener la negra (R1)	to be out of luck
tocarle a uno la negra (R1)	to have bad luck
pasarlas negras (R1)	to have a tough time of it
ponerse negro	to look gloomy/bleak
trabajar como un negro (R1)	to work like a slave

NOTE: this idiom does not currently appear to have any racist association in the Spanish-speaking world.

| verse uno negro para hacer algo | to have great difficulty in doing something |

rojo

rojo de ira	crimson/red with anger
estar en números rojos	to be in the red
estar al rojo vivo	to be in a passionate state of mind

verde

un chiste verde	a dirty joke
poner verde a^{PERS} uno (R1) (Pen)	to say nasty things about someone / to give someone a dressing down
a buenas horas mangas verdes	you've/she's, etc, missed the opportunity

8.3   Some idioms based on numbers

uno

ser un cero a la izquierda (R1)	to be useless
una y no más, Santo Tomás	I don't trust him further than I can throw him

dos

cada dos por tres	very frequently
estar entre dos fuegos	to be caught in the cross fire
estar entre dos aguas	to fall between two stools
estar a dos velas	to be without a bean
como dos y dos son cuatro	as sure as eggs is eggs

tres

dar tres cuartos al pregonero	to publicize a secret
buscar tres pies al gato	to split hairs, to make things more complicated than they are
donde Cristo dio las tres voces	in a very distant, solitary place
A la tercera va la vencida	Third time lucky
Ni a la de tres (R1)	Nothing doing!
no ver tres en un burro (R1)	to see nothing (it's so dark)

cuatro

echar un cuarto a espadas	to intervene, give an opinion
estar a la cuarta pregunta	to be penniless
Estaban/había cuatro gatos	There was no one there (at the event)

cinco

Choca esos cinco (R1)	Shake on it!
estar en el quinto coño (R1*)	to be a helluva way away

siete

hacerse un siete en la ropa	to tear your shirt (literally)
estar en el séptimo cielo	to be in seventh heaven
andar/recorrer las siete partidas	to keep going over (an idea)
tener siete vidas	to have nine lives
pícaro de siete suelas (R1)	helluva rascal

diez

hacer las diez de últimas	to end up with nothing

once

meterse en camisa de once varas	to poke your nose in (where it is not your concern)

trece

mantenerse en sus trece — to stick to your guns, not to shift in an opinion

martes y trece — Tuesday the thirteenth (considered an unlucky day, like Friday the thirteenth in the English-speaking world)

cuarenta

cantarle las cuarenta (R1) — to give someone a piece of your mind

cien

poner a[PERS] **uno a cien** (R1) — to (cause to) get in a state of high excitement

Dentro de cien años todos calvos — One day everyone'll be the same

mil, millón

Mil gracias / Un millón de gracias — Many thanks

Vendrá a las mil y quinientas (R1) — (S)he'll come well beyond the agreed time

8.4 Similes based on adjectives

más [†]astuto que la zorra	as cunning as a fox
más blanco que la nieve	as white as snow
[†]bueno como un ángel	as good as gold
más [†]bueno que el pan	goodness itself
tan claro como el agua	as clear as crystal
más [†]contento que unas Pascuas	as happy as a lark
más duro que un mendrugo / una [†]piedra	as tough as nails
más feo que Picio	as ugly as sin
más frío que el hielo / un témpano	as cold as ice
[†]fuerte como un roble	as strong as an ox
tan negro/oscuro como boca de lobo	as black as pitch
más [†]pobre que una [†]rata	as poor as a church mouse
más sordo que una [†]tapia	as deaf as a post
[†]viejo como el mundo	as old as the hills

NOTE: The patterns **más** ADJ **que** and **(tan)** ADJ **como** are interchangeable.

8.5 Similes based on verbs

†**aburrirse como una ostra/almeja**	to be bored to tears
bailar como una peonza	to spin like a top
beber como una †**cuba**	to drink like a fish
†**caer / venir como** †**anillo al dedo**	to fit like a glove
†**cantar como un jilguero**	to sing like a canary
†**comer como una** †**lima**	to eat like a horse
†**correr como un galgo**	to run like a greyhound
†**dormir como un lirón / una** †**piedra / un** †**tronco / un leño**	to sleep like a log
fumar como un carretero	to smoke like a chimney
†**hablar como un loro**	to talk like a parrot
†**llorar como un** †**niño / una Magdalena**	to cry like a baby
nadar como un †**pez**	to swim like a fish
venderse como churros / pan bendito	to sell like hot cakes

8.6 Proverbs and proverbial expressions

Agua pasada no mueve molino	It's all water under the bridge
En casa del ahorcado no se ha de nombrar la soga	*lit* You shouldn't mention the rope in the house of a hanged man, ie *Avoid talking about things that may cause embarrassment*
Arrancada de caballo y parada de asno	*lit* starting like a horse and stopping like an ass, ie *If you set off too quickly you get tired*
Uno piensa el bayo, y otro el que lo ensilla	*lit* The bay horse thinks one thing, and the person who saddles him thinks another, ie *Everyone sees things from their own point of view*
Quien mala cama hace, en ella se yace	*You made your bed, now lie in it!*
A mal tiempo buena cara	*lit* a good face to bad weather, ie *Grin and bear it*
Empezar la casa por el tejado	*lit* to begin the house with the roof, ie *to put the cart before the horse*
Antes que te cases, mira lo que haces	*lit* Before you marry, look what you are doing, ie *Marry in haste, repent at leisure*, or *Look before you leap*

Eso es el cuento de la lechera	*counting one's chickens before they are hatched* (refers to the story of the milkmaid who planned what to do with the money she would get for her milk, but dropped the pitcher on the way to market)
Del dicho al hecho hay gran trecho	*There's many a slip 'twixt cup and lip*
Poderoso caballero es don Dinero	*Money talks*
Los dineros del sacristán, cantando se vienen y cantando se van	*Easy come, easy go*
Dios aprieta pero no ahoga	*lit* God squeezes but he doesn't stifle, ie *Keep calm, all will come right in the end*
Dios los cría y ellos se juntan	*Birds of a feather flock together*
A Dios rogando y con el mazo dando	*lit* asking God and wielding the mallet, ie *God helps those who help themselves*
Gato escaldado del agua fría huye	*lit* A scalded cat avoids cold water (as well), ie *Once bitten, twice shy*
Hablando del rey de Roma por la puerta asoma	*lit* When you speak of the king of Rome he appears at the door, ie *Talk of the devil (and in he comes)*
A lo hecho, pecho	*It's no use crying over spilt milk*
A quien madruga, Dios le ayuda	*lit* God helps the early riser, ie *The early bird catches the worm.* The answer often given to this is **No por mucho madrugar amanece más temprano** = *It doesn't dawn any earlier because you get up earlier*
Ojos que no ven, corazón que no siente	*Out of sight, out of mind*
Más vale pájaro en mano que cien volando	*A bird in the hand is worth two in the bush*
De tal palo, tal astilla	*a chip off the old block*
Las paredes oyen	*Walls have ears*
El que quiere peces que se moje el culo (R1)	*lit* He who wants fish must get his bottom wet, ie *If you want to be successful you must take risks*
El que se pica ajos come	*lit* He who is cross eats garlic, ie *If the cap fits, wear it*
El puchero dijo a la sartén: 'Apártate de mí que me tiznas'	*the pot calling the kettle black*

A cada puerco llega su San Martín	*lit* To every pig comes his Martinmas (the day on which the pig is killed), ie *There is a day of reckoning for everyone*
No se puede repicar y andar en la procesión	*lit* You cannot ring the bells and walk in the procession, ie *You cannot do two things at once*
Al río revuelto ganancias de Pescadores	*lit* Fishermen gain from a turbulent river, ie *It's an ill wind that blows nobody any good*
Cuando el río suena agua lleva	*lit* When the river makes a noise there's a lot of water, ie *There's no smoke without fire*
Cuando a Roma fueres / Allí donde fueres, haz como vieres	*When in Rome, do as the Romans do*
El sapo a la sapa tiénela por muy guapa	*lit* The male toad considers the female toad very pretty, ie *Beauty is in the eye of the beholder*
Sarna con gusto no pica	*lit* Mange with pleasure does not sting, ie *that's his / her choice; (s)he's made her / his bed, let her / him lie on it*
Ir a vendimia y llevar uvas de postre	*lit* to go to the grape harvest and take grapes as a dessert, ie *to take coals to Newcastle*
En una hora no se ganó Zamora	*Rome wasn't built in a day*
Mucho sabe la zorra pero más el que la toma	*lit* The vixen is clever, but the one who catches her is cleverer

9 Proper names

Wherever a Spanish equivalent for a foreign name exists, Spanish uses it. Christian names are regularly adapted. For example, Catherine the Great is **Catalina la Grande**; Queen Elizabeth and Prince Charles are always **la Reina Isabel** and **el Príncipe Carlos** in the Spanish press. Spanish has in the course of history hispanized a number of foreign personal and place names, many of which survive in current usage. The following lists, though long, are by no means exhaustive; they include the commonest of such names and those which are not immediately recognizable, together with the English equivalent (which is frequently an anglicized name). It should be stressed that Spanish-speakers expect these forms to be used: for example, it would be odd to refer to New York as anything other than **Nueva York** in a Spanish-speaking context.

NOTE: English has anglicized some Spanish names, eg Corunna (**La Coruña**), Havana (**La Habana**), Majorca (**Mallorca**), Minorca (**Menorca**), Biscay (**Vizcaya**), Saragossa (**Zaragoza**).

9.1 Names of people

9.1.1 The Ancient Greek world

Alejandro (Magno)	*Alexander (the Great)*
Aquiles	*Achilles*
Ariana	*Ariadne*
Aristófanes	*Aristophanes*
Aristóteles	*Aristotle*
Arquímedes	*Archimedes*
Edipo	*Oedipus*
Esopo	*Aesop*
Esquilo	*Aeschylus*
Euclides	*Euclid*
Eurípides	*Euripides*
Febo	*Phoebus*
Homero	*Homer*

Ilíada	*Iliad*
Odisea	*Odyssey*
Jenofonte	*Xenophon*
Jerjes	*Xerxes*
Leandro	*Leander*
Pitágoras	*Pythagoras*
Platón	*Plato*

9.1.2   The Ancient Roman world

Adriano	*Hadrian*
Aníbal	*Hannibal*
Augusto	*Augustus*
Boecio	*Boethius*
Cartago	*Carthage*
Catón	*Cato*
(Julio) César	*(Julius) Caesar*
Cicerón	*Cicero*
Escipión	*Scipio*
Horacio	*Horace*
Marco Antonio	*Mark Antony*
Nerón	*Nero*
Ovidio	*Ovid*
Plinio	*Pliny*
Tito Livio	*Livy*

9.1.3   The Bible: Old Testament

Adán	*Adam*
Baltasar	*Belshazzar*
Dalila	*Delilah*
Isaías	*Isaiah*
Jehová	*Jehovah*
Jonás	*Jonah*
Josué	*Joshua*
Judá	*Judah*
Matusalén	*Methuselah*
Moisés	*Moses*
Nabucodonosor	*Nebuchadnezzar*
Noé	*Noah*
Rut	*Ruth*
Saba	*Sheba*
Saúl	*Saul*

NOTE: the New Testament Saul (later Paul) = **Saulo**.

9.1.4   The Bible: New Testament

Andrés	*Andrew*
Herodes	*Herod*
Jesucristo/Jesús	*Jesus Christ / Jesus*
José	*Joseph*
Juan Bautista	*John the Baptist*
Lucas	*Luke*
Magdalena	*Mary Magdalene*
Marcos (cf Marco Antonio, above)	*Mark*
el Mesías	*the Messiah*
Poncio Pilato	*Pontius Pilate*
Satanás	*Satan*

NOTE ALSO the place names **Belén**, *Bethlehem*; **Jerusalén**, *Jerusalem*; **Nazaret**, *Nazareth*; **Sión**, *Zion*.

9.1.5   People in the medieval and Renaissance world

Colón	*Columbus*
Durero	*Dürer*
Lutero	*Luther*
Magallanes	*Magellan*
Mahoma	*Mohammed*
Maquiavelo	*Machiavelli*
Miguel-Ángel	*Michelangelo*
Petrarca	*Petrarch*
Ticiano OR Tiziano	*Titian*

9.2   Names of places

9.2.1   Europe

Amberes	*Antwerp*
Aquisgrán	*Aachen/Aix-la-Chapelle*
Atenas	*Athens*
Aviñón	*Avignon*
Basilea	*Basle*
Baviera	*Bavaria*
Berna	*Berne*
Borgoña	*Burgundy*
Brujas	*Bruges*
Bruselas	*Brussels*
Burdeos	*Bordeaux*
Cerdeña	*Sardinia*

NOTE: do not confuse with **Cerdaña**, an eastern Pyrenean valley.

Colonia	*Cologne*
Copenhague	*Copenhagen*
Córcega	*Corsica*
Cornualles	*Cornwall*
Cracovia	*Cracow*
Dresde	*Dresden*
Edimburgo	*Edinburgh*
Estambul	*Istanbul*
Estocolmo	*Stockholm*
Flandes	*Flanders*
Florencia	*Florence*
Francfort (del Meno)	*Frankfurt (am Main)*
Friburgo	*Freiburg*
Gante	*Ghent*
Gascuña	*Gascony*
Génova	*Genoa*
Ginebra	*Geneva*
Gotinga	*Göttingen*
Islas Orcadas	*Orkneys*
La Haya	*The Hague*

NOTE: **La** is the article, despite the normal rule that **el** precedes nouns beginning with a stressed **a-** or **ha-**.

Liorna	*Livorno*
Lisboa	*Lisbon*
Londres	*London*
Lovaina	*Louvain/Leuven*
Madera	*Madeira*
Maguncia	*Mainz*
Malinas	*Mechlin/Mechelen/Malines*
Mantua	*Mantua/Mantova*
Marsella	*Marseilles*
Micenas	*Mycenae*
Milán	*Milan/Milano*
Moscu	*Moscow*
Munich	*Munich/München*
Nápoles	*Naples*
Nicosia	*Nicosia*

NOTE: the difference in stress

Padua	*Padua/Padova*
París	*Paris*
Provenza	*Provence*
Ratisbona *also* Regensburgo	*Regensburg*
Rodas	*Rhodes*
Roma	*Rome*
Rosellón	*Roussillon*
Ruán	*Rouen*

Saboya	*Savoy*
Sajonia	*Saxony*
el Sarre	*The Saar*
Tesalónica	*Thessaloniki (Salonica)*
Tolosa	*Toulouse*
Tréveris	*Trier*
Turín	*Turin / Torino*
La Valeta	*(La) Valletta*
Varsovia	*Warsaw*
Venecia	*Venice*
Versalles	*Versailles*
Viena	*Vienna*

9.2.2   Asia

Antioquía	*Antioch*

NOTE: do not confuse with **Antioquia** in Colombia.

La Meca	*Mecca*
Pekín	*Beijing*
Seúl	*Seoul*
Singapur	*Singapore*

9.2.3   Africa

Addis-Abeba	*Addis Ababa*
Alejandría	*Alexandria*
Argel	*Algiers*
el Cairo	*Cairo*
Ciudad del Cabo	*Cape Town*

NOTE: **en la Ciudad del Cabo**

(el) Sáhara	*Sahara (desert and state)*
Tánger	*Tangier*
Túnez	*Tunis / Tunisia*

9.2.4   North America

Carolina del Norte / del Sur	*North / South Carolina*
Columbia Británica	*British Columbia*
Filadelfia	*Philadelphia*
La Guadalupe	*Guadeloupe*
Islas Lucayas *also* Bahamas	*Bahamas*
Luisiana	*Louisiana*
La Martinica	*Martinique*
Nueva Brunswick	*New Brunswick*
Nueva Escocia	*Nova Scotia*
Nueva Orleáns	*New Orleans*

Nueva York	*New York*
Nuevo Méjico/México	*New Mexico*
Pensilvania	*Pennsylvania*
Tejas	*Texas*
Terranova	*Newfoundland*

9.2.5   South America

Islas Malvinas	*Falkland Islands*

9.3   Names of rivers

Amazonas (m)	*Amazon*
Misisipí (m)	*Mississippi*
Misuri (m)	*Missouri*
Nilo	*Nile*
Rin (m)	*Rhine*
Ródano	*Rhone*
Sena (m)	*Seine*
Tajo	*Tagus*
Támesis (m)	*Thames*

9.4   Names of mountains and volcanoes

Alpes (m pl)	*Alps*
Apalaches (m pl)	*Appalachians*
Apeninos	*Apennines*
Himalaya (m)	*Himalayas*
Las Montañas Rocosas	*The Rockie Mountains*
Pirineos	*Pyrenees*
Vesubio	*Vesuvius*

10 Adjectives pertaining to countries and towns

Spanish has a wealth of special adjectives for inhabitants of countries and towns. By contrast with similar adjectives in English (Mancunian, Liverpudlian, etc), the Spanish ones are in extremely common use. It is difficult to predict which of the several suffixes available will combine with a particular name, and sometimes the adjective will be unrelated to the name, or derive from an older name.

The following list includes the commoner of these adjectives, and those which are not immediately recognizable.

10.1 *España* → *español* or *hispano* (R3)

NOTE the use of **hispano-** in compounds, eg **hispanoárabe**.
NOTE: Spain is frequently referred to as **la Península** *(peninsula)*, especially when distinguishing between the mainland and **Baleares** and **Canarias**.

10.1.1 Regions

Andalucía → **andaluz**
Aragón → **aragonés** OR **maño/mañico** (R1)
(las Islas) Baleares → **balear**
(las Islas) Canarias ⟶ **canario** OR **guanche**
NOTE: The Canaries are also referred to simply as **Las Islas**.
Cantabria → **cántabro**
NOTE: **la Cordillera Cantábrica, el Mar Cantábrico**
Castilla → **castellano**
Cataluña → **catalán**
Extremadura → **extremeño**
Galicia → **gallego**
el País Vasco → **vasco** OR **euskadi** (invariable), the latter preferred by Basques
NOTE: **Vascongado** is used chiefly in the expression **las Provincias Vascongadas**. **Vascuence** is used for the Basque language (also **euskera**).

10.1.2 Towns

Alcalá de Henares → **complutense**
NOTE: **complutense** is also used of the Madrid University which was transferred from Alcalá.
Ávila → **abulense**
Barcelona → **barcelonés**
NOTE: Barcelona is also frequently referred to, especially in journalistic R3, as **la Ciudad Condal**.
Burgos → **burgalés**
Cádiz → **gaditano**
Córdoba → **cordobés**
Elche → **ilicitano**
Granada → **granadino**
Huelva → **onubense**
Huesca → **oscense**
Jaén → **jaenés** OR **jienense**
Madrid → **madrileño**
Málaga → **malagueño**
Oviedo → **ovetense**
Salamanca → **salmantino**
San Sebastián → **donostiarra**
Santander → **santanderino**
NOTE: Santander (Colombia) has the adjective **santandereano**.
Santiago de Compostela → **compostelano** OR **santiagués**
NOTE: The Santiagos of Latin America all have different adjectives: see the Latin American list.
Sevilla → **sevillano**, **hispalense** (R3)
Tarragona → **tarraconense**
Valencia → **valenciano**
Valladolid → **vallisoletano**
Zaragoza → **zaragozano**

10.1.3 Islands

Ibiza → **ibicenco**
Mallorca → **mallorquín**
Menorca → **menorquín**
Tenerife → **tinerfeño**

10.2 *América Latina / Latinoamérica → (latino)americano*

The following names should be distinguished:
América Latina / Latinoamérica → **latinoamericano** = Spanish- and
   Portuguese-speaking America

América del Sur / Sudamérica → **sudamericano** = South America
    (ie from isthmus of Panama south)

América Central / Centroamérica → **centroamericano** = Central
    America (ie Panama to Mexico)

Hispanoamérica → **hispanoamericano** = Spanish-speaking America
    (ie not including Brazil, etc)

Iberoamérica → **iberoamericano** = América Latina

NOTE: The adjective **americano** may correspond to English
Latin-American; English *American*, which usually refers to North
America, is often **norteamericano**. **El hemisferio**, a term often
used in journalistic American Spanish, refers to the entire American
continent.

(la) Argentina → **argentino**
    Buenos Aires → **porteño** OR **bonaerense**

NOTE: **porteño** is used of other ports as well, notably of Valparaíso
(Chile).

    Patagonia → **patagón**
    Santa Fe → **santafecino**
    Santiago del Estero → **santiagueño**
    Tierra del Fuego → **fueguino**

Bolivia → **boliviano**
    La Paz → **paceño**
    Potosí → **potosino**
    Sucre → **sucrense**

Brasil → **brasileño**

Colombia → **colombiano**
    Bogotá → **bogotano**
    Medellín → **medellinense**

Costa Rica → **costarriqueño** OR **costarricense**
    San José → **josefino**

Cuba → **cubano**
    La Habana → **habanero**
    Santiago → **santiaguero**

Chile (m) → **chileno**
    Concepción → **penquisto** OR **pencón**
    Santiago → **santiaguino**
    Valparaíso → **porteño**

(el) Ecuador (m) → **ecuatoriano**
    Quito → **quiteño**

Guatemala → **guatemalteco**
    Honduras → **hondureño**
    Tegucigalpa → **tegucigalpense**

México (Am) / Méjico (Pen) → **mexicano** (Am) / **mejicano** (Pen)
    Guadalajara → **guadalajarense**

NOTE: Guadalajara (Spain) has the adjective **guadalajareño**.
    Mérida → **meridano**

NOTE: Mérida (Spain and Venezuela) has the adjective **merideño**.

Nicaragua → **nicaragüense**
  Managua → **managüense**
Panamá **(m)** → **panameño**
(el) Paraguay **(m)** → **paraguayo**
  Asunción → **asunceno**
(el) Perú (m) → **peruano**
  Callao → **chalaco**
  (el) Cuzco → **cuzqueño**
  Lima → **limeño**
Puerto Rico → **puertorriqueño** OR **portorriqueño**
El Salvador (m) → **salvadoreño**
(el) Uruguay (m) → **uruguayo**
  Montevideo → **montevideano**
Venezuela → **venezolano**
  Caracas → **caraqueño**
  Maracaibo → **maracaibero**

10.3 *Europa → europeo*

Albania → **albanés**
Alemania → **alemán**
  Berlín → **berlinés**
  Hamburgo → **hamburgués**
Andorra → **andorrano**
Austria → **austríaco** or **austriaco**
Bélgica → **belga**
Bielorrusia → **bielorruso**
Bosnia-Herzegovina → **bosnio**
Bulgaria → **búlgaro**
Cerdeña → **sardo**
Chipre (f) → **chipriota**
Córcega → **corso**
Creta → **cretense**
Croacia → **croata**
Dinamarca → **danés** OR **dinamarqués** (R3)
Escocia → **escocés** (but see **Gran Bretaña** below)
Eslovenia → **esloveno**
Estonia → **estonio** OR **estoniano**
Finlandia → **finlandés**
Francia → **francés** or **galo** (R3)
NOTE: the use of **franco** in compounds, eg **franco-belga**
  París → **parisiense** or **parisino**
Gales (m) → **galés**
Gran Bretaña / (el) Reino Unido → **británico**
NOTE: Spanish-speaking people often use **inglés** for any inhabitant of the British Isles.
  Londres → **londinense**

Grecia → **griego**

NOTE: The now obsolete adjective **greco** is still used in compounds, eg **grecolatino**, and in the name of the painter **El Greco**.

Atenas → **ateniense**

Holanda / (los) Países Bajos → **holandés**

Hungría → **húngaro**

Inglaterra → **inglés**

Irlanda del Norte / el Úlster → **irlandés** (but see **Gran Bretaña** above)

Irlanda del Sur / República de Irlanda → **irlandés** (but see **Gran Bretaña** above)

Italia → **italiano**

Letonia OR Latvia → **letón** OR **latvio** (**letonés** is also widely used)

Lituania → **lituano**

Vilnius → **Vilna**

Luxemburgo → **luxemburgués**

Macedonia → **macedonio**

Malta → **maltés**

Montenegro → **montenegrino**

Noruega → **noruego**

Polonia → **polaco**

Portugal (m) → **portugués** OR **lusitano** (R3)

NOTE: the use of **luso-** in compounds, eg **luso-hispano** (R3)

Lisboa → **lisboeta**

República Checa → **checo**

República Eslovaca → **eslovaco**

BUT **checoslovaco**

Romanía / Rumania → **rumano**

Rusia → **ruso**

Moscú → **moscovita**

Serbia → **serbio**

NOTE: the use of **serbo-** in compounds, eg **serbocroata**

Suecia → **sueco**

Suiza – **suizo**

Turquía → **turco**

Ucrania → **ucraniano** (preferred) or **ucranio**

10.4 *África* → *africano*

África del Sur / Sudáfrica / Suráfrica → **sudafricano** OR **surafricano**

NOTE: África Meridional = Southern Africa

Angola → **angoleño**

Argelia → **argelino**

Benín (m) → **beninés**

Burkina Faso (m) → **burkinés**

(el) Camerún → **camerunense** OR **camerunés**

Chad (m) → **chadiense**
Costa de Marfil → **(costa)marfileño**
Egipto → **egipcio**
Etiopía → **etíope**
Gabón (m) → **gabonés**
Ghana → **ganés**
Guinea → **guineo**
Kenia → **kenyata** OR **keniano**
Liberia → **liberiano**
Libia → **libio**
Madagascar (m) → **malgache**
Magreb (m) → **magrebí**
Malawi (m) → **malawi**
Mali (m) → **malagués**
Marruecos (m sg) → **marroquí**
Mauritania → **mauritano**
Mozambique (m) → **mozambiqueño** OR **mozambicano**
Namibia → **namibiano** OR **namibio**
Níger (m) → **nigerino**
Nigeria → **nigeriano**
(la) República Centroafricana → **centroafricano**
(el) Senegal → **senegalés**
Sierra Leone → **sierraleonés**
Somalia → **somalí**
(el) Sudán → **sudanés**
Tanzania → **tanzano**
Togo (m) → **togolés**
Túnez (m) → **tunecino**
Ugandan → **ugandés**
Zaire (m) → **zaireño**
Zambia → **zambiano**
Zimbabwe/Zimbabue (m) → **zimbabuo** OR **cimbabués**

10.5   *Asia → asiático y Australia → australiano*

Afganistán (m) → **afgano**
Bangladés / Bangla Desh (m) → **bengalí**
Birmania → **birmanés**
Corea del Norte → **norte-coreano**
Corea del Sur → **surcoreano**
(la) China → **chino**
(las) Filipinas → **filipino**
la India → **indio**
NOTE: **Hindú** is also widely used in R1.
Indonesia → **indonesio**
(el) Japón → **japonés** OR **nipón** (R3)
Kampuchea → **camboyano** OR **kampucheano**

Laos (m) → **laosiano**
Malasia → **malayo**
(el) Nepal → **nepalés**
Nueva Caledonia → **neocaledoniano**
Nueva Zelanda → **neozelandés** OR **neocelandés**
(el) Pakistán → **pakistaní**
Sri Lanka (m) → **srilanqués**
Tailandia → **tailandés**
(el) Tibet → **tibetano**
(el) Vietnam → **vietnamita**

10.6 *Oriente Medio*

Arabia Saudita → **arabesaudí** OR **saudí**
(el) Irak → **iraquí**
(el) Irán → **iraní**
Israel (m) → **israelí**
Jordania → **jordano**
Siria → **sirio**

10.7 *América del Norte* → *norteamericano*

(el) Canadá → **canadiense**
(los) Estados Unidos → **(norte)americano** OR **estadounidense**
(often spelt **estadunidense** in Mexico); ALSO **yanqui**, **gringo** (R1–2
Am)
NOTE: **Estados Unidos** used without the article is generally treated as
singular, eg **Estados Unidos suspendió sus garantías defensivas
hacia Nueva Zelanda, a las que está comprometido . . .**
Nueva York → **neoyorquino**

11 Abbreviations

Abbreviations and acronyms *(siglas)* abound in the Spanish-speaking world, and it is beyond the scope of this book to provide a comprehensive survey. In practice, many abbreviations relating to political parties and commercial organizations are not recognized outside their immediate area of relevance, and they tend to be shortlived; when they are used in the press, for instance, they are usually explained when they first appear. A selection of the more important of these is given in the third list below. The majority of the abbreviations given here, however, are those which, unless stated otherwise, are used throughout the Hispanic world, and which are frequently used without explanation.

   A more comprehensive list of abbreviations used in the Spanish-speaking world may be found in *Diccionario de siglas y abreviaturas. Dictionary of Spanish-Language Abbreviations and Acronyms*, by Thomas L. West (Atlanta, GA: Intermark Language Publications, 2002), and an older list in *Diccionario de siglas y abreviaturas*, edited by M. Alvar and A. Miró (Madrid: Alhambra, 1983).

NOTE: The pronunciation of an abbreviation which is pronounced as if it were a word in its own right is given in conventional spelling in brackets, eg **SEAT** (séat). An abbreviation pronounced letter by letter is marked with an asterisk. In all other instances the words to which the abbreviation relates are spoken in full.

11.1 Abbreviations of titles and common words

*****ADN**	ácido desoxirribonucleico	*DNA*
Apdo.	apartado (de correos)	*(post office) box*
Arz.	arzobispo	*Archbishop: Abp*
Av(da).	avenida	*avenue (street name): Ave.*
c/	calle	*street (street name): St*
cap. **capº.** }	capítulo	*chapter: Ch.*
c/c	cuenta corriente	*current account: c/a*
c.c.p.	con copia para	*cc*

*CD	cede(rrón)	*CD*
c/d	casa de	*care of (address): c/o*
cfr.	confróntese	*compare: cf*
Cía.	compañia	*company: Co.*
cta.	cuenta	*account: a/c*
cte.	corriente	*instant (month): inst.*
D.	Don (title)	
Dª.	Doña (title)	
dcha.	derecha	*right-hand (apartment)*
dupdo.	duplicado	*duplicate (often used with house numbers in a street)*
*DVD	disco de vídeo digital	*DVD*
E	este	*east: E.*
e.p.d.	en paz descanse	*rest in peace: RIP*

NOTE: *RIP (= *requiescat in pace*) is also used.

Exc.	Excelencia (title)	*Excellency*
Excmo.	Excelentísimo (title)	*Most Excellent*
FC	ferrocarril	*railway*
Fr.	Fray	*Brother (religious): Br.*
Hnos.	hermanos	*brothers: Bros.*
íd.	ídem	*ditto: do*
Ilmo.	Ilustrísimo (title)	*Most Illustrious*
izq(da).	izquierda	*left-hand (apartment)*
a. de J. C.	antes de Jesucristo	*before Christ: BC*
d. de J. C.	después de Jesucristo	*after Christ: AD*
Lic.	licenciatura	*equivalent of bachelor's degree: cf BA, BSc, BS, etc*
Mons.	Monseñor	*Monsignor: Mgr*
N	norte	*north: N.*
N. A.	nota del autor	*author's note*
N. (de la) R.	nota de la redacción	*editor's note: Ed.*
N.ªS.ª	Nuestra Señora	*Our Lady*
n.º, núm.	número	*number: no.*
N. S.	Nuestro Señor	*Our Lord*
N. T.	nota del traductor	*translator's note*
O	oeste	*west: W.*
P.	Padre	*Father (religious): Fr*
p.ª	para	*for*
pág(s).	página(s)	*page(s): p, pp*
P. D.	postdata	*postscript: PS*
pdo.	pasado	*last (month): ult.*
p.ej.	por ejemplo	*for example: eg*
pmo.	próximo	*next (month): prox.*
P.º	paseo	*(street name)*

rte.	remite/remitente	*sender (put on back of envelope)*
S	sur	*south: S.*
S., Sta., Sto.	San, Santa, Santo	*Saint: St*
S. M., SS.MM.	Su Majestad, Sus Majestades	*Your/His/Her Majesty, Their/Your Majesties: HM*
s/n	sin número	*unnumbered (address)*
Sr.	Señor	*Mr*
Sra.	Señora	*Mrs*
Srta.	Señorita	*Miss*

NOTE: There appears to be as yet no Spanish equivalent for English *Ms.*

SS	Santos	*Saints: SS*
tel., teléf.	teléfono	*telephone: tel.*
Ud., Uds. **Vd., Vds.** } **V., VV.**	usted, ustedes	*you*
v.gr.	verbigracia	*namely: viz.*
*****VIH**	virus de inmunodeficiencia humana	*HIV*
V.(º), B.(º)	visto bueno	*approved: OK*

NOTE ALSO: the Spanish custom in referring to significant dates: **el 11–S** (9/11, 11 September 2001, the date of the terrorist attack on the World Trade Center), **el 11–M** (11 March 2004, the date of the terrorist attack in Madrid)

11.2 Abbreviations of weights and measures (see also Chapter 19)

cm^2	centímetro(s) cuadrado(s)	*square centimetre(s): sq cm* OR *cm^2*
cm^3	centímetro(s) cúbico(s)	*cubic centimetre(s): cc* OR *cm^3*
cs	centavos	*centavos*
*****C.V.**	caballos de vapor	*horse power: h.p.*
gr.	gramo(s)	*gram(s): g*
h.	horas	*o'clock; hours*
Ha.	hectárea(s)	*hectare(s): ha*
kg.	kilogramo(s): kt	*kilogram(s): kg*
km.	kilómetro(s)	*kilometre(s): km*
km/h.	kilómetros por hora	*kilometres per hour: cf mph*
kv. OR **kW.**	kilovatio(s)	*kilowatt(s)*
m.	metro(s)	*metre(s): m*
m^2	metro(s) cuadrado(s)	*square metre(s): sq m* OR *m^2*

m³	metro(s) cúbico(s)	*cubic metre(s): cu m* OR *m³*
$	Used not only for American dollars but also for **pesos** in many Latin American countries (see **19.7**).	
T.m.	tonelada(s) métrica(s)	*metric ton(s): t*

11.3 Abbreviations of major national and international organizations

ALA . . .	*used in many siglas, standing for* Asociación latinoamericana de . . .
ALADI (aladi)	Asociación latinoamericana de integración
ALASEI (alasei)	Agencia latinoamericana de servicios de información
BID (bid)	Banco interamericano para el Desarrollo
***CD**	Cuerpo diplomático
***CELAM** (celam)	Consejo episcopal latinoamericano
CEPAL (cepal)	Comité Económico para América Latina
CF	Club de Fútbol
EE.UU.	Estados Unidos
FAR . . .	*used in many siglas, standing for* Fuerzas armadas revolucionarias . . .
FMI	Fondo Monetario Internacional: *IMF*
FRE . . .	*used in many siglas, standing for* Frente . . .
ODECA (odeca)	Organización de estados centroamericanos
***OEA**	Organización de estados americanos: *OAS*
***OLP**	Organización para la liberación de Palestina: *PLO*
OMS (oms)	Organización Mundial de la Salud: *WHO*
ONU (onu)	Organización de las Naciones Unidas: *UNO*
OPEP (opep)	Organización de los Países Exportadores de Petróleo: *OPEC*
OTAN (otan)	Organización del Tratado del Atlántico Norte: *NATO*
***OUA**	Organización de la Unidad Africana: *OAU*
***PNB**	Producto nacional bruto: *GNP*
RAE	Real Academia Española
***SA**	Sociedad Anónima *(cf Ltd, PLC, Inc.)*
. . . SA	*used in many siglas, with the above meaning*
SELA (sela)	Sistema económico latinoamericano
***UE**	Unión Europea: *EU*

11.4   Other abbreviations from Spanish-speaking countries

Here is a selection of other abbreviations currently in use in Spanish-speaking countries:

*AA	Aerolíneas argentinas
ANAPO (anapo)	Alianza Nacional Popular *(Colombia)*
*AVE	Alta Velocidad Española: *high-speed train (Pen)*
AVENSA (avensa)	Aerovías venezolanas
Av. Pte.	Avenida Presidente *(Arg)*
BANAMEX (banamex)	Banco Nacional de México
BANPAIS (banpaís)	Banco del País *(Mex)*
BANXICO (banjico)	Banco de México
Bs. As.	Buenos Aires
BUP (bup)	Bachillerato unificado y polivalente *(Pen): corresponds to British GCSE (taken at sixteen years of age)*
Cap. Fed.	Capital Federal *(Arg)*
CC.OO	Comisiones Obreras *(Pen)*
CONACYT (conacit)	Consejo Nacional de Ciencia y Tecnología *(Mex)*
COU (cou)	Curso de orientación universitaria *(Pen): corresponds to British A-Level / high school diploma*
*CVG	Corporación venezolana de Guayana
*D. F.	Distrito Federal *(Mex)*
*DNI	Documento nacional de identidad *(Pen)*
*EGB	Educación general básica *(Pen)*
FAS (fas)	Fuerzas armadas *(Pen)*
*FDR	Frente Democrático Revolucionario *(El Salvador)*
*FNM/FF.NN.	Ferrocarriles Nacionales de México *(also referred to as* Ferronales)
GEO (geo)	Grupo especial de operaciones *(Pen): anti-terrorist squad*
ICETEX (icetex)	Instituto colombiano de especialización técnica en el exterior
IMSS	Instituto Mexicano del Seguro Social *(Mex)*
INSALUD (m)	Instituto Nacional de la Salud *(Pen)*
ISSSTE	Instituto de Seguridad y Servicios Sociales para los Trabajadores del Estado *(Mex)*
IVA (iva)	Impuesto sobre el valor añadido *(Pen): VAT (value added tax)*

LAN (lan)	Línea aérea nacional *(Chile)*
la N uno, etc	la carretera nacional número uno, etc *(Pen): the Spanish classification of main roads*
*****NIF**	número de indentificación fiscal *(Pen)*
ONCE (once)	Organización de Ciegos Españoles *(Spanish organization for the blind, which runs one of the national lotteries)*
OVNI (ovni)	objeto volante no identificado: *UFO*
PEMEX (pémex)	Petróleos mexicanos
PETROVEN (petroven)	Petróleos de Venezuela
*****PM**	Policía militar *(Pen)*
*****PP**	Partido Popular *(Pen)*
PRI (pri)	Partido Revolucionario Institucional *(Mex)*
*****PSOE**	Partido Socialista Obrero Español *(Pen)*
PVP	precio de venta al público *(Pen): RRP (Recommended Retail Price)*
PYMES (pimes)	pequeñas y medianas (empresas) *(Pen)*
RENFE (renfe)	Red Nacional de Ferrocarriles Españoles *(Pen)*
*****RNE**	Radio Nacional de España
*****RTVE**	Radio Televisión Española
SEAT (séat)	Sociedad Española de Automóviles de Turismo
SECTUR (sectur)	Secretaría de Turismo *(Mex)*
SENA (sena)	Servicio nacional de aprendizaje *(Colombia)*
SIDA (sida)	síndrome (m) de inmunodeficiencia adquirida: *AIDS*
SIDERMEX (sidermex)	*Mexican steel corporation (appears never to have had a full name)*
SIDOR (sidor)	Siderurgia del Orinoco *(Venezuela)*
*****S. S.**	Seguridad Social
SSA	Secretaría de Salubridad y Asistencia *(Mex)*
TELMEX (telmex)	Teléfonos de México
UNAM (unam)	Universidad Nacional Autónoma *(Mex)*
UVI	Unidad de Vigilancia Intensiva: *Icu*
VIASA (viasa)	Venezolana Internacional de Aviación
el día X	*red-letter day*

11.5   Truncated words

Speakers often shorten common words in R1.

la bici	la bicicleta
el boli	el bolígrafo
el bus	el autobús *(which is often used in preference)*
el cole	el colegio
la compe	la competición
un crono	cl cronometraje *(time recorded in a race)*
el fisio	el fisioterapeuta
el frigo	el frigorífico
la info	la información
el logo	el logotipo
la mili	la milicia *(military service)*
la peli	la película
el/la poli	el/la policía *(both individual officers and the police force)*
el porno (NOTE *that the abbreviated form is masculine, and that as an adjective* porno *is invariable:* una película porno)	la pornografía
el/la profe	el profesor / la profesora
la tele	la televisión

12 Latin expressions

There are a number of Latin expressions in common use in modern Spanish, particularly in educated R2 speech and in R3.

R3

ad hoc	a propósito: un argumento ad hoc	*for the purpose*, ad hoc
a fortiori	con mayor razón	*with all the more reason*, a fortiori
ex aequo	con igual mérito: tres ex aequo	*equals*
in extremis	en caso extremo	*in an extreme case*, in extremis
modus vivendi	arreglo entre dos o varias personas	*arrangement, compromise*, modus vivendi
non plus ultra (N)	el no va más, el tope	*the absolute limit, the* ne plus ultra
persona non grata	persona indeseable	*undesirable, unwelcome person*, persona non grata
sine qua non	imprescindible: una condición sine qua non	*essential condition*; NOTE: *in English*, sine qua non *is used as a noun.*

R2 (and R3)

a posteriori	después: un juicio a posteriori	*after the event*, a posteriori
a priori	antes: un juicio a priori	*before the event*, a priori
exabrupto (N)	brusquedad: contestar con un exabrupto	*abrupt remark, outburst*
ex cáthedra	en tono magisterial: hablar ex cáthedra	*authoritatively*, ex cathedra
ex profeso	expresamente	*deliberately, expressly*
ex voto (N)	ofrenda dedicada a Dios	*offering*
(a) grosso modo	de forma general	*in a general way*
ipso facto	inmediatamente; por el mismo hecho	*immediately; by the very fact* NOTE: *English* ipso facto *is used only in the second sense.*

statu quo (N)	el estado en que se hallan las cosas	*status quo*
ultra (N) (m)	extremista	*extremist*
vice versa	al revés	*the opposite way, vice versa*
vía crucis (N) (m)	camino de la cruz, calvario	*way of the Cross (a path laid out with the stations of the Cross)*

NOTE: **Vía crucis** is masculine, although **vía** is feminine.

All registers

etcétera (etc)	y lo demás	*and the others, et cetera*

13 Anglicisms

Modern Spanish has many borrowings from English. Although some
of these may prove to be only fleeting additions to the Spanish
vocabulary, others appear to have been very firmly adopted into the
language and are not necessarily to be avoided, despite the strictures of
some purists. A number of anglicisms do not correspond exactly in
meaning to the original English words. There have even been some
coinings of pseudo-English words (especially those ending in **–ing**).
Attention should also be paid to pronunciation, which is not always
obvious either from the English original or the current Spanish
spelling. Note also the gender and plural form of nouns (see also **22.1**).
The following are all in common use: pronunciation, which is often
not obvious from the Spanish spelling on the English original, is
indicated by standard International Phonetic Alphabet Symbols.

Anglicism	Meaning	Other Spanish equivalents
casting ['kastin] (m) • **Más de 200 personas se presentaron al casting**	casting, selection	**(selección)**
cátering ['katerin] (m) • **un servicio de cátering para fiestas**	catering	no other equivalent
fan(s) (m/f)	fan	**seguidor, aficionado, hincha**
fax(es) (m)	fax	no other equivalent
flash(es) [flas] (m) or **flas**	news flash; flash (photograph); flash (computing)	no other equivalent
footing ['futin] (m) • **Cada mañana hago footing**	jogging	no other equivalent
glamour [gla'muɾ] (m) • **un toque de glamour** = a touch of glamour	glamour	**(encanto)**
hobby(ies) ['xoβi] (m)	hobby	**afición, pasatiempo**
jet–set [jet set] (f)	jet set	no other equivalent

Anglicism	Meaning	Other Spanish equivalents
kit(s) (m) • **un kit de construcción**	(1) (construction) kit	no other equivalent
	(2) kit = collection of tools, etc	**equipo**
• **un kit de herramientas** = a toolkit		
	(3) (sports) kit = clothes	**ropa**
• **nuestros kits están personalizados**		
NOTE: Meaning (3) is relatively recent; **kit** is not used to refer to clothes in general.		
†**laptop(s)** ['laptop] (m)	laptop computer	**ordenador portátil**
†**líder(es)** (m/f)	leader (esp political and commercial)	firmly established, but also **dirigente**, **jefe**
lifting ['liftin] (m)	face lift	no other equivalent
light	(1) light (= containing fewer calories, less damaging to health);	no other equivalent
	(2) watered down (esp in politics)	
• **una gaseosa light**, **una política light**		
look (m) • **el nuevo look del verano**	look	**imagen**, **aspecto**
manager(s) ['manajer] (m/f)	manager (sport, arts, etc)	**representante**
NOTE: manager (gen) = **director**, **gerente**		
†**marketing** ['marketin] (m)	marketing	no native equivalent
mis (f)	winner of a (female) beauty contest	no native equivalent
míster (m) • **el nuevo míster de Real Madrid**	(1) soccer trainer	**entrenador**
	(2) winner of a (male) beauty contest	no other equivalent
NOTE: Meaning (1) is extending to mean a boss in general, eg **el nuevo míster de Intel**.		
pack(s) (m) • **Compré un pack de seis botellas**	pack (of tins, bottles, etc)	**lote** (m)
puénting (m)	bungee-jumping	no other equivalent
ránking ['rankin] (m)	ranking (sport, etc)	**lista**
récord(s) ['rekor] (m) • **Batió el récord del mundo en el lanzamiento de peso**	record (esp sport)	**plusmarca**, **marca**

Anglicism	Meaning	Other Spanish equivalents
sándwich(es) [ˈsaŋgwitʃ] (m)	sandwich made with sliced bread, toasted sandwich	**emparedado**, **bocadillo**
sexy [ˈseksi]	sexy	**erótico**
shock [ʃok] (m) • **en un estado de choque** = in a state of shock • **el shock de lo nuevo** = the shock of the new	(1) shock (medical) (2) shock (general)	**shock** **choque**, **susto**
show(s) [ʃoṷ] (m) • **montar un show** = to make a scene	(1) (variety) show (entertainment) (2) scene, public display	**espectáculo** **escena**
spot(s) (publicitario(s)) [esˈpot] (m)	slot, space (for commercial on TV)	no other equivalent
stand(s) [esˈtan] (m)	stand (at a fair or exhibition)	no other equivalent
stock(s) / estock(s) [esˈtok] (m)	stock (= goods in store awaiting sale or use)	no other equivalent
star(s) [esˈtaɾ] (f)	(film)star	**estrella**
suspense (m) • **una película de suspense** = a thriller	suspense (eg in a drama)	**suspenso** is used in this sense in Am.
top-less [ˈtoples] (m) • **bañarse en top-less**	topless	no other equivalent
top-model(s) (f) • **Muchas jóvenes quieren ser top-model**	a top model	no other equivalent
underground [andeɾˈgraṷn] (usu ADJ) • **un movimiento underground**	underground (literature, writer, etc)	no other equivalent
web (f) • **una página web** = a webpage	(worldwide) web	**red** (f) (= net)
zoom(s) [θum] or [sum] (m)	zoom; zoom lens	**teleobjetivo**

The influence of English is not restricted to single words. In English, nouns can be used quite freely as adjectives (*paper money*, *road map*, *bank account*), and while this was not impossible in Spanish, it is noticeable that the number of noun + noun combinations has substantially increased in recent years, perhaps as a result of the influence of English models. Some, however, must be native creations, since they do not correspond exactly, if at all, to English:

bomba lapa	limpet mine
bomba trampa	booby-trap bomb
buque (m) **escuela**	training ship
café (m) **concierto**	café with live music
café (m) **teatro**	café in which short plays are staged
cama nido	truckle bed (Brit), trundle bed (US)
camión (m) **cisterna**	tanker
cárcel (f) **modelo**	model prison
célula madre	mother cell
ciudad (f) **dormitorio**	dormitory town
ciudad (f) **modelo**	model town
coche (m) **bomba**	car bomb
coche (m) **cama**	sleeping car
coche (m) **patrulla**	patrol car
crédito puente	bridging loan (Brit), bridge loan (US)
elemento clave	key element
etapa reina	A Spanish term for the most difficult stage in a cycling competition
exposición (f) **estrella**	major exhibition
factor (m) **sorpresa**	surprise factor
fecha límite	deadline
fecha tope	sell-by date
gas (m) **ciudad**	town gas
hora punta	rush hour
lengua madre	mother tongue
localidad (f) **dormitorio**	dormitory town
luz (f) **piloto**	pilot light
madre (f) **patria**	mother country
obra cumbre	greatest work
papel (m) **moneda**	paper money
piso piloto	showhouse
radio (f in Pen, m in Am) **receptor**	radio receiver
retrato robot	identikit picture
tiempo récord	record time
vehículo todo terreno	4 × 4
zona euro	Eurozone

Plurals of these nouns: generally add **–s/–es** to the first noun –
ciudades dormitorio, coches bomba, factores sorpresa.

14 Grammatical terms

In talking about the Spanish language, you will find the following terms, which are in common use among educated Spanish-speakers, useful.

Grammatical terms *Términos gramaticales*

el acento (ortográfico)	*(written) accent*
tónico (ADJ)	*stressed*
átono (ADJ)	*unstressed*
palabra aguda	*word stressed on final syllable, eg* **hablar**
palabra llana *or* grave	*word stressed on next to last syllable, eg* **sale**
palabra esdrújula	*word stressed on antepenultimate syllable, eg* **clínico**
la consonante	*consonant*
la †sílaba	*syllable*
la †vocal	*vowel*
el adjetivo	*adjective*
el adverbio	*adverb*
el complemento	*object*
la conjunción	*conjunction*
la †frase, la oración	*sentence*
el género	*gender*
masculino (ADJ)	*masculine*
femenino (ADJ)	*feminine*
el †nombre, el sustantivo	*noun*
la ortografía	*spelling*
el participio	*participle*
el pronombre	*pronoun*
posesivo (ADJ)	*possessive*
demostrativo (ADJ)	*demonstrative*
relativo (ADJ)	*relative*
el sufijo	*suffix*
diminutivo (ADJ)	*diminutive*
despectivo (ADJ)	*pejorative*

aumentativo (ADJ)	*augmentative*
superlativo (ADJ)	*superlative*
el verbo	*verb*
el tiempo	*tense*
los tiempos †simples/ compuestos	*simple/compound tenses*
†presente	*present* (**hablo**)
futuro	*future* (**hablaré**)
pretérito (*also* pretérito indefinido)	*preterite* (**hablé**)
imperfecto	*imperfect* (**hablaba**)
pretérito anterior	*past anterior* (**hube hablado**)
futuro perfecto	*future perfect* (**habré hablado**)
condicional	*conditional* (**hablaría**)
condicional perfecto	*conditional perfect* (**habría hablado**)
(pretérito) pluscuamperfecto	*pluperfect* (**había hablado**)
el subjuntivo	*subjunctive*
el indicativo	*indicative*
el imperativo	*imperative* (**¡habla!, ¡hablad!**)
el infinitivo	*infinitive* (**hablar**)
el gerundio	*gerund* (**hablando**)
el participio pasado	*past participle* (**hablado**)

Punctuation marks *Signos de puntuación*

el aparte	*new paragraph*	
el asterisco	*asterisk*	*
la †coma	*comma*	,
las comillas	*quotation marks*	≪ ≫ or " "
las comillas simples	*single quotation marks*	' '
los corchetes	*square brackets*	[]
la diéresis	*diaeresis*	¨
la exclamación	*exclamation mark*	¡!
el guión	*hyphen*	–
la interrogación	*question mark*	¿?
las (letras) mayúsculas	*upper-case letters*	
las (letras) minúsculas	*lower-case letters*	
el †paréntesis	*brackets*	( )
el párrafo	*paragraph*	
el punto	*full stop, dot* (see Chapter 18)	
el punto y coma	*semicolon*	;
los dos puntos	*colon*	:
los puntos suspensivos	*suspension marks*	. . .
la †raya	*dash*	——
la tilde	*mark above* **ñ**; *the written accent*	∼ or ´

15 Interjections

Interjections are typical of the spoken language, and are most common in the 'lower' registers. In the following table, the interjections most frequently used in modern Spanish are listed according to general meaning, with an indication of their register value. Particular attention should be paid to those marked as R1*: these are generally considered indecent, and should only be used with great care. Of course, the use of such expressions, in Spanish-speaking countries as in English-speaking countries, varies with personality and environment.

	R2	R1	R1*
Admiration	†¡estupendo! ¡hombre! ¡qué maravilla! ¡qué barbaridad! ¡(muy) bien! ¡bien bien! ¡extraordinario! ¡madre mía!	¡caray! ¡chachi! ¡híjole! (*Mex*) ¡olé! ¡de narices! †¡jo! ¡jolín!/¡jolines! ¡demasiado! ¡ostras!	†¡cojonudo! †¡coño! ¡de pelotas! †¡joder! ¡de puta madre! ¡hostia(s)! ¡de cojones!
Agreement	†¡de acuerdo! ¡muy bien! ¡perfecto! ¡vale!	¡OK! (oké) ¡por qué no!	¡de puta madre!
Annoyance	¡maldición! ¡maldito sea!	¡caray! ¡qué asco! ¡por Dios! ¡qué caramba! ¡a la porra! ¡mecachis!	¡carajo! ¡mierda! †¡coño! †¡joder! ¡me cago en Dios / diez /la leche / la puta! ¡hijo de puta! ¡cojones! ¡(a) la mierda!

	R2	R1	R1*
Disbelief	†¡imposible! †¡increíble! ¡qué va! ¡no me digas! †¡ni hablar!	¡de narices! ¡ca! ¡ja! †¡venga (venga)! ¡no trago! ¡anda ya! ¡no cuela! ¡vamos, hombre!	
Joy	¡(qué) caramba! ¡qué bien! ¡qué alegría! †¡hombre! NOTE: ¡Hombre! is used to both men and women †¡mujer!	¡demasiado! ¡como enrolla! ¡qué pasada! ¡pipudo! ¡qué marcha!	¡carajo! ¡de puta madre! †¡coño! †¡joder!
Objection	¡que no! ¡qué caramba! ¡para nada!	†¡nada, nada!	
Surprise	¡Dios mío! ¡caramba! ¡cielos!	†¡huy! ¡porras! ¡mecachis! ¡qué pasa! ¡ostras!	¡carajo! ¡hostia(s)!
Warning	†¡cuidado! ¡atención!	¡ojo! ¡tate! ¡al loro!	

16 Fillers

In conversation, speakers often need time to formulate what they are
going to say, and therefore make use of a range of introductory
'hesitation formulae' or 'fillers'. While overuse of such words can be
annoying, their judicious use adds authenticity to a foreigner's speech –
as well as giving time to think! The following are the most common
such expressions in Spanish. English equivalents are suggested, but
really their 'meaning' is minimal.

- **al fin y al cabo** *in the end, when all is said and done*
  Al fin y al cabo tuvo algo de razón
- **†bueno** *well*
  Used almost automatically when answering a question; also to call
      attention, eg: ¿Cuándo piensas volver? – Bueno, no sé . . .
      Bueno, ¿estás listo?
- **¿cómo se diría?** *how shall I put it?*
  Pues (¿cómo se diría?), es como una fruta
- **digamos** *let's say*
  Digamos que, al fin y al cabo, todo tiene relación
- **digámoslo así** *as it were*
  El alcohol es otra manera de escaparse, digámoslo así
- **en fin** *so, there it is*
  Often used in isolation to conclude a point.
  En fin, no sé qué decirte
- **entonces** *then*
  Frequently with **pues** (see below).
  Pues entonces, le daremos un aprobado
- **es que** *the thing is, was*
  Es que estaba enferma mi madre
- **esto** *er*
  Signifies deliberation.
  Esto . . . bueno, ya veremos
- **†hombre** *goodness, really*
  Hombre, pues cuesta mucho
- **†mira/mire** *look here*
  Mira, no tengo ni idea

- **no sé** *I don't know*
  No sé, digamos que vendrá mañana
- **o sea** *or, that is*
  Also used as a general hesitation.
  Se puede hacer esta tarde, o sea, si vienes después del almuerzo
  Bueno, es que . . . o sea, no te puedo decir nada
- **podríamos decir** *as one might say*
  Podríamos decir, es un mamífero
- **por decirlo así** *so to speak*
- †**pues** *well, then*
  The most frequent filler in Spanish, it is used meaninglessly at the
  beginning of any sentence and before other fillers.
  Pues tienes que pagar
  ¡Vámonos, pues!

N O T E : **Pues** corresponds to English *then* only in the 'weak' logical
sense; it should not be used for *then* as a time adverb, which
corresponds to Spanish **entonces**, **después**, etc.

- **vamos a ver** *let me see, let's see*
  Vamos a ver, si contesto a la pregunta

17 Transition words

It is most useful to be familiar with the following words in speaking or writing Spanish, particularly in those registers where longer sentences are used and arguments sustained. They express a 'logical' relation between one proposition and another, and, although frequently used, they are not simply 'fillers' as are the expressions in Chapter 16.

- **ahora bien** (i) *but* (ii) *now*
  (i) Te puedes llevar el coche; ahora bien, a las diez lo necesito
  (ii) Ahora bien, volvió su padre, y le dijo lo contrario
- **al / por el contrario** *on the contrary*
  No está claro; al / por el contrario está confuso
- **†a pesar de N, a pesar de que . . .** *in spite of*
  Comimos, a pesar de que no teníamos ganas
- **así** *and*
  Quedamos aquí, así luego iremos al cine
- **así mismo** *also*
  La paella es plato típicamente español; así mismo lo es la fabada
- **†aunque** *although, even though*
  Está bien, aunque se podrá superar
- **claro que** *of course*
  Sucedió así; claro que las consecuencias fueron inesperadas
- **de cualquier manera** *anyway*
  Te puede resultar difícil; de cualquier manera, hay que hacerlo.
- **†dado que** (R2–3) *since, given that*
  Dado que se sentía mal, no era de extrañar que suspendiese el examen
- **de modo/manera/forma que** *so* (see p 398)
  Llegaremos a las ocho, de modo que nos tendrán que esperar
- **de tal modo que** *in such a way that, so*
  Arregló el coche de tal modo que no tuvimos problemas después
- **empero** (R3) *however*
  Baroja escribe muy bien; empero, se encuentran en sus novelas faltas gramaticales
- **en efecto / en (la) realidad** *indeed, in fact*
  Tiene razón; en efecto / en realidad es como dice

- [†]**en resumen** *in short*
  La conferencia fue agradable; en resumen, estuvo acertada
- **es decir** *that is, that means*
  Hace calor, es decir, se puede salir sin abrigo
- **no obstante / sin embargo** *nevertheless*
  Pensábamos ir; no obstante / sin embargo, si llueve nos quedamos
- **(o) . . . o bien / o . . . o . . . / bien . . . bien . . .** (R3)
  either . . . or . . .
  (O) vas a Madrid o bien vas a Santander
  O lo lees ahora o lo lees más tarde
- **ora . . . ora . . .** (R3) *now . . . now . . .*
  Ora sonríe, ora llora
- **pero** *but*
  Hay que correr, pero con precaución
- [†]**Por consiguiente /** [†]**en consecuencia / por lo cual / por lo que** *so, consequently*
  No ganó mucho dinero, por lo cual no puede irse de vacaciones
- [†]**Por lo tanto** *so, therefore*
  Tenemos un problema, por lo tanto hay que resolverlo
- **porque** *because*
  No puedo venir porque me he roto el brazo
- [†]**por una parte . . . por otra (parte) . . . /** [†] **por un lado . . . por otro (lado) . . .** *on the one hand . . . on the other . . .*
  Por una parte creo que está bien, por otra (parte) creo que está mal
- **sino** *but* (contrastive: what follows **sino** must deny what precedes)
  No es así sino al contrario
- **tanto . . . como . . .** *both . . . and . . .*
  Tanto los ingleses como los italianos se opusieron al proyecto
- **ya que** *since*
  Ya que estás aquí, vamos a tomar algo

18 Numerals

Spanish uses a comma **(coma)** where English uses the decimal point, and a dot where English uses a comma in partitioning thousands. Thus Spanish **29,107 (veintinueve coma uno cero siete)** = English *29.107 (twenty-nine point one zero seven)*, and Spanish **7.654.321 (siete millones, seiscientos cincuenta y cuatro mil, trescientos veintiuno)** = English *7,654,321 (seven million, six hundred and fifty-four thousand, three hundred and twenty-one)*.

Spanish practice with telephone numbers varies. It is increasingly common now to read the digits one by one, as in English, so 00 34 9412568 is **cero cero tres cuatro nueve cuatro uno dos cinco seis ocho**. More traditionally the digits are paired off as far as possible: 412568 is often written 41 25 68 or 41.25.68 and read **cuarenta y uno, veinticinco, sesenta y ocho**, and when there is an odd number of digits in the number, the first is given in isolation: eg 369 47 11 is **tres sesenta y nueve, cuarenta y siete, once**. There is quite a range of possibilities with longer numbers, so 00 34 9412568 can be read **cero cero treinta y cuatro novecientos cuarenta y uno veinticinco sesenta y ocho** or **cero cero treinta y cuatro noventa y cuatro doce quinientos sesenta y ocho**.

19 Measurements

Even though the metric system is gradually being accepted in the English-speaking world, the imperial system is entrenched in the minds of many English-speakers. The Spanish-speaking world uses the metric system exclusively, at least officially, although older units of measurement may survive locally (see **19.8**). It is important to realize that, although Spanish equivalents of some English terms do exist (eg **yarda**, **pie**), they are not generally understood, and measurements must be converted. While precise mathematical calculation will be necessary in some cases (eg height on a passport, a baby's birth-weight), for everyday purposes round numbers and rough equivalents are adequate. In translation it is particularly important to imitate such rounding up (or down): *200 yards away* is not to be rendered as **a 182,88 metros** but rather as **a (unos) 200 metros**.

The following sections give the standard equivalences to facilitate calculation, but also give typical rough equivalences for everyday use.

NOTE: numbers in English text below are given with the English decimal point; thousands are partitioned by a comma.

19.1 Length

Standard equivalences	
1 in (**pulgada**) = 2.54 cm	1 cm = 0.3937 in
1 ft (**pie**) = 30.48 cm	1 m = 3.28084 ft
1 yd (**yarda**) = 0.9144 m	1 km = 0.62137 miles
	(very nearly $\frac{5}{8}$ mile)
1 mile (**milla**) = 1.6093 km	

NOTE: **milla** in a purely Spanish context is a nautical mile (1,852 km or 6,076 ft).

> *Rough equivalences*
>
> 10 cm – 4 in   1 km – $\frac{1}{2}$ mile
> 50 cm – 1$\frac{1}{2}$ ft   100 km – 60 miles
> 1 m – 1 yd
> 100 m – 100 yds

Examples

una niña de noventa centímetros
a child 3 feet tall
un hombre de un metro ochenta
a man 6 feet tall
cien kilómetros por hora
60 miles an hour

Expressing length

Note the following ways of expressing measurements of length, etc:
Esta carretera tiene dos kilómetros de longitud (R3) / de †largo: Es
  una carretera de dos kilómetros de longitud / de largo
La casa tiene cinco metros de altura (R3) / de alto: Es una casa de
  cinco metros de altura / de alto
Este pozo tiene diez metros de profundidad (R3) / de profundo: Es
  un pozo de diez metros de profundidad / de profundo
La autopista tiene treinta metros de anchura (R3) / de ancho: Es una
  autopista de treinta metros de anchura / de ancho
Este acero tiene diez centímetres de espesor (R3) / de grueso: Este
  acero es de diez centímetros de espesor

19.2   Weight

> *Standard equivalences*
>
> 1 oz **(onza)** = 28.35 g   1 g = 0.03527 oz
> 1 lb **(libra)** = 0.4536 kg   1 kg = 2.20462 lb
> 1 stone / 14 lbs = 6.35 kg   1 metric ton/tonne = 1,000 kg =
>   0.9842 tons
> 1 cwt = 50.8kg
> 1 ton **(tonelada)** = 1016.05 kg

NOTE: in a Spanish context, **tonelada** would normally mean a metric
ton or tonne.

> *Rough equivalences*
> 1/4 kilo − 1/2 lb
> 1/2 kilo − 1 lb
> 1 kilo − 2 lb

Examples

un hombre de sesenta kilos
a 10-stone man
un hombre de ochenta kilos
a 13-stone man

19.3 Area

> *Standard equivalences*
> 1 sq in = 6.4516 cm^2 1 cm^2 = 0.155 sq in
> 1 sq ft = 0.0929 m^2 1 m^2 = 10.764 sq ft
> 1 sq yd = 0.8361 m^2 1 km^2 = 0.3861 sq miles
> 1 sq mile = 2.589 km^2 or 258.9 ha   1 ha (=10,000 m^2) = 2.471 acres
> 1 acre = 4,046.72 m^2 or 0.405 ha

> *Rough equivalences*
> 6 cm^2 − 1 sq in   1 ha − 2 1/2 acres
> 1 m^2 − 1 sq yd   50 ha − 125 acres
> 1,000 m^2 − 1/4 acre   250 ha − 1 sq mile

Example

una finca de cuarenta hectáreas
a 100-acre estate

19.4 Volume

> *Standard equivalences*
> 1 pint = 0.5682 litres (UK) / 0.47 litres   1 litro = 1.759 pints (UK)
>   (USA)   / 2.128 pints (USA)
> 1 quart = 1.1364 litres (UK) / 0.946 litres
>   (USA)
> 1 gallon = 4.546 litres (UK) / 3.785 litres
>   (USA)

> *Rough equivalences*
> 1 litre – 2 pints
> 4 litres – 1 gallon
> 16 litres – 4 gallons
> 24 litres – 5 gallons

Examples

Mi coche gasta/consume seis litros a los cien (kilómetros)
My car does 50 (miles) to the gallon
once litros a los cien
25 to the gallon
medio litro de cerveza
a pint of beer

19.5   Temperature

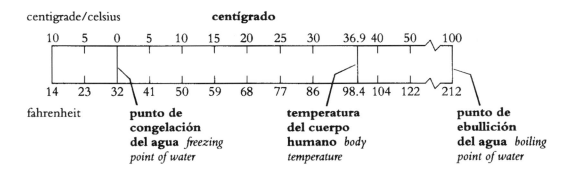

19.6   Time

The 24-hour system is used for official business, timetables, radio, etc, although more informally the 12-hour system is used, as in English. In Peninsular Spanish **de la madrugada**, **de la mañana**, **de la tarde**, **de la noche** are often used to resolve any resulting ambiguity; in Latin America, **am** and **pm** may also be used, as in English.

19.7 Currencies

Argentina	**peso**
Bolivia	**boliviano**
Chile	**peso**
Colombia	**peso**
Costa Rica	**colón** (m)
Cuba	**peso**
Ecuador	**sucre** (m)
El Salvador	**colón** (m)
Guatemala	**quetzal** (m)
Honduras	**lempira** (m)
México	**peso**
Nicaragua	**córdoba** (m)
Panamá	**balboa** (m)
Paraguay	**guaraní** (m)
Perú	**(nuevo) sol** (m)
Puerto Rico	**dólar** (= US $) (m)
República Dominicana	**peso**
Spain	**euro** (formerly **peseta** (**pela** (R1)))
Uruguay	**(nuevo) peso**
Venezuela	**bolívar** (m)

19.8 Traditional measurements

Some traditional measurements are still used in some rural areas and persist in some expressions. The most common of these are the **arroba** (about 11 $\frac{1}{2}$ kg, and also used as a measure of capacity), the †**cuadra** (a measure of length; in Latin America it also means 'a block of houses' and is frequently used as an informal measure of distance in this sense, eg **vive a tres cuadras de aquí**), the **fanega** (just over $\frac{1}{2}$ ha as a measure of area, or about 50 litres as a measure of capacity), the **legua** (= English *league*, about 4–5 km or 3 miles), the **quintal** (formerly 100 lbs, now about 45 kg) and the †**vara** (just under 1 m).

20 Semi-technical vocabulary

Technical dictionaries can be very daunting for students, though it is increasingly important to have some knowledge of the vocabulary of specialized fields. The following lists collect together some common words and expressions.

20.1 Banking

20.1.1 Buildings, people and things

†**banca**	banking (system)
sistema (m) **bancario**	banking system
†**banco**	(individual) bank
banco comercial	commercial bank
ente (m) **bancario, entidad** (f) **bancaria** (R3)	banking establishment
caja de ahorros	savings bank
banquero/a	banker
cajero/a	cashier
empleado/a de banco	bank employee
mostrador (m)	counter
†**ventanilla**	window (for service in bank)
cristal (m) **anti-balas**	bullet-proof glass
caja	cash desk
†**cámara acorazada**	strongroom, vault
caja fuerte	strong box
fajo de billetes	roll of bills, wad of notes
tira magnética / banda magnética (Mex)	magnetic strip
cajero (automático)	cash dispenser
calcular	to calculate

20.1.2 Opening an account

abrir una cuenta	to open an account
cerrar una cuenta	to close an account
tener cuenta en banco	to hold a bank account
número de cuenta	account number
número de †sucursal (f)	branch number

20.1.3 Accounts: types of account

cuenta bancaria	bank account
cuenta personal	personal account
cuenta corriente	current/checking account
cuenta conjunta	joint account
cuenta de ahorros	savings account
cuenta de depósito	deposit account
cuenta de crédito	credit account
cuenta presupuestaria	budget account
cuenta vivienda	mortgage account

20.1.4 Accounts: cheques (Brit), checks (US) / etc

cheque (m), **†talón** (m)	cheque/check
talonario de cheques, chequera	cheque/check book
cheque en blanco	blank cheque
cheque cruzado	crossed cheque
cheque al portador	bearer cheque
cheque sin fondos, cheque rebotado (Mex), **cheque de hule** (R1)	dishonoured cheque, cheque that bounces
cobrar un cheque	to cash a cheque
ingresar un cheque	to pay in a cheque
abonar el cheque en caja	to pay the cheque in at the cash desk
dar un cheque en blanco	to give a blank cheque
pagar con talón	to pay by cheque
Adjunto talón a nombre de . . .	I enclose a cheque in the name of . . .
libreta de ahorros	passbook, bank book
cartilla de ahorro	savings book
tarjeta de débito	debit card
tarjeta de crédito	credit card

20.1.5 Accounts: management

gestionar una cuenta	to manage an account
estado de cuenta	bank statement
saldo acreedor	credit balance
saldo deudor	debit balance
saldo a favor de	balance in favour of
orden (f) **permanente de pago**	standing order
pago (m) **automático**	direct debit
domiciliación (f)	payment by direct billing/debit
hacer una transferencia	to transfer
abonar mil dólares en una cuenta	to pay a thousand dollars into an account
domiciliar su sueldo mensual	to have your salary paid directly into the bank
debitar una cantidad de una cuenta (R2–3)	to debit a sum from an account
depositar dos mil pesos en una cuenta	to pay two thousand pesos into an account
retirar cien euros	to take out one hundred euros

estar en números rojos	to be in the red
estar en/al descubierto	to be overdrawn

cargar a la cuenta de	to charge to the account of
carta/nota de crédito	credit note
cobrar intereses	to charge interest
comisión (f) **de administración**	administration charges
cuantía máxima	maximum sum
giro	draft
límite (m) **de crédito**	credit limit
Me cargaron doscientos dólares	They charged me two hundred dollars

20.1.6 Saving

ahorrador/-ora	saver
ahorrar dinero	to save money

interés (m) **de crédito**	interest on credit
acumulación (f) **de interés**	accumulation of interest

20.1.7 Cash

pagar al contado / en efectivo / en metálico / en cash (Mex)	to pay cash

20.1.8 Changing money

cambio de moneda extranjera	foreign currency exchange
†**divisas** (pl)	foreign exchange
divisas convertibles	convertible currency
divisas fuertes	hard currency
divisas inconvertibles	unconvertible currency (like the rouble)
reservas de divisas	currency reserves
cambista (m/f)	money changer
control (m) **de divisas**	currency control
revaluación (f) **de la moneda**	currency revaluation

20.1.9 Loans

préstamo/empréstito (R3)	loan
prestar una cantidad	to loan a sum
pedir prestada una cantidad de dinero	to borrow a sum of money
pedir un crédito	to ask for credit
†**amortizar un préstamo**	to repay a loan
recibir un préstamo subsidiado (R2–3)	to receive a subsidized loan
crédito hipotecario, crédito vivienda	mortgage
solicitar un préstamo (R3)	to apply for a loan
llenar una solicitud de préstamo (Mex)	to fill in a form for a loan
hacer un adelanto, un anticipo	to make an advance
ventas (pl) **a crédito**	instalment plan, hire purchase
pagaré (m)	IOU, promissory note
pago inicial	down payment
pagar por adelantado	to pay in advance
pagar una cuota de mil dólares al mes	to pay a rate of a thousand dollars a month
amortización (f)	repayment
†**plazo de amortización**	repayment instalment on loan
amortizaciones (f pl) **susceptibles de desgravación**	tax-deductible repayments
bajo fianza	against a deposit
con capacidad (f) **de pago / solvente**	credit-worthy
valoración (f) **crediticia**	assessment as to whether a person is credit-worthy

tipo (m) **de interés**	interest rate
tasa real del orden de trece **por ciento**	real rate of the order of thirteen per cent
cuota mensual	monthly quota
mantener un saldo de mil **euros**	to keep a balance of one thousand euros
restricciones (f pl) **de crédito**	credit restrictions

20.1.10   Investment

inversión (f)	investment
inversionista (m/f)	investor
†**(sub)invertir**	to (under)invest
valores (m pl) **en cartera**	investments, holdings
interés (m) **fijo**	fixed interest
interés (m) **variable**	variable interest
†**renta fija**	fixed income
renta variable	variable income
baja de los valores	drop in the value of stocks/securities
beneficios fiscales	tax benefits
datos macroeconómicos	macroeconomic data
especulación (f) **inmobiliaria**	property speculation
valores (m pl) **de renta variable**	variable yield securities
valores (m pl) **inmobiliarios**	real estate

20.2   The Stock Exchange

20.2.1   Buildings, people and activities

la †**Bolsa**	the Stock Exchange
BMV (Bolsa Mexicana de **Valores)** (Mex)	Mexican Stock Exchange
parqué (m)	floor (in Stock Exchange)
sala de la Bolsa	Stock Exchange hall
tablón (m) **con las** **cotizaciones bursátiles**	(Stock Exchange) prices board
accionista (m/f)	shareholder
accionariado	stock/shareholders
agente (m/f) **de la Bolsa,** **bolsista** (m/f), **corredor** (m) **de Bolsa**	stockbroker
capitalista (m/f)	capitalist
suscriptor/-ora	underwriter
invertir en Bolsa	to invest on the Stock Exchange

251

20.2.2 Stocks and shares

acción (f)	share
tramo	share issue
gestionar una cartera	to manage a portfolio
Las acciones se cotizan a mil pesos	Shares are quoted at a thousand pesos
obligaciones (f pl)	bonds, debentures
lanzar una emisión de obligaciones	to launch an issue of bonds
título de portador	bearer bond
invertir en bonos del Estado	to invest in Government bonds
vender títulos	to sell securities/bonds
páguese al portador	pay the bearer
plusvalía	capital gain, added value

20.2.3 Market activity

actividad (f) **bursátil**	activity on the stock market
contratación (f)	transactions, trading
estar cotizado en Bolsa	to be listed/quoted on the Stock Exchange
cotización (f) **de apertura**	opening price
cotización (f) **de cierre / de clausura**	closing price
índice (m) **de la Bolsa**	Stock Exchange index
ampliación (f) **de capital**	capital increase
La Bolsa sube	The market / Stock Exchange is becoming bullish
experimentar une ligera subida	to go up slightly
experimentar una subida acusada	to go up sharply
caída de los valores	drop in value of stocks/shares
La Bolsa baja	The market / Stock Exchange is becoming slack
experimentar una ligera baja	to drop slightly
El precio fluctúa	The price fluctuates
evolución (f) **del índice de cotizaciones**	change in the price index
fluctuación (f) **de la moneda**	currency fluctuation
gráfica de estadísticas	statistics graph

20.2.4 Speculation

especulaciones (f pl)	speculation
especular en Bolsa	to speculate on the Stock Exchange
jugar a la baja	to speculate on a price fall
jugar al alza (f)	to speculate on a price rise

20.2.5 Takeovers

oferta pública de adquisición	takeover bid
oferta pública hostil	unfriendly takeover bid

20.3 Commerce

20.3.1 General

dirigir un comercio	to run a business
gestionar una compañía	to run a company
montar una sociedad	to set up a company
dirigente (m/f) **de una empresa**	company director
dirigente (m/f) **gerente**	managing director
ejecutivo/a	executive
socio/a	partner, shareholder
empresario/a	businessman/-woman
patronal (f)	management, employers
pequeños comerciantes	small traders
empresariales (f pl); **estudios** (m pl) **empresariales**	business studies
estudios mercantiles	commercial studies
El tiempo es oro	Time is money
Dinero llama dinero	Money makes money

20.3.2 Production and distribution

acopiar	to stockpile
acopio	stock
almacenar mercancías	to stock goods
tener un artículo en estock	to have an article in stock
materias primas	raw materials
código de barras	bar code

oferta y demanda	supply and demand
tener mucha demanda	to be in great demand (a product)
volumen (m) de cobros y pagos	turnover
volumen (m) de ventas	turnover
†superávit (m)	surplus
expansión (f)	expansion
incremento de ocho mil unidades	increase (in output) by eight thousand units
moderar el consumo	to dampen down consumption
rendimiento anual	annual output

distribución (f) de los productos	distribution of products
red (f) de distribución	distribution network
embarcar un producto	to ship a product
venta al contado	cash sale
subasta pública	public auction
embargar bienes	to seize goods

cupo de pesca	fish quota
explotar yacimientos de carbón (m)	to exploit coal seams

20.3.3 Marketing

marketing (m) / comercialización (f)	marketing
comercializar un producto	to market a product
propaganda	advertising
lanzamiento de un modelo	launch of a model
consolidar una red comercial	to consolidate a commercial network
mercado internacional	international market
promocionar la exportación	to promote exports
cuota de ventas	sales quota
liquidación (f) por cierre	closing down sales

20.3.4 Prices

precio (in)asequible	(un)affordable price
precio calidad	value for money
precio competitivo	competitive price
precio de la plata	price of silver
precio del oro	price of gold

fijar un precio	to fix a price
contener los precios	to hold down prices
aumento/subida/incremento/ **escalada de precios**	increase in prices
Los precios se elevan	Prices are rising
baja/disminución (f) **de** **precio**	drop in price
índice (m) **de precios**	price index
correr a/por mil pesos la **unidad**	to sell at a thousand pesos the unit
caro / salado (R1 Arg)	costly, expensive
ser un timo (Pen) / **un afano** (Arg) (R1)	to be a rip-off

20.3.5   Finance

20.3.5.1   *General*

institución (f) **financiera**	financial institution
operación (f) **financiera**	financial operation
medios financieros	financial means/resources/circles
equilibrio monetario	monetary stability
crisis (f) **financiera**	financial crisis
estabilidad (f) **financiera**	financial stability
control (m) **monetario**	monetary control

20.3.5.2   *Bills and payment*

factura	invoice, bill
pagar una factura	to pay a bill
pago atrasado	delayed payment
percibir un pago	to receive payment
pagar a plazos	to pay in instalments
pagar dentro del plazo **establecido**	to pay at an agreed time
cancelar el crédito	to settle the account
demanda de pago	demand for payment
demanda final	final demand
depósito inicial / enganche (m) (Mex)	down payment, initial deposit
desembolso	outlay
recibo / boleta (Arg)	receipt
dar la †**vuelta** (Pen) / **el vuelto** (Am)	to give change

20.3.5.3   Debt

contraer una deuda	to contract a debt
agravamiento de los déficits presupuestarios	worsening of the budget deficit
atender peticiones de crédito	to deal with credit requests
bienes (m pl) **inmuebles**	real estate, property
bienes (m pl) **muebles**	personal assets

20.3.5.4   Money

comisión (f)	commission
derechos aduaneros	customs duties
dividendo	dividend
dinero caliente	hot money
blanqueamiento del dinero	money laundering
blanquear el dinero	to launder money

20.3.5.5   Credit

crédito a corto plazo	short-term credit
crédito a largo plazo	long-term credit
crédito a medio plazo	medium-term credit
crédito instantáneo	instant credit

20.3.5.6   Interest

fijación (f) **de intereses**	fixing of interest rates
fondos públicos	public funds
tipos de interés	rates of interest

20.3.5.7   Profit and loss

solvencia	solvency
solvente	solvent
rentabilidad (f)	profitability
rentable	profitable
sobrepasar el listón de los dos millones de dólares	to exceed the two million dollar mark
pérdidas netas	net loss
hacer bancarrota	to go bankrupt
quiebra	bankruptcy
hundimiento	collapse
insolvencia	insolvency

20.3.5.8 *Exchange*

movimiento de capitales	movement of capital
transferencia de fondos	transfer of funds
letra de cambio	bill of exchange
vale (m)	voucher
hacer de intermediario	to act as an intermediary

20.3.6 Salaries

salario anual	annual salary
salario bruto	gross salary
salario libre de impuestos	tax-free salary
salario neto	net salary

20.3.7 Competition

mejorar la competencia	to improve competitiveness
cuota de mercado	market share/quota
monopolio	monopoly
adquisición (f)	takeover
competencia	competition
fusión (f) **de dos entidades financieras**	merger between two financial institutions
oferta pública de adquisición	takeover bid
perder competitividad (f)	to lose a competitive edge
regatear	to haggle, to bargain

20.3.8 The economy

auge (m) **económico**	economic peak
boom (m) **(económico)**	economic boom
crecimiento	growth
desarrollo económico	economic development
política (f) **monetaria**	monetary policy
presiones (f pl) **alcistas**	upward pressure
presiones (f pl) **bajistas**	downward pressure
economía de servicios	services economy
fomentar el aumento de empleo	to boost employment
mejorar el nivel de vida	to improve the standard of living

recesión (f)	recession
marasmo	slump
declive (m) **económico**	economic decline
crac(k) (m)	(economic) collapse
La economía se frena	The economy is slowing down
La economía se recalienta	The economy is overheating
sobrecalentarse	to overheat

reactivar la economía	to reactivate the economy
saneamiento	improvement
recuperación (f) **del sector**	sector recovery
repunte (m) **leve**	slight recovery

inflación (f)	inflation
deflación (f)	deflation
devaluación (f)	devaluation
desequilibrio monetario	monetary instability
deterioro de la balanza comercial	worsening in the balance of payments
deterioro del crecimiento económico	slackening of economic growth
situación (f) **deficitaria**	loss-making situation
levantar una barrera proteccionista	to put up a protectionist barrier
nacionalizar	to nationalize
poder (m) **adquisitivo**	buying power
valor (m) **del dólar / del euro**	value of the dollar / euro

20.4 Insurance (general)

20.4.1 General

adaptar necesidades a su medida	to tailor to your needs
agente (m/f) **de seguros**	insurance broker
anular un contrato	to cancel a contract
asegurado	(the) insured
aseguradora	insurance company
asegurar un capital	to insure a sum
cobertura	cover
comisión (f) **de seguro**	insurance commission
compañía aseguradora	insurance company
corredor/-ora de seguros	insurance broker
demanda de seguro	request for insurance
entidad (f) **aseguradora**	insurance company
número de póliza	policy number

póliza de seguro	insurance policy
recargo de la prima	surcharge on the premium
seguro	insurance
suma asegurada	sum assured
tasador/-ora de seguros	insurance assessor
tipo de seguro	insurance rate
titular (m/f) **de la póliza**	policy holder

20.4.2   Taking out an insurance policy

formalizar un seguro	to draw up an insurance policy
presupuesto más bajo	lowest quotation
suscribir una póliza de seguros	to take out an insurance policy
cerrar un contrato	to take out / sign a contract
elegir la forma de pago	to choose the form of payment
mayor cobertura	greater cover
modalidad (f) **de seguro**	type of insurance
pagar cotizaciones (f pl)	to pay premiums
pagar una prima fija	to pay a fixed premium
rellenar los datos necesarios	to fill out/in the necessary data/information
renovar una póliza	to renew a policy
requisito médico	medical requirement
rescindir un contrato	to cancel/rescind a contract

20.4.3   Terms

accidente (m) **corporal**	physical injury
anticipo del 25% de la suma asegurada	advance of 25% on the sum inssured
asistencia jurídica	legal assistance
asistencia psicológica	psychological counselling
beneficiario/a	beneficiary
bonificación (f) **por carencia de reclamaciones** (f pl)	no claims bonus
casa asegurable	insurable house
condiciones (f pl) **de la póliza**	conditions of the policy
contratar un seguro	to take out a contract
costes (m pl) **funerarios**	funeral costs
cotización (f)	statement of value
cubrir al máximo	to take out maximum cover
dañar los bienes	to damage possessions, property
descuento sobre la primera	discount on the first instalment

incapacidad (f) **profesional**	professional disability
invalidar un contrato	to invalidate a contract
obtener anticipo sobre póliza a bajo interés	to obtain an advance on a low-interest policy
plazo de carencia	repayment holiday (period free of interest payments and debt repayments)
prestaciones (f pl) **del servicio contratado**	benefits of the service paid for / agreed
prestaciones (f pl) **en caso de accidente**	benefits in case of accident

20.4.4   Claims

en caso de fallecimiento	in case of death
en caso de invalidez (f)	in case of disability
fallecimiento traumático	sudden death
indemnización (f) **conforme al baremo**	compensation in accordance with the rates
indemnización (f) **inicial**	down / initial compensation payment
indemnización (f) **mensual**	monthly compensation payment
informe / reporte (Mex) (m) **del perito**	expert's report
invalidez (f) **permanente**	permanent disability
lugar (m) **del fallecimiento**	place of death
pago inmediato	immediate payment
pérdida sufrida en (la) propiedad	damage/loss suffered by property
perito de la Aseguradora	insurance expert, assessor from the insurance company
presentar los justificantes	to provide supporting evidence
recibir una cantidad global	to receive a lump sum
reclamar al seguro	to make an insurance claim
reembolso de gastos médicos	reimbursement of medical expenses
reembolso entero	full reimbursement
robo por expoliación	theft, burglary
tasar los daños	to assess the damage
trámite rápido del siniestro	accident claim speedily resolved

20.4.5   Different kinds of insurance

seguro de vivienda	home insurance
seguro de incendio	fire insurance
seguro de tarjeta de crédito	insurance for loss of credit card
seguro de enfermedad	health insurance
seguro médico	medical insurance
seguro de automóvil/vehículo	automobile/car/vehicle insurance
póliza de seguro de vida	life insurance/assurance policy
seguro de viaje	travel insurance
seguro de la vejez	pension plan/scheme
multirriesgo del comercio	commercial all-risks policy
seguro de compensación por accidentes laborales	compensation insurance for industrial injury
seguro responsabilidad civil	civil liability insurance

20.4.6   Home insurance policy

asegurar el continente y el contenido	to insure the home and contents
asegurar la casa contra incendios	to insure the house against fire
asegurar una vivienda	to insure a home/dwelling
multirriesgo del hogar	comprehensive home insurance
proteger el valor de la vivienda	to protect the value of the home
proteger el valor del mobiliario	to protect the value of household goods
seguro contra el robo	insurance against theft
seguro de casa con cobertura amplia (Mex)	comprehensive house insurance
allanamiento de morada	breaking and entering, burglary
escalamiento	housebreaking, burglary
contenido mobiliario	contents
robo del contenido	theft of contents
bienes (m pl) **asegurables**	insurable possessions
objetos de seres queridos	objects of sentimental value
aparatos sanitarios	bathroom fittings
daños materiales	material damage
daños por agua	water damage
daños por helada	frost damage
sustitución (f) **de llaves y cerraduras**	replacement of keys and locks

reposición (f) **de artículos**	replacement of articles
reposición (f) **de documentos**	replacement of documents
localización (f) **de la avería**	locating the breakdown/damage
reemplazo de artículos	replacement of articles
reparación (f) **de la tubería**	pipe repairs
reventón (m) **de la tubería**	pipe burst
rotura de cristales	breakage of windows
rotura de espejos	mirror breakage
rotura de servicio de mesa	breakage of set of dishes
rotura de vajilla	breakage of chinaware
salvamento y desescombro	clearing of site

garantía de incendio y robo	guarantee against fire and theft
gastos de extinción	fire extinction costs
incendio y riesgos complementarios	fire and other risks
honorarios de peritos	assessor's fees

parada / paralización (f) / **descompostura** (Mex) **de cámaras frigoríficas**	fridge and freezer breakdown

20.4.7   Financial planning and pensions

planificación (f) **económica**	financial planning
plan (m) **de seguro**	insurance plan
plan (m) **de jubilación**	retirement plan
garantizar sus ingresos	to guarantee your income
garantizar una jubilación asegurada	to guarantee a retirement insurance
†**avalar un plan de pensiones**	to guarantee a pensions plan
garantizar el futuro	to guarantee the future
realizar un presupuesto personalizado	to take a personal budget plan
ventajas fiscales	tax advantages

20.5   Tax

20.5.1   General

fiscalidad (f)	taxation, tax regulations
sistema (m) **tributario**	tax system
imponer contribuciones a	to tax
tributar	to pay taxes

pagar fuertes contribuciones (f pl)	to pay heavy taxes
presión (f) **fiscal**	tax burden
percepción (f) **de impuestos**	tax collection
recaudación (f) **de impuestos**	tax collection

gravamen (m)	tax burden
gravar con un impuesto	to burden with taxes

tasador/-ora de impuestos	tax assessor
agente tributario/a	tax agent/inspector
asesor/-ora contable	tax advisor/accountant
contable (m/f) **especializado/a en asuntos tributarios**	tax specialist/advisor
Delegación (f) **de Hacienda**	local tax office
Inspección (f) **de la Hacienda Pública**	Tax Inspector's Department

evasión (f) **fiscal / tributaria**	tax evasion
fraude (m) **fiscal**	tax fraud/evasion
paraíso (m) **fiscal**	tax haven

exiliado/a por motivos fiscales	tax exile
refugio fiscal	tax haven
vivir sin pagar contribuciones	to live tax free

20.5.2   Types of tax

tasa de aeropuerto	airport tax
impuesto sobre apuestas	betting tax
impuesto de plusvalía	capital gains tax
impuesto sobre el capital	capital levy
impuesto sobre sociedades (f pl)	corporation tax

impuesto sobre espectáculos	entertainment tax
impuesto sobre las sucesiones / los bienes heredados	death/estate duty
impuesto de lujo	luxury tax
impuesto sobre la propiedad	property / real estate tax
contribución (f) **territorial / impuesto de radicación**	property / real estate tax
impuesto de venta	sales tax
impuesto del timbre	stamp duty
impuesto sobre la renta de las personas físicas	tax on an individual's income
impuesto revolucionario	tax paid to revolutionary groups
Impuesto sobre la Renta (ISR) (Mex)	tax taken from source

impuesto al / sobre el valor añadido (IVA)	Value Added Tax (VAT)
impuesto de circulación (f)	vehicle tax
impuesto sobre la riqueza	wealth tax
impuesto de actividades económicas	tax on commercial and professional activities
tasa por vados	tax on garage entrance (to keep it free)
tasación (f) **de los activos de una compañía**	assessment of a company's assets
gravar una vivienda	to tax a house/dwelling

20.5.3 Filling in a tax return

realizar la declaración de impuesto sobre la renta	to fill out/in a tax return
cumplimentar los datos en el impreso por triplicado	to fill out/in the forms in triplicate
declaración (f) **de renta**	income-tax return
PADRE = Programa de Ayuda para la Declaración de la Renta	(in Spain) computer program for on-line filing of a tax return
presentar las declaraciones tributarias	to make a tax declaration
cumplir sus obligaciones tributarias	to meet your tax obligations
tramitación (f) **de los expedientes**	processing of the dossiers
banda impositiva	tax band
base (f) **de cálculo de retención**	basic rate of tax
tipo impositivo	tax coding/bracket
ingreso gravable	taxable income
ingreso sujeto a impuesto	taxable income
ingresos no imponibles	non-taxable income
beneficios antes de impuestos	profits before tax
†**capital** (m) **mobiliario**	personal assets
cometer una infracción tributaria	to defraud the Treasury / Inland Revenue
comprobación (f) **de los hechos imponibles**	proof of taxable matters
concepto deducible	sum/amount deductible
renta bruta anual	annual gross income
renta imponible	taxable income

pasivo circulante/corriente	current liabilities
pasivo diferido	deferred liabilities
rendimiento del capital inmobiliario	returns on property

familiar (m/f) dependiente	family dependent
gastos deducibles	deductible expenses
gravamen (m) de una hipoteca	mortgage liability
tener personas a su cargo	to have dependents

ordenación (f) de pagos	order to pay
fecha de devengo del impuesto	final date for payment of tax
aplazamientos devengan interés de demora	late payments attract interest

defraudar a Hacienda	to defraud the Treasury / Inland Revenue
falsear los datos de la declaración	to make a false declaration on the tax form/return
inventar gastos	to invent/concoct expenses
justificantes (m pl) de gastos y deducciones	supporting documentation for expenses and deductions
omitir ingresos	to fail to declare income

20.5.4 Assessment

arancel (m)	tariff
cuota del impuesto de la renta	tax scale
cuota tributaria	tax dues
desgravación (f) fiscal	tax relief
desgravable del 17% en el impuesto de renta	17% relief on taxable income
privilegio tributario	tax concession
reducción (f) de impuestos	tax reduction
desgravación (f) personal	personal allowance, personal tax relief
desgravar el interés sobre la hipoteca	to allow tax relief on mortgage repayments
devolución (f) de impuestos	reimbursement of tax
reembolso fiscal	tax reimbursement
disfrutar de beneficios fiscales	to enjoy tax benefits

exento de contribuciones	tax exempt
exento de impuesto	tax free
eximir de impuestos	to exempt from tax
exento del pago de impuestos	exempt from the paying of tax
libre de gravamen (m)	free from encumbrance (debts, tax liability, etc)
vacaciones (f pl) **fiscales**	provisional suspension of tax payment

contribuyente (m/f) **con cónyuge a cargo**	taxpayer with dependent spouse
contribuyente (m/f) **divorciado/a**	divorced taxpayer
contribuyente (m/f) **separado/a legalmente**	legally separated taxpayer
contribuyente (m/f) **soltero/a**	unmarried taxpayer
perceptor/-ora de haberes pasivos	pensioner

hechos que resultan gravados	matters attracting tax liability
sujeto al pago de	liable for the payment of

liquidar el impuesto	to pay off your taxes
fraccionamiento de pago	payment by instalments
ingresar una cantidad al tesoro	to pay a sum to the Treasury
deducir previamente	to deduct at source

20.5.1 Taxation policy

legislación (f) **fiscal**	tax legislation
ley (f) **reguladora del impuesto**	tax-governing law
ordenanzas fiscales	tax regulations
régimen (m) **de impuesto / tributario**	tax rules/system

aprobar los presupuestos generales del Estado	to approve the State budget
erario	public treasury/purse
financiar la producción de bienes y servicios públicos	to finance government services and property

20.6   Social Security

20.6.1   General

trabajos de asistencia social	social work
gozar de protección social	to enjoy social welfare
Instituto Nacional de la Salud (Spain) / **Secretaría de Salud** (Mex)	Ministry of Health
escasez (f) **de viviendas**	housing shortage
ingreso mínimo	minimum wage
trabajo temporal	temporary employment

20.6.2   People

asegurados (sociales)	those insured with social security
envejecimiento de la población	ageing population
familia monoparental / hogar (m) **sin pareja**	one-parent family
huérfano/a	orphan
parados de larga duración	long-term unemployed
perceptor/-ora de subsidio de desempleo	person drawing unemployment benefit
prejubilación (f)	early retirement
prejubilado/a	person who has retired early

20.6.3   Benefits

tener derecho a prestaciones	to have a right to benefits
intervenciones (f pl) **al cargo del Estado**	state pay-out
indemnización (f) **de desempleo**	unemployment benefit
cobrar un subsidio de desempleo	to receive unemployment benefit
cobrar el seguro de desempleo	to receive unemployment benefit
ayuda oficial a la vivienda	grant for public housing / council accommodation
cobrar la incapacidad (Mex)	to receive sick pay
cobrar la incapacidad por maternidad (Mex)	to receive maternity pay

prestaciones (f pl) **económicas en caso de invalidez**	financial help in case of disability
prestaciones (f pl) **en asistencia social**	social welfare/benefits
recibir prestaciones de la Seguridad Social	to receive Social Security benefits
reclamar una subvención	to claim benefit / a grant
subsidio de enfermedad	sick pay/benefit
subsidio de natalidad (f)	maternity benefit
subsidio de vejez (f)	old-age pension
subsidio por discapacidad (f)	disability benefit
servicios de comida	meals service, meals delivered to your home, meals on wheels
vivir a cargo de la asistencia social	to live on social welfare
beneficio de justicia gratuita	entitlement to legal aid
bienestar de los niños	children's welfare

ayuda familiar / ayudas en el hogar	home help
casa de reposo	rest home
centro de asistencia social	social welfare centre
clínica de reposo	convalescent home
club (m) **de pensionistas**	pensioners' club
subvenir a los gastos	to meet the expenses
sufrir una contingencia social	to meet with unforeseen circumstances

guardería infantil	crèche
asilo de huérfanos / orfanato / orfelinato	orphanage
vivienda protegida / de renta limitada	public housing, council house
vivienda para obreros	workers' housing
residencia de ancianos	old people's home
casa para personas de la tercera edad (Mex)	home for elderly people

20.6.4   Assessment

averiguar los recursos económicos	to assess income
comprobar medios de vida	to means-test
cotizaciones (f pl) **a la Seguridad Social**	Social Security contributions

cotizaciones (f pl) **patronales /** **cuota patronal**	employers' contributions
aumento de las cotizaciones	subscription increase
beneficios relacionados con **los ingresos**	earnings-related benefits
continuidad (f) **del ingreso** **profesional**	continuation of professional income
empleo a tiempo parcial	part-time work
en función de los ingresos **profesionales**	depending on professional income

20.6.5   Policy

política sanitaria	health policy
subvención (f) **estatal**	state subsidy
subvencionar	to subsidize
reducir al mínimo las **intervenciones sociales**	to minimize state intervention
ampliar beneficios sociales	to expand social benefits
revalorizar pensiones	to increase benefits/allowances
revaluar subsidios	to increase pensions
financiar un sistema de **cobertizo**	to finance a comprehensive system
privatizar el sistema	to privatize the system
desmantelar el sistema	to terminate / wind up the system
problema (m) **de la vivienda**	housing problem
pronóstico demográfico	demographic forecast
situación (f) **precaria de las** **finanzas públicas**	precarious state of public finances

20.6.6   Charitable work

beneficiencia social	charitable work
obra de beneficiencia	charitable organization
concierto de beneficiencia	charity concert

20.7   Justice

20.7.1   General

legal	legal
ilegal	illegal
íntegro	upright, honest
jurisprudencia	jurisprudence
instancia	authority
código penal	penal code
causa (civil)	lawsuit
demanda	lawsuit
pleito	action, lawsuit
recurrir a la vía judicial	to have recourse to law
enzarzarse en pleitos	to get involved in lawsuits
asesoría jurídica	legal advice/consultancy
bufete (m)	lawyer's office, legal practice
ejercer la abogacía	to exercise the law
hacer justicia	to dispense justice
orden (m) público	public order
reforma judicial	legal reform
ser del dominio público	to be in the public interest/domain
novela policíaca	thriller (novel)

20.7.2   People

abogado/a (R2)	lawyer
jurista (m/f) (R2–3)	lawyer, jurist
letrado/a (R3)	lawyer
togado	lawyer
picapleitos (m) / leguleyo/a (R1)	shyster, pettifogging lawyer (pej)
procurador/-ora	attorney, lawyer
notario/a	notary, solicitor
fiscal (m/f)	district attorney, public prosecutor
fiscalía	district attorney's office, public prosecutor's office
licenciado/a en derecho	law graduate
juez (m/f) (also jueza (f))	judge
juez (m/f) de instrucción / juez instructor(a)	examining magistrate
juez (m/f) de paz	justice of the peace
magistrado/a	magistrate
magistratura	post of judge, magistracy

defensor/-ora	defence counsel/lawyer
demandado/a	defendant
inculpado/a	(the) accused
defender a[PERS] **un(a) cliente** (m/f) (also **clienta** (f))	to defend a client
defensa	defence
demandante (m/f) / **querellante** (m/f)	plaintiff
fuerzas del orden	police force
defensor/-ora del pueblo	ombudsman
[†]**testigo** (m/f, but always **-o**)	witness
testigo (m/f) **de cargo**	witness for the prosecution
testigo (m/f) **de descargo**	witness for the defence
testigo (m/f) **de vista / testigo ocular**	eye witness
testimoniar	to testify, to bear witness
jurado/a	jury, juror
[†]**miembro** (m/f, but always **-o**) **del jurado**	member of the jury
capellán (m)	chaplain
persona (always f) **física y jurídica**	individual (in a legal context)

20.7.3 Crimes

delinquir (R3)	to offend, to commit an offence
cometer una infracción (R2–3)	to commit an offence
crimen (m) **premeditado**	premeditated crime
amenaza	threat
amenazar	to threaten
conducta punible (R2–3)	punishable behaviour
preso/a convicto/a y confeso/a	a convicted and self-confessed prisoner

20.7.4 Investigation and apprehension

encuestas policiales	police enquiries
investigación (f)	investigation
inspección (f) **ocular**	inspection of the scene (by going there)
pieza de convicción (f)	piece of evidence
amañar pruebas	to tamper with the evidence

equipo forense	forensic team
medicina legal	forensic medicine
hacer una deposición	to make a deposition/statement
antecedentes (m pl) **penales**	police record

sospecha	suspicion
prontuariar (Am)	to open a file (on)
perseguir	to hunt, to pursue, to persecute
orden (f) **de busca y captura**	arrest warrant
coger/sorprender/pillar en flagrante delito / in fraganti (R3)	to catch *in flagrante delicto* / redhanded

interrogar	to question, to interrogate
interrogatorio policial	police grilling/interrogation
imputar delitos a	to accuse (someone) of offences
confesar	to confess
confesión (f)	confession
sumario	indictment
enjuiciar	to indict, to commit for trial
inculpar	to indict, to charge
encausar	to charge
instruir diligencias	to institute proceedings
instruir un sumario	to present an indictment
orden (f) **de comparencia**	court order (to appear)
pleitear (R3)	to go to litigation/court

escapar(se)	to escape

20.7.5 Courts

tribunal (m)	court
†**audiencia**	hearing, court
juzgado de instrucción (f) / **de primera instancia**	court of first instance
juzgado de menores	minors' court
tribunal (m) **supremo**	supreme/high court
procedimiento	proceedings
procesamiento	prosecution, trial

celebrar sesión	to hold a session
†**comparecer**	to appear (in court)
comparencia	appearance (in court)
galería pública	public gallery

20.7.6   Proceedings

vista (f)	hearing
abrir una vista (R3)	to begin a hearing
levantar la sesión (R2–3)	to suspend the session
bajo la jurisdicción de	under the jurisdiction of
lenguaje jurídico	legal language
acusación (f)	accusation
acusado	accused
acusar	to accuse
autor/-ora presunto/a	alleged perpetrator
en el banquillo de los acusados	in the dock
entablar un proceso contra	to put on trial
ser procesado	to be put on trial
instrucción (f)	hearing, preliminary investigation
juicio/proceso	trial
juicio a puerta cerrada	trial *in camera*
presentar una demanda contra	to sue
procesar	to take to court, to sue
†**querella**	lawsuit, action
recurrir a la ley	to resort to the law
remitir al juez competente	to refer to the competent judge
remitir al tribunal	to refer to the court
someter a un careo	to confront, bring face to face (two parties)
partes (f pl) **contratantes**	contracting parties
equidad (f)	equity
declararse culpable	to plead guilty
declararse inocente	to plead innocent
presunción (f) **de inocencia**	presumption of innocence
negar haber cometido el crimen	to deny having committed the crime
exigir fianza	to demand bail
atestiguar	to testify
audición (f) **de los testigos** (R3)	hearing of the witnesses
audiencia (f) **de los testigos**	hearing of the witnesses
citar/emplazar	to summon
entregar una citación	to subpoena, to hand in a summons
mandamiento judicial	court order / warrant
mandar comparecer	to order to appear (in court)
comparecer a requerimiento de	to appear at the request of

deposición (f)	statement (in court)
examinar	to examine
repreguntar	to cross-examine
jurar	to swear
prestar declaración	to make a statement
prestar juramento	to swear an oath

evidencia	proof, evidence
alegato	submission
caso litigioso	contentious issue
coartada	alibi
probar la coartada	to prove the alibi

abuso de confianza	breach of trust/confidence
contumacia	contempt of court
contumaz (m/f)	person who is in contempt of court

culpable	guilty
culpabilidad (f)	guilt
inocente	innocent

absolución (f)	acquittal
absolver	to acquit
apelar contra	to appeal against
recurso de casación	appeal for annulment

gastos judiciales	legal expenses
informe (m)	report

20.7.7   Verdict and sentencing

condena / sentencia	sentence
dictar una sentencia	to pass / hand down a sentence
condenar a quince años de cárcel (f)	to sentenced to fifteen years' imprisonment
condenar a seis meses de prisión (f)	to sentence to six months' imprisonment
condena condicional	conditional sentence
sentencia firme	unappealable sentence
condenado a daños y perjuicios	ordered to pay damages
condenado en rebeldía	convicted in his/her absence
estar condenado a muerte	to be sentenced to death
estar en libertad provisional	to be on bail
circunstancias atenuantes	attenuating circumstances
gracia	clemency
conmutar la pena	to commute a sentence
cumplir su condena	to complete your sentence

juzgar a^{PERS} un delincuente	to judge a criminal
veredicto	verdict
dar un veredicto / fallar	to give a verdict
pronunciar una sentencia de culpabilidad	to pronounce a verdict of guilty
veredicto inapelable	final verdict
fallar a favor de	to rule in favour of
fallo	ruling, judgement, verdict

indultar	to reprieve
indulto	reprieve
indemnizar	to indemnify, to compensate

justo	just, fair
injusto	unjust
imparcial	impartial

20.7.8   Punishments

†castigar / punir (R3)	to punish
castigo / punición (f) (R3)	punishment
aplicar la ley con todo su rigor	to apply the full weight of the law
certificado de penales	certificate of criminal record
reivindicar justicia	to appeal for justice
sanción (f) penal	penal sanction
suplicio	punishment
ejecución (f) / pena capital	capital punishment
pena de muerte	death penalty
sentencia de muerte	death sentence
ahorcamiento	hanging
fusilar	to shoot
decapitar	to behead
cadalso/patíbulo	scaffold
ajusticiar/ejecutar	to execute
corredor (m) de la muerte	death row
abolir la pena de muerte	to abolish the death penalty
garrote (m)	garrotte
inyección (f) letal	lethal injection
silla eléctrica	electric chair
verdugo	executioner
picota	pillory

custodia	custody
sistema (m) **penitenciario**	prison system
detención (f) **preventiva**	protective custody
detención (f) **provisional**	remand
cárcel (f) **modelo**	model prison
celda	cell
mazmorra	dungeon
interno/a, recluso/a	inmate
entre rejas	behind bars
trabajos forzados	hard labour
intento de fuga	attempt at escape
población (f) **penal**	penal population
prisión (f) **de alta seguridad**	high-security prison
reclusión (f) **perpetua**	life imprisonment
deportar	to deport
desterrar	to exile
destierro, exilio	exile
expulsar	to expel
confiscación (f)	confiscation
decomisar	to seize, to confiscate
embargo	seizure, sequestration
expropriación (f)	expropriation
incautación (f)	confiscation
incautarse de	to confiscate
estar sujeto a una multa	to be subject to a fine
rehabilitación (f)	rehabilitation
reinserción (f) **social**	social rehabilitation

20.7.9   Policy

aprobar un proyecto de ley	to approve a bill
derogar una ley	to abolish a law
atentar contra los intereses ajenos	to threaten other people's interests
denuncia pública	public report

20.8   Computing

20.8.1   General

ordenador (m) (Pen), **computadora** (Am)	computer
ordenador (m) **de mesa**	desktop computer

ordenador (m) **portátil**	portable, laptop
laptop (m in Spain, f in Am)	laptop
micro-ordenador (m)	micro-computer
computar	to compute
informática, computación (f) (Am)	computing
informático	computing engineer
cyberespacio	cyber-space
globalización (f)	globalization

20.8.2   System

sistemas (m pl) **multimedia**	multimedia systems
†**iniciar**	to start
apagar el sistema	to shut down the system
cerrar sesión	to shut down
reiniciar / resetear	to restart
colgarse	to crash
fallar	to be down, to crash
quedarse colgado	to crash
actualizar un sistema	to upgrade a system
código de entrada	access code
contraseña	password
mandato	command
memoria central	central memory
panel (m) **de control**	control pannel
almacenar	to store
bit (m)	bit
byte (m), **octeto**	byte
software (m)	software
sujetadatos (m)	clipboard
trabajo en serie	batch job
bicho (m)	virus, bug
depurar	to remove the virus, to debug

20.8.3   Hardware and peripherals

unidad (f) **central de proceso**	central processing unit
chip (m), **plaqueta**	chip
consola	console, control panel

unidad (f) **de discos**	disk drive
disco compacto	compact disk
disco duro	hard disk
disco flexible	floppy disk
disquetera	disk drive
floppy (m)	floppy disk
servidor (m)	server
impresora	printer
impresora de puntos	dot printer
tinta de impresora	printing ink
cartucho (m)	cartridge
tóner (m)	toner
imprimir	to print
módem (m)	modem
código de barras	bar code

20.8.4   Display, keyboard and mouse

monitor (m)	monitor
pantalla	screen
icono	icon
cursor (m)	cursor
barra de herramientas	tool bar
menú (m)	menu
menú (m) **de visualización** (f)	display menu
ventana	window
ampliar	to maximize
minimizar	to minimize
visualizar	to visualize
tecla	key
teclado	keyboard
apretar / pulsar una tecla	to press a key
teclear	to press the keys
espaciador (m)	space bar
tecla de entrada	enter key
teclas de función	function keys
teclas de las letras	letter keys
teclas de los números	number keys
ratón (m)	mouse
chasquear, hacer clic (m)	to click

20.8.5 Files

archivo, fichero (less used)	file
†**carpeta**	folder
archivar	to file
guardar, salvar	to save
borrar, cancelar	to delete
copiar	to copy
cortar y pegar	to cut and paste
propiedades (f pl)	properties
recuperar	to get back
respaldo	backup
respaldar un archivo	to back up a file

20.8.6 Programs

†**acceder / accesar** (Mex) **a una aplicación**	to access an application
salir	to exit
salida	exit
programador/-ora	programmer
videojuegos (m)	video games
hoja de cálculo	spreadsheet

20.8.7 Internet

ponerse en línea	to go on line
en Internet	on the Internet
hojear	to browse
visitar un sitio web	to visit a web site
explorar hacia atrás	to backtrack
alias (m)	alias
buscador (m)	search engine
†**buscar**	to search
booleano	Boolean
descargar	to download
bajar archivos	to download files
contraseña / palabra de paso	password
pirata (m/f) **informático/a**	hacker
proveedor (m)	provider
red (f) **comunitaria**	freenet
servicios en línea	on-line services
surfear	to surf

20.8.8   Word processing

procesamiento/tratamiento de textos	word processing
procesar	to process
cabecera de página	page heading
formatear	to format
justificar	to justify
poner en cursiva	to italicize
poner en negrita	to put in bold
subrayar	to underline
marcar una frase	to block a sentence
seleccionar un párrafo	to block a paragraph
retroceder	to backspace
tabulación (f)	tabulation
columna	column
reticulado	grid
plantilla de caracteres	character template
referencia cruzada	cross reference

20.8.9   Graphics and fax

escáner (m)	scanner
escanear un documento	to scan a document
gráfico	graphic
representación gráfica	graphic display
flujograma (m)	flow chart
faxear un documento	to fax a document

20.8.10   E-mail

correo electrónico, e-mail (m), **emilio** (R1)	e-mail
buzón (m) **electrónico, dirección** (f) **electrónica**	e-mail address
abrir un anexo	to open an attachment
chatear	to chat
salón (m) **de chat(eo)**	chat room
decodificar	to decode
arroba	'at' sign (@)

Part II Grammar

21 Gender

NOTE: In this book, the gender of nouns is indicated *only* when it is not predictable from the principles given in this section.

Spanish nouns all belong to one of two genders, masculine or feminine, and articles and adjectives agree in gender with the noun to which they refer. It is sometimes said that Spanish has a neuter gender (see **21.10** below), but no noun belongs to this.

Feminine nouns beginning in stressed **a-** or **ha-** take the articles **el** and **un (el agua fría, un ave nocturna)**. In R1, such nouns are often treated as masculine; eg: **mucho** ! **hambre, hambre epidémico** ! , **asma alérgico** ! . (Before a feminine adjective beginning in stressed **a-** or **ha-**, however, **la** and **una** are used: **la Alta Edad media, una amplia falda.**)

BUT NOTE: **la hache** *(letter)* h, **la a personal** *personal* a, **La Haya** *The Hague.*

21.1 Gender and sex

Nouns referring to people of the male sex are nearly always masculine. Nouns referring to people of the female sex are usually feminine. This principle can override the gender of a noun which otherwise does not refer to a person, eg **la piel roja** *(red skin)*, but **un piel roja** *('redskin' = Native American)*.

Exceptions

The generic words **la persona, el individuo, la víctima** *(victim)* and **la estrella** *(film-star)* are invariable in gender.

El desnudo *((picture of a) nude)* is always masculine.

Similar gender distinctions are made in nouns referring to animals, eg **el toro** *(bull)*, **la vaca** *(cow)*, although one word is usually used to refer generically to the animal, eg **el caballo** *(horse in general)*, **la yegua** *(mare)*. Where the names of animals do not have distinct masculine and feminine forms, [†]**macho** and **hembra** (invariable) are used to make the distinction when necessary, and the gender of the noun does not change:

las ardillas macho
male squirrels
el ratón hembra
female mouse

21.2 Gender associated with types of noun

Masculine

rivers	el Ebro, el Guadiana, el Amazonas, el Paraná
months	(el) enero *January*, (el) abril *April*
mountains and volcanoes	el Etna, el Mulhacén, el Aconcagua
cars	el Mercedes, el Seat, el Ford
watches	el Seiko, el Longines
ships	*el Reina Isabel*
planes	el Concorde, el Boeing
languages	el guaraní, el vascuence OR el euskera *Basque*
metals	el hierro *iron*, el cobre *copper*
many trees	el olmo *elm*, el fresno *ash*, el roble *oak*
	BUT NOTE: el haya (f) *beech*, la encina *holm oak*, la higuera *fig tree*
musical notes	fa sostenido *F sharp*
cheeses	el Cabrales, el Brie
wines	el Borgoña *Burgundy (wine)* BUT la Borgoña *Burgundy (area of France)*, el Rioja *Rioja (wine)* BUT la Rioja *La Rioja (region of Spain)*

Feminine

islands	la apacible Barbados
letters of the alphabet	la i, la b
	NOTE ALSO: la consonante *consonant*, la †vocal *vowel*
firms	la Ford, la Siemens

21.3 Gender associated with noun ending

Masculine

-o   *Most common exceptions*
  • Some masculine nouns which do not change their endings when they denote females:
  la soprano *soprano*, la modelo *model*, la testigo *witness*, la miembro *member*

- Abbreviations of feminine nouns:

la moto(cicleta) *motor bike*, la foto(grafía) *photograph*, la
    †radio(difusión) (but **radio** is usually masculine in Am)
    radio

- Where a feminine noun is implied or understood:

la Gestapo (policía), la UNESCO (organización)

- Other:

la mano, la dínamo (but **dínamo** is often masculine in Am),
    la libido OR la líbido

-or	Denoting agent:
	el autor *author*, el conductor *driver*
-or	Not denoting agent:
	el calor *heat*, el licor *liquor*, el valor *value*
	Exception
	la labor *work*
-aje	el viaje *journey*, el linaje *lineage*, el andamiaje *scaffolding*
-én	el andén *platform*, el terraplén *embankment*
	Exception
	la sartén *fry(ing) pan* (BUT SEE **21.6**)
-men	el certamen *contest*, el volumen *volume*, el régimen *régime*
-gen	el origen *origin*
	Most common exceptions
	la imagen *image*, la †margen *margin* (SEE **21.6**)

Feminine

-a	*Exceptions*
	• Nouns denoting males (see above):
	el cura *priest*, el artista *artist*, el guardia *guard*, el jesuita *Jesuit*
	• Abstract nouns ending in **-ma**:
	el carisma *charisma*, el cisma *schism*, el *climate*, el prisma *prism*, el problema *problem*, el reuma *rheumatism*, el síntoma *symptom*, Contrast:
	la amalgama *amalgam*, la crema *cream*, la diadema *diadem*, la gema *gem*, *la* yema *egg yolk*
	NOTE:
	el asma (f) *asthma*, †la estratagema *stratagem*, †la trama *plot*
	• Other:
	el día *day*, el mapa *map*, el planeta *planet*, el tranvía *tram*, el †cometa *comet*, el †pijama *pyjamas*, el delta *delta (river)*, el pesticida *pesticide*
-ad	la verdad *truth*, la enfermedad *illness*, la majestad *majesty*

–ud	la virtud *virtue*, la longitud *length* *Exceptions* el ataúd *coffin*, el laúd *lute*
–ed	la merced *mercy* *Exceptions* el césped *lawn*, el huésped *quest*
–ión	Denoting abstraction: la ración *ration, portion*, la región *region* Contrast el gorrión *sparrow*, el avión *aeroplane*, el sarampión *measles*, el camión *truck*, etc
–umbre	la certidumbre *certainty*, la costumbre *custom*
–ie	la serie *series*, la planicie *plain*

–sis	la síntesis *synthesis*, la metamorfosis *metamorphosis*
	Exceptions
	el análisis *analysis*, el apocalipsis *apocalypse*, el énfasis
	    emphasis, el éxtasis *ecstasy*, el oasis *oasis*, el paréntesis
	    parenthesis, el piscolabis *snack*

21.4 Gender of compound nouns

Noun + noun combinations are usually feminine when both nouns
are feminine, eg:
>   la bocacalle *street entrance, turn*, la maniobra *manoeuvre*,
>   la madreselva *honeysuckle*

BUT
>   el/la purasangre *thoroughbred (horse, etc)*

NOTE ALSO:
>   la enhorabuena *congratulations*, la sinrazón *outrage*

Otherwise, compound nouns formed with other parts of speech are
usually masculine:
>   el terremoto *earthquake*, el abrelatas *can opener*, el paraguas *umbrella*,
>   el aguardiente *brandy*, el altavoz *loudspeaker* (altoparlante(Am)),
>   el rompecabezas *brain teaser*

21.5 Adjectives as nouns

In certain cases, a phrase consisting of a noun and an adjective has
undergone ellipsis of the noun, leaving only the adjective, which
retains the gender of the original noun.

Adjective	Noun	English meaning
amistoso (m)	partido	friendly (match)
comarcal (f)	carretera	minor road
coordinadora (f)	organización	coordinating body
eliminatoria (f)	prueba	eliminator
empresariales (m pl)	estudios	business studies
exteriores (m)	ministerio de asuntos	Ministry of Foreign Affairs
filial (f)	compañía/empresa	subsidiary
inmobiliaria (f)	agencia	estate agent
interior (m)	ministerio del	Ministry of the Interior
Internacional (f)	asociación	the (Socialist) International
legislativas (f pl)	elecciones	parliamentary elections
móvil (m)	teléfono	mobile
multinacional (f)	compañía	multinational
mundial (m)	campeonato	world championship
municipales (f pl)	elecciones	local elections
nacional (f)	carretera	major road
patronal (f)	asociación	employers' organization
plenaria (f)	asamblea	plenary session
pleno (m)	comité	full committee
portátil (m)	ordenador	portable/laptop computer
presidenciales (f pl)	elecciones	presidential elections
tabacalera (f)	compañía	tobacco company

21.6   Words of varying gender

arte	Masculine in its meaning of *individual art* (**el arte precolombiano, los artes de dibujar y de escribir**) but feminine in its collective plural *the Arts* (**las bellas artes**).
dote	Masculine or feminine (usually feminine) in singular *dowry*, but always feminine in plural *gifts* (**las dotes intelectuales**).
mar	Masculine in general (**el Mar Mediterráneo**), but sometimes feminine in R3, and always feminine in some set phrases, eg: la mar de + ADJ = *very* + ADJ (R1), alta mar *high seas*, mar gruesa *heavy sea*, hacerse a la mar *put to sea*, mar llena *high tide*
margen	Masculine in R1–2 but sometimes feminine in R3. In its meaning of *river bank* it is feminine.
masacre	Now generally feminine, though until recently it was often found as masculine.
sartén *fry(ing) pan*	Masculine in many areas of Latin America and Spain, although in standard Spanish it is feminine.

Both masculine and feminine

The following words are currently found as both masculine and feminine in all registers:

> cas(s)et(t)e *cassette*, doblez *deceitfulness*, interrogante *question*, lente *lens*, †linde *boundary*, maratón *marathon*, monzón *monsoon*, terminal *terminal*

21.7 Names of towns

Usually the gender is suggested by the form of the name:

> **en el Oviedo moderno**
> **en la Roma antigua**

But all towns can be thought of as feminine, since **ciudad** is feminine:

> **Madrid es bella**
> **la maravillosa Estambul**

However, **un**, **medio**, **todo** and **mismo** may be used in the masculine even with apparently 'feminine' towns:

> **todo Málaga**
> **el mismo Valencia**

NOTE: **El Barcelona**, **el Málaga**, etc, are the names of the towns' respective football teams.

21.8 Formation of masculine/feminine pairs

The commonest masculine/feminine pairs in Spanish are:

–o/–a	el †tío / la †tía *uncle/aunt*
–e/–a	el monje / la monja *monk/nun*
–or/–ora	el autor / la autora *author/authoress*

There are also one or two less common distinctive feminine endings, eg:

–esa	el abad / la abadesa *abbott/abbess*
–isa	el profeta / la profetisa *prophet/prophetess*
–riz	el actor / la actriz *actor/actress*

However, not all masculines have corresponding feminine forms:

> el/la hereje *heretic*
> el/la mártir *martyr*
> el/la testigo *witness*
> el/la cómplice *accomplice*
> el/la reo *convict*
> el/la edil *councillor*
> el/la cliente *customer*
> el/la cónyuge *spouse*
> el/la monarca *monarch*
> el/la pariente *relative*

el/la portavoz *spokesperson*
el/la suicida *suicide (victim)*
all nouns in **–ista**, eg: el/la violinista *violinist*

Problems occur in the following situations:

(a) when the feminine form is already in use with a distinct meaning:
el físico *physicist* / la física *physics*
el alcalde *mayor* / la alcaldesa *wife of the mayor*
el policía *policeman* / la policía *police*

(b) when there was no feminine form in existence:
ministro (*now also* ministra) *minister*
presidente (*now also* presidenta) *president*
cónsul (la cónsul *now used*) *consul*
agente (la agente *now used*) *agent*
piloto (la piloto *now used*) *pilot*

As women have taken on new rôles in society, Spanish has had to find new feminines, and many of these are by no means firmly established. The feminine form of professional nouns is now regularly used to denote women working in those professions. For example, **médica** means *woman doctor* and not *doctor's wife* (though **la médico** is still preferred); **alcaldesa** means *woman mayor* and not exclusively *mayor's wife*; **abogada** means *woman lawyer* and not *lawyer's wife*; and **la policía** is now regularly used to mean *the policewoman* as well as *the police*. But there is hesitation, particularly in R3. Margaret Thatcher, the British Prime Minister in the 1980s, was both **la primer ministro** and **la primera ministra** in the press (mainly the latter). Difficulties in category (a) above can be resolved by reinforcements, eg **una mujer policía** *policewoman*; and this may extend to other categories too, eg **una (mujer) candidata**.

The following are now accepted as female forms of the noun given, ie in the sense of 'female X':

alcaldesa *mayor*, árbitra *referee*, cacica *local boss*, candidata *candidate*, †catedrática *professor*, clienta *client*, diputada *member of Parliament*, jefa *head*, reportera *reporter*, sastra *tailor*, senadora *senator*, sirvienta *servant*

On the other hand, **el modisto** enjoyed some popularity as the masculine of **la modista**, *fashion designer*, but **el modista** now seems to be preferred.

21.9 Family relations and titles

With nouns denoting titles and family relations, a masculine plural in Spanish may correspond to a masculine and feminine pair, or to a 'genderless' plural in English:

¿Cuántos hijos tienes?
How many children (= sons *and* daughters) have you got?
los duques de Alba
the Duke and Duchess of Alba
los Reyes Católicos
the Catholic Monarchs (= Queen Isabel and King Fernando)

21.10 The neuter

The demonstratives and the third-person pronoun have a distinctive 'neuter' form: **esto**, **eso**, **aquello**; **ello**, **lo**. They are *always* used to refer to a proposition or general idea, *never* to a noun.

Contrast:

Un pacto social resulta casi imprescindible. Por ello, . . .
A social compact is almost essential. Because of this . . .

BUT

Lo he hecho por él
I've done it for him

Eso de no tener dinero me sorprendió
That business of not having any money surprised me

BUT

Nuestra idea es ésa
That is our idea

The definite article also has a 'neuter' form which is used *with adjectives only*, similarly to denote a general idea. Contrast:

Lo más difícil fue escapar
The most difficult thing was to escape

BUT

El último ejemplo fue el más difícil
The last example was the most difficult

21.11 Homonyms distinguished by gender

A number of Spanish nouns are both masculine and feminine, but have a different, though usually related, meaning according to gender.

(a) The feminine noun is collective, the masculine individual

	f	m
batería	battery (of guns); set (of lights); footlights; percussion section of orchestra; kitchen utensils	drummer (in band)
centinela	guard, watch (body)	sentry (individual)
defensa	defence (gen)	(full)back (football)
escolta	escort (body)	escort (individual)
†**guardia**	guard (body), custody	guard (individual), policeman
policía	police	policeman (but see **21.8**)

(b) The feminine noun is concrete, the masculine noun is a person or thing with an associated metaphorical function

	f	m
bestia	beast; uncouth woman (R1)	uncouth man, brute (R1)
cabeza	head	head of organization, leader
calavera	skull	madcap; good for nothing
†**cámara**	camera	cameraman
cava	(act of) digging; cellar	cava (sparkling wine)
caza	hunt	fighter plane
cura	cure	minister (having 'cure' of souls)
espada	sword	swordsman, matador
†**facha**	appearance, look (R1–2)	fascist (term of abuse) (R1)
génesis	origin	Book of Genesis
guia	guidebook	guide (person)
mañana	morning	future
meta	goal (= objective)	goalkeeper
pareja	couple (of people); female partner	male partner
recluta	recruitment	recruit
reserva	reserve (abstract); female reserve	male reserve; wine aged for at least three years
vigía	watchtower, female lookout	watchman, male lookout

(c)   Others

	f	m
canal	pipe	canal; channel
†**capital**	capital city (national or provincial)	financial capital
†**central**	head office; (telephone) exchange; **central hidroeléctrica/nuclear** = hydroelectric/nuclear power station	centre forward, central defender (football)
cólera	anger (R3)	cholera
†**coma**	comma	coma
cometa	kite	comet
corriente	flow, current, draught, course	current month
corte	(royal) court: **la Corte madrileña** = Madrid; **las Cortes** = Spanish Parliament	cut (gen), (power) cut
editorial	publishing house	lead article
fantasma	bogey	ghost
†**final**	final (match)	end (of street, etc)
frente	forehead	front, front part; (battle, political) front
granuja	grape seed	urchin, rogue
hincha	ill-will, grudge	supporter (sport)
†**moral**	ethics; morale	mulbery tree
†**orden**	order, command; military/religious order, eg **la Orden de Calatrava**	order, arrangement (eg **orden alfabético** alphabetical order); (civil) order (eg **las fuerzas del orden** the forces of law and order); field, style (eg **el orden dórico** Doric order)
ordenanza	ordinance, decree	office boy
†**panda**	gang	panda
†**parte**	part	report (eg **el parte meteorológico** the weather forecast)
†**pendiente**	slope	earring
†**pez**	pitch, tar	fish (alive)
†**radio**	radio	radius, spoke (of wheel); radium
	NOTE: **Radio** = radio is usually masculine in Am.	
†**vocal**	vowel	member of committee

21.12   Problem genders

The gender of the following words is especially liable to confusion by English learners.

(a)   Words ending in **-e**

m		f	
el auge	climax, boom	**la base**	base, basis
†**el avance**	advance	**la catástrofe**	catastrophe
el bache	pothole	**la élite**	élite
el balance	balance (accounting); assessment; result	**la gripe**	flu
el calambre	cramp	**la hélice**	propeller; helix
el cauce	(river) bed, course	**la higiene**	hygiene
el conclave OR **el cónclave**	conclave	**la índole**	disposition
†**el declive**	slope, incline	**la mole**	mass, bulk
el desmadre	chaos (R1)	**la pirámide**	pyramid
el eclipse	eclipse	**la pose**	pose
el enchufe	plug; contacts, influence	**la prole**	children, offspring (R1)
el enclave	enclave	**la sangre**	blood
el fraude	fraud	**la sede**	seat (of government), see (ecclesiastical)
el límite	limit	**la tilde**	tilde; written accent mark
el peine	comb	**la variable**	variable
el postre	dessert BUT **a la postre** (R3) in the end		
el romance	ballad; Romance (language)		
el síndrome	syndrome (and hence **el SIDA** AIDS)		
el timbre	bell; stamp, seal		
el tomate	tomato		

(b)   Words ending in **-al**

m		f	
el cereal	cereal	†**la cal**	lime
el zarzal	bramble, thicket	†**la central**	power station; (telephone) exchange
		las credenciales	credentials
		la digital	foxglove; digitalis
		la espiral	spiral
		la filial	subsidiary company
		la inicial	initial letter
		la multinacional	multinational company
		la postal	postcard
		la sal	salt
		la señal	sign
		la sucursal	branch (office)

(c) Words ending in **-ante** and **-ente**

m		f	
el componente	component	la constante	constant
el paciente	patient	la mente	mind
		la patente	patent
		la simiente	seed
		†la vertiente	slope
		la vacante	vacancy

(d) Words ending in **-z**

m		f	
el aprendiz	apprentice	la avestruz	ostrich
el cáliz	chalice; calyx	la coz	kick
el lápiz	pencil	†la faz	face, surface
el matiz	hue, shade	la hoz	sickle; gorge
†el pez	fish (alive)	la lombriz	worm
el regaliz	liquorice	la perdiz	partridge
		la tez	complexion

(e) A number of feminine words

la armazón	frame, framework; in Am = shelves, bookcase
la bilis	bile
la cárcel	prison
la circular	circular
la col	cabbage
la crin	horse's mane
la diabetes OR la diábetes	diabetes
la flor	flower
la metrópoli	metropolis
la miel	honey
la sien	temple (part of head)
la tos	cough
la tribu	tribe

There are also a number of other words with unpredictable endings, although once the ending is known the gender is obvious.

(f) English *-ive* corresponds to Spanish **-ivo** or **-iva**

la alternativa	alternative
la defensiva	defensive
la iniciativa	initiative
la misiva	missive
la negativa	negative, refusal
la ofensiva	offensive
BUT	
el objetivo	objective
NOTE ALSO:	
los preparativos	preparations

(g) English *-er* corresponds to Spanish **-or** or **-ora**

There is a good deal of variation in Spanish in the naming of new gadgets:

el aspirador / la aspiradora	vacuum cleaner
el batidor / la batidora	whisk
el computador (Pen) / **la computadora** (Mex)	computer
el contestador	answering machine
la freidora	deep-fat fryer
la lavadora	washing machine
el secador	hair dryer
BUT **la secadora**	tumble-dryer
el tostador / la tostadora	toaster

(h) Others

la característica	characteristic
la década	decade
la herramienta	tool
la paradoja	paradox
la sílaba	syllable

22 Number

22.1 Formation of plurals

(a) Nouns and adjectives ending in an unstressed vowel or stressed **e**, **o** or **u** add **-s**, eg:

    libro / **libros**, bueno / **buenos**
    carta / **cartas**, inglesa / **inglesas**
    estudiante (m/f) / **estudiantes**, triste / **tristes**
    pie (m) / **pies**
    bici (f) / **bicis**
    dominó/dominós
    tribu (f) / **tribus**

(b) Nouns and adjectives ending in a consonant (including y) add **-es**, eg:

    pared (f) / **paredes**
    cortés / **corteses**
    árbol (m) / **árboles**
    español / **españoles**
    rey (m) / **reyes**

(c) Nouns and adjectives ending in a stressed **-á**, **-í** or **-ú** have traditionally added **-es**, eg:

    bajá (m) / **bajáes**
    rubí (m) / **rubíes**
    marroquí / **marroquíes**
    esquí (m) / **esquíes**
    hindú / **hindúes**
    zulú / **zulúes**

but nowadays many such words simply add **-s**, eg:

    sofá (m) / **sofás**
    mamá (f) / **mamás**
    papá (m) / **papás**

NOTE: in the formation of plurals the place of the stress and the sound of the final consonant of the singular remain the same, and the spelling must reflect this, eg:

virgen (f) / **vírgenes**

lápiz (m) / **lápices**

(d)   Compound nouns

The plurals of compound nouns generally follow the above rules when the noun is a word in its own right, eg:

la bocacalle / **las bocacalles**

el altavoz / **los altavoces**

But in noun + noun groups which consist of two separate words, only the *first* noun pluralizes:

el coche patrulla / **los coches** patrulla

la fecha tope / **las fechas** tope

Exceptions

(a)   Nouns ending in unstressed vowel + **s** have no distinctive plural form, eg:

la crisis / **las crisis**

el lunes / **los lunes**

el virus / **los virus**

(b)   Family names optionally add **-s** or **-es** apart from those ending in **-s** or **-z**, which never do, eg:

los Moreno OR los Morenos

los Pérez

los Galmés

(c)   Some Anglicisms have the English plural form (though usage is rapidly changing in this area), eg:

el camping / **los campings**

el gángster / **los gángsters**

el póster / **los pósters**

el récord / **los récords**

el slip / **los slips**

el stand / **los stands**

BUT

el club / **los clubs** (R1–2) / **clubes** (R2–3)

el slogan / **los slogans** OR **slóganes**

See also **Chapter 13**.

(d)   One or two learned nouns which derive from Latin formulae have no distinctive plural form, eg:

el déficit / **los déficit**

el ítem / **los ítem**

el superávit / **los superávit**

el ultimátum / **los ultimátum**

(e)   One or two nouns have stress on different syllables in singular and plural:

el carácter / **los caracteres**

el régimen / **los regímenes**

el espécimen / **los especímenes**

22.2   Some Spanish plurals which correspond to English singulars

las agujetas	stiffness (of limbs)
por los aires	through the air
las algas	seaweed
las andas (sg in Am)	stretcher, bier, platform for religious tableaux
los aplausos	applause
†la(s) barba(s)	beard
las bodas	wedding
los cascotes / los escombros	rubble
los celos	jealousy
los conocimientos (also in sg)	knowledge
los consejos	advice
(los) Correos	Post Office
las cosquillas	tickling
con creces	with interest (financial), abundantly (gen)
los cubiertos	cutlery/silverware
los datos	information, data
los deberes	homework
¡Buenos días!, etc	Good morning!
las diligencias	procedure
los efectivos	effective force available (military)
las enaguas	petticoat
los escarceos (amorosos)	affair
a mis expensas, a expensas de	at my expense, at the expense of
las fuerzas	strength
los funerales (also in sg)	funeral
†los honorarios	fee
los informes	information
los ingresos	income
los intereses	interest (financial)
las investigaciones	research
las municiones	ammunition
las Navidad(es) / ¡Felices Navidades!	Christmas / Merry Christmas!
las nieves (R3)	snow
los pertrechos	gear; ammunition
las precipitaciones	rainfall
hacer †progresos	to make progress
los remordimientos (also in sg)	remorse
los restos	remains
las tinieblas	darkness

los transportes (públicos)	(public) transport (ie the transport system)
● el Ministerio de Transportes	
BUT	
● el transporte (de las mercancías)	transport (= act of transporting) of goods
los trapicheos	scheming, esp political manoeuvring
en vísperas de	on the eve of

22.3   Some Spanish singulars which correspond to English plurals

el alicate (ALSO los alicates)	pliers
la braga (ALSO las bragas)	panties, knickers
el calzón (ALSO los calzones)	shorts (Pen); trousers (US pants) (Am)
el calzoncillo (ALSO los calzoncillos)	pants (US underpants, shorts)
la escalera (ALSO las escaleras)	stairs
la estadística	set of statistics; statistics as a subject
la gente (ALSO las gentes (R3))	people
la malla (ALSO las mallas (R1))	tights (ALSO = bathing costume/suit in Am)
el pantalón (ALSO los pantalones)	trousers (US pants)
†el pijama	pyjamas
la pinza (ALSO las pinzas)	pincers (sg ALSO = peg; claw)
la ropa	clothes
la táctica	tactics
la tropa (ALSO las tropas)	troops
el vaquero	jeans

NOTE ALSO: **la física** (*physics*), **la política** (*politics*), etc, which appear to be plural (though in fact they are syntactically singular).

In R1, Spanish often uses a singular to refer to a great number: **mucho coche** *a lot of cars*, **tanta vaca** *so many cows*.

22.4   Number concord

Collective nouns

Expressions involving collective nouns are susceptible to some variation in usage:

Collective noun + de + plural noun

> **Es la primera vez que se reúne(n) un número de especialistas**
> **Un grupo de profesores está(n) preparando un estudio**
> **La mayor parte / La mayoría de las publicaciones está(n) escrita(s) en castellano**
> **La mitad de los chicos está(n) a favor de la reforma**

The higher the register, the more likely is the use of the singular in such constructions, but the plural seems now to be usual in R2.

Collective noun + de + singular noun

> **La mayoría / El †resto, etc de la gente dice que . . .**
> Here a plural verb is not acceptable, even in R3.

Noun – ser – noun

Ser agrees in number with a following plural noun:
> **El problema son los estudiantes**
> **El ejemplo más frecuente citado son los numerosos y múltiples avances tecnológicos derivados de la II Guerra Mundial**
> **La revolución eran simplemente unos festivos fuegos artificiales daneses**

23 Word order

Spanish is often said to have an extremely flexible word order. It is important to realize, however, that while there is a good deal of freedom which is manipulated for stylistic reasons, differences in word order very often correspond to important differences in meaning.

23.1 Subject and verb

In a Spanish sentence, the first element is usually the 'topic', ie what is already being talked about, while the remaining material is the new information being communicated. This can be very clearly seen in answers to questions which ask for new information:

–**¿Cómo reaccionó tu padre?**

–**Mi padre se puso contento.**

(**Mi padre** is the topic; **se puso contento** is the new information.)

–**¿Quién lo dijo?**

–**Lo dijo Enrique**.

(**Lo dijo** is the topic; **Enrique** is the new information.)

When the verb precedes the subject, therefore, more emphasis is laid on the subject. This order is especially frequent in the following contexts, where the subject is typically the new information.

(a) When the subject is much longer than the verb or verb phrase:

Durante estos siglos se fueron formando las lenguas castellana, catalana y galaico–portuguesa

The Castilian, Catalan and Gallaeco-Portuguese languages were formed during these centuries

(b) With verbs such as **faltar**, **sobrar**, **gustar**, **doler**, **encantar**, etc, which do not take a direct object:

Me sobra dinero

I've more than enough money

Nos hace falta dinero

We need money

Me encanta el cuadro

I love the picture

(c) When a plural subject is used without an article; these sentences are 'existential' in nature (compare the word order with the 'existential'

verb **hay/había**, etc: **Había cosas que nunca se mencionaban** =
There were things that were never mentioned):

> **Vivían lobos en el bosque**
> Wolves used to live in the wood (= There were wolves living
> in the wood)
> **Aquí se venden manzanas**
> Apples are sold here (= There are apples being sold here)

(d) With non-finite verbal constructions:

> **de haberlo sabido antes tu madre**
> if your mother had known beforehand
> **Procesado el sargento que mató a un soldado** (newspaper
> headline)
> The sergeant who killed a soldier [is] on trial

23.2 Subject, verb and object

The verb may come first according to the principles outlined in the
preceding section. Objects may also precede subject and verb, though
only one object at a time can be moved in this way, and generally a
corresponding pronoun must be used with the verb:

> **El atentado se lo atribuyó a la banda terrorista**
> The attack was attributed to the terrorist group
> **Al hombre le vino la idea de . . .**
> The idea of . . . came to the man
> **A mi hijo de dos años le picó una abeja**
> My two-year-old son was stung by a bee

Objects involving negative, indefinite and demonstrative pronouns and
tanto may also precede the verb, especially in R3:

> **el proyecto que tantos problemas nos ha planteado**
> the project which has caused us so many problems
> **Pero quienes se hallaban cerca de la explosion nada oyeron,
> al principio**
> But those who were near the explosion heard nothing at first
> **Todo eso, y algunas cosas más, le contó el sargento hace
> unos días a Santiago López**
> The sergeant said this, and a few more things, to Santiago López a
> few days ago

In R1 the fundamental tendency to place the 'topic' of a sentence first
can result in quite complex word orders:

> **Ahora, yo esa palabra todavía, su definición exacta, no la sé**
> Now I don't know the exact meaning of that word

(Cf R2–3: **Ahora, todavía, no se la definición exacta de esa
palabra**)

> **Desde un punto de vista . . . principios digamos . . . yo es
> que no estoy plenamente convencida que a la persona
> que le sacan el corazón, al donante, no creo que esté
> muerta . . .**

Let's say that from the point of view of principle, I'm not fully
convinced that the person whose heart they're taking out, the
donor, I don't think that person's dead . . .
(Cf R2–3: **Digamos que desde el punto de vista de principios,
yo no estoy plenamente convencida de que esté muerta la
persona a la que sacan el corazón, o sea el donante**)

23.3   Verb, objects and adverb

The adverb usually immediately precedes or immediately follows the
verb in Spanish, though it may, as in English, also follow the object:

**He leído con interés la noticia/He leído la noticia con
interés**
I have read the news with interest
Si no me acuerdo mal/Si mal no me acuerdo
If I remember rightly

23.4   Noun and adjective

23.4.1   One adjective

There are some adjectives in Spanish which have slightly different
meanings according to whether they precede or follow the noun. The
chief of these are:

†**antiguo**	costumbres antiguas	*old customs*
	un antiguo presidente	*a former president*
†**bárbaro**	los soldados bárbaros	*the Barbarian soldiers*
	los bárbaros soldados	*the barbaric soldiers*
cierto	indicios ciertos	*sure signs*
	cierta falta de confianza	*a certain lack of confidence*
	ciertas personas	*certain people*
†**diferente**	libros diferentes	*different books*
	diferentes libros	*several books*
†**distinto**	ideas distintas	*distinct ideas*
	distintas ideas	*various ideas*
†**grande**	una casa grande	*a big house*
	un gran escritor	*a great writer*
†**medio**	el hombre medio	*the man in the street*
	la clase media	*the middle class*
	el dedo medio	*the middle finger*
	medio litro	*half a litre*

mismo	Roma misma OR la misma Roma (*note the article*)	*Rome herself*
	su mismo pueblo OR su pueblo mismo	*his very village*
	el mismo sentido	*the same sense*
nuevo	una canción nueva	*a new(ly composed) song*
	nos trasladamos a una nueva casa	*we moved to another house*
†**pobre**	un barrio pobre	*a poor district*
	¡Pobre chico!	*Poor (= unfortunate) boy!*
propio	en defensa propia	*in self-defence*
	tiene casa propia OR tiene su propia casa	*he has his own house*
	sus propias palabras	*his very words*
	obra del propio Unamuno	*a work of Unamuno himself*
puro	la verdad pura	*the unadulterated truth*
	de pura envidia	*through sheer envy*
simple	un corazón simple	*a simple heart*
	de simple interés	*out of mere interest*
único	Eres una mujer única	*You're a unique woman*
	el único problema	*the only problem*
varios	razones muy varias	*very varied reasons*
	varias personas	*several people*

More complicated is the situation with other adjectives. Most adjectives in Spanish may be placed before or after the noun, and there is a growing preference among Spanish speakers for the preceding position. Nevertheless, there is usually a slight difference in meaning associated with different adjective positions.

Factors involving a preference for a following position

(a) An adjective following a noun usually has a 'distinctive' overtone, a nuance which is often conveyed in English by contrastive stress, eg:

–¿Cómo es tu casa?
What's your house like?
–Es una casa pequeña
It's a *small* house
BUT
Vivía en una pequeña casa cerca de la catedral
I lived in a small house near the cathedral
(here, nearness to the cathedral is the more 'distinctive' property)
Note the difference between the following sentences:
Las hojas secas se cayeron
The *dry* leaves fell (implies that the others didn't)

Las secas hojas se cayeron

The dry leaves fell (all the leaves were dry, and all fell)

The difference between preceding and following position is not always clearcut, however, as in the following examples:

Ayer dimos un paseo muy largo

We went for a very long walk yesterday

(may imply that we don't usually go for *long* walks)

Ayer dimos un largo paseo por el campo

We went for a long walk in the countryside yesterday

(that it was in the countryside is the 'distinctive' information; a walk in the countryside is normally long).

Some adjectives are always essentially 'distinctive' and rarely if ever precede the noun, except for a very special effect. Such adjectives typically denote nationality, membership of a political or religious group, colour, etc, eg:

la ejecutiva socialista

the socialist executive

de nacionalidad libanesa

of Lebanese nationality

vino tinto

red wine

However, for deliberate less 'distinctive' effect, even these may sometimes precede the noun, eg:

. . . apoyado contra la gris pared de una casa (C.-J. Cela)

leaning against the grey wall of a house

En mi propia casa estaban mis octogenarios padres

My 80-year-old parents were in my own house

Conversely, in some contexts an adjective cannot have a 'distinctive' value and must precede the noun, eg:

su admirable buen sentido

her admirable good sense (a person has only 'one' good sense)

tu adorable mujer

your adorable wife (a person has only one wife)

BUT

una mujer adorable

an *adorable* woman (as opposed to others)

(b) When a noun which has a very general meaning and an adjective which has a more specific (and hence more 'distinctive') meaning come together, the adjective tends to follow, eg:

la región craneal

the cranial region

el preso fugado

the escaped convict

dos puntos fundamentales

two fundamental points

un problema geométrico

a geometrical problem

Factors involving a preference for a preceding position

(a) When the adjective is an 'expected' attribute, eg:

un lamentable accidente
a lamentable accident
con enormes dificultades
with enormous difficulty

This usage is frequently employed for stylistic effect, eg:

El buque ofrece un esmerado servicio del que podemos disfrutar a lo largo de un maravilloso crucero de ocho inolvidables días (advertisement)
The ship offers high-class service which one can enjoy during a wonderful cruise of eight unforgettable days

It is extensively exploited in R3:

La feliz pareja pasó una agradable velada en un conocido restaurante
The happy couple spent a pleasant evening in a well-known restaurant
Las espontáneas y curiosas imágenes de los reyes de España
The spontaneous and curious pictures of the King and Queen of Spain

(b) When adjective and noun make a familiar or set phrase, eg:

los altos Alpes
the high Alps
un ligero aumento en el coste de la vida
a slight increase in the cost of living
su presunta responsabilidad
his presumed responsibility
el pasado mes de julio
last July
unas recientes declaraciones
recent statements

(c) Past participles which make reference back to something already mentioned:

la citada/mencionada medida
dichos individuos

NOTE: The use of such words in Spanish, while typical of R3, is much less formal than the corresponding English words *aforementioned* and *said*.

(d) A preceding position seems to be generally favoured for **difícil**, eg:

La extensión real de las propiedades es de difícil precisión
It is difficult to be precise about the true extent of the properties

More than one adjective

There are many possibilities available, but the rules for one adjective still basically hold. The most 'distinctive' adjectives will be placed after and furthest away from the noun, eg:

la política contemporánea mejicana
contemporary *Mexican* politics
la política mejicana contemporánea
contemporary Mexican politics

In cases where one or more of the adjectives may be placed before or after the noun, very subtle differences are possible. The adjective(s) which follow(s) the noun always has/have the more 'distinctive' value. The English translations given convey something of the differences of emphasis.

una muñeca manoseada y rota
a *worn, broken* doll
una manoseada y rota muñeca
a worn, broken *doll*
una manoseada muñeca rota
a *broken* worn doll
una rota muñeca manoseada
a *worn* broken doll

23.5 Numerals, quantifiers and *otro*

Numbers, ordinal numerals (**primero, segundo**, etc) and expressions of quantity normally precede the noun: **dos amigos, el sexto piso, menos dinero**. Note the order of these elements with respect to one another, which is sometimes different from the order of the corresponding English words:

los dos primeros/últimos años (more common) or **los primeros/últimos dos años**
the first/last two years
otros muchos chicos
many other young people
otros pocos chicos
a few other young people
otros tantos chicos
just as many other young people
otros dos chicos
two other / another two young people

23.6 Fixed order expressions

The fixed order of some Spanish expressions is different from that of the corresponding English expression:

de (los) pies a (la) cabeza = from head to toe
tarde o temprano = sooner or later
NOTE ALSO the expression of dates:
el martes 13 de setiembre = Tuesday the 13th of September

24 Prepositions

24.1 *a*

24.1.1 Basic meanings

> (a) *destination, direction; generally corresponds to English* to
> **Voy a la costa**
> I'm going to the coast
> BUT NOTE:
> **Ayer llegamos a Madrid**
> Yesterday we arrived in (= got to) Madrid
> **Cayó al suelo**
> It fell on (= to) the ground
> (b) *point in time* (see **24.1.2** below)

The preposition **a** also introduces the indirect object of the verb and the 'personal' direct object (see **24.1.9** below).

24.1.2 **a** in time expressions

Spanish **a** corresponds to English *in, at, on* in many time expressions. Note, however, that there are several time expressions which require no preposition; eg: **los sábados** *on Saturdays*, **el día quince** *on the fifteenth*, **el lunes pasado** *last Monday*. See also **en (24.8)**.

a las dos de la madrugada	at two in the morning
a(l) mediodía	at noon
a (la) medianoche	at midnight
a (las) primeras/altas horas de la noche	in the early hours of the morning
a última hora	at the last moment
al día siguiente / al otro día	on the following day
a la mañana siguiente	on the following morning
a la noche/mañana/tarde	tonight/tomorrow morning/this afternoon

a principios/comienzos del/de (R1) año/mes / de la semana	at the beginning of the year/month/week
a mitad del año	half-way through the year
a mediados de(l) año/mes	in the middle of the year/month
a finales de(l) año/mes	at the end of the year/month
a media mañana/tarde/ semana	in the middle of the morning/ afternoon/week
a los diecinueve años	at nineteen years of age
a los cinco minutos de llegar / haber llegado	five minutes after arriving
al poco rato	a little later
al mismo tiempo / a la vez	at the same time
a la par que	at the same time as
a corto/largo/medio plazo	in the short/long/medium term
trabajar a tiempo completo/parcial	to work full/part time
a deshora/destiempo	at the wrong time
a tiempo	in time
a primera vista	at first sight

24.1.3 **a** expressing rate

día a día (see also **tras, 24.16**)	day by day
uno a uno (ALSO de uno en uno)	one by one
paso a paso	step by step
a docenas/millares	by the dozen/thousand
dos veces a la semana (see also **por, 24.13.4**)	twice a week
a diario	daily
a razón de cinco por persona	at the rate of five per person
trabajo a destajo	piecework
¿A cuánto se vende el coche? (= ¿Cuánto es el coche?)	How much is the car being sold for?
a sesenta pesetas el kilo	at 60 pesetas a kilo
lo vende al litro (R1) (ALSO por litros (R2–3))	she sells it by the litre
vender al por menor/mayor	to sell retail/wholesale
tenemos libros a granel	we've got tons of books (often suggests disorder)
la cosecha ha sido a granel	there's been an abundant crop
a (una velocidad de) cuarenta km/h	at (a speed of) twenty-five mph
un empate a cero / a un gol	nil–nil/one-all draw

24.1.4   **a** expressing manner

a la española / a lo español /	in the Spanish style
al estilo español	

NOTE: **A lo español** is more abstract than **a la española** and is higher register.

a mi manera	in my own way
a la manera de X	in X's way, after the fashion of X
BUT: **de una manera/forma / de un modo elegante**	
pagar al contado	to pay cash
a mi costa / a toda costa	at my expense / at all costs
a la inversa / al revés	the opposite way, vice versa
a mi juicio/entender/	in my opinion
parecer / modo de ver	
BUT: **en mi opinión**	
†**a la larga**	in the long run
tomar algo a la ligera	to take sth lightly
a la perfección	perfectly, to perfection
a la moda (ALSO **de moda**)	in fashion
matar a cuchilladas	to stab to death

24.1.5   Adverbial idioms with **a**

There are many adverbial idioms of manner in Spanish formed on the patterns **a** + singular noun, **a** + plural noun (without an article) and **a** + feminine plural adjective or noun. Some of the most common are:

estar a sus anchas	to be at ease
Le mataron a balazos	They shot him dead
Se lo comió a bocado	She gulped it down by the mouthful
Salió a borbotones	It flooded out
a brazo perdido	fearlessly
a la buena de Dios	randomly, carelessly
a caballo (**de a caballo** in Am R1)	on horseback
Llueve a cántaros	It's pouring with rain
a ciegas	blindly
a ciencia cierta	for sure
estar al corriente	to be informed
a la corta o †**a la larga**	sooner or later
Le metieron a empellones	They pushed him through
Se abrió paso a empujones	He pushed his way through
a escondidas	covertly

a espaldas de uno	behind sb's back
a la fuerza	whether you, we, etc, like it or not
a gatas	on all fours
vivir a lo grande	to live like a king
estar a gusto	to be at ease
Entró a hurtadillas	He crept in
a instancias de (R3)	at the request of
un ataque a mano armada	an armed attack
a medias	partly
a lo mejor	perhaps
llorar a moco tendido (R1)	to cry one's eyes out
a los ojos de uno	in the eyes of sb
a oscuras	in the dark
La echaron a patadas / a puntapiés	They kicked her out
tomar a pecho	to take to heart
a duras penas	with great difficulty
a pie (de a pie in Am R1)	on foot
dormir a pierna suelta	to sleep soundly
saber a punto fijo	to know for certain
Le derribó a puñetazos	He hit him until he fell
a quemarropa	point-blank
a rajatabla	completely, strictly
a regañadientes	unwillingly
a sabiendas	knowingly
a solas	alone
Avanzó a tientas	He groped his way forward
Se enfrentaron a tiros	They shot at each other
a todo correr	at full speed
a todo gas (R1)	flat out, at full speed
a todo meter	with great intensity
a tontas y a locas	haphazardly
a trancas y barrancas	with great difficulty
a trechos	occasionally
a troche y moche	anyhow, helter–skelter
a trompicones	in fits and starts
un comunista a ultranza	an out–and–out communist
luchar a ultranza	to fight tooth and nail
a vista de pájaro	with a bird's-eye view
a voz en cuello/grito	at the top of one's voice

24.1.6 **a** expressing position

en (24.8) is the preposition used for the general expression of position, but **a** appears in many set phrases, eg:

caer al agua	to fall in the water

NOTE: in standard Spanish, **en** is generally used with verbs like **caer** if the 'destination' is uppermost in the speaker's mind; however, **a** is more commonly used in Am R1.

al aire libre	in the open air
al alcance de	within reach of
a bordo de	on board
a medio camino / a mitad de camino	half-way there
al/en contacto con	in contact with
al cuello	around his/her neck
llevar a cuestas	to carry on one's back
a la derecha	on the right
jugar a domicilio	to play at home (football, etc.)
a escala internacional	on an international scale
Se miró al espejo	He looked at himself in the mirror
al fondo de	at the bottom/end of
BUT **en el fondo** basically	
al hombro	on/over his/her shoulder
a hombros	on his/her back
a la intemperie	in the open air
a la izquierda	on the left
al otro lado	on the other side
a lo lejos	in the distance
a la luz de	in the light of (lit and fig)
a (R2–3) / **en** (R2) **la mesa**	at the table
a nivel literario	on the literary level
a orillas (R3) **del mar / del río**	at the seashore / by the river
NOTE: **En las orillas** = R2.	
tocar una melodía al (ALSO **en el**) **piano**	to play a tune on the piano
al raso	in the open air
varios kilómetros a la redonda	several kilometres around
a la sombra	in the shade
estar al teléfono	to be on the telephone
BUT **llamar por teléfono**	to telephone, to call (by telephone)

NOTE ALSO: the general expression of distance from something – **estar a (dos kilómetros) de (la Universidad)** to be (two kilometres) from (the University)

24.1.7 **a** expressing instrument

hecho a mano/máquina	made by hand/machine
un cuadro al óleo	an oil–painting
un dibujo a pluma/lápiz	a drawing in pen/pencil

24.1.8 Complex prepositional expressions with **a**

a la altura de	on the same latitude as (lit); abreast of (fig)
● **estar a la altura de las circunstancias**	● to rise to the occasion
a/por causa de	because of
a favor de	in favour of
a fuerza de	by dint of, by force of, by means of
● **Le convencí a fuerza de argumentos**	● I convinced him with persuasive arguments
a guisa de (R3)	by way of
al lado de	by the side of
a lo largo de	along
a nivel de	at the level of
a partir de	starting from (a point in time)
†**a pesar de**	in spite of
a raíz de	immediately after; as a result of, because of
a título de	by way of (eg excuse)
● **a título personal**	in my personal opinion
en lo concerniente a / tocante a / (con) respecto a	with regard to
BUT **respecto de**	
junto (invariable) **a**	close to, next to

24.1.9 'Personal' **a**

The preposition **a** precedes the direct object when the object refers to:

(a) a person, eg:
>**Yo quisiera ver al director**
>I would like to see the director
>**A mí no me interesa**
>It doesn't interest me
>**No vi a nadie**
>I didn't see anyone

(b) a personalized group, eg:
>**Los soldados defienden a la nación**
>The soldiers defend the nation
>**Van a reforzar al gobierno**
>They're going to strengthen the government

No haga el error de juzgar a Cuba
Don't make the mistake of judging Cuba

(c)   an animal which engenders affection, eg:

Llamó al perro
She called the dog

(d)   something 'personified', eg:

Llamó en vano a la muerte
He called in vain on death

a is also used to resolve ambiguity. In the following usages it often has a rôle in resolving the potential ambiguities caused by the relative freedom of Spanish word order:

Por fin ha vencido el joven su pasión por el juego
The young man has finally conquered his passion for gambling

Por fin ha vencido al joven su pasión por el juego
The young man's passion for gambling has finally conquered him

Se vio el hombre en el espejo
The man saw himself in the mirror

Se vio al hombre en el espejo
The man was seen in the mirror

But it may be used with objects of other kinds to resolve ambiguity, especially with verbs which express a relation of order of some kind, eg:

El silencio sigue al ruido
Silence follows the noise

El coche alcanzó a la bicicleta
The car overtook the bicycle

The 'personal' **a** is not used:

(a)   when a person referred to is treated not as an individual human being, but as a thing or a commodity, eg:

Los romanos arrojaban (a) los cristianos a las fieras
The Romans used to throw the Christians to the wild animals

Prefiero (a) Unamuno
I prefer Unamuno (as an author rather than as an individual)

NOTE: absence of **a** is more prevalent in R1; so strong is the association between a 'personal' object and the use of **a** that the **a** is often used in such cases in R2–3.

(b)   when an animal referred to does not engender affection, but is considered from the point of view of usefulness, or food, eg:

He comprado un caballo
I've bought a horse

Cogió un ratón
She caught a mouse

(c)   when a person referred to is not known and his or her function rather than 'personality' is being thought of, eg:

Espero un basurero
I'm waiting for a dustman (garbage-collector)

BUT:

Espero al basurero
I'm waiting for the dustman (garbage-collector)
Busco un médico que sepa curar a mi hijo
I'm looking for a doctor who can cure my son (any doctor will do)

BUT:

Busco a un médico que sabe curar a mi hijo
I'm looking for a doctor (who I already know of) who can cure my son

(d) sometimes when there is also a personal indirect object in the same sentence, since ambiguity might result, eg:

Presentó al director su hija María Amparo
She introduced her daughter María Amparo to the director

BUT NOTE:

Llevo a mis amigos a la estación
I'm taking my friends to the station

With this prepositional phrase there is no possibility of ambiguity.

The following verbs need special care in the use of **a** with their personal objects:

(a) tener

Tengo dos hermanos
I've got two brothers (OR a brother and sister)

BUT:

Tengo a mi esposa en la cama
I've got my wife (ill) in bed
Tuvo una hija
She had a daughter

BUT:

Tuvo a su hija hace seis meses
She gave birth to her daughter six months ago

(b) †querer

Quiere un hijo
He wants a son

BUT:

Quiere a su hijo
He loves his son

(c) perder

Este niño ha perdido su madre
This child has lost his mother

BUT:

Perdió a su hijo
She was the ruin of her son

24.2   *ante, delante de, antes de, antes que*

before *(position)*	**ante** face to face with, in the presence of; restricted to R3 in general meaning of 'before'; several fig usages	**delante de** before, in front of (gen and predominantly lit)
before *(time)*	**antes de** gen	**antes que** when a clause introduced by **antes que** is implied: note that pronouns following remain in the subject form (**yo**, **tú**, etc)

Compareció ante el capitán	He appeared before the captain
ante las circunstancias	in the circumstances
ante la posibilidad de	faced with the possibility of
ante todo	especially
delante de la casa	in front of the house
antes de las cuatro	before four o'clock
Lo hizo antes que yo (lo hiciera)	He did it before me (= before I did)

24.3   *bajo, debajo de*

Both **bajo** and **debajo de** have the basic meaning of *under.* **Bajo** tends to be restricted to R3 in its literal meaning, but appears in many set phrases in all registers with a figurative meaning.

dos (grados) bajo cero	two (degrees) below zero
bajo la batuta de	under the baton of
bajo la condición de que	on condition that
bajo control	under control
bajo cuerda	on the side, surreptitiously
bajo la custodia	in custody
bajo fianza	on bail
bajo la lluvia	in the rain
bajo el mando de	under the command of
bajo sus órdenes	at your command
bajo palabra	on sb's word
bajo pena de muerte	on pain of death
bajo ningún pretexto	on no account
bajo la protección de	under the protection of
bajo la recomendación de	on the recommendation of
bajo aquel rey	under that king

Debajo de is used in all registers with a predominantly literal meaning.

debajo de la mesa	under the table

24.4 *con*

24.4.1 Basic meanings

(a) association

café con leche
coffee with milk
una cartera con dinero
a wallet containing money

(b) instrument
Abrí la lata con un destornillador
I opened the can with a screwdriver

(c) cause
Estoy contento con usted
I'm pleased with you
Me cansé con tanto escribir
I got tired with writing so much

(d) with adjectives describing behaviour which affects someone else
amable con / para con (R3) **todos**
friendly towards everybody

24.4.2 **con** in complex prepositional expressions

con arreglo a la ley	in accordance with the law
con miras al futuro	with a view to the future
con motivo/objeto de escaparse	with the intention of escaping
con ocasión de	on the occasion of
con relación a	in relation to
(ALSO **en relación con**)	
(con) respecto a	with regard to
El barco salió (con) rumbo a Nueva York	The boat left for New York
con vistas a	with a view to

24.4.3 **con** expressing manner

con cabeza desnuda	bareheaded
con voz ronca	in a hoarse voice

con combines with many abstract nouns to create adverbial expressions, eg:

con claridad	clearly
con desagrado	with displeasure
con locura	madly
con sequedad	drily

NOTE: in Am R1 (especially Central American Spanish), **con** may replace **a**[10] or **a**, especially with verbs which take a personal direct object, eg:

Me presentó con el jefe [!]
He introduced me to the boss
¡Lléveme con un médico! [!]
Take me to a doctor!

24.5   *contra, en contra de*

These correspond to English *against* (lit and fig). **en contra de** is much more common than **contra** to denote the expression of contrary opinion.

Puso la silla contra la pared	She put the chair against the wall
un remedio contra la tos	a remedy for a cough
la lucha contra el enemigo	the struggle against the enemy
Las posibilidades son una contra diez	It's a ten to one chance
hablar/expresarse/pronunciarse en contra de una opinión	to speak / to express oneself against an opinion

NOTE: **contra** may have the meaning *near* in Am (especially Argentine Spanish); **¿contra qué? (= ¿para qué?)** is also an American usage.

24.6   *de*

24.6.1   Basic meanings

(a) possession; corresponds to English genitive ('s, s') or of
Esta casa es de mi padre
This house is my father's
una calle de Barcelona
a Barcelona street

(b) direction from; corresponds to English from
de Madrid a Segovia
from Madrid to Segovia
empezar de cero
to begin from nothing
NOTE ALSO: in time expressions –
de mañana en ocho días
in a week's time (= eight days from tomorrow)
and **de . . . en**, corresponding to English *from . . . to* –
de año en año
from year to year

de puerta en puerta
from door to door
de vez en cuando
from time to time

(c) origin (fig associated with (b))
Es de Caracas
He's from Caracas

(d) material from which something is made (again, fig associated with (b))
la estatua de mármol
the marble statue
NOTE ALSO:
Su dedicación hace de él un gran actor.
His dedication made (of) him a great actor.

---

*(e) introducing an agent (see also **por, 24.13.5**)*
Estaba cubierta de una lona
It was covered in/by a tarpaulin
manchado de sangre
bloodstained
Es amado de todos
He's loved by everyone
un cuento de García Márquez
a short story by García Márquez
This usage is found especially with past participles which would be
accompanied by **estar** (see **32.5**), but extends to others which
primarily express a mental state (the use of **por** indicating a
more active involvement by the agent).

(f) cause (esp with abstract nouns)
Murió de tristeza
He died of grief
Lloró de alegría
She cried out of / for happiness

(g) concern; corresponds to English about
No sé nada de eso
I don't know anything about that

(h) introducing a descriptive or specifying phrase

el chico del pelo largo	the long-haired boy
la casa de al lado	the house next door
sordo del oído izquierdo	deaf in his left ear
español de nacimiento	Spanish by birth
peluquero de profesión	a hairdresser by trade
un instrumento de percusión/cuerda/viento	a percussion/string/woodwind instrument

The phrase may indicate type, purpose or content:

un buque de (also **a** R1 Pen and R1–2 Am) **vapor**	a steamship
una máquina de escribir	a typewriter
una taza de té	a cup of tea

(i) linking nouns in apposition

la ciudad de Buenos Aires	the city of Buenos Aires
el bribón de mi hermano	my rogue of a brother

24.6.2 **de** in adverbial expressions of time

de antemano	beforehand
de día	by day
de inmediato	immediately
de joven	as a youngster
(muy) de mañana	(very early) in the morning
embarazada de tres meses	three months pregnant
de momento	for the moment
de niño	as a child
de noche	by night
estar de exámenes/regreso/ vacaciones	to be in the middle of exams / on the way back / on holiday

24.6.3 **de** in adverbial expressions of position

estar de pie	to be standing
estar de rodillas/hinojos (R3)	to be kneeling

24.6.4 **de** in expressions of price and measurement

un sello (Pen) / **una estampilla** (Am) **de (a) treinta pesetas/pesos**	a thirty-peseta/peso stamp
El precio del coche es de ocho mil dólares	The price of the car is eight thousand dollars
El aumento es del diez por ciento	The increase is 10 per cent
La distancia es de cien km	The distance is a hundred km
El peso es de cinco kilos	The weight is five kilos
más de diez (see **35.1**)	more than ten

24.6.5 **de** with professions

Hace de camarero	He works as a waiter
ejercer de gerente/	to work as a manager/presenter
presentador(a) (R3)	
Empezó de ayudante	She began as an assistant
See also **estar**, **meterse (32.9)**	

24.6.6 **de** in adverbial expressions of manner

de todas formas/maneras /	in any case
de todos modes	
(BUT: **en todo caso**)	
de cierto modo / de cierta	in a certain way
manera	
(BUT: **en cierto modo**)	in some way or other (see **24.8.5**)
NOTE: **la manera como (R1–2)**	the way in which Sara does it
/ en la que (R2–3) lo hace	
Sara	
vestido de luto/paisano/	dressed in mourning, in civilian
militar/marinero	clothes, in military naval
	uniform
La conozco de vista/nombre	I know her by sight/name
tirarse de cabeza / de pie	to dive, to jump (into the water)
(al agua)	
marcar de penalti/cabeza	to score from a penalty/header

24.6.7 Common idioms and expressions involving **de**

Me lo dio de balde	He gave it to me free
SEE ALSO **en balde (24.8.5)**	
caer de bruces	to fall on one's face
de buenas a primeras	suddenly
de costumbre	usually
de buena fe	in good faith
de buena/mala gana	willingly/unwillingly
de golpe	suddenly
de buen grado (R2–3)	willingly
mirar de hito en hito	to stare at
de improviso	unexpectedly
de un lado, . . . , de otro, . . .	on the one hand, . . . , on the other, . . .
Es de lejos el mejor	It's the best by a long way
de memoria	by heart, from memory
estar de moda	to be in fashion
de nuevo	again
de oídas	by hearsay

de oído	by ear
de ordinario	usually
estar abierto de par en par	to be wide open
venir de perillas	to come at an opportune moment
de pronto	suddenly
Me lo dieron de regalo	They gave it to me as a present
de repente	suddenly
Tengo tiempo de sobra	I've more than enough time
de un tirón	all in one movement
Lo bebió de un trago	He gulped it down in one mouthful
de trecho en trecho	occasionally
de veras/verdad	truly
estar de viaje	to be travelling
estar de visita	to be visiting

24.6.8 de expressing direction to or from

el camino de la ciudad	the way to the town
el tren de Valencia	the Valencia train (ie to Valencia)
el autocar procedente de Córdoba	the bus from Córdoba
de acá para allá (R1)	here and there
más acá de Salamanca	this side of Salamanca
más allá de Zamora	the other side of Zamora

24.6.9 'Grammatical' uses of de

(a) Before **que** with some verbs, adjectives and nouns (see **25.4** and **31.10**):

Me extraño de que no lo sepa
I'm surprised he doesn't know
Estoy seguro de que vendrá
I'm sure she will come
Pronto me di cuenta de que habían salido
I soon realized that they'd gone

NOTE: In R1, **de** is often omitted. In journalistic R3, on the other hand, **de** is sometimes erroneously used between a verb and a following que . . . (eg **se dice de que** ⏹); this is known as **dequeísmo**.

(b) In constructions involving adjectives meaning *easy* and *difficult*:

Este libro es muy difícil de leer (= Es muy difícil leer este libro)
This book is very difficult to read

(c) In superlative constructions:

el edificio más alto del mundo
the highest building in the world

24.6.10 Complex prepositions with **de**

acerca de	concerning
alrededor de	around
cerca de (cerca a Am R1)	near

ALSO: **el embajador cerca de la corte inglesa** — the ambassador to the English court

BUT NOTE: **junto a** (p 182) and the adjectives **cercano a**, **contiguo a** and **inmediato a**. The adjective **vecino** is found with **a**, though **de** is preferred.

enfrente de	opposite
de parte de	on behalf of
● **de mi parte**	● on my behalf

24.7 *desde*

desde has the basic meaning of *from* (a particular point) and hence overlaps with basic meaning (b) of **de (24.6.1)**. It is used in expressions of position and time, and may also be used figuratively:

Desde la habitación se ve la costa
From the room you can see the coast
Está descontento desde ayer
He's been unhappy since yesterday
No lo hago desde hace tres meses
I haven't done it for three months
desde el más rico hasta el más pobre (R2–3)
from richest to poorest
NOTE: **De . . . a** is preferred to **desde . . . hasta** in R1.
desde mi punto de vista
from my point of view
desde muy antiguo
from olden times
In Am R1 **desde** is sometimes used to mark a point in past time:
Desde el lunes llegó $\boxed{!}$
He arrived on Monday

24.8 *en*

24.8.1 Basic meanings

(a) position above; corresponds to English on *(see also* **encima de** *(24.9) and* **sobre** *(24.15))*

en el tejado	on the roof

(b) position within; corresponds to English in

en/dentro de la caja in the box

NOTE: **Entre** is sometimes used in R1 in this sense.

en primera división in the first division

means of transport

en tren/coche/bici(cleta)/ moto(cicleta)/ barco/ avión/autobús

BUT: **en el avión del presidente**

reference to a point within a period of time; corresponds to English in *or* at

en la actualidad	at present
en la antigüedad	in antiquity
en aquel entonces / en aquellas fechas	at that time
en breve (R2–3)	soon
en (el (R2–3)**) invierno**	in (the) winter
en junio	in June
en Semana Santa / Navidad(es)	in Holy Week / at Christmas
en tiempo de guerra	in time of war
en tiempos del rey	in the king's time
No he dormido en toda la noche	I haven't slept all night
No he hecho tal cosa en toda mi vida	I haven't done such a thing in my life

metaphorical position; corresponds to English in (a state)

en estado de crisis	in a state of crisis
el gobierno en el poder	the government in power
en paro	on strike
en plural	in the plural

(c) location; corresponds to English at *and* in

en la cárcel / en prisión	in prison
en casa	at home
en la estación	at the station
en Málaga	in Málaga
en todas partes	everywhere

reference to a point in time (see also **a**, *24.1.2); often corresponds to English* on

en el día trece	on the 13th
el día en que (el día que (R1)**)**	the day when / on which
de hoy en cuatro días	in four days' time

(d) movement within; corresponds to English into

El tren entró en el túnel	The train went into the tunnel
poner en órbita	to put into orbit

NOTE: By comparison with English, no article is used after **en** if the noun has a generic sense. In a recipe, for example, one would be likely to see the instruction **dejarlo en frigorífico**, while referring to a specific situation in conversation one would say **déjalo en el frigorífico**. In recent years there has also been a strong tendency to omit the article with the noun following **en** in a large number of common expressions:

en ambiente desértico/ doméstico/ escolar/ hospitalario/rural	in a desert/domestic/school/ hospital/rural environment
pagar en caja/taquilla	to pay at the cashier's desk/box office
estar en laboratorio/estudio	to be in the lab/studio
ver algo en Internet	to see sth on the Internet
preguntar en Información	to ask at the Information desk
estar en tercera ronda / primera división	to be in the third round (of competition) / the first division
estar en estado grave	to be in a serious condition
escribir en lengua castellana	to write in the Spanish language
en primera/segunda lectura	on the first/second reading
estar/entrar en coma	to be in / go into a coma
estar en estado de confusión	to be in a state of confusion
correr en pista	to run on the track
La película todavía está en cartelera	The film is still in the listings (= still showing)
estar en primera página / portada	to be on the front page/cover
estar en reunión / conferencia de prensa	to be in a meeting/press conference
BUT:	
en la práctica	in practice

24.8.2 **en** in expressions of measurement

aumentar, disminuir, etc, **en un diez por ciento**	to increase, decrease, etc, by 10 per cent
firme en mal estado en diez km	bad road surface for ten km

24.8.3 **en** indicating material (see also **de, 24.6.1**)

La estatua es en mármol
The statue is made from marble

en focuses attention on the material, while **de** is more a simple description: **una estatua en mármol** = *a statue made out of marble*, **una estatua de mármol** = *a marble statue.*

24.8.4 **en**, corresponding to English *from*, with nouns indicating receptacles

fumar en pipa	to smoke a pipe (as a habit)
beber café en una taza	to drink coffee from a cup
comer en un plato	to eat from a plate

24.8.5 Common idioms and expressions involving **en**

en antena	on the air
en ausencia de	in the absence of
en balde	in vain
(SOMETIMES **de balde** in R1)	
en beneficio de	for the benefit of
en busca de	in search of
BUT: **a la búsqueda de**	
en cabeza	in the lead
en calidad de colega	as a colleague
en cambio	on the other hand
en carnes (vivas)	(stark) naked
en carretera	on the (main) road
en todo caso	in any case
en concreto	in fact, specifically
†**estar en condiciones de**	to be in a position to
en consecuencia	consequently
BUT: **por consiguiente**	
en contestación/respuesta a	in reply to
en correo aparte	under separate cover
en cuanto a (algo / hacer algo)	as for (sth/doing sth)
en cuclillas	squatting
en cueros (vivos)	(stark) naked
en derredor de	around
emisión en diferido	recorded broadcast
emisión en directo	live broadcast
en especial	especially
en esto	thereupon
licenciado en filosofía y letras	bachelor of arts
en función de	in terms of
el presidente en funciones	the acting president
en honor de	in honour of
en lugar/vez de	instead of
asesino en masa/serie	mass/serial killer
en cierto modo	in some way or other
en nombre de	on behalf of
en mi opinión	in my opinion
BUT: **a mi juicio, a mi entender**	
en parte	in part
en pie de guerra	on a war footing

salieron en plan de reyes	they went out like royalty
en presencia de	in the presence of
fue el primero / segundo, etc / último en hacerlo	he was the first / second, etc / last to do it
arguyó en pro de la reforma	he argued for (the) reform
en la †radio	on the radio
en razón de	by reason of, because of
en recuerdo de	in memory of
en relación con (ALSO con relación a)	in relation to
†en resumen	in short
frenar en seco	to brake sharply
en seguida	immediately
en serio	seriously
en (la) televisión (ALSO por la televisión)	on (the) television
en torno a	with regard to, concerning
en trance de	in the process of
en tropel	in a mass
en lo que va de año	as far as this year is concerned
en vano	in vain
en virtud de	by virtue of
en vivo	live (eg television broadcast)
en voz alta/baja	aloud / in a low voice

24.9 *encima de*

encima de has the basic literal meaning of *on, above, on top of,* and is preferred to **en (24.8)** and **sobre (24.15)**, where a high position is involved. **arriba de** is often used for **encima de** in this sense in Am.

encima de mi cabeza	above my head
Saltó encima de la cama	She jumped on (to) the bed

It also has the figurative meaning corresponding to **además de**:

Encima de ser tonto, es desobediente

As well as (on top of) being stupid, he's disobedient

24.10 *enfrente de, frente a*

In its basic meaning of *opposite,* **frente a** is slightly higher register than **enfrente de**, eg:

enfrente de / frente a (R2–3) **la casa**

opposite the house

NOTE ALSO: the following special meaning of **frente a** (all registers):

Hubo un accidente frente a Bilbao

There was an accident off (the coast of) Bilbao

24.11 *hacia*

direction	literal		figurative	
	hacia Cáceres	towards Cáceres	**sus sentimientos hacia los animales / su padre**	his feelings towards animals / his father
	miró hacia atrás/arriba	she looked back/up		
in time expressions	**hacia octubre** towards (= about) October			

24.12 *hasta*

direction	literal		figurative	
	hasta allí/aqui	there (= to there) / here (= to here)	**Estaba cansado hasta tal punto que . . .**	I was so tired that . . .
	desde Lisboa hasta Madrid (see **24.7**) (R2–3)	from Lisbon to Madrid		
time	**¡Hasta luego!**		So long!	
	hasta entonces		up till then	
	No lo habrá terminado hasta mañana		He won't have finished until tomorrow	

NOTE: the use of **no** in this construction, and consequently its meaning, vary considerably with register and regional variety, eg:

Hasta las tres no iré (standard)
I'll not go until three o'clock
Hasta las tres iré (R1–2, esp Central America, Colombia)
I'll not go until three o'clock
No saldré hasta que llegue (standard)
I'll not leave until he comes
No saldré hasta que no llegue (R1 Pen and Am)
I'll not leave until he comes

24.13 *para* and *por*

Since **para** and **por** are both the equivalents of English *for* in some of their meanings, English speakers do not always know which one to use. For this reason, it is helpful to present them contrastively, although they are quite different in their basic meanings.

24.13.1 Basic meanings

para	*por*
(a) purpose	*(a) cause*
¿Para qué sirve?	**¿Por qué lo hiciste?**
What is it for?	Why did you do it?
He venido a la biblioteca para estudiar	**La castiga por no estudiar**
I've come to the library to study	He punishes her for not working
	Le han despedido por perezoso
	They've dismissed him for being lazy
	Por tu culpa he perdido el tren
	It's your fault I've missed the train
	Las víctimas murieron por asfixia
	The victims died of suffocation
	Te felicito por tu nombramiento
	I congratulate you on your appointment
(b) destination	*(b) on behalf of, for the sake of, in substitution for*
Lo compré para ti	**Lo hice por ti**
I bought it for you	I did it for you (= for your sake)
un garaje para dos coches	**una misa por su alma**
a garage for two cars	a mass for (the sake of) his soul
	Hazlo por caridad
	Do it for (the sake of) charity
	Firma por su esposa
	He signs for (= on behalf of) his wife
	Lo cambiaron por un coche nuevo
	They exchanged it for a new car
	Le envié por (a por (R1)) vino
	I sent him for wine
	Pasa por lista
	She is considered intelligent

NOTE: the following constructions with **razón** –

la razón de/para su salida
the reason for his leaving
la razón por (la)
que / por la cual salió
the reason why he left

(c) in expressions of place, **para**
again indicates destination

Sale para Madrid
He's leaving for Madrid
Voy para casa
I'm going home
Caminé para el árbol
I walked towards the tree

(c) through, along, around

Fui a Madrid por Valladolid
I went to Madrid via Valladolid
Mire por la ventana
Look out of the window
Se paseaba por la calle
She was walking along the street
¿Hay un banco por aquí?
Is there a bank (around) here?
Está por Pamplona
It's near Pamplona

24.13.2 **para** and **por** in time expressions

para	*por*
Se va para una semana He's going away for a week (= he intends to be away for a week)	**Viene por tres días** He's coming for three days (= for a period of three days' duration)
	Vamos a aplazarlo por un mes Let's put it off for a month
Vendré para el veinticinco de mayo I'll come (in time) for 25 May	**Vendré por el veinticinco de mayo** I'll come about 25 May
	por la noche at night
	por el momento (ALSO **de momento**) for the moment
	por primera vez / por vez primera (R3) for the first time
	Es todo por ahora That's all for the time being
Va para dos años que murió (R1) It's been nearly two years since he died	
Nos veremos para el año que viene (R1) We'll see each other some time next year	

24.13.3   Other uses of **para**

para is the equivalent of English *to* and *for* in expressions of excess (*too . . . to/for*) and sufficiency (*enough . . . to/for*), eg:

Eso es demasiado para mí
That's too much for me
No tengo dinero suficiente (como) para comprártelo
I don't have enough money to buy it for you
Es para volverse loco
It's enough to drive you mad
No es para creerlo
You really can't believe it

24.13.4   **por** expressing rate (see also **a, 24.1.3**)

por docenas	by the dozen
día por día	day by day
ocho por ciento	8 per cent
a cien km por hora	at a hundred km an hour

24.13.5   **por** expressing agent (see also **de, 24.6.1**)

La carta fue escrita por un holandés
The letter was written by a Dutchman

24.13.6   **por** in expressions of manner and means

por adopción	by adoption
por aire/carretera/ ferrocarril/mar/tierra	by air/road/rail/sea/land
por carta	by letter
por correo	by mail
por (la) radio / (la) televisión (ALSO **en (la) televisión**)	on (the) radio / (the) television
Lo conocí por el sombrero	I knew him by his hat
llamar por teléfono	to telephone
BUT: **estar al teléfono (24.1.6)**	to be on the telephone (momentarily)

24.13.7   **por** in adverbial idioms of manner

por cierto	certainly; of course
por consiguiente	consequently
BUT: **en consecuencia (24.8.5)**	
por el (ALSO **al**) **contrario**	on the contrary
por desgracia	unfortunately
por escrito	in writing
por fortuna	luckily

por lo general / por regla general	in general
por un lado / una parte	on the one hand
por otro lado / otra parte	on the other hand
por separado	separately
por supuesto	of course
por lo tanto	therefore
por último	at last
por lo visto	apparently

24.13.8 **por** with other prepositions

por used before a preposition indicating location adds the idea of movement:

Corrieron por entre los coches
They ran among the cars
Pasó por detrás de la silla
He passed behind the chair
El avión voló por debajo del puente
The plane flew under the bridge
Saltó por encima de la mesa
He jumped over the table

24.13.9 Complex prepositions with **por**

mi abuelo por parte de mi padre
my grandfather on my father's side
Me lo pidió por mediación de su amigo
He asked me for it through his friend

24.14 *sin*

sin corresponds to English *without*, but is also often used in a general negative sense:

Lo harás sin mí / sin mi cooperación	you'll do it without me / my cooperation
Lo dije sin pensar	I said it without thinking
He estado un mes sin fumar	I haven't smoked for a month
Sigo sin recibir respuesta	I still haven't had a reply
¡Sin problema!	No problem!

For the use of **sin** with an infinitive, see **27.2**.

24.15 *sobre*

sobre has the basic meaning of *on top of*, and is an alternative to **en** in basic meaning (a) (**24.8.1**) and to **(por) encima de** (**24.9** and **24.13.8**), eg:

Hay un libro sobre/en la mesa	There's a book on the table
Puso un ladrillo sobre/ encima de otro	He put one brick on top of another
mil metros sobre el nivel del mar	a thousand metres above sea level
un grado sobre cero	one degree above zero
sobre (R3) / **en el cielo español**	in the Spanish sky
El reactor voló sobre / por encima de la ciudad	The jet flew over the town

In addition, **sobre** has a range of figurative usages, many, but not all, of which correspond to English *on*:

un libro sobre Cervantes	a book on Cervantes
sobre las cinco de la tarde (ALSO **a eso de las cinco**)	at about five o'clock
ocho sobre diez	eight out of ten
Dice tontería sobre tontería	He says one stupid thing after another

Adverbial phrases with **sobre**

sobre ascuas	on tenterhooks
sobre aviso	on one's guard
sobre manera	exceedingly
sobre todo	especially

24.16 *tras (tras de* in Am R1), *detrás de (atrás de* in Am R1), *después de, después que*

after (position)	**detrás de**	**tras**
	behind (gen and predominantly lit)	gen R3, but R1–3 in some set expressions (see below)
	Caminaron uno tras otro (R1–3)	*They walked one behind the other*
	tras (R3) / **detrás de la puerta**	*behind the door*
	Iba tras (R3) **el** / **detrás del caballo**	*She followed on after the horse*
after (time)	**después de**	**tras**
	gen	gen R3, but R1–3 in some set expressions (see below)
	después que	
	when a clause introduced by **después que** is implied	

NOTE: Pronouns following **después que** remain in subject form (**yo**, **tú**, etc).

día tras día (R1–3)	*day after day*
(ALSO **a, 24.1.3**)	
Leía libro tras libro (R1–3)	*He read book after book*
tras (R3) / **después de las seis**	*after six o'clock*
tras (R3) / **después de dos meses de ausencia**	*after two months' absence*
Lo hice tras (R3) / **después que él**	*I did it after him*

24.17 *a través de*

a través de corresponds to English *through* in most senses:

a través de una celosía
through a blind

Lo supe a través de la radio
I found out through the radio

Se puede hacer a través del banco
You can do it through the bank

Lo puedes encargar a través de mi profesor
You can order it through my teacher

It is also equivalent to English *across* when this implies a vague distance from one side of something to the other, eg:

Corrió a través de los campos / del bosque
She ran across the fields / the wood

Compare:

una carrera campo a través
a cross-country race

NOTE: Where a precise distance is implied, the notion of *across* requires a different construction (see **Chapter 26**), eg:

Cruzó la calle corriendo
She ran across the road

Atravesó el río nadando / a nado
She swam across the river

NOTE: *Across* in the sense of *on the other side* is usually rendered by Spanish **al otro lado de**, eg:

El transatlántico estaba anclado al otro lado de la bahía
The liner was anchored across (= on the other side of) the bay

24.18 Accumulation of prepositions

Prepositional phrases may sometimes be used rather like nouns, and be preceded themselves by other prepositions. Such usage is most common in R1, eg:

No es de por aquí (R1)
He's not from around here
Estará la casa arreglada para dentro de dos meses (R1)
The house will be sorted out within two months
Fue a por vino (R1)
He went to get wine
de a ratos (Am R1)
from time to time
No se meta usted de por medio
Don't poke your nose in here
la casa de al lado
the house next door

25 Prepositional constructions with verbs, nouns and adjectives

This is one of the most complex areas of Spanish grammar. The following sections outline some general principles and draw attention to the many differences between Spanish and English. All verbs, nouns and adjectives listed in this section are included in the Spanish word index at the end of the book.

NOTE: The raised equals sign by a verb ($=$) indicates that in order for the verb to take an infinitive or gerund complement the subject of the verb and the implied subject of its dependent infinitive or gerund must be identical. For example, in **aprendí (yo) a hacerlo (yo)**, yo is the subject of both **aprendí** and **hacer** (cf English *I learned how **I** should do it*).

25.1 Verbs with no preposition before an infinitive

25.1.1 Infinitive as subject of the verb

If the infinitive is the subject of the verb, no intervening preposition is used: [†]**aburrir (a[IO] uno)** *(to be boring (to sb))* is such a verb. In the sentence **Me aburre hacer eso**, **hacer eso** is the subject of **me aburre**. Notice that the most usual English equivalent of such sentences is often not parallel in structure: **Me aburre hacer eso** might be translated as *I'm bored doing that* in preference to the more literal *Doing that bores me*.

agradar a[IO] uno	to please sb
[†]**alegrar a[IO] uno**	to gladden sb
[†]**antojarse a[IO] uno**	
• Se me antoja hacerlo	• I feel like doing it
apasionar a[IO] uno	to arouse passion/enthusiasm in sb
apetecer a[IO] uno	to appeal to sb
atraer a[IO] uno	to attract sb
[†]**bastar a[IO] uno**	to be enough for sb
[†]**caber**	to fit, to be appropriate
• **Cabe destacar que . . .**	• It should be pointed out that . . .
[†]**convenir a[IO] uno**	to be fitting for sb

[†]**corresponder a**^{IO} **uno**	to be up to sb
● **Me correspondió contestar**	● It was up to me to reply
costar a^{IO} **uno**	to cost sb effort
● **Cuesta manejar tantas cifras**	● It's difficult to cope with so many figures
[†]**cumplir a**^{IO} **uno hacer algo**	to behove sb to do sth
[†]**encantar a**^{IO} **uno**	to be pleasing/delightful to sb
[†]**entusiasmar a**^{IO} **uno**	to arouse enthusiasm in sb
[†]**extrañar a**^{IO} **uno**	to surprise sb
[†]**hacer falta a**^{IO} **uno**	to be lacking to sb (lit)
● **Hace falta matricularse**	● You have to register
fascinar a^{IO} **uno**	to fascinate sb
[†]**fastidiar a**^{IO} **uno**	to annoy sb
[†]**gustar a**^{IO} **uno**	to be pleasing to sb (lit)
● **Me gustaría saberlo**	● I would like to know

NOTE: **gustar de hacer algo / algo**, *to like doing sth / sth*, is restricted to R3; **gustar hacer algo / algo**, with the same meaning, is common, however, in Am R1.

[†]**importar a**^{IO} **uno**	to be important / to matter to sb (lit)
● **¿Te importa cerrar la ventana?**	● Would you mind closing the window?
incumbir a^{IO} **uno** (R3)	to be incumbent upon sb
interesar a^{IO} **uno**	to interest sb
merecer/valer la pena	to be worthwhile
[†]**molestar a**^{IO} **uno**	to be a nuisance to sb
[†]**ocurrirse a**^{IO} **uno**	to occur to sb (lit)
● **Se me ocurrió ir**	● I made up my mind to go
[†]**quedar a**^{IO} **uno**	to remain for sb
[†]**sobrar a**^{IO} **uno**	to be superfluous
[†]**tocar a**^{IO} **uno**	to fall to sb (fig)
● **Te toca pagar**	● It's your turn to pay

25.1.2 Infinitive as direct object

When the following infinitive has essentially the same function as a direct object noun, there is no intervening preposition:

> [†]**Fingió**⁼ **tener miedo**
> He pretended to be afraid

Compare:

> **Fingió sorpresa**
> He feigned surprise

Other verbs of this class are:

[†]**aceptar**⁼	to undertake (to do sth / sth)
[†]**acordar**⁼	to agree (to do sth / on sth)
anhelar⁼ (R2–3)	to long (to do sth / for sth)

BUT: **el anhelo por/en**
ansiar=   to long (to do sth / for sth)
BUT: **el ansia (f) de/para**
añorar=   to yearn for
[†]**aparentar**=   to make as if (to do sth / to feign sth)
[†]**conseguir**=   to manage (to do sth) / to succeed (in doing sth) / to obtain (sth)
[†]**desear**=   to want (to do sth / sth)
BUT: **el** [†]**deseo de; deseoso de**
[†]**escoger**=   to choose (to do sth / sth)
[†]**evitar**=   to avoid (doing sth / sth)
[†]**intentar**=   to try (to do sth) / to attempt (sth)
BUT: **el intento de/por/para**
jurar=   to swear (to do sth / sth)
lamentar=   to regret (doing sth / sth)
[†]**lograr**=   to succeed (in doing sth) / to get (sth)
[†]**necesitar**=   to need (to do sth / sth)
BUT: **la** [†]**necesidad de**
[†]**parecer**=   to seem (to do sth / sth)
[†]**pedir**=   to ask (to do sth / for sth)
planear=   to plan (to do sth / sth)
[†]**preferir**=   to prefer (to do sth / doing sth / sth)
[†]**pretender**= (R2–3)   to want (to do sth) / to try (to do sth) / to claim (to do sth) / to seek (sth)
prever= / **tener**=**previsto**   to foresee (doing sth)
[†]**probar**= (R3 with inf)   to try (to do sth / sth)
[†]**procurar**=   to try (to do sth / sth)
prometer=   to promise (to do sth / sth)
[†]**proponerse**=   to propose (to do sth / doing sth) / sth)
[†]**proyectar**=   to plan (to do sth / sth)
BUT: **el proyecto de hacer algo**
[†]**querer**=   to want (to do sth / sth)
[†]**resolver**=   to resolve (to do sth)
BUT: **resolverse**= **a/para hacer algo, estar resuelto a hacer algo**
[†]**saber**=   to know (how to do sth / sth)
[†]**sentir**=   to regret (doing sth / sth)
[†]**solicitar**=(R3)   to ask (to do sth / for sth)
[†]**temer**=   to fear (doing sth / to do sth / sth)

25.1.3   Verbs of ordering

A number of verbs of ordering take an infinitive without a preposition as an alternative to the **que** + subjunctive construction (see **31.2.2**), eg:

†**aconsejar a**^{IO} **uno**	to advise sb (to do sth)
†**consentir a**^{IO} **uno**	to allow sb (to do sth)
†**dejar a**^{IO} **uno**	to let sb (do sth)
†**hacer a**^{IO} **uno**	to make sb (do sth)
†**impedir a**^{IO} **uno**	to prevent sb (from doing sth)
†**mandar a**^{IO} **uno**	to order sb (to do sth)

BUT: **Mandar a uno a hacer algo** = *to send sb to do sth*. In Am R1 the distinction is sometimes obscured, **a** being used in both constructions.

†**ordenar a**^{IO} **uno**	to order sb (to do sth)
†**permitir a**^{IO} **uno**	to allow sb (to do sth)
†**prohibir a**^{IO} **uno**	to forbid sb (to do sth)
†**sugerir a**^{IO} **uno**	to suggest (doing sth) to sb

25.1.4   Verbs of perception (eg **oír** and †**ver**)

Examples:
Oí cantar a María
I heard Mary sing(ing)
Oí cantar una canción
I heard a song (being) sung
Oí cantar una canción a María
I heard Mary sing(ing) a song

25.1.5   Verbs of saying

Several verbs of saying may take an infinitive in R2–3 with no intervening preposition as an alternative to the **que** + clause construction, eg:
Confirmó que lo había hecho / Confirmó haberlo hecho (R2–3)
He confirmed that he had done it / having done it
Other verbs of this class:

afirmar=	to affirm that . . .
asegurar=	to maintain that . . .
• **Aseguraron no saber nada de lo sucedido**	• They maintained that they knew nothing about what had happened
confesar=	to confess doing sth / that . . .
†**creer**=	to think that . . .
†**decir**=	to say that . . .

- **Destruyen lo que dicen defender**
- **declarar**[†]=
- **demostrar**[†]=
- **Ha demostrado tener gran paciencia**
- **denunciar**[†]=
- **Denunció ser víctima de malos tratos**
- **dudar**[†]=
- **manifestar**[†]=
- **negar**[†]=
- **pensar**[†]=
- **reconocer**[†]=

- They destroy what they say they defend
- to declare that . . .
- to show that . . .
- She showed that she had great patience
- to report
- He reported that he was a victim of ill-treatment
- to doubt if/whether/that . . .
- to state that . . .
- to deny doing sth / that . . .
- to think that . . .
- to recognize that . . .

25.1.6 Other verbs

dignarse[†]=	to deign (to do sth)
osar= (R2–3)	to dare (to do sth)
rehuir= (R2–3)	to avoid (doing sth)
rehusar= (R3)	to refuse (to do sth)

25.2 *a* before an infinitive

As with the use of **a** in isolation (see **24.1.1**), there is often the notion of metaphorical movement towards a goal; **a** tends to be used with verbs which carry a 'positive' meaning.

25.2.1 Attainment and figurative motion

acertar= **a**	to manage to (do sth) / to succeed in (doing sth)

NOTE: **acertar a hacer algo** = *to happen to do sth*: **Un cartero acertó a pasar** *A postman happened to pass.*

alcanzar[†]= **a**	to manage to (do sth) / to succeed in (doing sth)
aprender= **a**	to learn (how) to (do sth)
apresurarse[†]= **a** (ALSO **por, con**)	to hasten to (do sth)

ALSO **apresuramiento a** (ALSO **en**) **hacer algo**

arriesgarse[†]= **a**	to risk (doing sth)
aspirar= **a**	to aspire to (do sth)
atinar[†]= **a**	to manage to (do sth) / to succeed in (doing sth)

†**atreverse**⁼ **a**	to dare to (do sth)
†**buscar**⁼ **a**	to seek to (do sth)
†**decidirse**⁼ **a**	to decide to (do sth)

ALSO **estar**⁼ **decidido a** = *to be decided on doing sth*

BUT: **decidir**⁼ **hacer algo** with same meaning, and **la** †**decisión de hacer algo**

†**llegar**⁼ **a**	to succeed in (doing sth) / to end up (doing sth)
†**matarse**⁼ **a**	to kill oneself (doing sth)
†**precipitarse**⁼ **a** (ALSO **en**)	to hasten to (do sth)
rebajarse⁼ **a**	to stoop to (doing sth)
tender⁼ **a**	to tend to (do sth)

25.2.2 Verbs of beginning

†**comenzar**⁼ **a**
†**echarse**⁼ **a**
†**empezar**⁼ **a**
†**meterse**⁼ **a**
†**ponerse**⁼ **a**
†**principiar**⁼ **a** (R3)

See also *empezar* in **Chapter** 5.

ALSO:

†**lanzarse**⁼ **a**	to rush into (doing sth)
†**pasar**⁼ **a**	to go on to (do sth)
• **Pasó a leer el periódico**	• He went on to read the newspaper
†**romper**⁼ **a**	to burst out (doing sth)
• **Los niños rompieron a llorar**	• The children burst out crying

25.2.3 Agreement

†**acceder**⁼ **a** (R2–3)	to agree to (do sth) / to (doing sth)
†**avenirse**⁼ **a** (R3)	to agree to (do sth) (of two or more people)

See also *acordar* in **Chapter 5.**

25.2.4 Encouragement, help or other influence

†**acostumbrar a**ᴾᴱᴿˢ **uno /** **acostumbrarse**⁼ **a**	to accustom sb/oneself to (doing sth)
†**animar a**ᴾᴱᴿˢ **uno a**	to encourage sb to (do sth)
autorizar aᴾᴱᴿˢ **uno a** (ALSO **para**)	to authorize sb to (do sth)

†**ayudar a**^{PERS} **uno a**	to help sb to (do sth)
brindarse= **a** (ALSO **para**)	to offer to (do sth)
comprometerse= **a (also para)**	to undertake to (do sth)
BUT: **un** †**compromiso de ir**	an undertaking to go
condenar a^{PERS} **uno a**	to condemn sb to (do sth) / to (doing sth)
consagrarse= **a**	to devote oneself to (doing sth)
contribuir= **a**	to contribute towards (doing sth)
†**convidar a**^{PERS} **uno a** (ALSO with no PREP in Am R1)	to invite sb to (do sth)
dedicarse= **a**	to dedicate oneself to (doing sth)
†**determinar a**^{PERS} **uno a**	to determine sb to (do sth)
disponerse= **a** (ALSO **para**)	to prepare to (do sth)
emplazar a^{PERS} **uno a** (ALSO **para**) (R3)	to summon sb to (do sth)
empujar a^{PERS} **uno a**	to push sb into (doing sth)
†**enseñar a**^{PERS} **uno a**	to teach sb to (do sth)
entregarse= **a**	to devote oneself to (doing sth)
exhortar a^{PERS} **uno a** (R3)	to exhort sb to (do sth)
†**forzar a**^{PERS} **uno a** (R2–3)	to force sb to (do sth)
habituar a^{PERS} **uno a** / **habituarse**= **a**	to accustom sb/oneself to (doing sth)
impulsar a^{PERS} **uno a**	to impel sb to (do sth)
incitar a^{PERS} **uno a**	to incite sb to (do sth)
inclinar a^{PERS} **uno a**	to incline sb to (do sth)
inclinarse= **a**	to be inclined to (do sth)
ALSO **inclinación a** (ALSO **por**)	
inducir a^{PERS} **uno a**	to lead sb to (do sth)
instar a^{PERS} **uno a** (R3)	to urge sb to (do sth)
†**invitar a**^{PERS} **uno a** (ALSO **para**;	to invite sb to (do sth)
ALSO with no PREP in Am R1;	
ALSO **invitación a** (ALSO **para**))	
estar = †**listo a** (ALSO **para**)	to be ready to (do sth)
†**llevar a**^{PERS} **uno a**	to lead sb to (do sth)
†**mentalizarse**= **a** (ALSO **para**)	to make up one's mind / to decide to (do sth)
†**mover a**^{PERS} **uno a**	to move sb to (do sth)
obligar a^{PERS} **uno a**	to oblige sb to (do sth)
BUT: **la obligación de hacer algo**	
†**ofrecerse**= **a** (ALSO **para**) (R2–3)	to offer to (do sth)
†**persuadir a**^{PERS} **uno a** (ALSO **para**) (R3)	to persuade sb to (do sth)
†**prepararse**= **a** (ALSO **para**)	to prepare to (do sth)
ALSO **estar** = †**preparado a** (ALSO **para**) = *to be prepared to (do sth)*	

prestarse= **a**	to lend oneself to (doing sth)
proceder= **a** (R2–3)	to proceed to (doing sth)
†**tentar a**^{PERS} **uno a**	to tempt sb to (do sth)

25.2.5   With verbs of motion

†**Fui a verla**
I went to see her
†**Salió a recibirme**
He came out to welcome me
†**Se sentó a pensar**
She sat down to think
†**Vengo a decirte que . . .**
I've come to tell you that . . .

25.2.6   **a** for **para** and **por**

In R1, and increasingly in R2–3, **a** may be used for **para** and **por** (see **25.5.3**) in the following types of construction:

una cuestión a ⌊!⌋ (R1) / **para** (R2–3) **resolver**
una †**cuenta a** ⌊!⌋ (R1) / **por** (R2–3) **pagar**

25.2.7   **a** + infinitive as imperative

a + infinitive has the force of an imperative in R1:

¡**A comer!**
Let's eat!
¡**A dormir!**
Let's sleep!
¡**A ver!**
Let's see!
¡**A pasarlo bien!**
Have a good time!

25.3   *a before a noun*

25.3.1   Indirect object **a** rendered by a preposition other than *to* in English

With verbs which have the general meaning of 'to take away', Spanish **a**^{IO} corresponds to English *from*, eg:

Lo compré a^{IO} **un gitano**
I bought it from a gipsy

Other verbs of this class are:

arrebatar (R2–3)	to snatch away
confiscar	to confiscate
disimular	to hide
escamotear (R1–2)	to whisk away
esconder	to hide
[†]**exigir**	to demand
[†]**ganar**	to win
[†]**hurtar**	to steal
ocultar	to hide
ocupar	to seize
[†]**pedir**	to ask for
[†]**pedir prestado**	to borrow
[†]**quitar**	to take away
[†]**reclamar**	to claim
[†]**restar**	to take away
[†]**robar**	to steal
[†]**sacar**	to get out of
[†]**solicitar** (R2–3)	to ask for
sonsacar	to extract (eg information)
[†]**sustraer** (R2–3)	to take away

a^{IO} may also be rendered by other prepositions in English, eg:

imponer (R2–3)		to impose sth on sb
inculcar (R2–3)	} **algo a**^{IO} **uno**	to inculcate sth in sb
infundir (R2–3)		to instil sth in sb
producir una impresión a^{IO}**uno**		to make an impression on sb
[†]**regatear**		to keep sb short of sth
	} **algo a**^{IO} **uno**	
reprochar		to reproach sb for sth

25.3.2 Noun + **a** + noun

Several nouns which represent actions or attitudes require **a** before a noun which functions as the direct object of the corresponding verb, eg:

su apoyo al primer ministro
his support for the Prime Minister

Compare:

Apoyó al primer ministro
They operated on the Prime Minister

Other examples:

su [†]**afición al dinero** (ALSO **por**)	his love of money
ALSO **estar aficionado a algo**	
la agresión a Nicaragua (ALSO **contra**)	aggression against Nicaragua

el amor a un hijo (ALSO por)	love for a child
el asalto a Cádiz	the attack on Cadiz
un ataque al gobierno	an attack on the government
un atentado a la seguridad nacional	an attack against national security
un atraco a un banco	a bank raid
una ayuda a los habitantes	help for the inhabitants
el boicot a África del Sur	the boycott of South Africa
un †comentario al *Quijote* (ALSO del)	a commentary on the *Quixote*
Hizo muchas críticas a los medios informativos	He made many criticisms of the media
el culto al ejercicio físico	the cult of physical exercise
su †denuncia a los responsables	his denouncing of those responsible
la entrevista al primer ministro (ALSO con)	the interview with the Prime Minister
la explotación a los inmigrantes	exploitation of immigrants
un †interrogatorio al sospechoso	an interrogation of the suspect
maltrato a animales	mistreatment of animals
mi odio a los dictadores	my hatred for dictators
una operación al paciente / al ojo	an operation on the patient / an eye operation
NOTE: Le operaron (d)el ojo	They operated on her eye
la opresión a los judíos (ALSO sobre)	the oppression of the Jews
el rechazo a los liberales (ALSO de)	the rejection of the liberals
el reconocimiento a Shakespeare (ALSO por, de)	recognition of Shakespeare
su †renuncia a la sucesión (ALSO de)	his renunciation of the succession
un repaso a la lección (ALSO de)	a review of the lesson
una repulsa a la idea	a rejection of the idea
el respeto a las leyes	respect for the law
el robo a una bolsa	the theft of a handbag
mi †temor a la muerte (ALSO de) SEE ALSO tener miedo, 25.9.	my fear of death
un veto al proyecto	a veto for the project

NOTE: With such nouns, **de** marks the subject of the corresponding verb; contrast the following examples with those given above:

el amor de un hijo	a son's love
el odio de clases	class hatred (ie hatred of one class by another)

25.3.3 With verbs of smell and taste

oler a algo	to smell of sth
†**saber a algo**	to taste of sth
tener †**gusto a algo**	

25.4 *de* before an infinitive or noun

de may be thought of as the 'opposite' of **a**. It tends to be associated with metaphorical movement away from something.

25.4.1 Cessation

†**abstenerse⁼ de**	to abstain from (doing sth / sth)
†**acabar⁼ de**	to have just + PP / to finish (doing sth)

NOTE: †**acabar de** has the meaning of *to have just* when used in the Present and Imperfect; in other tenses it has the meaning of *to finish* –

Acabo de llegar
I've just arrived
Acababa de llegar
I'd just arrived
Cuando acabó de vestirse . . .
When he had finished dressing . . .

NOTE ALSO: **no acabar de** = to *fail to* (see **27.1**) –

Estudio mucho pero no acabo de entenderlo
I study a lot but I fail to understand it

†**dejar⁼ de**	to stop (doing sth)
desistir⁼ de	to desist from (doing sth / sth)
†**despedirse de**	to take one's leave of (sb/sth)
†**parar⁼ de**	to stop (doing sth)
†**terminar⁼ de**	to stop (doing sth)

25.4.2 'Negative' idea

A number of verbs have unfavourable or 'negative' meanings.

†**acusar a^PERS uno de**	to accuse sb of (doing sth)
†**burlarse de**	to make fun of (sb/sth)
ALSO **burlar a^PERS uno** (R3)	= to *deceive sb*
†**cuidarse bien de**	to take good care not to (do sth)

culpar a^{PERS} uno de	to blame sb for (doing sth / sth)
desconfiar de	to distrust (sb/sth)
BUT: desconfianza en algo/uno	
†desesperarse= de	to despair of (doing sth /(sb/sth)
desinteresarse= de (ALSO por)	to lose interest in (doing sth / sth)
BUT: desinterés por algo	
†disuadir a^{PERS} uno de (R3)	to dissuade sb from (doing sth / sth)
excusarse= de hacer algo / algo (ALSO por algo)	to apologize for (doing sth / sth)
†guardarse= de	to be careful not to (do sth)
librarse de	to escape from (sb/sth)
mofarse de (R2–3)	to make fun of (sb/sth), to scoff at (sb/sth)
privar a^{PERS} uno de	to forbid sb to do (sth) / to deprive sb of (sth)
privar(se) de	to deprive (oneself) of (sth)
†quejarse de	to complain about (sth)
recelar de (R2–3)	to be suspicious of (sb)
†renegar de	to forsake (sb/sth; esp faith)
resarcirse de	to make up for (sth)
vengarse de	to take revenge on (sb)/for (sth)
zafarse de	to dodge (sth)
BUT NOTE:	
†negarse= a	to refuse to (do sth)
†negativa a	refusal to (do sth)
†renunciar a	to renounce (sth)
†renuncia a	renunciation of (sth)
†resistirse= a	to resist doing (sth / sth)

25.4.3 Causation

†aburrirse de (ALSO con)	to be bored by (sth)
admirarse de	to wonder at (sth)
†alegrarse de (ALSO por, con)	to be gladdened by (sth)
†arrepentirse= de	to repent of (doing sth / sth)
asombrarse de	to be amazed at (sth)
asustarse de (ALSO por, con)	to be frightened by (sth)
†avergonzarse= de	to be ashamed of (doing sth / sth / sb)
†cansarse= de	to tire of (doing sth / sth / sb)
ALSO cansarse con uno	
estar †contento de (ALSO con)	to be happy with (sth/sb)
estar †descontento de (ALSO con)	to be unhappy with (sth/sb)

enamorarse de	to fall in love with (sb)
escandalizarse de	to be scandalized by (sth)
espantarse de	to be scared of (sth)
[†]**extrañarse de**	to be surprised at (sth)
[†]**fatigarse= de**	to get tired of (doing sth / sth)
[†]**gloriarse de**	to be proud of (sth)
hartarse= de	to be fed up with (doing sth / sth)
ALSO **estar= [†]harto de**	
[†]**jactarse= de** (R2–3)	to boast of (doing sth / sth)
maravillarse de	to marvel at (sth)
preciarse= de (R2–3)	to pride oneself on (sth) / to boast of (doing sth)
[†]**preocuparse de** (ALSO **con, por**)	to worry about (sth) / to give special attention to (sth) (Am)
[†]**reírse de**	to laugh at (sth)
[†]**sonreírse de**	to smile at (sth)
sorprenderse de	to be surprised at (sth)
ufanarse= de (R3) (ALSO **con**)	to be proud of (doing sth / sth)

25.4.4 'Advantage'

[†]**aprovecharse de**	to take advantage of (sth)
beneficiarse de	to benefit from (sth)
[†]**disfrutar de**	
[†]**gozar de**	} ALSO with no PREP to enjoy (sth)
incautarse de	to confiscate (sth)

25.4.5 'Instrument' (**de** is often the equivalent of English *with*)

apercibirse de (R3)	to provide oneself with (sth), to realize (sth)
colmar a[PERS] **uno de**	to fill sb up with, to overwhelm sb with (sth)
concienciar/concientizar a[PERS] **uno de**	to make sb aware of (sth)
encargar a[PERS] **uno de**	to entrust sb with (sth) / (sth) to sb

ALSO **encargar algo a uno** with the same meaning; and **encargarse de** = *to take charge of (sth)*

henchirse de (R2–3)	to swell (intr) with (sth)
mentalizar a[PERS] **uno de**	to make sb realize (sth)
pertrecharse de	to equip oneself with (sth)
saciarse de	to be satisfied with (sth), to have one's fill of (sth)
vestir a[PERS] **uno de** (ALSO refl)	to dress sb in (sth)
vivir de	to live on (sth)

25.4.6 With verbs of change

†**cambiar**	to change
• **Quieren cambiar de casa**	• They want to change house(s)
mudar	to change
variar	to vary in sth
• **Las dos paredes varían de color**	• The two walls vary in colour

25.4.7 Other uses of **de**

†**el deber de hacer algo**	the duty to do (sth)
tener ganas de hacer algo	to want to do sth
†**Ya es hora de hacer algo**	It's time to do sth
la voluntad de hacer algo	the will to do sth
digno de algo / hacer algo	worthy of sth / doing sth
seguro de algo / hacer algo	sure of sth / of doing sth
†**susceptible de hacer algo**	capable of doing sth

25.5 *por* before an infinitive or noun

Although many of the uses of **por** can be related to the basic meanings of the preposition (**24.13.1**), it is sometimes difficult for English speakers to perceive the connection.

25.5.1 **por** = *on account of*

†**apurarse⁼ por**	to worry about (sth / doing sth)
ser curioso por	to be curious about (sth)
felicitar aᴾᴱᴿˢ **uno por**	to congratulate sb on (doing sth / sth)
(dar las) gracias por	(to give) thanks for (doing sth / sth)
indignación por	indignation, anger about (sth)
†**indignarse por**	
†**irritarse por** (ALSO **con, contra**)	to get angry about sth
interesarse por/en algo	to be interested in (sth)
interesarse por uno	to enquire about (sb)
obsesión por (ALSO **para**)	obsession for (doing sth / sth)
BUT **tener la obsesion de** = *to be obsessed by (sth / doing sth)*	
una pasión por	a passion for (doing sth / sth)
†**preocuparse⁼ por** (ALSO **de, con**)	to worry about (doing sth / sth)
una protesta por	a protest about (sth)
†**protestar por**	to protest about (sth)

25.5.2 **por** = *by*

With verbs of beginning and ending, **por** + inf or ger alone may be used, eg:

> **Acabé por leerlo** or **acabé leyéndolo**
> I ended up by reading it

†**acabar**= **por** (ALSO + ger) to end up (doing sth)

†**comenzar**= **por** (ALSO + ger)

†**empezar**= **por** (ALSO **con** + ger) } to begin by (doing sth)

†**terminar**= **por** (ALSO + ger) to end up (doing sth)

25.5.3 **por** = *in favour of*

abogar por (R3)	to plead for (sb)
apostar por	to bet on (sth)
†**brindar por** (ALSO **a**)	to drink to (sb)
†**decidirse**= **por**	to decide in support of / on (doing sth / sth)
BUT: **la** †**decisión de** = *the decision to (do sth)*	
optar= **por**	to opt for (doing sth / sth)
†**votar**= **por**	to vote in support of / for (doing sth / sth)

25.5.4 With verbs and nouns of 'effort'

afanarse= **por** (ALSO **en**)	to strive to (do sth)
ALSO **afán** (m) **por** (ALSO **de**)	
†**apurarse**= **por** (ALSO **en**)	to hasten to (do sth)
una comezón (R3) **por**	an itch to (do sth)
†**entusiasmarse**= **por** (ALSO **con**)	to get enthusiastic about (doing sth / sth)
ALSO **entusiasmo por** (ALSO **para**)	
†**esforzarse**= **por** (ALSO **en**)	to strive to (do sth)
ALSO **esfuerzo por** (ALSO **en, para**)	
†**esmerarse**= **por** (ALSO **en**)	to take pains to (do sth)
ALSO **esmero en**	
†**hacer** = **por**	to try to (do sth)
tener= **ilusión por** (ALSO **para**)	to look forward to (doing sth)
luchar= **por** (ALSO **para**)	to fight to (do sth)
ALSO **lucha por**	
†**matarse**= **por**	to kill oneself (doing sth) / for (sth)
†**morirse**= **por**	to be dying to (do sth), to be crazy about (sth / sb)

hacer⁼ **lo posible por** (ALSO **para**)	to do one's utmost to (do sth)
†**darse**⁼ / †**tener**⁼ **prisa por** (ALSO **en** (**25.7**) and **a**)	to hasten to (do sth)
pugnar⁼ **por** (R2–3)	to fight to (do sth) / for (sth)
rabiar⁼ **por**	to be dying to (do sth) / for sth
reventar⁼ **por** (R1–2)	to be bursting to (do sth) / for (sth)
suspirar⁼ **por**	to long to (do sth) / for (sth)

NOTE ALSO:

mil cosas por hacer	a thousand things to be done

Compare: **estar por** (**25.9**, **32.9**) and **quedar por** (**25.9**).
See also: **a** (**25.2.6**).

25.6 *para* before an infinitive or noun

25.6.1 Ability and inability

aptitud para	aptitude for (doing sth / sth)
autorizar aᴾᴱᴿˢ **uno para** (ALSO **a**)	to authorize sb to (do sth)
ALSO **autorización para**	
tener⁼ **capacidad para**	to have talent for (doing sth / sth)
ALSO **la (in)capacidad para** (ALSO **de**), †**capaz para** (ALSO **de**)	
estar⁼ **capacitado para** (ALSO **a**)	to be qualified to (do sth)
tener⁼ **dificultad para**	to have difficulty in (doing sth)
tener⁼ **facilidad para**	to have a gift for (sth)
estar⁼ **facultado para**	to be empowered to (do sth)
†**hábil para**	competent to (do sth) / at (sth), qualified to (do sth)
ALSO **tener**⁼ **la habilidad para** = *to have the capacity to (do sth) / for (sth)*, **habilitar a**ᴾᴱᴿˢ **uno para** = *to qualify sb to (do sth) / for (sth)*	
imposibilitar aᴾᴱᴿˢ **uno para**	to make it impossible for sb to (do sth)
impotencia para	inability to (do sth)
tener⁼ **libertad para** (ALSO **de**)	to be free to (do sth)
permiso para	permission to (do sth)
prepararse⁼ **para** ALSO **preparado para** (ALSO **a**)	to prepare oneself to (do sth) / for (sth)
estar pronto / presto (R3) **para** (ALSO **a**)	to be ready, quick to (do sth)
tener voluntad para	to have the willpower to (do sth)
NOTE: **tener voluntad de**	to be willing to (do sth)

25.6.2 Sufficiency (see also **24.13.3**)

†**bastar para**	to be enough to (do sth)
• **Me bastan cien pesos para hacerlo**	• A hundred pesos are enough for me to do it
†**faltar para**	to be necessary to (do sth) / for (sth)
• **Me falta una para las cien**	• I need another one to make a hundred
• **Me faltan dos días para terminarlo**	• I need two days to finish it

25.6.3 Persuasion

convencer a uno para	to persuade sb to (do sth)

25.7 *en* before an infinitive or noun

25.7.1 **en** corresponding to English *in, into, on*

†**apoyarse en**	to lean on (sth) (lit and fig)
hacer= bien en	to do well in (doing sth) / to do (sth)
†**coincidir= en**	to coincide in (doing sth) (lit)
• **Coincidimos en no decir nada**	• We both said nothing
BUT: **El papel coincide con el patrón** = *The paper matches the pattern*	
complacerse= en (R2–3)	to take pleasure in (doing sth)
concentrarse= en	to concentrate on (doing sth / sth)
†**creer en**	to believe in (sb/sth)
NOTE: **creer a**PERS **uno** = *to believe sb (ie to believe what sb says)*	
†**deleitarse= en** (R3) (ALSO **con** + ger)	to delight in (doing sth / sth)
ejercitarse en	to practise (sth), to train in (sth)
†**embarcarse en**	to get involved in (sth) / to get on (sth) (eg a bus) (Am)
empeñarse= en ALSO **empeño en**	to insist on (doing sth / sth), to persist in (doing sth / sth)
entrar en (ALSO **a** (R1, esp Am), but see **25.9**)	to enter (sth)
†**entretenerse= en**	to pass the time (in) (doing sth)
†**esperar en**	to hope, to believe in (sb/sth)
†**incidir en**	to fall on (sth) (eg light on water) (lit); to have an effect on (sb/sth) (fig)

incurrir en (R2–3)	to incur (sth) / to commit (sth) (fig)
• **Incurrimos en el error**	• We committed an error to
influir en (ALSO **sobre**)	influence (sb/sth)
BUT: **influir con uno para que haga algo** = *to influence sb to do sth*	
ingresar en (ALSO **a** (R1 Am))	to go into (sth), to be admitted to (sth) (eg hospital), to enlist in (sth) (eg army)
insistir⁼ en (ALSO **para**)	to insist on (doing sth / sth)
ALSO **insistencia en**	
tener = interés en (ALSO **por**)	
interesarse⁼ en (ALSO **por**)	to be interested in (doing sth / sth)
estar⁼ interesado en (ALSO **por**)	
ser⁼ lento en	to be slow in (doing sth / sth)
†**participar en**	to participate in (sth)
penetrar en (ALSO **a** (R1, esp Am))	to penetrate (sth) (lit)
perseverar⁼ en	to persevere in (doing sth / sth)
persistir⁼ en	to persist in (doing sth / sth)
ser⁼ el primero, último en	to be the first, last in (doing sth)
†**darse⁼/**†**tener prisa en** (ALSO **por**)	to hurry in (doing sth)
†**recrearse⁼ en** (ALSO + ger) (R3)	to amuse oneself (in) (doing sth)
ser⁼ unánime en (R3)	to be unanimous in (doing sth)

25.7.2   With verbs of 'persistence'

obstinarse⁼ en ALSO **obstinación en**	to persist in (doing sth)
perseverar⁼ en (R2–3)	to persevere in (doing sth)
persistir⁼ en (R2–3) ALSO **persistencia en**	to persist in (doing sth)

25.7.3   With verbs of 'hesitation'

†**dudar⁼en**	to hesitate in (doing sth) / to (do sth)
vacilar⁼ en (ALSO **para**)	
ALSO **vacilación en** (ALSO **para**)	

25.7.4   With verbs of 'noticing'

fijarse en	to notice (sth)
†**reparar en**	
NOTE also:	
†**consentir⁼ en**	to consent to (doing sth / sth)

25.8 Verbs followed by the gerund

†**continuar**$^=$
†**seguir**$^=$ $\Big\}$ to continue (doing sth)

†**llevar**$^=$ **(tiempo)** (see also **29.6**)

- **Llevo dos horas escribiendo**
- I've been writing for two hours

25.9 Varying prepositions

Several Spanish verbs, nouns and adjectives have a range of prepositional structures with following infinitives and nouns. Change of preposition usually involves a change of meaning.

†**acabar**	**acabar de** (p 346), **por / + ger** (p 350) AND **Acabó con palabras de agradecimiento** He ended with words of thanks **Las palabras que acaban con/por 'a'** The words which end in 'a' **Acabó con las malas costumbres** He put an end to the evil customs **La fiesta acabó en desastre** The party ended in disaster
acostumbrar	**acostumbrar a**^{PERS} **uno a** (p 341) AND **Acostumbro**$^=$(R3) **acostarme tarde** I usually go to bed late
aferrarse	**¿Por qué te afierras a esta hipótesis?** Why do you stick to this theory? **Se aferró en su error** He persisted in his error
†**amenazar**	**Amenaza**$^=$ **con llover** It's threatening to rain **Me amenazó de** (ALSO **con**) **un machete** He threatened me with a machete
†**apoyar**	cf †**apoyarse** and †**apoyo** **Apoyo esta opinion** I support this view **La columna apoya sobre el pedestal** The column is supported on the pedestal

†armarse	**Se armó con un fusil** (lit) He armed himself with a rifle **Se armó de valor** (fig) He armed himself with courage
arriesgarse	**arriesgarse a** (p 340) AND **Se arriesgó en una misión desesperada** He ventured upon a desperate mission
†asirse	**Se asió a la cuerda** (R2–3) He seized the rope NOTE: **Asió la cuerda** is more common in R1–2. **Se asió con el intruso** He grappled with the intruder **Se asió de provisiones** She got hold of provisions
atinar	**atinar a** (p 340) AND **Has atinado⁼ en decir eso** You were right to say that **Atinó con la solución** She hit on the answer
†atreverse	**atreverse a** (p 341) AND **Se atrevió con el director** He was rude to the principal
†avenirse	**avenirse a** (p 341) AND **Tenemos que avenirnos en una solución** We must agree on a solution **No se aviene con mi amigo** He doesn't get along with my friend
†bastar	**bastar hacer algo** (p 336), **para** (p 352) AND **Basta con telefonearle** (R1–2) You need only telephone him **Basta con tu presencia** (R1–2) Your presence is enough
†hacer caso	**¡Haz caso a las señales de tráfico!** Pay attention to the road signs! **Hace caso del niño** He looks after the child
coincidir	**coincidir en** (p 352) AND **Coincide con usted** I agree with you
comenzar	**comenzar a** (p 341), **por** / + ger (p 350)

compensar	**compensar algo / una cosa con otra** (p 363) AND
	Le compensaron de sus esfuerzos
	They compensated him for his efforts
	Le compensaron con 20 euros por el reloj perdido
	They gave him 20 euros compensation for the lost watch
†concordar	**El verbo concuerda con el sujeto**
	The verb agrees with the subject
	Todos concordamos en que no será aconsejable
	We all agree that it would not be advisable
†confiar	**Confió la carta a su hija**
	He entrusted the letter to his daughter
	Confío en mi amigo
	I trust my friend
	ALSO **su †(des)confianza en su amigo**
	BUT: **Me confié a mi amigo** = *I confided in my friend*
consentir	**consentir a**^{IO} **uno / hacer algo** (p 339), **consentir**$^=$ **en** (p 353)
†convenir	**convenir** (p 336) AND
	Convine$^=$ **con él en ir**
	I agreed with him to go
	Convinieron en un precio
	They agreed on a price
tener cuidado	**¡Ten**$^=$ **cuidado de escribir de forma legible!**
	Take care to write legibly!
	Hay que tener cuidado con el perro
	You must be careful of the dog
	ALSO **el †cuidado en** (ALSO **con**) **hacer algo** = *care in doing sth*
cuidar	**Mi hermana cuida a**^{PERS} **los niños**
	My sister looks after the children
	Cuida de nuestra casa cuando estamos ausentes
	She looks after our house while we're away
	ALSO **†cuidarse de algo** = *to take care of sth*
chocar	**chocar con, contra** (p 366) AND
	chocar con uno
	to fall out with sb
	chocar a^{PERS} **uno**
	to shock sb

dar	**Le dio por regresar temprano**
	He took it into his head to come back early
	Lo dio por terminado
	He considered it finished
	Di con él en la calle
	I bumped into him in the street
	Di con una ocupación
	I found a job
	Mi habitación †da al mar
	My room looks onto the sea
	El coche dio contra un árbol
	The car struck a tree
	Has †dado con/en la solución
	You've found the answer
†decidir	**Decidí= ir**
	I decided to go
	but la †decisión de ir = *the decision to go*
	decidir de/sobre algo
	to decide (about) sth
	(Cf **decidirse a** (p 341), **por** (p 350))
dejar	**dejar** (p 339), **dejar= de** (p 346)
desesperarse	**desesperarse= de** (p 347) AND
	desesperarse por algo
	to despair at sth
	la desesperación por la falta de empleo
	despair about the lack of work
determinar	**determinar a** (p 342) AND
	Determiné= hacerlo en seguida
	I decided to do it immediately
†dudar	**dudar= en** (p 353) AND
	Dudo de su buena voluntad
	I doubt his good will
	Duda= entre aceptar y rechazar
	He's hesitating between accepting and refusing
†echar	**Echó= a correr**
	He began to run
	Se echó= a llorar
	She began to cry
	Echaron por el camino de . . .
	They took the direction of . . .
	NOTE: the idiom **echarse de ver** = *to be obvious*
†empezar	**empezar= a** (p 341), **por** / +ger (p 350)

entender	**No entiendo de matemáticas** I don't understand mathematics **Se entiende en inglés** He can make himself understood in English **Me entiendo a la perfección con ella** I get along perfectly well with her
entrar	**entrar en (a)** (p 352) AND **Entró al colegio el año pasado** She started school last year
†**esperar**	**esperar** (p 363), **en** (p 352), **a** (p 363)
†**estar**	**Estoy= por salir ahora** I'm inclined to go out now **Lo demás está por escribir** The rest remains to be written **Estaba= para morirse** He was on the point of death **No estoy para chistes** I'm not in the mood for jokes **Las manzanas están a dos euros** The apples are two euros **Está con fiebre muy alta** She's got a high fever **Una gran parte de la población estaba con los gobernantes** Much of the population was on the side of the governors **estar de camarero** to have a job as a waiter
†**faltar**	**faltar para** (p 352) AND **Faltaron a la cita** They didn't turn up for the date **Falta a su palabra** He breaks his promise **Faltan dos cucharas** There are two spoons missing ALSO **estar falto de** (R3) = *to be lacking in*
†**fatigarse**	**fatigarse= de** (p 348) AND **fatigarse=** +ger / **en** + inf to get tired (in) doing sth

gusto	**gusto a** (p 346) AND **¡Mucho gusto en conocerle!** Pleased to meet you! **el gusto por/de la música** the taste for music
†hacer	**hacer** (p 339), **por** (p 350) AND with nouns: **Hace de camarero** He works as a waiter **No me hago al calor** I can't get used to the heat **Los militantes se hicieron con el poder** The militants took power
†indignarse	**indignarse por** (p 349) AND **Se indignó conmigo** He became indignant with me
inspirar	**inspirar algo a^{IO} uno** to inspire sth in sb **inspirarse en/de algo** to be inspired by sth
†ir	**Tu corbata no va bien con el color del traje** Your tie doesn't go with the colour of your suit **Va para primer ministro** He hopes to be Prime Minister **En lo que va de año . . .** As far as this year goes . . .
libre	**El hombre no es libre de matar** Man is not free to kill (axiomatic) **Está libre para marcharse** He is free to go (permission)
†echar mano	**echar mano a algo** to get hold of sth **echar una mano a uno** (R1) to give sb a hand **echar mano de algo** to have recourse to sth
†meterse	**meterse= a** (p 341) AND **¡No te metas conmigo!** Don't provoke me! **Se metió de secretaria** She took a job as a secretary

†tener miedo	**Tengo miedo al/del profesor** I'm afraid of the teacher **Tengo miedo de que no lo haga** I'm afraid he won't do it **Tengo= miedo de hacerlo** (ALSO, though less commonly, **a**) I'm afraid of doing it
†mirar	**mirar** (p 364) AND **mirar a algo** to contemplate, to think about sth **mirar por uno/algo** to look after (sb) / to be concerned about sth
motivo	**el motivo de su rechazo** the reason for its rejection **No tienes motivo para quejarte** You've no reason to complain
ocuparse	**La madre se ocupó de la cena** Mother dealt with dinner **Me ocupaba en/de enviar cartas a todos mis amigos** I spent my time sending letters to all my friends
†participar	**participar en** (p 353) AND **Participan de la misma opinión** They share the same opinion
†pasarse	**Se pasó de lista** She was just a bit too clever **Me paso sin pan** I do without bread
†pensar	**Pienso= hacerlo esta tarde** I intend to do it this afternoon **Estoy pensando en mis estudios** I'm thinking of my studies **¿Qué piensas de la película?** What do you think of the film? **Hay que pensarlo bien** A lot of thought must be given to it
†persuadir (R3)	**persuadir** (p 342) AND **persuadir a**PERS **uno de algo / de que . . .** to persuade sb of sth / that . . .

†poner	**La pusieron a estudiar en el instituto**
	They sent her to study at the institute
	Lo han puesto a cinco euros
	They have priced it at five euros
	Le pusieron de dependiente
	They found him a job as a shop assistant
†protestar	**protestar por** (p 349) AND
	Protesta de su inocencia
	He protests his innocence
	Vamos a protestar contra la reforma
	Let's protest against the reform
quedar	**Le quedaron veinte duros al^{IO} chico**
	The boy had twenty duros left
	Hemos quedado^= en (de (R1 Am)) aplazarlo
	hasta mañana
	We've agreed to put it off until tomorrow
	Quedamos en el día trece
	We agreed on the thirteenth
	Quedamos para mañana
	We arranged to meet tomorrow
	Quedan diez páginas por leer
	There are ten pages left to read
	Quedan seis semanas para Navidad
	It's six weeks to Christmas
†quedarse	**Se quedó con el coche**
	He kept the car
	La fiesta se quedó^= en beber
	The party was reduced to drinking
tener razón	**Tuvo^= razón para hacerlo**
	She had reason to do it
	Tuvo^= razón en hacerlo
	She was right to do it
rebajarse	**rebajarse^= a** (p 341) AND
	El alumno se rebajó de la clase de latín
	The pupil was excused from the Latin class
†reclamar	**reclamar a^{IO}** (p 344) AND
	reclamar contra algo
	to protest against sth
†reparar	**reparar en** (p 353) AND
	reparar algo
	to repair sth

responder	**Voy a responder a la pregunta** I'll answer the question **Este responde a la descripción** This man answers the description **No respondo de mi hermano** I'm not responsible for my brother **Respondo por él** I can vouch for him
servir	**Esta herramienta no sirve para nada** This tool is good for nothing **Puede servir de plato** It can serve as a plate
†**temor**	**su temor a la oscuridad** his fear of the dark **mi temor de que lleguen a saberlo** my fear that they will get to know
†**tentar**	**tentar a**ᴾᴱᴿˢ **uno a** (p 343) ᴀɴᴅ **tentar= (a) hacer algo** (R2–3) to try to do sth ʙᴜᴛ: **la tentativa de hacer algo**
†**terminar**	**terminar= de** (p 346), **por / +** ger (p 350); ᴀʟˢᴏ with **con** as **acabar**
†**tratar**	**tratar= de hacer algo** to try to do sth **Me trató de mal educado** He called me ill-bred **El conferenciante trató de/sobre un tema apasionante** The lecturer dealt with a fascinating subject **tratar con uno** to have dealings with sb **tratar en algo** to deal in sth
†**ver**	**ver** (p 339) ᴀɴᴅ **Veré= de terminarlo** I'll try and get it finished

25.9.1   No preposition in Spanish: preposition in English

Spanish verbs not listed above which take no preposition before a following infinitive or noun but correspond to English verbs which do:

†**acordar algo**	to agree on sth
†**agradecer algo a^{IO} uno**	to thank sb for sth
BUT NOTE: **estar agradecido a^{IO} uno por algo** = *to be grateful to sb for sth*	
†**aguardar algo / a^{PERS} uno**	to wait for (sb/sth)
BUT: **aguardar a que** + subj	
ambicionar hacer algo / algo	to have the ambition of doing sth / to strive after doing sth / sth
†**aprobar algo**	to approve of sth
†**aprovechar algo**	to take advantage of sth
BUT: **aprovecharse de algo** with the same meaning	
buscar algo / a^{PERS} uno	to look for sth/sb
†**callar algo**	to keep quiet about sth
comentar algo	to comment on sth
BUT: **un comentario a algo** (p 345)	
compadecer a^{PERS} uno	to sympathize with sb
BUT: **compadecerse de uno** with the same meaning	
†**compensar algo / una cosa con otra**	to compensate for sth / for sth with sth else
SEE ALSO **25.9**	
contratar algo / a^{PERS} uno	to sign a contract for sth / to take sb on
costear algo	to pay for sth
†**desaprobar algo**	to disapprove of sth
discriminar a^{PERS} uno	to discriminate against sb
equivocar algo	to make a mistake about sth
BUT: **equivocarse de algo** with the same meaning	
• **Equivocamos la fecha / Nos equivocamos de fecha**	• We got the date wrong
escuchar algo	to listen to sth
†**esperar algo / a^{PERS} uno**	to wait for sth/sb
BUT: **esperar a que** + subj	
NOTE: **esperar que** + indic/subj (**31.3, 31.8**) = *to hope that*	
impactar algo / a^{PERS} uno	to hit / to make a profound impression on sth/sb
incendiar algo	to set fire to sth
†**intervenir a^{PERS} uno**	to operate on sb
llorar algo	to weep over sth

†**mirar algo / a**^{PERS} **uno**	to look at sth/sb

BUT: **mirar a algo** = *to gaze at sth*

operar a^{PERS} **uno**	to operate on sb
padecer algo	to suffer from sth
pagar algo	to pay for sth

BUT: **Pagué uno con cincuenta por el periódico** = *I paid one euro fifty cents for the newspaper*

pedir algo a^{IO} **uno**	to ask sb for sth
†**pisar algo**	to tread on sth
†**pisotear algo**	to trample on sth
presidir algo	to preside over sth
†**profundizar (en) algo**	to go deeply into sth
†**recorrer una ciudad**	to go round (= visit) a town
suscribir algo	to subscribe to sth

BUT: **suscribirse a algo** with the same meaning

velar a^{PERS} **uno** (ALSO **por**)	to watch over sb
votar algo	to vote for sth

BUT: **votar por uno** = *to vote for sb* (**25.5**)

25.9.2 Preposition in Spanish: no preposition in English

Spanish verbs taking a preposition before a following infinitive or noun corresponding to English verbs which take no preposition:

†**abusar de algo**	to abuse sth
†**acordarse de algo (de** often omitted $\boxed{!}$ in R1)	to remember sth

NOTE: **recordar algo** with same meaning, and see **recordar** below. In Am R1 **recordarse de** and **recordar de** are often used.

†**amenazar**⁼ **con hacer algo** (see p 354)	to threaten to do sth
anteponerse a algo	to precede sth
anticiparse a algo	to anticipate, to get there before sth
ALSO **anticipar algo**	
†**apoderarse de algo**	to take hold of sth
†**apropiarse de algo**	to appropriate sth
asemejarse a uno	to resemble sb
†**asirse a algo**	to seize sth
†**asistir a algo**	to attend sth
carecer de algo	to lack sth
†**cargar con algo**	to take sth
• **Debo cargar con la responsabilidad**	• I must take the responsibility
casarse (see **34.3**) **con uno**	to marry sb
condescender⁼ **en hacer algo** (R3)	to condescend to do sth

contactar con algo/uno	to contact sth/sb
†contestar (a) una carta	to answer a letter

NOTE: **Contestar algo** has the additional meaning of *to contest sth*.

contravenir a algo	to contravene sth
†cumplir con algo	to fulfil sth

BUT: **su cumplimiento de la orden** = *his execution of the order*

†disponer de algo	to have sth at one's disposal
†dudar de algo (see 25.9)	to doubt sth
†encaramarse a/en algo	to climb sth
ensayarse= a/para hacer algo	to practise doing sth
enterarse de algo	to find sth out
†entrevistarse con uno	to interview sb

BUT: una †entrevista a/con uno

excederse en algo	to overdo, to exceed sth
fiarse de algo/uno	to trust sth/sb
incorporar algo a algo	to incorporate sth into sth
†jugar a(l tenis, etc)	to play (tennis, etc)
motejar a^{PERS} uno de algo	to label sb sth
†necesitar de algo/uno	to need sth/sb

ALSO **necesitar algo / a^{PERS} uno** with same meaning

BUT: la †**necesidad de algo / uno** = *the need for sth/sb*

†negarse= a hacer algo	to refuse to do sth

ALSO la †**negativa a hacer algo**

obsequiar a^{PERS} uno con algo (**con** often omitted in Am)	to give sb sth as a present
olvidarse de hacer algo / algo	to forget to do sth / sth

NOTE: the following constructions with **olvidar** and **olvidarse** −

Olvidé las llaves Se me olvidaron las llaves	} I forgot my keys
Me olvidé de hacerlo Se me olvidó hacerlo	} I forgot to do it
parecerse a uno	to resemble sb
percatarse de algo	to notice sth
†posesionarse de algo	to take possession of sth, to seize sth
†precisar de algo (R3)	to need sth
presumir de algo/ADJ	to think oneself sth/ADJ
• Presume de artista/listo	• He thinks himself an artist/clever
†protestar de algo	to protest sth
• Protesta de su inocencia	• He protests his innocence
†recordar algo a uno	to remind sb of sth

[†]**renunciar**⁼ **a hacer algo /**   to renounce doing sth / sth
  algo
ALSO **la** [†]**renuncia a hacer algo / algo**
[†]**resistirse**⁼ **a hacer algo / algo**   to resist doing sth / sth
rivalizar con uno/algo   to rival sb/sth
servirse de algo   to use sth
sobrevivir a uno/algo   to survive sb/sth
[†]**sustituir a algo/uno**   to substitute for sth/sb
unirse a algo   to associate oneself with sth

25.9.3   Some prepositions which do not correspond in Spanish and English

[†]**agarrarse a algo** (ALSO **de**   to cling on to sth
  (R1))
apiadarse de uno   to take pity on sb
arremeter contra uno   to charge sb
atenerse a algo/uno   to abide by sth / to rely on sb
atentar contra algo/uno   to make an attempt on sth/sb
• **Atentó contra la vida del**   • He made an attempt on the
rey ALSO **un atentado contra**   king's life
  algo/uno
calificar algo / a^{PERS} **uno de**   to describe sth/sb as ADJ
  (ALSO **como**) ADJ
[†]**chocar con/contra algo/uno**   to bump into sth/sb
[†]**compadecerse de uno**   to sympathize with sb
hacer compañía a uno   to keep sb company
confinar con algo (R3)   to border on sth
[†]**consentir en hacer algo /**   to consent to doing sth / sth
  algo
ALSO **el consentimiento**   (ALSO **para**, de) = *consent to sth*
  en algo
consistir en hacer algo/algo   to consist of doing sth / sth
BUT: **constar de hacer algo /**   with similar meaning
  algo
contar con uno/algo   to count on sb/sth
depender de uno/algo   to depend on sb/sth
[†]**diferente a** ($\boxed{!}$, but common) /   different from sth
  de algo
dimitir de (presidente)   to resign as (president)
ALSO **dimitir (la presidencia)** = to resign (from) (the presidency)
disparar a/contra uno   to fire at/on sb
NOTE: **disparar un tiro / un fusil** = *to fire a shot / a rifle*
[†]**distinto a/de algo**   different from sth
[†]**encararse con/a algo/uno**   to face up to sth/sb

†**encontrarse con algo/uno**	to meet sth/sb
†**enfrentarse con / a** $\boxed{!}$ **algo/uno**	to face up to sth/sb
examinarse de (**en** R1 Am) **algo**	to take an exam in sth
†**informar de/sobre algo**	to report on sth
informarse sobre algo	to enquire into sth
†**inquirir (sobre) algo**	to enquire into sth
†**lindar con algo**	to border on sth
†**pasar de (diez)**	to be more than, to exceed (ten)
†**preguntar por uno**	to ask for/after sb
prescindir= **de hacer algo / uno / algo** (R3)	to do without doing sth / sb / sth
rebasar de (diez)	to be more than, to exceed (ten)
responsabilizarse de algo	to make oneself responsible for sth
ALSO †**responsable de algo**	
soñar con uno/algo (often with no preposition in Central American R1)	to dream of (sb/sth)

NOTE: **soñar en hacer algo / algo** = *to daydream about* + ger/ *sth*

†**sustituir X por Y**	to substitute Y for X (lit to substitute X with Y)
†**tardar**= **en hacer algo**	to take time to do sth / in doing sth
ALSO **tardanza en hacer algo**	
tirar de algo†	to pull on sth

NOTE: **tirar algo** = *to throw sth*

toparse con algo (R2–3)	to run up against sth
traducir a (un idioma)	to translate into (a language)
†**tropezar con uno/algo**	to bump into sb/sth
†**vecino de algo**	next door to sth
ALSO **vecino a** (p 323)	

26 Constructions with verbs of movement

English and Spanish differ greatly in the ways they express *manner* and *direction* of movement. English tends to use a verb to express *manner* and a preposition to express *direction*; in Spanish, the verb normally expresses *direction* while a gerund or other adverbial phrase expresses *manner*. For example:

She ran / across the road
manner   *direction*
Atravesó la calle / corriendo
direction   *manner*

Other examples:

He crawled towards the wall
Avanzó a gatas hacia la pared
She hobbled back to the kitchen
Volvió cojeando a la cocina
He burst in
Entró volando
She swam across the river
Cruzó el río nadando / a nado
I crept downstairs
Bajé de puntillas la escalera
He cycled back
Volvió en bicicleta
They climbed over the wall
Pasaron por encima del muro

The chief *direction* verbs of Spanish are:

atravesar	(to go) across
avanzar hacia algo	(to go) towards sth
†**bajar**	(to go) down
†**continuar**	(to go) on
cruzar	(to go) across
†**dar la vuelta a algo**	(to go) around sth
†**entrar en algo**	(to go) in(to) sth
†**pasar**	(to go) past
pasar por debajo de algo	(to go) under sth

pasar por encima de algo	(to go) over sth
†**salir de algo**	(to go) out of sth
†**seguir**	(to go) on
†**subir**	(to go) up
†**volver**	(to go) back

Spanish does, however, have some *direction* adverbs, eg:

Anduvieron calle abajo
They walked down the street
Corrieron escaleras arriba
They ran up the stairs
Anduvieron campo a través
They went across the fields

and many *manner verbs*, eg:

Gateó hacia la valla
She crawled towards the fence
Irrumpió en la casa
He burst into the house
Pasearon a lo largo del río
They walked along the river

27 Negation

27.1 General

A Spanish sentence is negated by placing **no** before the verb or auxiliary (and associated pronouns, if any), eg:

Juan no lo hizo
John didn't do it
No quiero volver a verte
I don't want to see you again

'Scope' of negation can be limited by placing **no** in front of individual elements, eg:

No todos acudieron
Not everyone came
Estoy dispuesto a no hacerlo
I'm ready not to do it
Te lo digo no porque tu madre esté enfadada sino porque quiero saber la verdad
I'm telling you not because your mother is angry but because I want to know the truth

NOTE, however, that in one or two verbal expressions **no** does not give an exactly opposite meaning, eg:

†**Acabo de entender por qué lo hizo**
I've just realized why he did it

BUT

No acabo de entender por qué lo hizo
I fail to understand why he did it
†**Dejé de fumar**
I gave up smoking

BUT

No dejé de rezar las oraciones (R3)
I didn't neglect to say my prayers

27.2 Negation of adjectives

Often an adjective can be negated by using a negative prefix **in-** or **des-**, eg **cómodo/incómodo**, **conocido/desconocido.** If such a ready-made word does not exist (always check in a dictionary if you are uncertain), a variety of negatives, **no**, **nada** and **poco**, can be used.

no is used for straightforward negation:

un corazón no corrompido

an uncorrupted heart

objetivos no logrados

unattained objectives

poco is used where there is a sense of gradation, and means roughly *not very*, eg:

una idea poco original

an unoriginal idea

un paisaje poco típico

an atypical countryside

nada is stronger than **poco** and means roughly *not at all*, eg:

una costumbre nada frecuente

a not at all frequent custom

un empleo nada lucrativo

a not at all well-paid job

NOTE ALSO: the use of **sin** + inf in an adjectival sense, meaning *not yet*, eg:

una cuestión sin resolver

an unresolved question

una calle sin pavimentar

an unpaved street

27.3 Negative pronouns, adjectives and adverbs

These expressions (**nada**, **nadie**, **jamás**, **nunca**, **tampoco**, **ni**, **ni siquiera**, **ni . . . ni . . . ,** **ninguno** (**alguno** R3 following the noun)) are inherently negative. If used after a verb, the verb has to be preceded by **no** or another negative pronoun or adjective, eg:

No encontró nada BUT **Nada encontró** (R3)

He found nothing

No lo supo nadie BUT **Nadie lo supo**

No one knew

No había leído ningún libro / libro alguno (R3)

He had not read any books

No tengo ni bolígrafo ni lápiz

I have neither a ballpoint pen nor a pencil

BUT

Ni tú ni yo sabemos hacerlo
Neither you nor I know how to do it
NOTE: **ni . . . ni . . .** may be used with verbs –
Ni fumo ni bebo
I neither smoke nor drink

27.4 Expressions which require *no* before the verb

Spanish has a number of other expressions which have the value of a negative and require **no** before the verb:

No dijo palabra
He didn't say a word (anything)
No he dormido en toda la noche
I haven't slept all night
En mi vida no vi tal cosa
I've never seen such a thing
No me gustó en absoluto
I didn't like it at all

27.5 Other negative contexts

The negative and inherently negative expressions referred to in the preceding sections are also required in the following contexts – **sin, antes de, más . . . que, ser imposible**:

sin decir nada a nadie
without saying anything to anyone
antes de hacer ningún gesto
before making any expression
más alto que nunca
taller than ever
Es imposible contestar nada
It's impossible to answer anything

28 Use of tenses

Tenses in Spanish have three kinds of function: (a) temporal (referring to times: past, present, future, etc), (b) modal (representing attitudes: commands, politeness, supposition, etc) and (c) aspectual (the way in which an action or state is viewed: continuous, repeated, within 'fixed' limits, etc). The following table gives a summary of the main functions of the Spanish tenses within these categories.

28.1 Present tense (*hago*, etc)

Temporal functions	*Modal functions*
Any kind of PRESENT, including reference to a general state of affairs which includes the PRESENT, eg:	IMPERATIVE (see also **28.2** and **31.2**)
Ahora terminan su trabajo	**¿Me hace el favor de repetirlo?**
They're finishing their work now	Would you please repeat it?
Ahora sé qué hacer	'DUENESS' in FUTURE, eg:
Now I know what to do	**Mañana vamos a la playa**
Leo el periódico	Tomorrow we are going (= we have arranged to go) to the beach
I'm reading the newspaper	INTENTION in FUTURE, eg:
Hoy hace mucho frío	**¿Qué escribo?**
It's very cold today	What shall I write?
Siempre llego a las cinco	ABILITY in general PRESENT, eg:
I always arrive at five	**Habla tres idiomas**
Los Andes son muy altos	She speaks three languages
The Andes are very high	**Desde esta ventana se ven las montañas**
FUTURE (especially R1; see also modal functions), eg:	From this window you can see the mountains
El tren sale a las seis	
The train leaves at six	
IMMEDIATE PAST (especially R1), eg:	

Temporal functions

¿Qué me cuentas?
What have you just told me?
Te traigo un regalo
I've brought you a present
PAST continuing to PRESENT, eg:
**Vivo aquí desde hace dos
    meses**
I've been living here for two
    months
PAST (as R1 equivalent for
    Preterite and Imperfect), eg:
**Luego salgo del bar y estoy en
    la calle**
Then I left the bar and was in the
    street
Also regularly with **por poco
    (no)**, eg:
Por poco le mato
I nearly killed him

28.1.1 Present and Perfect

With adverbs marking a period of time back from the PRESENT
(English *for*, Spanish **desde**, **desde hace**, etc) standard Spanish uses the
Present when the action or state is continuous, eg:

Te espero aquí desde hace una hora **Hace una hora que te espero aquí** **Llevo esperándote aquí una hora** **Tengo una hora esperándote aquí** (Am, esp R1)	I've been waiting here for you for an hour

But where the period of time is that of something which has *not*
happened, either Present or Perfect can be used, and in R1 the
Imperfect may be used, eg:

Hace dos meses que no te veo / he
    visto
Hace dos meses que no te veía (R1)
Hace(n) dos meses a que no te veía
    (R1 (Am))
	It's two months since
	I saw you

28.2   Future tense (*haré*, etc)

Temporal function	Modal functions
FUTURE (but increasingly rare in R1), eg: **Mañana lo sabremos** Tomorrow we'll know	INTENTION, eg: **De eso no te diré más** I won't say any more to you about it IMPERATIVE (see also **28.1** and **31.2**), eg: **¡Sí que lo harás!** Oh yes you *will* do it! SUPPOSITION in PRESENT, eg: **Ahora estará aquí** He must be here now

28.3   Future Perfect tense (*habré hecho*, etc)

Temporal function	Modal functions
Anteriority in FUTURE, eg: **Lo habré terminado cuando le veamos** I will have finished it when we see him	SUPPOSITION (anterior to PRESENT), eg: **Habrá llegado ahora** He must have arrived now

28.4   Conditional tense (*haría*, etc)

Temporal function	Modal functions
FUTURE in PAST, eg: **Dijo que pronto lo sabríamos** She said that we would soon know	POLITENESS, eg: **¿Tendría usted la bondad de contestarme?** Would you be kind enough to answer me? SUPPOSITION (in PAST), eg: **Serían las ocho cuando salimos** It must have been eight o'clock when we left HYPOTHESIS in PRESENT OR FUTURE (see **31.7**), eg: **Se lo diría de buena gana si lo supiera, pero . . .** I would willingly tell you if I knew, but . . .

28.5   Conditional Perfect tense (*habría hecho*, etc)

Temporal function	*Modal functions*
Anteriority to FUTURE in PAST, eg: **Dijo que lo habría terminado antes de que llegara** She said she would have finished before he arrived	SUPPOSITION (anterior to PAST), eg: **Ya habría llegado cuando salimos** She must have arrived when we left HYPOTHESIS in PAST (see **31.7**), eg: **Se lo habría dicho, pero tú me lo impediste** I would have said so, but you stopped me

28.6   Imperfect and Preterite (*hacía*, etc; *hice*, etc)

The basis of the contrast between Imperfect and Preterite is aspectual. Both tenses can represent a single action or state or the repetition of an action or state.

The Preterite is basically the aspect of sequential action ('what happened next'); it implies that the action, state, or repeated action or state is thought of:

(a)   as taking place within a single 'closed' period of time, eg
   Estuve dos meses en Madrid
   I spent two months in Madrid
   Aquella semana fui cada día a la universidad
   That week I went to the university every day

(b)   as beginning at a particular moment, eg
   Luego supimos la verdad
   Then we got to know the truth

(c)   as being part of a sequence of events, eg
   Felipe V fue el primero de los Borbones (otros le sucedieron)
   Philip V was the first of the Bourbons (others succeeded him)
   Entonces hubo un estrépito grande (seguido de un silencio)
   Then there was a loud noise (followed by silence)

The Imperfect is basically the aspect of an ongoing action or state ('description in the past'). It represents actions, states, or repetitions of actions or states as being in progress and hence situated in an 'open' period of time, eg:

Estaba en Madrid (ya había estado allí unos meses) cuando
oí las noticias
I was in Madrid (I had been there some months) when I heard the
news
Ya lo sabíamos (antes que nos lo dijeras)
We already knew (before you told us)
Felipe V era típicamente Borbón
Philip V was a typical Bourbon
Iba muchas veces al río porque me gustaba nadar
I went to the river a lot because I liked swimming
Había un estrépito grande (ya había empezado) cuando
entré en la sala
There was a loud noise going on (it had already started) when I
went into the room
NOTE: the Imperfect is often used in journalistic R3 in place of the
Preterite, eg
El trece de febrero de 1939 atravesaba la frontera francesa
He crossed the French border on 13 February 1939

28.6.1 Imperfect tense (**hacía**, etc): other uses

Modal function

POLITENESS, eg:
Quería saber si . . .
I wanted to know if . . .

28.6.2 Preterite tense (**hice**, etc): other uses

Aspectual function

SUDDENNESS (idiomatic, with **acabarse**) (R1), eg:
Otros dos, y se acabó
Two more, and that's it

28.7 Perfect tense (*he hecho*, etc)

Temporal function

PAST where relevance to the PRESENT is implied, typically with
adverbs such as **hoy, este año, ahora mismo**, which include
reference to the PRESENT (understood), eg:
¿Todavía no has terminado?
Haven't you finished yet?
No le he visto esta semana
I haven't seen him this week

28.7.1 Perfect and Preterite

In general, the distinction between Perfect and Preterite in Spanish corresponds to that made in English between the Perfect and Simple Past (*have done / did*). But there are slight differences in register and regional variety in both languages. British English *I've already done it* corresponds to American English *I already did it*; American Spanish prefers **¿qué pasó?** to Peninsular **¿qué ha pasado?** Standard Peninsular and American usage prefer the Preterite for PAST events which are not related to the PRESENT, ie where adverbs such as **ayer**, **el año pasado**, **hace . . .** , etc, can be understood, although amongst Madrid speakers there is currently a preference for **lo he hecho ayer** over **lo hice ayer**.

28.8 Pluperfect tense (*había hecho*, etc)

Temporal function	*Modal functions*
Anteriority to PAST, eg: **Lo había terminado cuando llegó** I had finished when she arrived PAST in the PAST, eg: **Dijo que ya lo había hecho** He said he had already done it	SURPRISE (R1 Arg), eg: **¡Había sido usted!** So it's you!

28.9 Past Anterior tense (*hube hecho*, etc)

Temporal function	*Modal functions*
In a temporal clause, anteriority to PAST expressed by the Preterite, eg: **Cuando lo hubo terminado, salió** (R3 only; in R1–2 the Preterite or an alternative construction tends to be used) When he had finished, he left	SUDDENNESS in PAST, eg: **En un instante lo hubo terminado** (R2–3 only) He had finished it in an instant

28.10   -ra tense (*hiciera*, etc)

Temporal function	*Modal functions*
PAST (R3 Am), eg:	POLITENESS (restricted to **querer** in Pen), eg:
La noticia que este diario diera (= dio, ha dado) tiene confirmación	**Quisiera saber si . . .**
The news this paper gave has been confirmed	I would like to know if . . .
Anteriority in PAST (R3, esp Am), eg:	**¿Adónde fuéramos esta noche?** (Am)
Le entregó la carta que escribiera (= había escrito)	Where should we go tonight?
She gave him the letter she had written	HYPOTHESIS (see **28.5**), eg:
	Hubiera jurado que era él
	I could have sworn it was him

29 Periphrastic verb forms

The following periphrastic verb forms are used to a certain extent in all registers, but are especially common in R1, often replacing the verb forms in **28.1–10** above. They tend to be fairly specific in temporal, modal or aspectual value, and there are often restrictions on the tenses in which they can be used.

The English translations offered in this section are necessarily approximate, and do not always bring out the full value of the Spanish.

29.1 *ir a* + infinitive

Only used in Present and Imperfect.

Temporal functions	*Modal function*
FUTURE, and FUTURE in PAST, eg:	OBLIGATION, eg:
Voy a salir	**¡Cómo lo voy a saber!**
I'm going to leave	How should I know!
Iba a salir	
I was going to leave	

29.2 *acabar de* + infinitive

Only used in Present and Imperfect: otherwise it has the meaning of *to finish* + ger.

Temporal functions	*Modal function*
RECENT PAST, and RECENT PAST in PAST, eg:	POLITENESS (in negative), eg:
Acabo de salir	**No acabamos de entender**
I've just left	**por que . . .**
Acababa de salir	We can't understand why . . .
I'd just left	

29.3   *estar* + gerund

Aspectual value

CONTINUOUS action, eg:
Estoy leyendo
I'm reading
NOTE: **Estar** + gerund exists in all tenses, even in the Preterite, eg
Toda aquella mañana estuvimos haciendo visitas = *We were visiting all that morning.* Note, however, that the Spanish Present Continuous *cannot* refer to the future, as can English, eg: **Lo estoy haciendo** = I'*m doing it (now)*; but *I'm doing it tomorrow* = **Lo voy a hacer mañana.**
NOTE: many purists condemn **estar siendo**, although it is in common usage, especially in R1, eg **Esta lectura está siendo** (R1) / **resultando** (R2) **muy difícil** = *This reading is proving very difficult.*

29.4   *ir* + gerund

Aspectual values

GRADUAL action (implying adverbs such as **cada vez más/menos, poco a poco**, etc), eg:
El tiempo va mejorando
It's clearing up
GRADUAL BEGINNING of an action, eg:
Ya voy viendo
I'm beginning to see

29.5   *venir* + gerund

Only used in Present and Imperfect.

Temporal values	*Aspectual value*
PAST continuing to PRESENT (Present), FAR PAST continuing to PAST (Imperfect), eg: **Vengo diciéndolo desde hace mucho tiempo** I've kept saying so for some time	REPETITION

29.6 *llevar* + gerund

Aspectual function

The STAGE reached by a CONTINUOUS action or state, eg:
Lleva estudiando en Madrid dos meses
She's been studying for two months in Madrid

29.7 *tener* + past participle

Aspectual functions	*Modal value*
COMPLETION (only with transitive verbs; the PP agrees with the object), eg:	MORAL 'HOLD', eg:
Lo tengo bien pensado	**Te tengo prohibido que**
I've got it thought out	**digas cosas así**
Tengo escritas dos cartas	I've forbidden you to say things
I've got two letters written	like that
REPETITION (with transitives and intransitives), eg:	
Ya te tengo dicho que no hagas eso	
I've told you repeatedly not to do that	

29.8 *llevar* + past participle

Aspectual function

The STAGE reached in a REPEATED action or state, eg:
Llevamos publicados tres libros de la serie
We've got three books in the series published

29.9   *ir* + past participle

Aspectual functions

The STAGE reached in a REPEATED action or state (a kind of passive
   equivalent of **llevar** + PP), eg:
Van publicados tres libros de la serie
Three books in the series have been published
A RESULTANT STATE (comparable with **estar** + PP – see **32.5**), eg:
Van preparados para un desastre
They're prepared for a disaster

---

30 Modal auxiliaries

English has a relatively large number of auxiliary verbs (eg *will*, *would*, *may*, *might*, *shall*, *should*, *must*, *ought*) and verbal expressions (*to be to*: 'we were to arrive at nine'; *to have to*: 'we had to go'). Their main function is to express intentions or opinions (commands, possibility, etc). There is no straightforward match between these and their Spanish equivalents: Spanish has a rather smaller number of auxiliary verbs (eg **deber**, **poder**, **querer**) and verbal expressions (**tener que hacer algo**, **haber de hacer algo**). The major differences between Spanish and English are:

1 Spanish auxiliaries may usually be used in all tenses (eg **puede**, **podía**, **podría**, **ha podido**, **pudo**, etc) while English auxiliaries have a maximum of two (which may in any case have independent modal values, eg *may*, *might*) and sometimes only one (eg *must*).

2 In English, the Perfect auxiliary *have* is used only with the dependent infinitive (*He may have done it*), whereas in Spanish **haber** is used either with the dependent infinitive (**podría haberlo hecho**) or with the modal auxiliary (**Habría podido hacerlo**). There is a good deal of overlap in the values of modal auxiliaries in both Spanish and English: English *It will be six o'clock* or *It must be six o'clock*; Spanish **Debes hacerlo** or **Tienes que hacerlo**. Also, an auxiliary may have several modal functions: English *can* is associated with ABILITY and POSSIBILITY; Spanish **deber** with OBLIGATION and INFERENCE.

The following tables are presented according to categories of meaning rather than taking each modal auxiliary separately, and the equivalences given are necessarily rather vague. They are not exhaustive but cover the most problematic areas of usage. Judgements about 'strength' and 'weakness' of meaning derive from native speakers, but it is unlikely that all speakers would agree about these.

30.1 Obligation

	weakest	
You might (at least) tell him!	↑	**(Por lo menos) podrías/ podías decírselo**
You should tell him		**Has de** (R3 and regional) /
You ought to tell him		**Deberías / Debieras** (R3)
You are to tell him		**decírselo**
You have to tell him		**Debías decírselo**
You must tell him	↓	**Tienes que decírselo**
		Debes decírselo
	strongest	

	weakest	
You might (at least) have told him	↑	**(Por lo menos) podrías / podías / pudieras** (R3) / **has podido / pudiste habérselo dicho**
You should have told him		**(Por lo menos) podías / podrías / pudiste / habrías podido / hubieras podido** (R3) **/ habías podido / has podido decírselo**
You ought to have told him		**Habrías debido** (R3 preferred) **/ Hubieras debido** (R3) **/ Habías debido** (R3 preferred) **/ Has debido** (R3 preferred) **decírselo**
You were to tell him		**Debiste/Debías decírselo**
You had to tell him		**Debiste habérselo dicho**
You *should* have told him	↓	**Tenías que decírselo / Tenías que habérselo dicho** (R2)
		Deberías/Debías/Debieras (R3) **habérselo dicho**
	strongest	

Notes

1   The choice of tense for the auxiliary in Spanish (eg **has debido**, **debías**, **debiste**, etc) corresponds to the tense that would be appropriate for a simple verb, eg:

> **Se lo dije ayer**
> I told him yesterday
> **Se lo debí haber dicho ayer**
> I should have told him yesterday

NOTE: **Se lo debía haber dicho ayer** is also possible when thought of as an 'ongoing state' (see **28.6**).

> **Pudiste decírselo ayer**
> You might have told him yesterday!
> **Estaban en Nueva York**
> They were in New York
> **Debían estar en Nueva York**
> They had to be in New York
> **Ha ayudado a mucha gente**
> He's helped lots of people
> **Ha debido ayudar a mucha gente**
> He's had to help lots of people

2   **Debía** and **podía** may additionally function as alternatives to **debería** and **podría** in modal auxiliary expressions.

3   Tenses other than those given in the above examples may be used if the context demands them; for example, a future tense may be used for the modal auxiliary when reference is to the future:

> **Deberás hacerlo la semana que viene**
> You'll have to do it next week

30.2   Ability

Man cannot fly	**El hombre no puede volar**
They could not come	**No pudieron venir**

	weakest	
He could not have known	↑	**No podría haberlo sabido**
		No habría podido saberlo
		No podía haberlo sabido
	↓	**No podía saberlo**
	strongest	

NOTE: A learned ability is rendered in Spanish by **saber hacer algo**, eg

> I can swim
> **Sé nadar**

Poder hacer algo is used only for a physical ability, eg:
I can swim a kilometre
Puedo nadar un kilómetro
A general property is rendered in Spanish by a simple verb, eg
From here you can see the sea
Desde aquí se ve el mar

30.3 Inference

	least sure	
She should be in London now	↑	**Debe (de) estar ahora en Londres**
She must be in London now	│	
She ought to be in London now	│	
She will be in London now	↓	**Estará ahora en Londres**
	most sure	

	least sure	
She should have arrived by now	↑	**Ha debido llegar ahora**
She must have arrived by now	│	
She ought to have arrived by now	│	**Debe (de) haber llegado ahora**
She will have arrived by now	↓	**Habrá llegado ahora**
	most sure	

	least sure	
She should have arrived yesterday	↑	**Debió haber llegado ayer**
She ought to have arrived yesterday	│	
She would have arrived yesterday	↓	**Debió llegar ayer**
	most sure	

	least sure	
She should have finished by eight	↑	**Habrá debido terminar antes de las ocho**
She must have finished by eight	│	
She ought to have finished by eight	│	
She will have finished by eight	↓	**Habrá terminado antes de las ocho** (more frequent)
	most sure	

NOTE: Purists draw a distinction between **deber hacer algo** and **deber de hacer algo** on the basis that **deber de hacer algo** indicates inference and **deber hacer algo** obligation. While **de** is admitted by speakers in certain cases, as above, it appears always to be optional and is sometimes considered clumsy and pedantic, especially with compound tenses of **deber**.

30.4 Possibility

They may come	**Pueden venir**
They might come They could come	**Podrían venir**
They may have come	**Pueden haber venido**
They might have come They could have come	**Podrán haber venido** **Pudieron haber venido**

31 The Subjunctive

It should be stressed that in the Spanish of all registers and regions all the tenses of the Subjunctive are actively used today. In the Imperfect and Pluperfect Subjunctive, the **–ra** form is commoner than the **–se** form, especially in R1, and particularly in R1 Am. However, there *are* alternatives to many Subjunctive constructions which tend to be preferred in R1–2.

There are various uses of the Subjunctive, and it is essential *not* to think of the Subjunctive itself as having one characteristic 'meaning'. Having said that, it is helpful to bear in mind that the Subjunctive is largely confined to subordinate clauses and is strongly associated with many contexts in which the speaker is not committed to the truth of that clause, and so it is used to express doubt, hypothesis, lack of agreement, emotional attitude, etc. It is also helpful to realize at the outset that in Spanish there are both contexts in which the Subjunctive is obligatory (in the same way that a plural adjective is obligatory with a plural noun) and contexts in which there is a choice between Subjunctive and Indicative. In the former case, the Subjunctive itself is automatically required and so has no distinctive meaning; in the latter case, there is usually a difference in meaning between Subjunctive and Indicative, and English speakers sometimes find this difficult to grasp.

In the following sections, the uses of the Subjunctive are grouped according to the meaning or syntax of the contexts in which they are found. The possibility of choice between Subjunctive and Indicative is indicated by an asterisk (*), and explained more fully in notes. Alternatives to the Subjunctive constructions are also given, and are of two kinds: (a) optional alternatives which are on the whole more commonly used in R1–2, though unless otherwise indicated both constructions are actively used in all registers, and (b) obligatory alternatives which are demanded by certain conditions. The chief kind of obligatory alternative is the use of an infinitive when the subject of the main verb and the subject of the complement verb are identical, for example with **querer**. **Quiero que lo haga** could never be used to mean *I want to do it* (where **yo** is the subject of **quiero** and also of **haga**): this notion must be rendered by **Quiero hacerlo** or **Lo quiero hacer**.

NOTE: Only a brief account of usage with infinitive complements is included in this section; see **Chapter 25** for further information.

31.1 Sequence of tenses in Subjunctive constructions

The basic sequence-of-tense patterns are given in the following table:

main clause	subordinate clause
Present/Perfect Future / Future Perfect	Present/Perfect Subjunctive
Imperfect/Pluperfect-Preterite Conditional / Conditional Perfect	Imperfect/Pluperfect Subjunctive

Examples:
Pide que se lo digamos
She asks us to tell her
Me gustaría que lo hicieses
I'd like you to do it
Me alegro de que hayas llegado temprano
I'm glad you've arrived early
No había pensado que fuera tan difícil
I hadn't thought it was so difficult
Negó que lo hubieran hecho
He denied that they had done it
However, this sequence of tense may sometimes be broken if there is a shift in point of view in the course of the sentence (the same thing may happen in English in parallel structures), eg:
Negó (in the past) **que existiera/exista** (universal principle) **una relación directa entre la gravedad y el magnetismo**
He denied that there was/is a direct relationship between gravity and magnetism
Se pidió (in the past) **al presidente que buscara/busque** (he hasn't done it yet) **una solución**
The president was asked to find a solution
See also the note on sequence of tense on pp 410–11.

31.2 Commands and related structures

31.2.1 Direct commands

The Subjunctive is used for all direct commands except the **tú** and **vosotros** (Pen) positive imperatives **(haz**, **haced)**.

Subjunctive expression	*Alternative/Remarks*
¡Hága(n)lo!	**¡A hacerlo!** (R1–2), **¡Lo harás!** (R1–3), **¡Haciéndolo!** (R1), etc
¡No lo hagas! **¡No lo hagáis!** (Pen) **¡No lo haga(n)!**	**¡No lo harás!**, etc (R1–3), **¡Ni hacerlo!** (R1), **¡Nada de hacerlo!** (R1), **¡Sin hacerlo!** (R1)
¡Que venga(n)! **¡Empecemos ahora!** (R2–3) but with **ir(se)**: **¡Vámonos!**	**¡Vamos a empezar ahora!** (R1–2)

Notes

1 The Subjunctive may be used as an alternative to the **tú** and **vosotros** (Pen) imperatives to express a wish: **¡Que te diviertas mucho!** or **¡Diviértete mucho!**

2 The infinitive is increasingly used as an imperative

(a) in place of the rather odd-sounding Peninsular **vosotros** imperative: **¡Sentaros!** for **¡Sentaos!**

(b) to soften the tone of the imperative: **¡Escribirme!**, **¡Telefonearme mañana!**

(c) in formal instructions where it has the advantage of avoiding the choice between the polite and informal second-person forms: **Consumir preferentemente antes de la fecha indicada.** It is regularly used in recipes:

> **Poner en un cazo la leche, el agua, la mantequilla . . .**
> **Mezclar la harina. Añadir huevos . . .**

3 There are a number of other expressions involving imperatives which may conveniently be mentioned here, eg:

> **hágalo o no lo haga**
> whether she does it or not
> **dijera lo que dijera**
> whatever she might have said
> **viniera de donde viniera**
> wherever he came from
> **sea como sea/fuere**
> be that as it may

NOTE: **Fuere** is the old Future Subjunctive, still occasionally preserved in this expression.

> **venga cuando venga**
> come when he may / whenever he comes
> **Te vistas como te vistas**
> Dress as you like

The use of the Subjunctive after **como** and **cuando** in the last three examples is related to the use with *-ever* expressions (see **31.9**).

31.2.2   Indirect command, request, necessity

The Subjunctive is used in the complements of verbs and verbal expressions which express influence.

Subjunctive-requiring expression	*Alternative / Remarks*
†**aconsejar que** *to advise*	**aconsejar a uno** + inf
• **le aconsejé que lo hiciese**	• **le aconsejé hacerlo**
† **agradecer que** *to thank, to be grateful*	BUT NOTE the infinitive construction when the complement refers to the past:
• **Le agradezco (que) me escriba** I would be grateful if you would write to me	• **Le agradezco el haberme escrito** I am grateful to you for writing
† **animar a uno a que** *to encourage*	**animar a uno a** + inf
† **conseguir que** *to manage, to get*	BUT: **conseguir hacer algo** obligatory when subjects of main verb and complement verb are identical
†*†*decidir que** *to decide*	BUT: **decidir** + inf obligatory when subjects of main verb and complement verb are identical
• **Decidí que lo hiciese** I decided that he should do it	• **Decidí hacerlo** I decided to do it
† *decir que** *to tell*	See p 339 for **decir** + inf
†*declarar que** (R3) *to state*	See p 340 for **declarar** + inf
decretar que (R3) *to decree*	

Subjunctive-requiring expression	Alternative/Remarks
† **desear que** *to want, to wish, to desire*	BUT: **desear** + inf obligatory when subjects of main verb and complement verb are identical
† **disponer que** *to stipulate*	
es esencial que (impersonal) *it is essential*	**es esencial** + inf
*****establecer que** *to establish*	
† **evitar que** *to avoid*	BUT: **evitar** + inf obligatory when subjects of main verb and complement verb are identical
† **exigir que** *to demand, to require*	NOTE ALSO: **exigir a uno** + inf, eg: ● **Exigí al chico volver en seguida**
† **hace falta que** (impersonal) *it is necessary* ● **Hace falta que llegue a tiempo** I need to arrive in time	**hace falta** + inf, eg: ● **Hace falta llegar a tiempo** It's necessary to arrive in time NOTE: that the infinitive construction avoids specification of a subject
hacer que *to make, to mean* ● **La presencia del ministro hizo que la ceremonia revistiera más importancia** The minister's presence meant that the ceremony had greater importance	NOTE: that, where the subject of the second verb can be expressed as a personal pronoun, an infinitive construction is more usual: ● **Le hicieron firmar el contrato** They made him sign the contract
es imperative que (impersonal) *it is imperative*	**es imperative** + inf
es importante que (impersonal) *it is important*	**es importante** + inf
†**lograr que** *to manage, to get*	BUT **lograr** + inf obligatory when subjects of main verb and complement verb are identical

Subjunctive-requiring expression	Alternative/Remarks
†**mandar que** *to order*	**mandar** + inf NOTE these constructions: • **Le mandé hacerlo / Se lo mandé hacer** I ordered him to do it • **Lo mandé hacer / Mandé hacerlo** I ordered it to be done
†**es mejor que** (impersonal) *it is better*	**es mejor** + inf
motivar que *to motivate* • **El deseo de la unidad motivó que llegaran a un acuerdo** The desire for unity motivated them to come to an agreement	NOTE ALSO: the construction: • **El profesor motivó a los alumnos para estudiar** The teacher motivated the pupils to study
es necesario que (impersonal) *it is necessary*	**es necesario** + inf
†**necesitar que** *to need*	BUT **necesitar** + inf obligatory when subjects of main verb and complement verb are identical
†**ordenar que** *to order*	**ordenar a uno** + inf
†**pedir que** *to ask*	BUT **pedir** + inf obligatory when subjects of main verb and complement verb are identical
† **precisa que** (impersonal) (R3) *it is necessary*	**precisa** + inf
precisar que (R3) *to need*	BUT **precisar** + inf obligatory when subjects of main verb and complement verb are identical
es preciso que (impersonal) *it is necessary*	**es preciso** + inf
presionar para que *to press*	
†***pretender que** *to expect, to suggest*	See p 338 for **pretender** + inf

Subjunctive-requiring expression	*Alternative/Remarks*
† **querer que** *to want*	BUT **querer** + inf obligatory when subjects of main verb and complement verb are identical
† **reclamar que** *to demand, to require*	
recomendar que *to recommend*	
†**resolver que** (R2–3) *to resolve*	BUT **resolver** + inf obligatory when subjects of main verb and complement verb are identical
†**rogar que** *to ask*	**rogar a uno** + inf
†**suplicar que** *to ask, to implore*	**suplicar a uno** + inf
† **urge que** (impersonal) (R3) *it is urgent*	**urge** + inf
es urgente que (impersonal) *it is urgent*	**es urgente** + inf
más vale que (impersonal) *it is better, it is preferable*	**más vale** + inf

Notes

1 When the asterisked verbs listed above do not express a command, the Indicative is used. Contrast the following pairs of examples:

Decidí que dimitiera
I decided he should resign
Decidí que eso era mejor
I decided that was better
Juan me dijo que saliera
John told me to leave
Juan me dijo que saliste
John told me that you left
Ha declarado que los impuestos sean abolidos
He has declared that taxes should be abolished
Ha declarado que el Gobierno no sirve para nada
He has declared that the government is no good
**Hemos establecido que todos los ciudadanos tengan
    derecho a su opinión**
We have established that all citizens shall have a right to their opinion
Hemos establecido que el hidrógeno es combustible
We have established that hydrogen burns

Pretende que todos estén de acuerdo
He expects everyone to agree
Pretende que todos estaban de acuerdo
He claims that everyone was in agreement

2 **Que** is often omitted after **agradecer, pedir, rogar** and **suplicar** in R3, eg:

Rogamos se sirva contestar cuanto antes
Please reply as soon as possible

31.2.3 Suggestion

This may be viewed as a kind of weak or polite command.

Subjunctive-requiring expression	Alternative/Remarks
†**basta que** (impersonal) *it is enough*	**basta** + inf (as for **hace falta** + inf, p 337)
*****convencer a uno para que** *to persuade*	**convencer a uno para** + inf
†**convidar a uno a que** (R2–3) *to invite*	**convidar a uno a** + inf (R1–3)
†**conviene que** (impersonal) *it is fitting, it is advisable*	**conviene** + inf (as for **hace falta** + inf, p 337)
estar dispuesto a que *to be prepared for* • **No estamos dispuestos a que la gente se comporte de esta manera** We are not prepared for people to behave in this way	
†**disuadir a uno de que** *to dissuade*	**disuadir a uno de** + inf
†**importa que** (impersonal) *it matters*	**importa** + inf (as for **hace falta** + inf, p 337)
†*****indicar que** (R2–3) *to indicate*	
*****insinuar que** (R2–3) *to insinuate, to hint*	
†**invitar a uno a que** (R2–3) *to invite*	**invitar a uno a** + inf (R1–3)
†**persuadir a uno que** *to persuade*	**persuadir a uno a/para** + inf
†**proponer a uno que** *to propose*	**proponer a uno** + inf

Subjunctive-requiring expression	Alternative/Remarks
proponerse que *to propose* (in Perfect) *to be determined* • **Te has propuesto que no lo sepa** You're determined she won't know	BUT **proponerse** + inf obligatory when subjects of main verb and complement verb are identical • **Me propongo salir** I propose to go out
es suficiente que (impersonal) *it is sufficient*	**es suficiente** + inf (as for **hace falta** + inf, p 337)
†***sugerir que** *to suggest*	**sugerir a uno** + inf

Notes

When the asterisked verbs listed above do not have the force of a weak command, the Indicative is used. Contrast the following pairs of examples:

> **Le convencí para que fuese**
> I persuaded him he should go
> **Le convencí de que tenía razón**
> I convinced him that he was right
> **Me indicó/insinuó/sugirió que me sentara**
> He indicated/hinted/suggested that I should sit down
> **Me indicó/insinuó/sugirió que quería hacerse profesor**
> He indicated/hinted/suggested that he wanted to become a teacher

31.2.4   Permission and prohibition

Subjunctive-requiring expression	Alternative/Remarks
†**aprobar que** (R2–3) *to approve*	
†**consentir que** *to allow, to tolerate* • **No consiento que hable** I won't allow him to speak	**consentir a uno** + inf BUT **consentir en** + inf obligatory when subjects of main verb and complement verb are identical • **No le consiento salir** I won't allow him out • **Consiento en ir** I agree to go
†**dejar que** *to allow, to let*	**dejar a uno** + inf

Subjunctive-requiring expression	Alternative/Remarks
†**desaprobar que** (R3) *to disapprove* • **Desaprueba que lo haga yo** She disapproves of my doing it	
†**impedir que** *to prevent*	**impedir a uno** + inf
oponerse a que (R2–3) *to oppose*	BUT **oponerse a** + inf obligatory when subjects of main verb and complement verb are identical
†**permitir que** *to permit, to allow*	**permitir a uno** + inf
†**prohibir que** *to forbid, to prohibit*	**prohibir a uno** + inf
propiciar que *to favour, bring about* • **La situación económica propició que se invirtiera más dinero en la empresa** The economic situation favoured investing more money in the firm	

31.2.5 Conjunctions expressing purpose or intention

Subjunctive-requiring expression	Alternative/Remarks
a fin de que (R2–3) *in order that*	
*de forma/manera/modo que *so that*	
para que *in order that*	**para** + inf (R1) • **Lo hizo para saberlo yo** He did it so that I would know BUT **para** + inf obligatory when subjects of main verb and complement verb are identical

Notes

1 **De forma/manera/modo que** take the Indicative when they express consequence. Contrast the following:

Lo recité muy despacio, de forma/manera/modo que lo aprendieran

I recited it very slowly in order that they might learn it

Lo recité muy despacio, de forma/manera/modo que lo aprendieron

I recited it very slowly, so (consequently) they learned it

NOTE: Rather oddly, **de ahí que**, which always expresses consequence, takes the Subjunctive:

La niña tenía miedo a la oscuridad, de ahí que nunca se apagaran la luces

The little girl was afraid of the dark, so the lights were never switched off

2 **Para que** introducing a complement of sufficiency (see **24.13.3**) also takes the Subjunctive, eg:

Faltan/Quedan dos horas para que lleguen

It'll be two hours before they arrive

31.2.6 Other expressions of influence

Subjunctive-requiring expression	Alternative/Remarks
ayudar a uno a que *to help*	**ayudar a uno a** + inf
†forzar a uno a que *to force*	**forzar a uno a** + inf
†hacer a uno que *to make*	**hacer** + inf NOTE these constructions: • **Le hice leerlo / Se lo hice leer** I made him read it • **Lo hice leer / Hice leerlo** I had it read
obligar a uno a/para que *to oblige, to compel*	**obligar a uno a** + inf
ser partidario de que *to be in favour of*	BUT **ser partidario de** + inf obligatory when subjects of main verb and complement verb are identical
preferir que *to prefer*	BUT **preferir**+inf obligatory when subjects of main verb and complement verb are identical
tratar de que *to try and make sure* • **Trata de que no caiga** Try and make sure it doesn't fall	

399

31.3 Expressions of emotion

Spanish uses a Subjunctive in the complement of the following verbs and verbal expressions, whatever the truth or otherwise of the complement. Expressions of emotion should be carefully distinguished from expressions of opinion, which are dealt with in **31.5** below.

Subjunctive-requiring expression	Alternative/Remarks
†**alegra a uno que** (impersonal) *it makes sb happy*	**alegra a uno** + inf
†**alegrarse de que** *to be happy, to be glad*	BUT **alegrarse de** + inf obligatory when subjects of main verb and complement verb are identical
es bueno que (impersonal) *it is nice, it is good*	**es bueno** + inf
†**celebrar que** (R3) *to be glad*	BUT **celebrar** + inf obligatory when subjects of main verb and complement verb are identical
†*****confiar en que** (R2–3) *to trust*	
†**encanta a uno que** (impersonal) *it delights*	**encanta a uno** + inf
†*****esperar que** *to hope*	BUT **esperar** + inf obligatory when subjects of main verb and complement verb are identical
es de esperar que (impersonal) *it is to be hoped*	
extraña a uno que (impersonal) *it surprises*	**extraña a uno** + inf
es de †**extrañar que** (impersonal) *it is surprising*	
extrañarse de que *to be surprised*	
es †**extraño que** (impersonal) *it is surprising*	**es extraño** + inf

Subjunctive-requiring expression	Alternative/Remarks
es inevitable que (impersonal) *it is inevitable*	**es inevitable** + inf
es inútil que (impersonal) *it is useless*	**es inútil** + inf
es justo que (impersonal) *it is right*	**es justo** + inf
lamentar que *to be sorry*	BUT **lamentar** + inf obligatory when subjects of main verb and complement verb are identical
es (una (R1)) lástima que (impersonal) *it is a pity*	**es lástima** + inf
es lógico que (impersonal) *it is natural*	**es lógico** + inf
†**es mejor que** (impersonal) *it is better*	**es mejor** + inf
†**tener miedo que** *to be afraid*	BUT **tener miedo de** + inf obligatory when subjects of main verb and complement verb are identical
†**molesta a uno que** (impersonal) *it annoys*	**molesta a uno** + inf
es natural que (impersonal) *it is natural*	**es natural** + inf
tener pánico a/de que *to be terrified*	BUT **tener pánico de** + inf obligatory when subjects of main verb and complement verb are identical
es una pena que *it is a shame*	**es una pena** + inf
es raro que (impersonal) *it is odd*	**es raro** + inf

reprochar que
to reproach
• **Me reprochó que no dijera nada**
She reproached me for not saying anything

Subjunctive-requiring expression	Alternative/Remarks
hay el riesgo de que *there's the risk* • **Hay el riesgo de que se rompa** There's the risk that it will break	BUT **hay el riesgo de** + inf obligatory when the infinitive has an indefinite subject: • **Hay el riesgo de no llegar a tiempo** There's the risk of not arriving in time
estar satisfecho de que *to be satisfied*	
†**sentir que** *to regret*	BUT **sentir** + inf obligatory when subjects of main verb and complement verb are identical
†***temer que** *to fear*	BUT **temer** + inf obligatory when subjects of main verb and complement verb are identical
es de temer que (impersonal) *it is to be feared*	
es triste que (impersonal) *it is sad* NOTE, however, **lo triste es que** + Indicative: • **Es triste que no lo sepa** It's sad she doesn't know • **Lo triste es que no lo sabe** The sad thing is that she doesn't know	**es triste** + inf

Note

Confiar en and **esperar** frequently, but by no means always, take the Indicative when the complement is in the future; in such circumstances there is a choice between Indicative and Subjunctive which is often difficult to appreciate from an English point of view:

> **Espero/Confío en que haya tenido / tenga éxito**
> I hope/trust he has been / will be successful
> **Espero/Confío en que tendrá éxito**
> I hope/trust he'll be successful (I'm sure he will)

† **Temer(se)** takes the Indicative when the 'fear' is only conventional or polite and not a genuine emotion:

> **Temo que vaya a caer**
> I'm afraid (genuinely) that he'll fall
> **(Me) temo que usted no tiene razón**
> I'm afraid (polite) that you're wrong

31.4   Expressions involving a negative idea

31.4.1   Verbs and verbal expressions of denial and doubt

Subjunctive-requiring expression	*Alternative/Remarks*
no es casual que (impersonal) *it's no accident that*	
no es †cierto que (impersonal) *it is not certain*	NOTE: **no es cierto** (impersonal) **si** + Indicative
no comprender que *not to understand*	
descartar que (R2–3) *to rule out*	
desmentir (R3) **que** *to deny*	BUT **desmentir** + inf obligatory when subjects of main verb and complement verb are identical
†dudar que *to doubt* • **Dudo que tenga mucho dinero** I doubt he has much money NOTE: Perhaps because of the mixing of these constructions, **dudar que** sometimes takes the Indicative in R1 ⃞!	NOTE: **dudar si** + Indicative (R1–2) • **Dudo si llegará a tiempo** I doubt if he will arrive in time
es dudoso que (impersonal) *it is doubtful*	NOTE: **es dudoso** (impersonal) **si** + Indicative
no entender que *not to understand*	
no es que (impersonal) *it's not (the case)* • **No es que salgamos mucho** It's not that we go out a lot	
†ignorar que *to be unaware* NOTE: as for **dudar**	NOTE: **ignorar si** + Indicative
es inaudito que *it is beyond belief*	
es †increíble que (impersonal) *it is incredible*	

Subjunctive-requiring expression	Alternative/Remarks
†**negar que** *to deny*	BUT **negar** + inf obligatory when subjects of main verb and complement verb are identical

NOTE: **Negar que** sometimes takes the Indicative in R1 [!].

no querer decir que *not to mean*	

rechazar que *to reject (the idea)*	

• **Rechazamos que este procedimiento sea lícito**
We reject the idea that this procedure is justifiable

Subjunctive-requiring expression	Alternative/Remarks
no es seguro que (impersonal) *it is not certain*	NOTE: **no es seguro** (impersonal) **si** + Indicative

• **No es seguro que vaya**
It's not certain that she will go
See **32.6** for **ser/estar seguro** with a personal subject.

no es verdad que (impersonal) *it is not true*	

31.4.2   'Negative' conjunctions

Subjunctive-requiring expression	Alternative/Remarks
sin que *without*	**sin** + inf
• **Lo hizo sin que yo lo supiera** He did it without my knowing	• **Lo hizo sin saberlo yo** He did it without my knowing BUT **sin** + inf obligatory when subjects of main verb and complement verb are identical • **Lo dije sin darme cuenta** I said it without realizing

31.5   Expressions of opinion and thought

Verbs of thinking such as **admitir, comprender, concebir**, †**creer**, †**figurarse**, †**imaginarse**, †**parecer** (impersonal), †**pensar** and †**suponer** normally have Indicative verbs in their complements (but see **31.7** below). There are circumstances, however, in which the Subjunctive is used.

31.5.1   Apparent negation

When the verb is apparently negated, eg **No creo que sea verdad**. In fact, this is simply the equivalent of the construction **Creo que no es verdad**, and it is not **creer** itself that is being negated. This 'transferring' of the negative element from the complement verb to the main verb necessitates in Spanish the complement verb going into the Subjunctive, eg:

Me [†]parece que este problema no tiene solución
No me parece que este problema tenga solución
} I don't think this problem has a solution

Me [†]imagino que no ha salido todavía
No me imagino que haya salido todavía
} I don't suppose he's left yet

31.5.2   Doubt or hesitation

The Subjunctive is used where there is a strong element of doubt or hesitation concerning the complement, eg:

Creo que sea verdad (especially R1)
I think it may be true
Admito que no tenga razón
I admit he may not be right

Conversely, the 'negative-transferred' constructions discussed in the previous section may have the Indicative if the truth of the complement is being strongly asserted, eg:

Pedro no cree que la Tierra es redonda
Pedro doesn't think the Earth is round (but it is)

Extreme care should be taken in using constructions such as these.

31.5.3   Emotional overtone

The Subjunctive is used where the verb has an emotional overtone, eg:

Comprendo que no lo hayas querido hacer
I can understand that you shouldn't have wanted to do it

Extreme care should be taken in using constructions such as these.

31.6   Expressions of possibility and probability

Subjunctive-requiring expression	Alternative/Remarks
acaso (R2–3) *perhaps*	
es posible que (impersonal) *it is possible*	**es posible** + inf
posiblemente *possibly*	
prever que *to expect, foresee* • **Se prevé que empeore la situación** It is expected that the situation will get worse	
estar previsto que *to be due, expected*	
es probable que (impersonal) *it is probable*	
puede (ser) que (impersonal) *maybe, perhaps* NOTE: **Pueda (ser) que** + Subjunctive is also encountered in R1 (Pen) and R1–2 (Am).	BUT **poder** + inf obligatory when subjects of main verb and complement verb are identical
***quizá(s)** *perhaps*	
***tal vez** *perhaps*	

Note

Both Subjunctive and Indicative are used with **quizá(s)** and **tal vez**, the choice depending on the 'remoteness' of the possibility; this distinction is difficult to gloss in English:

Quizá(s) / Tal vez viene
Perhaps he's coming
Quizá(s) / Tal vez venga
Perhaps he may come
Quizá(s) / Tal vez ha venido
Perhaps he has come (I'm not sure)
Quizá(s) / Tal vez haya venido
He may have come (but I rather doubt it)

The Indicative is used when **quizá(s) / tal vez** follows the verb parenthetically, eg:

   Iré, tal vez / quizás
   I'll go, perhaps

Note that the other common expression with the meaning of *perhaps*, **a lo mejor**, takes the Indicative, and is the commonest in R1.

31.7 Hypothetical expressions

31.7.1 Verbs and expressions of imagining and wishing

Subjunctive-requiring expression	*Alternative/Remarks*
†***figurarse que** *to imagine*	
†***imaginarse que** *to imagine*	
¡ojalá (que)! (in R1 **que** is usually omitted) *if only* **¡Ojalá tuviéramos tiempo!** If only / I wish we had time!	
se presume que (impersonal) *it is presumed*	
es de presumir que (impersonal) *it is to be presumed*	
***suponer que** *to suppose*	NOTE ALSO that the Future and Conditional tenses can express the idea of supposition (see **28.2** and **28.4**).

Notes

1 The verbs marked with an asterisk also function as verbs of thinking (see **31.5**), in which function they normally take the Indicative.
2 Notice the sequence of tense with the following expressions:
   ¡Figúrate que venga mañana!
   Imagine he's coming tomorrow!
   ¡Suponga que estuviera aquí!
   Suppose he were here!
   ¡Ojalá hubiera podido venir!
   I wish he could have come!

31.7.2   Conjunctions of supposition, provision and concession

Subjunctive-requiring expression	Alternative/Remarks
a (la) condición (de) que *on condition that*	**si** (pp 410–11) will often have the same value
a no ser que *unless*	
*__a pesar de que__ *in spite of*	BUT **a pesar de** + inf is more usual when subjects of main verb and subordinate verb are identical, eg: • **A pesar de ser rico, no quería darme nada** In spite of being rich, he wouldn't give me anything
*__aun cuando__ *even if, even though*	**si bien** + Indicative (= *while, although*) is closely related in meaning
*__aunque__ *although*	Compare **si bien** (as above)
bien que *although*	Compare **si bien** (as above)
*__como__ *if* • **Como lo vuelvas a hacer, te castigaré** If you do it again I will punish you	**si** (pp 410–11) will often have the same value
como si *as if*	Always with the Imperfect or Pluperfect Subjunctive **como si lo supiera todo** as if she knew everything
*__con que__ *provided that* • **Con que se haga con antelación, no hay problema** Provided you do it in advance, there's no problem	**si** (pp 410–11) will often have the same value BUT **con** + inf is more usual when subjects of main verb and subordinate verb are identical, eg: • **Con levantarse temprano puede verlo** If you get up early you may see him
con tal (de) que *provided that*	**si** (pp 410–11) will often have the same value

Subjunctive-requiring expression	*Alternative/Remarks*
dado que *given that*	
en caso de que *in case*	BUT **(en) caso de** + inf is more usual when subjects of main verb and subordinate verb are identical
en el supuesto de que *supposing that*	
excepto que *unless*	
independiente de que *irrespective of* • **independiente de que sean franceses o españoles** irrespective of whether they are French or Spanish	
más que (R1 Am) *although*	
a menos que *unless*	
ni aunque (R1–2) *even though*	
ni que (R1) • **Ni que fuera tuyo** Anyone would think it was yours	
pese a que *in spite of*	
salvo que *unless*	
siempre que *provided that*	
supuesto que *supposing that*	**si** (pp 410–11) will often have the same value

Notes

1 **A pesar de que**, **pese a que**, **aun cuando**, **aunque** and **dado que** take the Indicative when they introduce an established fact rather than a hypothesis, eg:

A pesar de que me lo dijo ayer, no me acuerdo de su nombre
Despite the fact she told me yesterday, I can't remember her name

Aun cuando no tenía el menor interés en el tema, criticó a todos
Even though he hadn't the slightest interest in the matter, he criticized everyone

Aunque está aquí, no lo quiero ver
Even though he's here, I don't want to see him

Dado que es tan inteligente, ¿por qué no sabe contestar?
Given that he's so bright, why doesn't he know the answer?

2 **Como, conque** (note the spelling) and **supuesto que** take the Indicative when expressing cause, eg:

Como no tengo dinero, no puedo ir
Since I've no money, I can't go

¿Conque quieres escapar?
So you want to escape?

Supuesto que no quiere venir, vamos a salir sin él
Since he doesn't want to come, we'll go without him

31.7.3 Conditional sentences

The Imperfect or Pluperfect Subjunctive (but never the Present Subjunctive) is used after **si** when the condition is unlikely or impossible. The commonest patterns are:

FUTURE: **Si viniera mañana, se lo diríamos**
If he came tomorrow, we would tell him
PRESENT: **Si estuviera aquí, se lo diríamos**
If he were here, we would tell him
PAST: **Si hubiera estado allí, se lo habríamos dicho**
If he had been there, we would have told him

In the **si** clause, the **–ra** form may be replaced by the **–se** form in R2–3, and in the main clause, the Conditional is sometimes replaced by the **–ra** form. The several other combinations of tenses in conditional sentences which were to be found in Spanish literature until quite recently should nowadays be avoided.

There are, however, several equivalents in R1 which involve other tenses:

Si viniera mañana, se lo decíamos ⌊!⌋ (FUTURE)
If he came tomorrow, we would tell him
Si vendría ⌊!⌋ **mañana, se lo diríamos** (R1 Arg) (FUTURE)
If he came tomorrow, we would tell him
Que estuviera aquí ahora, se lo decíamos ⌊!⌋ (PRESENT)
If he were here now, we would tell him

NOTE ALSO: the many more specific conditional conjunctions on pp 408–9 above, and the common **de** + inf construction

De haberlo sabido, se lo habríamos dicho (PAST)

If we had known, we would have told him

NOTE: The Subjunctive is not used when the condition is open, eg:

Si viene, se lo diremos

If he comes, we shall tell him

Si sabe la respuesta, nos la dirá

If he knows the answer, he will tell us

Si viene aquí, lo vemos

Whenever he comes here, we see him

Si iba allí, lo veíamos

Whenever he went there, we saw him

Dije que si venía, se lo diríamos (reporting 'si viene, se lo diremos')

I said that if he came, we would tell him

Dije que si sabía la respuesta, nos la diría (reporting 'si sabe la respuesta, nos la dirá')

I said that if he knew the answer, he would tell us

31.8 Temporal clauses

The Subjunctive is used in all temporal clauses which refer to the FUTURE, eg:

En cuanto / Una vez que / Cuando, etc, venga Juan, vamos a avisarle de lo ocurrido

As soon as / Once / When, etc, John comes, let's tell him what happened

NOTE: The 'future' idea may be in reported speech or envisaged from a 'past' point of view, eg:

Dije que en cuanto llegáramos a casa, íbamos a telefonear a nuestros amigos

I said that as soon as we arrived home, we would telephone our friends

Iba a esperar en la estación hasta que viniera el autobús

She was going to wait at the station until the bus came

Compare the use of the Indicative when the temporal clause refers to the PAST or to a repeated action:

En cuanto vino Juan le avisamos de lo ocurrido

As soon as John came we told him what had happened

Siempre espero aquí hasta que viene el autobús

I always wait here until the bus comes

Siempre esperaba allí hasta que venía el autobús

She always waited there until the bus came

Antes (de) que is the only temporal conjunction which is *always* followed by the Subjunctive, eg:

Voy a salir antes de que llegue
I'm going before she arrives
Oí las noticias antes de que llegara
I heard the news before he got here
Siempre oigo las noticias antes de que llegue
I always hear the news before he gets here

Notes

1 **Antes de**, **después de**, **hasta** and **luego de** are preferably followed by an infinitive when the subjects of the main verb and temporal clause verb are identical, eg
   Lo supimos después de llegar
   We found out after arriving
   and, increasingly, may be followed by an infinitive and subject pronoun even when the subjects are not identical, eg
   Lo supimos después de llegar él
   We found out after he had arrived

2 **Desde que and luego que** are increasingly used with the **–ra** form, and occasionally with the **–se** form, of the Subjunctive, in journalistic and literary R3, eg:
   Es ésta la segunda crisis de Gobierno desde que fuera elegido en junio pasado
   This is the second government crisis since he was elected last June

3 **Después de que** is increasingly followed by the Subjunctive in all registers, eg:
   La reunion comenzó después de que acabara el Consejo de Ministros
   The meeting began after the Council of Ministers ended

4 A 'pleonastic' (logically superfluous) **no** is sometimes used with **hasta que** and **mientras**, eg:
   Me quedaré aquí mientras no lo haga ⟨!⟩
   I'll stay here while she does it

5 Notice also the complements of **aguardar** and **esperar** (see also p 363), which are similar to FUTURE temporal clauses:
   Estoy aguardando/esperando (a) que venga el autobús
   I'm waiting until the bus comes

31.9   Relative clauses

The Subjunctive is used in a relative clause which refers to a non-existent, indefinite or hypothetical antecedent. It is also used in R3, although more and more rarely, in a relative clause which refers to a superlative antecedent.

Non-existent antecedent

No hay nadie que sepa la respuesta
There's no one who knows the answer

Indefinite or hypothetical antecedent

Busco un (= cualquier) médico que me sepa curar
I'm looking for a doctor (= any doctor) who can cure me

Notes

1   The personal **a** is often omitted in this construction, since the object is not thought of as an individual (**24.19**). Contrast the above example with the following:
   Conozco a un médico que me sabe curar
   I know a doctor who can cure me

2   The Subjunctive construction is used in Spanish more often than might appear necessary to English speakers. It frequently has a more polite overtone than the Indicative, and avoids the presentation of the relative clause as a fact, eg
   Los que no hayan entendido pueden preguntar otra vez
   Those who haven't understood (if there are any) can ask again
   Nada de lo que diga me ofende
   Nothing of what she may say (if anything) offends me
   el incierto límite futuro que el destino nos tenga asignado
   the uncertain future limit which destiny may have assigned us

31.9.1   Superlative antecedent

el mejor libro que hayamos leído (R3)
the best book we have ever read
The Subjunctive is also used in the equivalent of English *-ever* expressions

quienquiera que sea/fuese	whoever it may be / might have been
dondequiera que ande/anduviera	wherever he goes/went
cuando quiera	when(ever) you wish
por estúpidos que sean/fuesen	however stupid they are/were

por más dinero que gane/ganara	however many she has/had
por muchos que tenga/tuviera	however much money he earns/earned
lo que me paguen	whatever they pay me
donde vayas	wherever you go

NOTE ALSO: the following idioms:

que yo sepa	as far as I know
que yo recuerde	as far as I remember

SEE ALSO **31.2**.

31.10 Noun clauses

The Subjunctive is used in noun clauses which correspond to the uses described in **31.2–7** above.

el deseo de que lo haga	the *wish* that she does it
la necesidad de que nos demos cuenta de lo ocurrido	the *necessity* of our realizing what has happened
la esperanza de que lo lea	the *hope* that he may read it
la duda de que lo sepa	the *doubt* whether she knows
la posibilidad de que se escape	the *possibility* he may escape
Había el peligro de que cayese	There was the *danger* of his falling

The Subjunctive is also regularly found after **el hecho de que**, even when the clause refers to an established fact about which no 'emotion' or 'opinion' is being expressed, eg:

El hecho de que los cristianos fueran mayoría era en gran parte sociológico

The fact that the Christians were a majority was largely sociological
Notice also:

†**Ya era hora de que hicieran lo que les diera la gana**

It was time they did what they liked

32 *ser* and *estar*

The idea that the contrast between **ser** and **estar** is based on considerations of 'permanence' and 'temporariness' seems to be entrenched in the minds of many English-speaking students. Although it has a limited usefulness where the adjectival complements of the two verbs are concerned, it is a very inadequate general principle. In fact, no single rule of thumb will satisfactorily describe the difference between **ser** and **estar** in English terms. The approach taken here is to examine the several contexts in which they appear and to look at the basis of the contrast, where there is one, within each of these.

32.1 With nouns, pronouns, infinitives and clauses

ser	estar
• Always used: **Soy médico** I am a doctor **¿Quién es el director?** Who is the head? **No es nada** It's nothing **Ver es creer** Seeing is believing **Eso es lo que quería saber** That's what I wanted to know NOTE:	• One or two idiomatic usages which derive from the use of **estar** with ADJECTIVES or PAST PARTICIPLES (see **32.5–6**), eg: **Estás (hecho) un hombre** (of a child) You've turned into a man **estar pez** (R1) to be an ignoramus

NOTE:
Durante la guerra mi padre fue coronel de artillería
During the war my father was a colonel in the artillery (though a 'temporary' state of affairs)

32.2 With adverbs of place

ser	estar
• Used with subjects which represent an event or other process, eg:	• Normally used, eg:
La clase es en la otra sala	**El Museo del Prado está en Madrid**
The class is (taking place) in the other room	The Prado Museum is in Madrid
El camino es por aquí	**¿Dónde estamos ahora?**
The road is (goes) this way	Where are we now?
• Reorganization of a sentence for the purposes of stress, using **ser**, may also result in its apparently being used with an adverb or adverbial phrase of place, eg:	**La misma idea está en la otra novela**
Donde te vi fue en la Calle Mayor	The same idea is in the other novel
It was in the Calle Mayor that I saw you	N O T E :
Fue en Londres donde nos conocimos	**La enciclopedia está siempre en el mismo estante**
It was in London that we met	The encyclopaedia is always on the same shelf
N O T E : These sentences are called 'cleft' sentences.	

N O T E : Adjectives indicating position, since they represent inherent characteristics (see **32.6** below), take **ser**:

    Mi país es lejano B U T **Mi país está lejos**
    Mi piso es cercano al Ayuntamiento B U T **Mi piso está cerca del Ayuntamiento**

32.3 With other adverbs

ser	estar
	• Always with **bien** and **mal**, eg:
	No está mal
	It's not bad

32.4 With a gerund

ser	estar
N O T E : **Fui llegando**, etc, are forms of **ir llegando** (see **29.4**)	• Always used in the formation of the progressive tenses, eg:
	Estaba leyendo el periódico cuando entró
	I was reading the paper when she came in
	(Estaba) llora que llora (R1)
	She was crying her eyes out

32.5   With a past participle

ser	estar
• Used to form the straightforward passive: **El árbol fue cortado por el leñador (= El leñador cortó el árbol)** The tree was cut down by the woodcutter • Many past participles can be used as adjectives, and **ser** is accordingly used where it would be the appropriate choice with an ADJECTIVE (see **32.6**), eg: **La ropa era muy usada** They were very worn clothes (**La ropa estaba muy usada** = The clothes had been worn a lot) **Este estudiante es muy instruido** This is a very well–informed student (**Este estudiante está muy instruido** = This student has been very well–educated) • Some adjectival past participles used with **ser** have an 'active' meaning, eg: **La película era aburrida** The film was boring **Tu propuesta es muy controvertida** Your proposal is very controversial **El joven es muy atrevido** The young man is very daring (BUT **atrevido** also has an 'active' meaning with **estar**: **El joven está muy atrevido** = *The young man is behaving very daringly*)	• With **estar**, the past participle indicates a state, never an action. The state **(a)** results from the action of a transitive verb, eg: **Este pan está vendido** This bread is sold (= has been sold and is awaiting collection) **El vaso está roto** The glass is broken (= has previously been broken) **La ventana estaba abierta** The window was open (= it had been opened) **(b)** is associated with a reflexive or intransitive verb, eg: **Está levantado** He is up (= **Se ha levantado**) **Estamos aburridos** We're bored (= **Nos aburrimos**) **Está muerto** He's dead (= **(Se) Ha muerto**) **Está callado** He's quiet (= **(Se) Ha callado**) BUT NOTE: **Es callado** = *He's a quiet (sort of) person.* NOTE: Many past participles in this category are translated by English present participles (the Spanish present participle is *never* used adjectivally):

acostado	*lying down*
acurrucado	*huddling, nestling*
agachado	*bending over*
agachapado	*crouching*
agarrado (a algo)	*grasping (sth)*
arrimado (a algo)	*leaning (on sth)*

417

NOTE ALSO in this category:

callado	*quiet*	**arrodillado**	*kneeling*
cansado	*tiring, tiresome*	**colgado**	*hanging*
confiado	*trusting*	**dormido**	*sleeping*
descreído	*disbelieving*	**echado**	*lying down*
disimulado	*cunning*	**inclinado**	*leaning*
†divertido	} *entertaining*	**repantigado**	*lolling*
entretenido		**sentado**	*sitting*
†osado	*daring*	**suspendido**	*hanging*
pesado	*dull, boring*	**tendido**	*lying down*
sufrido	*long-suffering*	**tumbado**	*lying down*

- Contrast the following:

Esta novela fue escrita por Galdós
This novel was written by Galdós (straightforward passive)

El grupo fue dividido en cuatro secciones
The group was divided into four sections (straightforward passive)

Esa niña es muy distraída
That girl is very absent-minded (adjective)

Aquí está escrito que . . .
It says here that . . .(= it has been written)

El capítulo está dividido en tres partes
The chapter is divided into three parts (description; it has been divided . . .)

Aunque intenté concentrarme, estaba muy distraído
Although I tried to concentrate, I was very absorbed in other things (my mind was wandering at that time)

NOTE: Many examples of contrast between **ser** and **estar** are extremely difficult to appreciate, and hence to render, in English, eg:

No es permitido decir cosas así
One isn't allowed to say things like that (it's not generally permissible)

¿Es usted casado o soltero?
Are you married or single? (Into which category do you fall?)

No está permitido salir
You can't go out (it's been forbidden)

No estoy casado todavía
I'm not married yet (**todavía** implies a change of state is possible)

32.6 With an adjective

ser	estar
(a) With adjectives which classify the subject into a category (typically nationality, religion, etc), eg:	**(a)** With adjectives which, like the past participles in **32.5**, represent a 'resultant' state, eg:
Mi mujer es francesa	**Este pastel está muy dulce**
My wife is French	This cake is very sweet (it tastes sweet)
Mi profesor de inglés es estructuralista	(**Este pastel es dulce** = This is a sweet kind of cake)
My English teacher is a structuralist	NOTE:
El tigre es carnívoro	**Estoy siempre tan nervioso**
The tiger is a carnivore	I'm always so nervous (though apparently 'permanent'; things are always making me nervous)
(b) Where the adjective is an inherent property of the subject, eg:	**(b)** With adjectives which do not represent a normally 'inherent' property of the subject, eg:
Es loco	**¡Estás loco!**
He's mad (literally insane)	You're crazy! (not literally insane)
La nieve es blanca	**La sala está vacía**
(All) snow is white, *not* The snow is white	The room is empty (rooms are not necessarily empty)
El hielo es frío	**Mi padre está ocupado**
(All) ice is cold, *not* The ice is cold	My father is busy (people are not necessarily busy)
(c) Where the adjective is a possible physical or moral property of the subject, even though this may not be 'inherent' or 'permanent', eg:	**El agua está fría**
	The water is/feels cold (water can be hot as well)
Juanito es muy alto	**Las uvas están verdes**
Johnny is tall	The grapes are/taste unripe (grapes are not necessarily unripe)
(**Juanito está muy alto** = Johnny looks tall)	**Está muy rica la comida**
Nuestros vecinos son ricos	The meal is (tastes) delicious
Our neighbours are rich	**¡Qué rica está la niña!**
Soy viejo	How lovely the little girl looks!
I'm old	NOTE:
El libro es triste	**Está enfermo desde niño**
The book is sad (its contents are sad)	He's been ill since he was a child (even though this is 'permanent', illness is not an inherent quality of people)
(d) Where the adjective expresses a measurement, quantity or comparison,	

eg:

Los tomates son muy caros
Tomatoes are very expensive
(BUT **Los tomates están muy**
caros = Tomatoes are very
expensive at the moment)
La calle es estrecha
The street is narrow
Juana es muy distinta de su
hermana menor
Juana is very different from her
younger sister
(e) Where the subject is a
proposition or its equivalent,
eg:
Este problema es dificilísimo
This problem is very difficult
Comunicarle eso sería
delicado
Telling him that would be difficult

(c) Where there is some
qualification or comparison of
an otherwise 'inherent'
notion, eg:
Este niño está muy alto para
su edad
This child is tall for his age
Estos zapatos me están
pequeños
These shoes feel tight
(d) Where it is desired to give an
impression of suddenness or
irony:
¡Qué alto estás!
How tall you look!
Hoy la nieve está blanquísima
The snow looks really white today
Está muy viejo ahora
He's looking very old now

NOTE: Again, there are examples of contrast between **ser** and **estar**
which are difficult to appreciate.

ser	estar
En este país todos somos libres We are all free in this country	**Este taxi ¿está libre?** Is this taxi free?
Este estudiante es muy listo This student is very clever	**¿Estamos listos?** Are we ready?
Es claro que no sabe It's clear he doesn't know	**¿Está claro?** Is that clear? (**estar claro** is generally more emphatic than **es claro**, and so more typical of R1–2)
La casa es nueva The house is newly built (**La casa está nueva** = The house still looks new)	**Este sombrero está todavía nuevo** This hat is still new (= unworn)
Esta muchacha es viva This girl is lively	**Todos estamos vivos** We're all alive (compare **estar muerto**, 32.5)
No es seguro de sí mismo He's unsure of himself (a characteristic)	**No está seguro de poder ir** He's not sure he can go (an attitude)
	Estoy muy contento aquí I'm very happy here (**contento** is never normally used with **ser**)

32.7   With a prepositional phrase

ser	estar
• As with ADJECTIVES, eg:	• As with ADJECTIVES, eg:
Ese libro es para mí	**Está con la gripe**
That book is for me	He's got flu
Soy de Málaga	**Estoy sin dinero**
I'm from Málaga	I'm without money
Eso es por el bien de todos	**Estamos en armonía**
That is for everyone's good	We're in harmony
	El cuarto está a oscuras
	The room is in darkness
	Hoy está de mal humor
	She's in a bad mood today
	Mi abuela estaba de luto
	My grandmother was in mourning

32.8   In isolation

ser	estar
• Implies existence or identity, eg:	• Implies location or state (of health), eg:
Todo lo que es	**¿Está D. Jaime?**
Everything that is (= exists)	Is D. Jaime there?
¿Quién es?	**¿Cómo estás?**
Who is it?	How are you?
	• It also appears in set phrases:
	¿Estamos?
	Are we agreed?
	Ya está
	That's it, it's finished
	Déjale estar
	Leave him alone

32.9 Idioms with prepositions, etc

ser	estar
● **ser de**: *to come from, to be made of, to belong to*, eg	● **estar a** + date, price or other measurement, eg:
La familia es de Madrid	**Estamos a quince de mayo**
The family is from Madrid	It's 15 May
La mesa es de madera	**Las manzanas están a veinte pesos el kilo**
The table is made of wood	Apples are twenty pesos a kilo
Los fantasmas no son de este mundo	**El termómetro está a cuarenta grados**
Ghosts are not of this world	The thermometer reads forty degrees
● †**ser de** (impersonal): *to become of*, eg	● **estar de** + profession, eg:
¿Qué será de mí?	**Estaba de profesor en una escuela de idiomas**
What will become of me?	He was doing the job of a teacher in a language school
● **ser para** (impersonal) (R1): *to be enough to*, eg	● **estar en**: *to consist of, to intend to*, eg
Es para morirse ya de risa	**El secreto está en no contestar**
It's enough to make you die of laughter	The secret lies in not answering
● **ser que** (impersonal): emphasis or question device, eg	**Estoy en decirle la verdad**
	I intend to tell you the truth
Es que no sé	● **estar a uno en** + quantity (R1): *to cost sb sth*
I don't really know	**Este traje me está en trescientos euros**
¿Es que el tren va a salir?	This suit cost me three hundred euros
Is the train going to leave?	● **estar con**: *to agree with*, eg
	En esta opinión estoy con usted
	In this view I'm in agreement with you
	● **estar para, estar a punto de, estar al** (R1) + inf: *to be about to*, eg
	El tren está para / a punto de / al salir
	The train is about to leave
	● **estar (como) para** (R1): *to be in the mood for*, eg
	No estoy para debates
	I'm not in the mood for arguments
	● **estar por** + inf: *to be inclined to*, eg
	Estamos por comenzar ahora
	We're inclined to start now
	● **estar por** (impersonal) + inf: *to remain to*, eg
	La novela perfecta está por escribir
	The perfect novel remains to be written
	● **estar por** + noun: *to be in favour of, to be keen on* (R1), eg
	Yo estoy por la playa
	I'm all for the beach
	Juan está por María
	Juan really likes María
	● **estar que** (R1): intensifying device, eg
	Estoy que me caigo
	I'm falling good and proper

33 Personal pronouns

In the following sections, pronouns are divided into two categories:

(a) UNSTRESSED: **me, te, se, le, lo, la, nos, os, les, los, las**. These pronouns never receive stress; they are always dependent upon a verb.

(b) DISJUNCTIVE: **yo, mí, tú, ti, usted, él, ella, ello, sí, nosotros/as, vosotros/as, ustedes, ellos, ellas**. These pronouns may be stressed, and they function as subjects of verbs or objects of prepositions. NOTE: After a preposition, choice between **yo** (subject) / **mí** (object), **tú** (subject) / **ti** (object) varies. The object form is used in the majority of cases (**para mí, detrás de ti**), but the subject form is used after **como, salvo, excepto** and **según (según yo, como tú**, etc), and effectively after **entre (entre tú y yo)**. In conjunction with another noun or pronoun, the subject form tends to be used, although it is preferable to repeat the preposition.

> **para mí** AND **para él y para mí** (preferred) BUT **para él y yo**
> **delante de mí** (ALSO **delante mío** (R1)) AND **delante de él y**
> **delante de mí** BUT **delante de él y yo**

33.1 Order

The order of unstressed pronouns relative to each other is governed by two principles.

Order by form

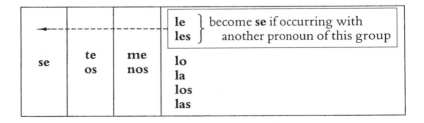

Te lo dije ayer
I told you yesterday
Se la envié
I sent it to him
Se me escapa la fecha
The date escapes me
¡Cómetemelo!
Eat it up for me!

Notes

1 **Se** sometimes follows **te/os**, **me/nos** in R1 |!| (see p 5).
2 **Se** (from **les**) **lo/la** sometimes becomes **se los/las** in R1 Am and even
R2 Am, eg:
Eso pasó como se los |!| digo a ustedes
It happened as I told you

Order by function

indirect object	direct object

If there is a conflict between the principles of order by form and order
by function, then a preposition and disjunctive pronoun construction
must in theory be used:
Te me recomendó
He recommended me to you
BUT
Te recomendó a mí
He recommended you to me
However, such cases are rare: a disjunctive pronoun construction is
generally preferred for all sequences involving first- and second-person
pronouns.

33.2 Pronouns and verb

The unstressed pronouns *precede* all finite verbs except the positive
imperative in all registers, eg:
me entiendes
se verá   BUT   **¡házmelo!**
¡no me digas!
NOTE: In R3, and (in some dialects) in R1, the pronoun(s) may follow
the first verb in a clause: eg the abbreviation **u.t.c.r.** in the *Diccionario
de la Real Academia Española*, which stands for **Úsase también como
reflexivo**. Some writers have cultivated this usage in other contexts,
eg:

Mi compañera, nuevamente fatigada, descansó la cabeza sobre el hombro de la que – lo sabíamos ahora – llamábase Rosario . . . (A. Carpentier)

My girl-friend, who was tired once again, rested her head on the shoulder of the woman who we now knew was called Rosario . . .

The unstressed pronouns *follow* all non-finite verbs (infinitive, gerund) and the positive imperative, eg:

viéndolo
al abrirla
¡Dígamelo!

(Pronouns are *never* attached to the past participle.)

The unstressed pronouns *either precede* the main verb *or follow* the infinitive or gerund in common verb + infinitive and verb + gerund groups. There is no difference in acceptability or register. Groups that allow such variation are:

†**acabar de** + inf	†**querer** + inf
†**continuar** + ger	†**seguir** + ger
†**deber (de)** + inf	†**soler** + inf
†**dejar de** + inf	†**terminar de** + inf
†**empezar a** + inf	†**tratar de** + inf
†**ir a** + inf	†**venir a** + inf
†**necesitar** + inf	†**volver a** + inf
poder + inf	

For example: **acaba de hacerlo** or **lo acaba de hacer**.

In the above constructions, groups of pronouns may not be split: eg, only **debe contármelo** or **me lo debe contar**. There are other constructions which allow the splitting of pronoun groups, since each verb has its own object, but which also allow the whole pronoun sequence to stand before the main verb:

te †**aconsejarán comprarlos**	OR	te los aconsejarán comprar
le †**hice leerlo**	OR	se lo hice leer
me †**permitió tocarla**	OR	me la permitió tocar

33.3 'Redundant' pronouns

Even when an object is expressed by a noun or a disjunctive pronoun, an unstressed pronoun is needed in Spanish in the following cases:

1 When a direct or indirect object is placed before the verb (see **23.2**), eg:

A Juan no le gustó la comida
John didn't like the food
Aquel libro lo leí en dos días
I read that book in two days

2 Very often when an indirect object is a person or animal or is felt to be personified, eg:

> **Le robó el collar a la chica**
> He stole the necklace from the girl
> **Se lo vendió a mi amigo**
> She sold it to my friend
> **Se lo mostró al público**
> He showed it to the audience
> **Le dio la comida al perro**
> She gave the dog food
> **(Se) lo di al banco**
> I gave it to the bank

N O T E : In the last example, the 'redundant' construction with **se** (= **le**) tends to be used if the people at the bank are known; without the 'redundant' pronoun, the bank is being thought of simply as an institution.

3 When a disjunctive personal pronoun is used, usually for emphasis or avoidance of ambiguity, eg:

> **Te llamaban a ti**
> They were calling you
> **Déselo a ella**
> Give it to her

33.4 Second-person pronouns

In Peninsular Spanish, four pronouns with second-person meaning are used:

	singular	*plural*
'familiar'	**tú**	**vosotros/as**
'polite'	**usted**	**ustedes**

The traditional labels 'familiar' and 'polite' do not adequately capture the circumstances in which the pronouns are used today. Since the 1970s it has become increasingly common to use **tú** and **vosotros/as** in 'polite' situations which might appear to require (and previously did require) the use of **usted** and **ustedes**. It is unthinkable to use anything but **tú** and **vosotros/as** in the following situations:

- addressing children or animals, or God
- among relatives, friends (of whatever ages), workmates, soldiers of the same rank, colleagues in the same profession

Tú is also used in the sense of *one*, *you* (general), especially in R1.

Nowadays it is normal to use **tú** and **vosotros/as** in the following situations:

- among young people, whatever the circumstances
- among people of different ages in almost any informal situation
- addressing priests

- wherever it is desired to establish a friendly note, even in 'semi-formal' situations (shops, banks, restaurants, etc)
- in public speeches, especially by politicians to their audience
- in advertisements where a 'matey' tone is required

In fact, it is not going too far to say that **usted**, **ustedes**, are used only:

- in formal, public situations
- when writing to strangers
- to old people not known to the speaker
- wherever it is desired to show (sometimes ostentatiously) respect

Some examples

Señores primeros ministros, señor presidente del Consejo, señores presidentes de las instituciones comunitarias, excelencias, señoras y señores, bien-venidos a España . . . El pueblo español *os* recibe satisfecho y consciente de la alta significación que este acto encierra.

(Speech of King Juan Carlos to visiting diplomats on the signing of the EEC membership treaty)

¿Has probado el nuevo X turbo? ¡Cómprate un Ford!
(advertisements)

Cuando pases por la biblioteca recógeme todos los libros
(student to student)

O Dios, ayúdame a aprobar mi examen (prayer)

¿Podría darme tres sellos y una postal? (to shopkeeper)

Oiga, Señor, ¿sabe usted dónde está el Paseo de la Castellana? (to stranger in street)

In American Spanish, the **vosotros/as** forms are completely absent, and **ustedes** is the only plural form. In the singular, some areas have **tú** as in Peninsular Spanish, while others use a form **vos** for the 'familiar' second person.

	singular	*plural*
'familiar'	**tú** or **vos**	
'polite'	**usted**	**ustedes**

The use of **tú, vos** and **usted** varies greatly from area to area in American Spanish. In general, the 'familiar' forms are not used in such a wide range of circumstances as in the Peninsular **usted** itself has a 'familiar' usage (parents to young children) in some areas, and is even used affectionately between husband and wife in Chile. There are register differences, too: speakers who use **vos** in R2 and below may revert to **tú** in R3.

NOTE: In areas which use the **voseo** (**vos** for **tú**), **vos** is the subject pronoun and prepositional object form; the possessives **tu** and **tuyo** survive. New verb forms for **vos** may be used: normal in Buenos Aires, for example, are Present Indicative **tomás, comés, vivís**; Present Subjunctive **tomés, comás, vivás**; Preterite **tomastes**, etc; Imperative **¡tomá!, ¡comé!, ¡viví!**. For example:

No hablemos de mí: hablemos de *vos*, de *tus* trabajos, de *tus* preocupaciones . . . Quiero saber qué *hacés* ahora, qué *pensás*, si has pintado o no.

(E. Sábato, *El túnel*)

33.5 Third-person (including *usted*, *ustedes*) object pronouns

There is a great deal of variation in the use of third-person object pronouns in the Spanish-speaking world, and no real agreement on a 'standard'. The following table summarizes the present situation:

subject	*direct object*	*indirect object*
él/ellos	**lo/los** referring to things **le/les** (Pen) ⎱ referring to **lo/los** (Am) ⎰ people (increasingly **lo/los** in Pen)	**le/les** (**lo/los** ! sometimes in R1)
ella/ellas	**la/las** referring to things **le/les** (Pen) ⎱ referring to **la/las** (Am) ⎰ people (increasingly **la/las** in Pen)	**le/les** (**la/las** ! sometimes in R1–2: more advanced than **lo/los** above)
usted/ustedes (m)	**le/les** (Pen) **lo/los** (Am)	**le/les**
usted/ustedes (f)	**le/les**	**le/les**

However, there are many regional departures from this scheme, both in Peninsular and American Spanish.

33.6   Personal pronouns expressing possession

Spanish personal pronouns are often used to express possession in preference to a possessive adjective.

Me lavé la cara

I washed my face

NOTE: The 'inalienable' possession (of parts of the body) is normally expressed in this way in Spanish.

Se me ha averiado el coche

My car has broken down

Le voy a arreglar el ordenador

I'm going to mend her computer

34 The reflexive

The Spanish reflexive has many different functions, several of which are not paralleled in English.

34.1 Genuine reflexives

Direct object, eg:

Me afeité
I shaved
Se estaba mirando en el espejo
She was looking at herself in the mirror

Indirect object, eg:

Me he cortado el dedo
I've cut my finger
Juan se lava las manos
John is washing his hands
NOTE: This is a common way of expressing possession, and with 'possessions' which are an integral part of the 'possessor' (such as parts of the body) this construction must be used instead of a possessive adjective.

The plural reflexive may also have a reciprocal meaning which may be made clear by the use of a reinforcing phrase, eg:
Se ayudaron los siniestrados
The victims helped each other
Se ayudan mutuamente
They help one another
Los políticos no se entienden entre sí
Politicians don't understand one another
Se critican unos a otros
They criticize one another

34.2 Inherent reflexives

Some verbs exist only in the reflexive and have no genuine reflexive interpretation, eg:

†**abstenerse (de)**	*to abstain (from)*
†**arrepentirse (de)**	*to repent (of, for)*
†**atreverse (a)**	*to dare (to)*
†**dignarse** (+ inf)	*to deign (to)*
†**gloriarse (de, en)**	*to boast (of)*
†**jactarse (de)**	*to boast (of)*
†**quejarse (de)**	*to complain (of)*
vanagloriarse (de)	*to boast (of)*

34.3 The reflexive as a marker of the intransitive

Use of the reflexive may convert a transitive verb into a corresponding intransitive:

	tr		*intr*
abrir	*to open*	†**abrirse**	*to open (intr)*
†**aburrir**	*to bore*	†**aburrirse**	*to get bored*
acercar	*to bring closer*	**acercarse**	*to get closer*
acostar	*to put to bed*	**acostarse**	*to go to bed*
†**alegrar**	*to make happy*	**alegrarse**	*to cheer up*
†**avergonzar**	*to put to shame*	**avergonzarse**	*to be ashamed*
†**cansar**	*to tire*	**cansarse**	*to get tired*
cerrar	*to close*	**cerrarse**	*to close*
desgarrar	*to tear*	**desgarrarse**	*to tear*
†**enfadar**	*to annoy*	**enfadarse**	*to get annoyed*
estremecer	*to shake*	**estremecerse**	*to tremble*
†**fundir**	*to melt*	**fundirse**	*to melt*
helar	*to freeze*	**helarse**	*to freeze*
†**hender**	*to split*	**henderse**	*to split*
†**levantar**	*to raise*	**levantarse**	*to get up*
mojar	*to wet*	**mojarse**	*to get wet*
pasear	*to take for a walk*	**pasearse**	*to go for a walk*
secar	*to dry*	**secarse**	*to get dry*
†**sentar**	*to seat*	**sentarse**	*to sit down*

So close is the association between intransitive and reflexive that several intransitive verbs have developed a reflexive form which is not perceptibly different in meaning. The reflexive in this function is especially preferred in R1 (Pen) and in American Spanish. Among such verbs are:

acabar (ALSO tr) / †**acabarse**	*to finish*	**acabarse** also = *to wear oneself out* in Am **Se ha acabado la guerra** (R1–2)
adelantar (ALSO tr) / **adelantarse**	*to go forward*	**adelantarse** preferred in Am
†**aparecer/aparecerse**	*to appear*	But **aparecerse** tends to be restricted to certain more striking expressions, eg **Se apareció el** **fantasma** = *The ghost appeared* **aparecer** is used for more ordinary appearance, eg **Apareció a la puerta** = *He appeared at the door*
†**bajar** (ALSO tr) / **bajarse**	*to go down*	**(Se** (R1)) **Bajó del autobús** = *She got off the* *bus*
†**callar** (ALSO tr) / **callarse**	*to be quiet*	**callarse** preferred
†**casar** (ALSO tr) / **casarse**	*to marry*	**casarse** is preferred in Pen, where **casar** belongs to R3
desayunar / **desayunarse**	*to have* *breakfast*	**desayunarse** is R3 in Pen, but preferred in some parts of Am
destacar (ALSO tr) / **destacarse**	*to stand out*	**destacarse** often has a rather stronger meaning than **destacar**: **La ciudad destaca por su riqueza** **monumental** = *The town stands out for the* *richness of its monuments* **El joven pianista se destacó entre los** **mejores de su categoría** = *The young* *pianist stood out among the best in his class*
enfermar (ALSO tr) / **enfermarse** !	*to fall ill*	Only **enfermar** in Pen, but **enfermarse** preferred in Am
entrenar ! (ALSO tr) / **entrenarse**	*to train*	NOTE: **Entrenar** used intransitively, though puristically castigated, is very widely used in this way.
†**imaginar** (ALSO tr) / **imaginarse**	*to imagine,* *to fancy*	**imaginarse** is R1–2
†**parar** (ALSO tr) / **pararse**	*to stop*	– ¿**Cuándo para el autobús aquí?** – **Para a** **las cinco.** = *When does the bus stop here? It* *stops at five.* But **El autobús se para a las** **cinco** = *The bus stops (for good) at five.*
pasear (ALSO tr) / **pasearse**	*to go for a walk*	
†**recordar** (ALSO tr) / **recordarse** !	*to remember*	Only **recordar** in Pen

regresar / **regresarse** $\boxed{!}$	*to go back,* *to return*	Only **regresar** in Pen; but **regresarse** is almost universal in Mex
reír/†**reírse**	*to laugh*	**reírse** is preferred when followed by **de** (p 212), eg: **Se rio de su estupidez** = *She laughed at his stupidity*
sonreír/†**sonreírse**	*to smile*	As **reír/reírse**
†**subir** (ALSO tr) / **subirse**	*to go up*	As **bajar/bajarse**
†**tardar/tardarse** $\boxed{!}$	*to take time*	Only **tardar** in Pen
terminar (ALSO tr) **/ terminarse**	*to finish*	

34.4   The reflexive as an intensifier

With many non-reflexive verbs, both transitive and intransitive, the addition of a reflexive pronoun gives a 'stronger', though essentially equivalent, meaning. The following list illustrates some of these differences:

	Non-reflexive	**Reflexive**
†**caer**	**Cayó de rodillas** He fell to his knees **Tiró la piedra, que cayó muy cerca** She threw the stone, which fell very close by **Cayeron muchos soldados en la batalla** Many soldiers fell (= died) in the battle **No caiga en la tentación** Don't fall into temptation (fig) **Su cumpleaños cae el lunes** His birthday is on Monday	**Juan se cayó del árbol** John fell out of the tree (implies an accident) **El libro se cayó de la mesa** The book fell off the table **¡Cuidado, te vas a caer!** Careful, you're going to fall! NOTE: The reflexive is favoured with a following **de** + noun phrase.
†**comer**	**He comido bien** I've eaten well	**Se lo comió** He ate it up
†**dormir**	**Duerme unas ocho horas** He sleeps about eight hours	**Se durmió en seguida** She went to sleep immediately

[†]encontrar	**No encuentro la calle** I can't find the street	**Se lo encontró en la calle** He found it (by chance) in the street
escapar	**Escapó a la policía** He avoided the police	**Se han escapado los presos** The prisoners have got out **El gas se escapa** The gas is escaping
[†]ir	**Voy a Nueva York** I'm going to New York	**Se fue a Argentina** She went off to Argentina
leer	**Leí cuatro libros** I read four books	**Me leí cuatro libros** (R1–2) I read four books
[†]llevar	**Llevaba una maleta** She was carrying a suitcase	**Se lo llevó a Francia** He took it off with him to France **El ladrón se llevó todo el dinero** The thief took all the money
[†]marchar	**Marcharon los soldados todo el día** The soldiers marched all day **No marcha bien el motor** The engine is not running well	**Se marcharon** They went off
[†]morir	**Murió su padre el año pasado** His father died last year	**Se está muriendo** She's dying
[†]ocurrir	**Ocurrió ayer el accidente** The accident happened yesterday	**Se me ocurrió regresar** It occurred to me to return
[†]pasar	**Los años pasaron** The years passed **¿Qué pasa?** What's happening?	**Se pasa todo el tiempo estudiando** (R1–2) He spends all his time studying **Se me pasó la oportunidad** The opportunity passed me by
[†]quedar	**El prado queda más allá** The field is further on **No queda ningún libro** There's not one book left **Quedan diez minutos** There are ten minutes left **Queda como un señor** He's shown himself to be a gentleman	**Me quedo en el coche** I'll stay in the car **Me quedo con el periódico** I'll keep the paper

†**salir**	**Salió del parque a las siete** She left the park at seven	**salirse** is associated with greater or unusual effort **Se enfadó y se salió del café** He got cross and walked out of the café **Se salió a mitad de la película** He went out in the middle of the film (may imply displeasure) **El coche se salió de la calzada** The car went off the road **La bombona se sale** The gas bottle is leaking
†**tomar**	**¿Qué vas a tomar?** What will you have to drink?	**Se tomó cuatro vasos de cerveza en cinco minutos** He gulped down four beers in five minutes
†**traer**	**Juana ha traído el lápiz** Juana has brought the pencil	**Dijeron que no, pero se trajo las tazas** They said not, but (still) he brought the cups (implies insistence)
†**venir**	**Vino a Inglaterra en 1948** He came to England in 1948	**Se ha venido a Inglaterra para abrir una nueva fábrica** He's come to England to open a new factory (implies more specific purpose)

34.5 The impersonal reflexive

The uses of the reflexive in **34.1–4** above apply to all persons. The third-person reflexive may also be used when the subject of the verb is left unexpressed: in this function it is often translatable by the English passive (but see **34.7**). Two constructions can be distinguished.

(a) The logical object of the verb appears to act as the subject, and the verb agrees with it in number, eg:

Se venden motos
Motor-bikes for sale
Se compran coches (see **23.1**)
Cars bought

(b) The verb is invariably in the singular and the logical object is also the grammatical object, eg:

Se les ayudó a los siniestrados
The victims were helped
Se le detuvo al hombre
The man was stopped

These two constructions are in practice often indistinguishable, though (b) is sometimes considered to be lower in register than (a):

Se me entregaron dos cartas (R2) / **Se me entregó dos cartas** (R1)
I was handed two letters

The impersonal reflexive can also be used with intransitive verbs, eg:

Cuando se tiene veinticinco años ya se está en edad para pasarse la vida tranquila
When you are twenty-five it's time to have a peaceful life

34.6 Further notes on *se*

1 The **se** which obligatorily replaces **le** or **les** in groups of more than one third-person pronoun is not a reflexive at all:

Le di el libro a Juan   **Se (= le) lo di**

2 In Spanish, not more than one **se**, of whatever kind (including (1) above), is allowed per verb. Many verb + infinitive and all verb + gerund structures also count as 'one' verb for this purpose, all the pronouns standing either before the finite verb or after the infinitive or gerund. Thus the notion *You cannot bathe here*, which might involve the 'clash' of two instances of **se** (one the impersonal reflexive, **se puede** . . . , the other the reflexive of **bañarse**), must be rendered in one of the following ways:

Uno no se puede bañar aquí
No está permitido bañarse aquí
No se permite bañarse aquí
(**bañarse** is here the subject of **permitir**, and therefore a separate clause)

34.7 The reflexive and the passive

Contrary to what is sometimes suggested, the passive (eg **fue escrito**) is very frequently used in Spanish, especially in R3. However, there are several circumstances in which, by comparison with the English passive, it either cannot be used or is not preferred. In such circumstances, it is often appropriate to use a reflexive construction instead. It is perhaps most important to appreciate where the Spanish passive and reflexive respectively *cannot* be used. In the following examples, suggested translations of the English sentences discussed are shown in brackets.

• The Spanish passive cannot be used as an equivalent to the English passive
  (a) where the subject of the passive verb is logically an indirect object or a prepositional object, eg:

I was taught Spanish by a Spaniard

(Me enseñó el español un español)

This bed was slept in by Henry VIII

(Enrique VIII durmió en esta cama)

(b) where the passive subject has no article, eg:

Pianos are sold here

(Se vende(n) pianos aquí)

(c) where the past participle has a different meaning as an adjective
with **ser**, eg:

The students were bored by the lecture

(La clase aburrió a los estudiantes OR **Los estudiantes
estaban aburridos por la clase** since **ser aburrido** = *to
be boring*)

(d) in the Present and Imperfect tenses where the verb denotes a
single action, eg:

Now the window is shut by the teacher

(Ahora la profesora cierra la ventana)

BUT the following are acceptable

**La ventana fue / será / ha sido, etc, cerrada por la
profesora**

La ventana es cerrada todos los días por la profesora

as are constructions with a verb denoting a quality, eg:

Es conocido por todos

He's known by everyone

NOTE: **La ventana es cerrada por la profesora** is also possible with
a 'commentary' interpretation: *The window is being shut by the teacher.*
This use is more frequent in journalistic R3 than in other registers.
The following are examples of captions from newspaper photographs:

Un obrero es socorrido por manifestantes en Tiananmen

A worker is aided by demonstrators in Tiananmen

**Asaltantes de supermercados son detenidos por la policía
argentina en la ciudad de Rosario**

Supermarket raiders are arrested by Argentine police in the city of
Rosario

• The Spanish reflexive cannot be used

(a) where a literal reflexive meaning is possible, eg:

The children were taught to read

(A los niños se les enseñó a leer)

NOT **Los niños se enseñaron a leer**, which would mean *The
children taught themselves to read.*

(b) where an agent is expressed, eg:

These books were sold by my uncle

(Estos libros los vendió mi tío)

NOT **Estos libros se vendieron por mi tío**

BUT NOTE: Reflexive + agent constructions appear to be being used
more often in Spanish; the following, for instance, are perfectly
acceptable

> **Este libro se editó por un catedrático muy conocido**
> This book was edited by a very well-known professor
> **La Academia se fundó por Felipe V**
> The Academy was founded by Philip V

(c) in the third person, where another **se** is needed or implied
(see **34.6**), eg:

> John wasn't asked for it
> **(No se lo pidieron a Juan – se** here = **le)**

NOT, of course, **No se se lo pidió a Juan. No se pidió a Juan** is
acceptable but means *He/She didn't ask John for it.*

35 Comparison

35.1 Comparison of inequality (more/less/fewer than)

- If a single part of speech is being compared, **que** is used, eg:

  Pedro es más/menos alto que Juan
  Pedro is taller/shorter than John

  La biblioteca tiene más/menos periódicos que revistas
  The library has more/fewer newspapers than magazines

  Da más que recibe
  She gives more (= to a greater extent) than she receives

  Ahora es más/menos pequeño que antes
  Now it's smaller than / not as small as before

  NOTE: In R1, a 'redundant' **no** is sometimes used after **que**, eg

  Tiene más libros que no $\boxed{!}$ **yo**
  He has more books than me

- Where the comparison is with an element in another clause, **de** +
  pronoun + **que** is used. If the pronoun refers back to a noun, it agrees
  with the noun; if it refers to a clause, **lo** is used, eg:

  Aquí hay más $\boxed{\text{libros}}$ **de** $\boxed{\text{los}}$ **que se puede leer (se puede**
  leer $\boxed{\text{libros}}$ **)**
  There are more books here than can be read

  Es más alto de $\boxed{\text{lo}}$ **que yo pensaba (pensaba** $\boxed{\text{que . . .}}$ **)**
  He's taller than I thought

  Contrast the following pairs of examples:

  Tiene más dinero de $\boxed{\text{lo}}$ **que dice (dice** $\boxed{\text{que . . .}}$ **)**
  She has more money than she says

  Tiene más $\boxed{\text{dinero}}$ **de** $\boxed{\text{el}}$ **que yo le di (Le di** $\boxed{\text{dinero}}$ **)**
  She has more money than I gave her

  Necesita más atención de $\boxed{\text{lo}}$ **que se sospechaba (se**
  sospechaba $\boxed{\text{que . . .}}$ **)**
  It needs more attention than was thought

  Necesita más $\boxed{\text{atención}}$ **de** $\boxed{\text{la}}$ **que se puede dar (se puede**
  dar $\boxed{\text{atención}}$ **)**
  It needs more attention than can be given

Notes

1 In R1, **de lo que**, **del que**, etc, are sometimes replaced by **que** alone ⟨!⟩

2 **Que lo que**, etc, are used in comparisons not involving a clause, eg:

Los libros que acabo de leer son más interesantes que los que tengo que leer ahora

The books I've just read are more interesting than those I've got to read now

With a numeral

With a numeral, **de** is used, eg:

Ha ganado más/menos de cien mil pesetas

He's earned more/less than a hundred thousand pesetas

Quedaron más/menos de dos meses

There were more/less than two months left

But **no más que** = *only*, and **que** is generally used before a numeral when a negative is present, eg:

No me quedan más que dos meses

I've only two months left OR I haven't more than two months left

35.2   *mayor / más grande, menor / menos grande*

These forms of the comparative are interchangeable *except* when they refer to people, when **mayor** and **menor** relate exclusively to age:

Es mayor que yo

He's older than me

BUT

Es más grande que yo

He's bigger than me

Esta calle es mayor / más grande que aquélla

This street is bigger than that one

NOTE: **mayor** also has the non-comparative sense of *elderly* – **una persona (muy) mayor** = a *(very) elderly person.*

35.3   Comparison of equality

Tanto + noun / **tan** + adjective or adverb + **como** . . . :

Me hace falta tanta comida como a él

I need as much food as he does

Este pueblo no tiene tantas casas como el otro

This village doesn't have as many houses as the other

Este chico me parece tan listo como su hermano

This boy seems to me as intelligent as his brother

Escribe tan bien como yo

He writes as well as I do

Notes

1   There is an alternative pattern with adjectives:

   Es blanco como (R2) / **cual** (R3) **la nieve**
   It's as white as snow

2   **Tanto . . . como . . .** is also frequently used as the equivalent of English *both . . . and . . .* , eg:

   tanto los ingleses como los españoles
   both the English and the Spanish
   (See **Chapter 17**.)

   Contrast the non–comparative **tan/tanto . . . que . . .** :

   Hacía tanto frío que no queríamos salir
   It was so cold that we didn't want to go out
   Era tan alta la torre que no quería subir a ella
   The tower was so high that he didn't want to go up it
   Llovía tanto que la carretera quedó inundada
   It was raining so much that the road became flooded

35.4   Comparison of clauses

Cuanto más lee, (tanto) más se divierte
The more he reads, the more he enjoys himself
Yo estuve tanto más contento cuanto que me resultó gratuita la comida
I was all the happier because the meal was free

36 Usage with names of countries

The vast majority of countries do not take the definite article unless they are qualified by an adjective or adjectival phrase:

Voy a España
I'm going to Spain
Es de México
He's from Mexico

BUT

en la Italia de hace cincuenta años
in the Italy of fifty years ago
en el Chile contemporáneo
in contemporary Chile

However, there are a number of countries, both masculine and feminine, which may be preceded by the definite article. They are indicated in **Chapter 10** as follows: **(el) Japón**, **(los) Estados Unidos**, **(la) Argentina**. Generally speaking, the use of the article is more typical of the written registers. One or two countries, notably **El Salvador**, have a definite article as part of their name, and it must always be used. As with names of towns **(eg El Ferrol)** where the article forms an integral part of the name, the article does not combine with **de** or **a** in very formal usage, eg:

en el norte de (la (R2–3)) **Argentina**
in the north of Argentina
el Primer Ministro de(l R2–3) **Japón**
the Prime Minister of Japan
la capital de El (R3) / **del** (R1–2) **Salvador**
the capital of El Salvador

Index

a 308–15, 413, 432
abajo 369
abalanzarse 176
abandonado 33
abandonar 33, 129
abarrotado 153
abastecer 128
abatido 179
abertura 55
abofetear 144
abogacía 270
abogado/a 270, 289
abogar 350
abolir 275
abonado 52
abonar 248, 249
aborigen 157
abrasar 80
abrazar 80
abrelatas 286
abrevar 55
abreviar 55
abrigo 108
abrir(se) 130, 431
absolución 274
absoluto, en 372
absolver 274
absorber 27
abstenerse 346, 431
aburrido 417
aburrir(se) 336, 347, 431
abusar 33, 364
acá
   de – para allá 322
   más – de 322
acabar(se) 346, 350, 354, 370,
    432
   de + inf 380
acaecer 158
acantilado 81
acaso 406
acatar 55
acaudalado 167

acceder 48, 110, 279, 341
accesar 279
accesible 55
accidentado 52
accidente 109, 259
acción 252
accionariado 251
accionista 251
acentazo 194
acento (ortográfico) 233
acepción 56
aceptación 56
aceptar 110, 337
acera 30, 102
acerca de 323
acercar(se) 431
acero 102
acertar 340
achacar la culpa 184
aclarar 56
acoger 90
acomodado 167
acompañante 56
acondicionar 56
aconsejar 339, 392
acontecer 158
acopiar 253
acopio 253
acorazada, cámara 247
acordar 110, 337, 363
acordar(se) 110, 364
acortar 91
acostado 417
acostar(se) 431
acostumbrar(se) 341, 354
acrecentarse 125
acrecer 125
acreedor, saldo 249
acta 94
activos 264
acto 94
actual 23
actualizar 277

acuerdo
   ¡de – ! 235
   estar de – 110
   estar de – con 26
   ponerse de – 110
acunar 81
acuñar 81
acurrucado 417
acusación 273
acusado 33, 52, 273
acusar 33, 273, 346
adelantado, pagar por 250
adelantar(se) 432
adelante
   sacar – 188
   salir – 188
adelanto(s) 155, 250
aderezar 56
adinerado 167
adjetivo 233
adjudicar 23, 81
admirable 142
admirarse 347
admitir 404, 405
adopción, por 331
adquisición 257
adquisitivo 258
aduaneros, derechos 256
adueñarse de 113
adverbio 233
advertir 115
afable 28
afán 350
afanar(se) 168, 350
afano 255
afectado 52
afectuoso 112
afeitar, maquinilla de 6
aferrarse 354
afición 344
   tener – 188
aficionado 344
afiliado 52

afirmar 339
aflicción 29
afligido 178
afrentar 56
afrontar 56, 139
afueras 32, 116
agachado 417
agachapado 417
agallas, tener (muchas) 195
agarrado 418
agarrar(se) 121, 366
agenda 23, 38
agente 289
agonía 23
agonizar 23
agosto, hacer su 195
agradar 336
agradecer 363, 392
agradecido 363
agrandarse 126
agravamiento 256
agresión 344
agresivo 32, 170
agreste 170
agrícola 18
agroindustria 18
agropecuario 18
agrupación 56, 146
agua
    al – 312
    estar con el – al cuello 195
aguardar 363, 412
aguardiente 286
agudo 152
    palabra aguda 233
agüero 56
agüita 192
agujero 110
agujetas 298
ahí
    de – que 399
ahíto 153
ahora bien 239
ahorcamiento 275
ahorita 7, 192
ahorrador/ –ora 249
ahorrar 249
ahorro
    caja de –s 247
    cartilla de – 248
    cuenta de –s 248
    libreta de –s 248
airarse 138
aire 113, 183
    al – libre 312
    por – 331
    por los –s 298

airecillo 193
ajusticiar 81, 275
alargarse 126
alberca 120
albergue juvenil 28
albornoz 109
alborozado 123
alcaide 81
alcalde 81
alcaldesa 289
alcance
    al – de 312
alcantarilla 81
alcanzar 145, 340
alcistas 257
aledaños 116
alegar 81
alegato 274
alegrar 336
alegrar(se) 347, 400, 431
alegre 123
alegría
    ¡qué – ! 236
alfombra 24
algas 298
alguno 371
alianza 112
alias 279
alicate(s) 299
aligerar 114
alimentario 57
alimenticio 57
allá
    de acá para – 322
    más – de 322
allanamiento de morada 261
allegados 45
allegar 81
alma
    caerse el – a los pies 195
    estar con el – en un hilo / en vilo
        195
almacén
    grandes –es 175
almacenar 277
    – mercancías 253
almeja, aburrirse como una – 204
almohada, consultar con la 195
alpinismo, hacer 172
alquiler 32
alrededor de 323
alrededores 116
alta, dar de 184
altanero 159
altavoz 286
alterar 33
altercado 135

alternativa 295
altivo 159
alto
    lo – 111
    pasar por – 184
altoparlante 286
altozano 122
altura
    a la – de 313
alumbrar 89
alumno/a 31
alza, jugar al 253
alzar 151
alzarse 166
amable 11, 111
amagar 81
amalgama 285
amañar 271
amanecer 185
amargar(se) 81
amarillo 201
amasar 33
ambicionar 185, 363
ambiente 57
ámbito 57
amenaza 271
amenazar 271, 354, 364
americana 108
ametralladora 57
amigote 194
amistoso 111, 287
amo/a 149
amolar, para acabarla de 6
amontonar 33
amor 57, 345, 346
amoratado 29
amorío(s) 57
amortiguar 57
amortización 250
amortizar 57, 250
amotinarse 166
ampliación 252
ampliar 19, 269, 278
ampliar(se) 126
amplio 29, 48
amplitud 13
amputar 125
análisis 286
anchas, a sus 310
anciano 183, 268
andar
    ¡anda ya! 236
andas 298
andinismo, hacer 172
anegar 87
anexo 280
anfitrión 48

ángel
  mal – 195
  tener – 195
ángulo 167
angustia 23
anhelar 337
anhelo 338
anilla 112
anillo 112
  – de boda 112
  – de matrimonio 112
  caer/venir como – al dedo 204
ánima 94
animado 57
animar 341, 392
ánimo 94
animoso 57, 180
aniquilar 133
ansia 338
ansiar 338
ante 316
antecedentes 272
antemano, de 320
antena, en 326
anteojos 144
anteponerse 364
anterior 48
antes
  – de 316, 372, 412
  – (de) que 412
  – que 316
anti-balas, cristal 247
anticipar(se) 364
anticipo 250, 259, 260
antiguo 183, 303
antojarse 189, 336
antológico 48
anular 49, 258
anunciar 115
anuncio 151
añejo 183
añicos, hacer 169
añorar 338
apachurrón 17
apaciguar 57
apagar 277
apalear 144
apañárselas 190
aparato 261
aparear 82
aparecer(se) 82, 113, 432
aparejar 82
aparentar 31, 338
aparición 57
apariencia 57, 113
apartarse 130
aparte 234

apasionar 336
apelar 274
apellido 158
apenado 179
apercibirse 348
apertura 55
apesumbrado 179
apetecer 336
apiadarse 366
aplausos 298
aplicación 33
apocalipsis 286
apoderarse 114, 364
apodo 158
aporrear 144
aposento 126
apostar (aposto) 33, 165
apostar (apuesto) 33, 350
apoyar 115, 354
apoyar(se) 352
apoyo 344
aprender 340
aprendiz 294
apresuramiento 340
apresurarse 114, 340
apretar 278
aprobado 52
aprobar 34, 93, 276, 363, 397
apropiarse 114, 364
aprovechar(se) 348, 363
aptitud 351
apuestas 263
apuntalar 82
apuntar 82
apunte 133
apurarse 114, 349, 350
apuro 31
ara 102
arancel 265
árbitra 289
arca 102
archivar 279
archivo 279
arco 102
ardid 140
arete 113
argolla 112
argot 150
argüir 34
argumento 34
arista 118
arma 114
armar 34
armarse 355
armazón 294
aro 102, 112, 113
arrabal 116

arrasar 132
arrebatar 344
arreglar 93
  – selas 190
arreglo
  con – a 317
arremeter 366
arrepentido 53
arrepentirse 347, 431
arrestado 53
arriba 369
  la parte de – 111
arriesgado 180
arriesgarse 340, 355
arrimado 418
arroba 246, 280
arrodillado 418
arrogante 159
arrojar 176
arrojarse 176
arrollar 133
arrostrar 139
arruinar 133
arte 287
artífice 24
artificio 24
artillería 114
artista 285
asaltar 168
asalto 345
ascender 171, 172
ascenso 44
asco 27
  causar/dar – 156
  dar – a 27
  ¡qué – ! 235
ascuas
  estar/tener a uno en – 195
  sobre – 333
asegurable 259, 261
asegurado 258, 259, 267
aseguradora 258
asegurar 258, 339
asemejarse 364
asentaderas 128
asentamiento 82
asentimiento 82
asequible 55, 254
asesinar 49
asesino 49
asesor/-ora 34, 263
asesoría 270
asestar, un golpe a 144
así 239
  – mismo 239
asignatura 46
asilo 268

asir(se) 121, 355, 364
asistencia social 259, 267, 268
asistir 24, 34, 115, 364
asma 283, 285
asolar 132
asombrarse 347
aspecto 113
aspirador/-ora 295
aspirar 340
asqueroso 28, 173
asterisco 234
astilla(s) 160
astuto 152
   más − que la zorra 203
asustarse 347
ataque 345
atascado 153
ataúd 286
¡atención! 236
atender 11, 24
atendido 53
atenerse 366
atentado 345, 366
atentar 276, 366
atenuante 274
atenuar 28
aterrar 82
aterrizar 82
atestado 153
atestar 34
atestiguar 273
atiborrado 153
atinar 340, 355
atisbar 181
átono 233
atracar 82
atracción 58
atraco 345
atractivo 58
atraer 336
atrancar 82
atrapar 121
atrás
   − de 333−4
   hacia − 279
atrasado, pago 255
atravesar 368
atreverse 341, 355, 431
atrevido 180, 417
atufarse 138
audición 34, 273
audiencia 34, 272, 273
auge 257, 293
augurio 56
aumentar 126, 171, 172
aumentativo 234
aumento 255

aun 82
   − cuando 408, 410
aún 82
aunque 239, 408, 410
   ni − 409
aupar 151
auscultar 49
ausencia
   en − de 326
auténtico 23, 49
autoabastecimiento 18
autobús 58
autocar 58
autóctono 49, 157
automóvil 17, 261
autonomía 49
autonómico 58
autónomo 58
autorización 351
autorizar 341, 351
autoservicio 24
auxiliar 115
avalar 89, 262
avance(s) 58, 155, 293
avanzada 58
avanzar 368
avenirse 110, 341, 355
avergonzado 27
avergonzar(se) 347, 431
avería 262
averiarse 83
averiguar 83, 268
aversión 27
avestruz 294
avión 286
avisar 83, 115
aviso, sobre 333
avispado 152
avistar 83
ayuda 345
ayudar 115, 342, 399
azar 174
azotar 144

baca 83
bache 110, 293
báculo 160
bailar como una peonza 204
baja 58, 252, 255
   dar de − 184
   jugar a la − 253
bajada 58, 122
bajar 279
bajar(se) 368, 432
bajista 257
bajito 192
bajo 316

bala 162
balance 58, 293
balanceo 58
balanza 58, 258
balar 170
balazos, a 310
balde
   de − 321, 326
   en − 326
   en − con 321
balido 170
balón 162
balsa 120
banca 94, 247
bancario 247
bancarrota, hacer 256
banco 35, 94, 247
banda 95
banda 146
   − impositiva 264
   − magnética 247
bandeja 83
bandera 83
bando 95, 146
banquero/a 247
banquillo 273
baño, (cuarto de) 127
barba 59, 298
barbaridad
   ¡qué − ! 235
bárbaro 35, 142, 303
barbilla 59
barca 95, 116
barco 95, 116
baremo 260
barra 102, 160, 278
barraca 24
barraco 10
barrancas, a trancas y 311
barras, código de 253
barreno 83
barreño 83
barrera 160, 258
barrio 32, 116
barritar 170
barrito 170
barro 102
barullo
   meterse en −s 198
base 293
bastar 189, 336, 352, 355, 396
basto 117
bastón 160
bata 109
batería 291
batidor/-ora 295
batir 131

batuta 160
baúl 47
baza 102
bazo 102
beber como una cuba 204
bellaco 155
bello 147
beneficiario/a 259
beneficiarse 348
beneficiencia 269
beneficio
   en – de 326
   –s 264, 265, 269
beneficioso 59
benéfico 59
benevolente 111
benévolo 111
benigno 112
berenjenal
   meterse en –es 198
besito 193
bestia 291
biberón 118
biblioteca 29
bibliotecario/a 29
bicho 277
bicho
   todo – viviente 195
bici 17, 226
bici-taxi 17
bien 416
   ¡– –! 235
   – ... – ... 240
   – que 408
   ahora – 239
   muy – 11
   ¡muy – ! 235
   (o) ... o – 240
   pasarla – 136
   pasarlo – 136
   ¡qué – ! 236
   tener a – 188
bienestar 268
bienintencionado 112
bienvenida, dar la 185
bigotazo 194
bilis 294
billete 17
birlar 168
bit 277
bizarro 24, 180
blanca
   estar sin – 201
   estar/quedarse sin – 195
blanco
   cheque en – 248
   ir de punta en – 201

más – que la nieve 203
   pasar la noche en – 201
blanqueamiento 256
blanquear 256
bledo, no importar un 196
bobo 177
boca
   a pedir de – 196
   hacerse la – agua– 196
   meterse en la – del lobo
   196
bocacalle 286
bocadillo 59
bocado 59
   a – 310
bocanada 59
bodas 298
bofetón 194
boicot 345
bola 102, 162
boleta 255
boleto 17
boli 226
bolita 192
bolo 102
bolsa 95, 251, 252
   corredor de – 251
bolsista 251
bolso 95
bomba 35, 103
   – lapa 232
   – trampa 232
   pasarlo – 136
bombo 103
bonachón 112
bondadoso 112
bonificación 259
bonito 147
bonos 252
booleano 279
boom 257
boqueada 59
boquete 110
boquiabierto, quedar 196
borbotones, a 310
bordar 24
borde 117
bordo
   a – de 312
Borgoña 284
borrar 279
borrasca 177
bosquejo 133
bota 118
botar 176
bote 116
botella 118

botellín 118
botellón 118
botija 118
botijo 118
braga(s) 299
bramante 127
bravío 59, 170
bravo 59, 170, 180
braza 103
brazo
   a – perdido 103, 310
brecha 110
bribón 154
brillar 118, 119
brindar 14, 350
brindarse 342
brioso 180
brisa 183
bronca 135
   echar la – 185, 196
   pegar la – 185
bronco 83
brotar 113
bruces, de 321
brújula 25
brutal 170
bruto 170, 257, 264
brutote 194
bucear 176
buenas
   de – a primeras 321
bueno 11, 112, 237, 400
   – como un ángel 203
   más – que el pan 203
bufete 270
buque 116
   – escuela 232
burdo 117
burlar 346
burlarse 346
burro 170
bursátil 251, 252
bus 226
busca 59
   en – de 326
   orden de – y captura 272
buscador 279
buscar 279, 341, 363
búsqueda 59
   a la – de 326
buzón 280
byte 277

¡ca! 236
caballeroso 180
caballete 192
caballito 193

caballo 170
  a – 310
cabecera 280
cabecilla 149
cabellera 161
cabello(s) 161
caber 189, 336
cabeza 291
  de – 321
  en – 326
cabezón 175, 194
cabezota 194
cable
  echar un – a 115
cabo, al fin y al – 237
cabrearse 138
cabrón 5, 194
caca 103
cacarear 170
cacareo 170
cacería 61
cacharro 83
cachetada, ponerse
  de la 6
cacho 168
cachondo 83
cachorro 83
cacia 289
cacica 149
cacique 149
caco 103
cadalso 275
caer 6, 90, 124
  – bien/mal 196
  dejar – 184
caer(se) 433
café
  – concierto 232
  – teatro 232
  tener mal – 197
cafetería 24
Caín, pasar las de 196
caja 247, 248
  – de ahorros 247
  – fuerte 247
cajero/a 247
cal 43, 293
calabazas, dar 196
calado
  estar – hasta los huesos
    197
calambre 293
calar 83
calavera 291
calcular 247
cálculo, hoja de 279
calentito 193

calidad 59
  en – de 326
  precio – 254
cálido 59
caliente 59
  dinero – 256
calificar 366
cáliz 294
callado 418
callar 83, 363
callar(se) 432
callejón
  meterse en un – sin salida 196
caluroso 59
calzada 95
calzado 95
calzón/calzones 299
calzoncillo(s) 299
cama nido 232
cámara 35, 291
  – frigorífica 262
camarilla 146
camarín 192
cambiar 60, 349
cambio 250, 257
  en – 326
cambista 250
camino, a medio/mitad de 312
camión 17, 286
  – cisterna 232
camisa, perder hasta la 199
camorra 135
campamento 60
campana 84
campaña 84
campera 108
campesino/a 30
camping 35, 60, 297
campo 60
cana 84
cana(s) 161
canal 292
canalla 154
cancelar 255, 279
canciller(a) 35
canción 60
candidata 289
canica 162
canino 133
canjear 60
canon 84
canónigo 84
cansado 418
cansar(se) 347, 431
cantar 60, 170, 171
  – como un jilguero 204
cántaro 81

  a –s 310
cante 60
cantera 81
cantimplora 118
canto 60, 117, 164, 170, 171
caña 84, 95
caño 95
cañón 84, 114
capacidad 351
capacitado 351
capaz 28
capellán 271
capital 134, 257, 263, 264,
    292
capitalista 251
capo 84
capó 84
captar 60
capturar 60
cara 119, 120, 150
  dar la – a 139
  hacer – a 139
  plantar – a 139
  ponerse de – a 138
  volver la – 138
carácter 35, 297
característica 295
¡carajo! 235, 236
¡caramba! 236
  ¡(qué) – ! 235, 236
caramelo 35
caravana 143
¡caray! 235
cárcel 276, 294
  – modelo 232
carecer 364
carencia, plazo de 260
careo 273
carga 95
cargamento 95
cargar 249, 364
  –selas 190
cargo 95, 265, 266
  testigo de – 271
cariñoso 112
carisma 285
carmín 29
carnes, en 326
caro 255
carpeta 24, 279
carrera 36
carreta 61
carrete 61
carretera
  en – 326
  por – 331
carretero, fumar como un 204

carretilla 61
carrito 61
carro 61
carromato 61
carta 35
  – de crédito 249
  dar – blanca a uno 201
  no saber a qué – quedarse 196
  por – 331
cartearse 185
cartel 36, 151
cartelera 151
cartera 251, 252
cartucho 278
casa 84, 103
casación 274
casarse 364
casca 103
cascar 129, 145, 169
casco 103
cascotes 298
cas(s)et(t)e 288
cash, pagar en 249
casita 192
caso 103
  en – de que 409
  en todo – 321, 326
  hacer – 185
castigar 24, 275
castigo 275
cásting 229
casual 403
casual(mente) 24
casualidad 174
casucha 194
catalejo 144
catar 55
catástrofe 293
catedrático/a 166, 289
cátering 229
cauce 293
caución 24
caudal 134
caudillo/a 149
causa
  – civil 270
  a/por – de 313
cautela 24
cautivar 60
cava 24, 291
caverna 24
cavidad 111
cavilar 25, 163
caza 61, 84, 103, 291
  ir de – 134
cazadora 108
cazar 134

cazo 103
celda 84, 276
celebrar 36, 400
celebrarse 158
celeste 61
celestial 61
celos 298
célula 84
  – madre 232
cemento 61
censurar 24
centavo, estar/quedarse sin un 195
centellear 119
centinela 291
central 61, 292, 293
céntrico 61
cepa 103
cepo 103
cerca 95, 416
  – de/a 323
cercanías 116
cercano 416
  – a 323
cercenar 125
cerco 62, 95
cereal 293
cero
  ser un – a la izquierda 202
cerrar 259, 277
cerrar(se) 431
cerro 122
certamen 28, 123
certificado 275
césped 286
cesta 96
cesto 96
¡chachi! 235
chamarra 108
chamba 6, 178
chapotear 62
chapucear 62
chapuzar 62
chaqueta 108
charca 96, 120
charco 96, 120
charlar 129
chasco, llevarse un 196
chasquear 278
chat(eo), salón de 280
chatear 280
chaval(a) 157
cheque 248
  – en blanco 248
chequera 248
chico/a 8, 157
chillar 121
china 164

chip 277
chirriar 121
chispa
  echar/arrojar/lanzar –s 196
¡chissst! 8
chistoso 146
chocar 145, 356, 366
chofer/chófer 17
chubasquero 108
chulo 159
chupado, está 196
churros, venderse como 204
chusco 168
ciberespacio 277
ciclón 183
ciegas, a 310
¡cielos! 236
cien
  dentro de – años todos calvos 203
  ponerle a uno a – 203
ciencia
  a – cierta 310
ciento, por 331
cierto 303, 403
  por – 331
cigala 85
cigarra 85, 103
cigarro 103
cima 85, 111
cimiento 61
cinco, Choca esos 202
cinta 96
cinto 96
cintura 62
cinturón 62
circo 62
circulación 264
circular 294
círculo 62, 112
circunstancias, ante las 316
cisma 285
citación 273
citar 273
ciudad 85
  – dormitorio 232
  – modelo 232
clarividente 152
claro
  – que 239
  tan – como el agua 203
clase 29
clic, hacer 278
cliente/a 271, 288, 289
clima 285
club 297
coagular 26
coartada 274

cobertizo 269
cobertura 258, 259, 261
cobrador(a) 25
cobrar 249, 267
　– un cheque 248
cobro 254
cochambroso 173
coche
　– bomba 232
　– cama 232
　– patrulla 232
cochecito 192
cochino 173
cocina 127
codazo 194
código
　– de barras 278
　– de entrada 277
　– penal 270
codo
　charlar por los –s 196
coger 90, 121
coherente 26
coincidir 352, 355
¡cojones! 235
　¡de – ! 235
¡cojonudo! 235
　pasarlo – 136, 142
col 294
colar 83
　¡no cuela! 236
cole 8, 226
colectivo 17
colegio 36
cólera 292
colgado 277, 418
colgarse 277
colina 122
collado 122
collar 25
colmado 153
colmar 348
colmillo 133
colocar 165
colonia 36
color 62
colorado 62, 201
colorido 62
columbrar 181
columna 280
coma 234, 292
comando 25
comarcal 287
comediante/-a 25
comedor 127
comentar 49, 363
comentario 345, 363

comenzar 136, 137, 341, 350, 355
comer como una lima 204
comer(se) 433
comercialización 254
comercializar 62, 254
comerciantes, pequeños 253
comerciar 62
comercio 175
cometa 285, 292
comezón 350
cómico 25, 146
comienzos
　a – de 309
comillas 234
　– simples 234
comino, no importar un 196
comisión 256, 258
　– de administración 249
comisura 167
como 408, 410, 441
　– si 408
cómo
　¿ – se diría? 237
comodidad 25
compadecer 363
compadecerse 363, 366
compañero/a 56
compañía, hacer 366
comparecer 113, 272, 273
comparencia 272
compás 25
compasivo 32
compe 226
compensación 261
compensar 356, 363
competencia 36, 123, 257
　hacer la – 184
competer 62
competición 28, 36, 122
competir 62
competitividad 257
complacerse 352
complementar 63
complemento 233
completo 152, 153
complicadillo 193
cómplice 288
componente 294
componer 92
comprar 343
comprender 403, 404, 405
comprensible 63
comprensivo 32, 63
comprobar 93, 268
comprometerse 342
compromiso 36, 342
compuesto, tiempo 234

computación 277
computador/-ora 276, 295
computar 277
comunicar 115
con 317–18
　– que 408
　estar – 422
concebir 163, 404
conceder 49, 128
concejal 63
concejo 63
concentración 37
concentrado 53
concentrarse 352
concepto 264
　por – de 19
concerniente
　en lo – a 313
concienciar/concientizar 187, 348
conciliar 63
conclave/cónclave 293
concordar 110, 356
concreto 25
　en – 326
concurso 123
condena 274
condenar 274, 342
condescender 364
condición
　a (la) – (de) que 408
　bajo la – 316
condicional 234
　– perfecto 234
condicionar 56
condiciones
　en – de 326
　estar en – (de hacer algo) 196
conducir 153
conducta 96
conducto 96
conductor/-ora 25, 30
conferencia 29, 37
confesar 272, 339
confesión 272
confeso 271
confiado 418
confianza 26, 63, 274
confiar 356, 400, 402
confidencia 26, 63
confinar 366
confirmar 339
confiscación 276
confiscar 114, 344
confrontar 139
confuso 27
congelar 26
congregado 53

conjunción 233
conjunta, cuenta 248
conjunto 146
conllevar 91
conmocionar 92
conmovedor 71
conmover 92
conmutar 274
conocer 169
conocimientos 298
conque 410
conquistar 131
consagrarse 342
consecuencia, en 240, 326, 331
consecuente 26
conseguir 93, 338, 392
consejero 63
consejo(s) 63, 298
consentimiento 366
consentir 110, 339, 353, 356, 366,
 397
conservante 31
consiguiente, por 240, 326, 331
consistente 26
consistir 366
consola 277
consonante 233, 284
constancia, dejar 188
constante 294
constar 366
consternación 26
constipado 8, 26
cónsul 289
consultado 53
consumación 63
consumar 63
consumición 63
consumir 49, 63
consumo 254
 artículo de – 25
contable 263
contactar 365
contacto
 al/en – con 312
contado
 al – 310
 pagar al – 249
 venta al – 254
contagiado 53
contar 366
 ¿qué me cuentas? 8
contener 255
contenido 261
contento 123, 347
 más – que unas Pascuas 203
contestación
 en – a 326

contestar 26, 365
contienda 135
contiguo a 323
continente 261
contingencia 268
continuar 354, 368
continuidad 269
contra 318
 en – de 318
contraria, llevar la 196
contrario
 al/por el – 239
 por – 331
contraseña 277, 279
contratación 252
contratante 273
contratar 259, 363
contratiempo 109
contravenir 365
contribuciones 262, 263
contribuir 342
contribuyente 266
control, bajo 316
controlar 37
controversia 135
controvertido 417
contumacia 274
contumaz 175, 274
convencer 352, 396, 397
convenios 18
convenir 110, 336, 356,
 396
conversar 129
convertir 49
convertirse 124
convicción 271
convicto 271
convidar 342, 396
convocar 31, 49
cónyuge 266, 288
¡coño! 235, 236
 estar en el quinto – 202
 ¡qué –! 5
coordinadora 287
copa 103, 111, 180
copia 37
copiar 279
copita 180
copo 103
coraje 37
corchetes 234
cordel 127
cordial 28
cordón 127
coro 85
corporal, accidente 259
corpulento 26, 145

corredor de la muerte 275
corredor/-ora de seguros 258
corregir 27
correo
 – electrónico 280
 en – aparte 326
 por – 331
Correos 298
correr 90, 255
 – como un galgo 204
 a todo – 311
corresponder 37, 110, 337
corriente 292
 al – 310
 cuenta – 248
 marchar/nadar/ir contra la –
 196
corrillo 146
corro 85
corta, a la 310
cortar 91, 125
 – y pegar 279
corte 118, 292
cosquillas 298
costa 64
 a mi – 310
 a toda – 310
costado 150
costar 337
coste 64
costear 363
costes 259
costo 64
costumbre, de 321
cota 104
cotización 251, 252, 259, 268,
 269
 – de apertura 252
 – de cierre 252
 – de clausura 252
cotizado 252
cotizar 252
coto 104
cotorrear 129
coz 294
crac(k) 258
crear 85
crecer 125
creces, con 298
crecimiento 257
credenciales 293
crediticia 250
crédito 249, 250, 251, 256
 – puente 232
 cuenta de – 248
 peticiones de – 256
 tarjeta de – 248

creer 85, 162, 339, 352, 404, 405
  ¡ya lo creo! 8
crema 285
crepitar 85
cresta 111
cretino 177
criar 85
criatura 37
crimen 131, 271
criminal 154
crin 294
crío 8
crispar 156
cristal 181, 182
  –anti-balas 247
cristiano, hablar en 197
criticar 24
críticas 345
crono 226
croquis 133
crujir 121
cruzada, referencia 280
cruzado, cheque 248
cruzar 368
cuadra 104, 246
cuadrilla 146
cuadro 104
cualidad 59
cuando 411
cuantía 249
cuanto
  en – a 326
  en – de que 411
cuánto
  ¿a – ? 309
cuarenta, cantarle las 203
cuarta
  estar a la – pregunta 202
cuartel 24
cuarto 126
  echar un – a espadas 202
cuartucho 194
cuatita 6, 7
cuatro
  Estaban/había – gatos 202
cuba 96
  beber como una – 204
cubiertos 298
cubo 96
cubrir 259
cuchilla 96
cuchilladas, a 310
cuchillo 96
cuclillas, en 326
cuco, ser un 196

cuello 25
  a voz en – 311
  al – 312
cuenca 96
cuenco 96
cuenta 97, 248, 249
  darse – de 31
  tener en – 188
cuentas, ajustar las 196
cuento 97
  venir a – 196
cuerda 127
  bajo – 316
  dar – 185
cueros, en 326
cuervo 170
cuesta 122
cuestas, a 312
cueva 24
cuidado 85
  tener – 356
¡cuidado! 236
cuidar 356
cuidarse bien 346
culebra 170
culo 128
culpa
  achacar la – 184
  echar la – 184
culpabilidad 274, 275
culpable 273, 274
culpar 347
culto 345
cumbre 111
cumplimentar 63, 264
cumplimiento 365
cumplir 63, 274, 337, 365
cuna 85
cuña 85, 104
cuño 104
cuota 250, 251, 254, 257, 265, 269
cupo 254
cura 285, 291
curioso 349
curita 6
curro 178
cursillo 193
cursiva 280
curso 37
cursor 278
curva 167
custodia 276
  bajo la – 316
cutis 49

dado que 239, 409, 410
damnificado 53

dañar 141, 259
daños 261
  – y perjuicios 274
dar 128, 138, 357
  – con 137
  – selas 190
  – un golpe a 144
dátil 26
dato 26
datos 298
de 318–23
  – + inf 411
debajo de 316
debate 34, 135
deber 349
deberes 178, 298
debitar 249
débito, tarjeta de 248
década 295
decaer 90
decaído 179
decapitar 275
decepción 26
dechado 30, 155
decidido 341
decidir 23, 341, 357, 392, 395
decidirse 341, 350
decir 129, 339, 392, 395
  digamos 237
  digámoslo así 237
  es – 240
  ni – tiene 188
  ¡no me digas! 236
  no querer – 404
  podríamos – 238
  por -lo así 238
decisión 341, 350
declaración 264, 274
declarar 340, 392, 395
declive 122, 258, 293
decodificar 280
decomisar 276
decretar 392
dedicación 64
dedicarse 342
dedicatoria 64
deducible 264, 265
deducir 266
defectivo 37
defectuoso 37
defender 271
defensa 271, 291
defensiva 295
defensor/-ora 271
déficit 18, 256, 297
deficitaria 258
deflación 258

defraudar 139, 265
dejar 31, 129, 339, 346, 357, 370, 397
delante de 316
deleitarse 136, 352
delgado 130
delicioso 147
delincuente 154
delinquir 271
delito 131, 272
delta 285
demanda 18, 254, 255, 258, 270, 273
   oferta y – 254
demandado/a 271
demandante 271
demandar 37, 161
¡demasiado! 235, 236
demente 29
demoler 132
demonios, un lío/ruido de todos los 196
demostrar 140, 340
demostrativo 233
denegar 92
denuncia 276, 345
denunciar 50, 340
deparar 128
departamento 38
departir 26, 129
dependencia 38
depender 366
deportar 276
deposición 272, 274
depositar 249
depósito 255
   cuenta de – 248
deprimido 179
depurar 277
derecha 97
   a la – 312
derecho 97
derivar(se) 38
derogar 276
derredor
   en – de 326
derribar 132
derrocar 85
derrochar 85, 154
derrotar 85, 131
derruir 132
derrumbar 132
desamparado 164
desaparecido 53
desaprobar 363, 398
desarrollarse 126
desarrollo 18, 257

desaseado 172
desayunar(se) 432
desbaratar 132
descargar 279
descargo, testigo de – 271
descarnado 130
descartado 53
descartar 403
descomponer 92
descompostura 262
desconcertar 27
desconfianza 347
desconfiar 347
desconsolado 178
descontento 178, 347
descorrer 90
descreído 418
descuarajingar 169
descubierto, estar en/al 249
descubrir 38, 137, 181
descuento 259
desde 323
   – que 412
desear 338, 393
desembolso 255
desenvolverse 126
deseo 338, 414
deseoso 338
desequilibrio 258
desértico 64
desescombro 262
desesperarse 347, 357
desfiladero 64
desfile 64, 143
desgarrar(se) 431
desgastar 91
desgracia 26
   caer en la – 26
   por – 331
desgraciado 164
desgravable 265
desgravación 250, 265
desgravar 265
deshacerse 27
deshonesto 26
deshonra 26
deshora, a 309
desierto 64
desinterés 347
desinteresarse 347
desistir 346
deslumbrar 89, 119
desmadre 293
desmantelar 132, 269
desmayo 26
desmentir 403
desmenuzar 169

desnudo 283
desolar 132
despabilado 152
despachar 141
despacho 40
despectivo 233
despedirse 185, 346
despejado 152
despeñarse 177
desperdiciar 154
despierto 152
despilfarrar 154
desplazarse 17
desplegar 140
despreocupado 24
después 238
   – de 333–4, 412
   – de que 412
   – que 333–4
desquite
   tomar el – (de algo) 196
destacar(se) 185, 432
destajo, a 309
destartalado 27
destellar 119
desterrar 276
destiempo, a 309
destierro 276
destinar 141
destino 38, 174
destitución 26
destrozar 132
destruir 132
desvalido 164
desvencijado 27
detención 276
detenido 53
deteriorar 141
deterioro 258
determinar 342, 357
detrás de 333–4
detrimento 19
deuda 104, 256
deudor, saldo 249
deudos 104
devaluación 258
devastar 132
devengar 265
devengo 265
devolución 265
devolver 94
día 285
   – a – 309
   – festivo 179
   – por – 331
   al – siguiente 308
   al otro – 308

día (*cont.*)
¡Buenos –s! 298
de – 320
todo el santo – 196
diabetes 294
diablo, mandar a uno al – 196
diadema 285
diagrama 133
diario 38
a – 309
dibujo 133, 156
dichoso 123
dictar 274
diente 133
dientecito 193
diéresis 234
diez
hacer las – de últimas 202
¡me cago en – ! 235
diferente 303, 366
diferido, en 326
dificultad 351
dificultar 187
digital 293
dignarse 185, 340, 431
digno 349
dilapidado 27
dilapidar 154
diligencia 38
diligencias 272, 298
diminutivo 158, 233
dimitir 366
dínamo 285
dineral 134
valer un – 200
dinero 134
– llama – 253
Dios
– mediante 196
¡– mío! 236
a la buena de – 310
armarse la de – 195
¡me cago en – ! 235
¡por – ! 235
diplomático/a 38
diputada 289
dirección 38, 280
directiva 97
directivo 97
directo, en 326
director/-ora 25, 27, 166, 230
dirigente 253
– gerente 253
dirigir 253
discapacidad 268
disco 278
– flexible 278

discriminar 363
discurrir 163
discusión 34, 135
discutir 34, 39
diseño 133, 156
disfrutar 136, 348
disgustado 27
disgustar 27
disgustarse 138
disgusto 27
disimulado 418
disimular 344
disminución 255
disminuir 28, 50
disparar 134, 176, 366
displicencia 30
disponer 27, 165, 365, 393
disponerse 342
dispuesto 396
disputa 31, 135
disquetera 278
distar 185
distinto 303, 366
distraerse 136
distribución 254
disuadir 347, 396
divertido 146, 418
divertirse 136
dividendo 256
dividir 86
divisar 27, 86, 181
divisas 134, 250
divorciado 266
doble 64
doblete 64
doblez 64, 288
docenas
a – 309
por – 331
dolencia 64
dolor 23, 64
doloroso 179
domiciliación 249
domiciliar 249
domicilio, a 312
dominar 131
dominio 270
don 166, 167
donación 166
donar 128
donativo 166
dondequiera 413
dormidito 192
dormido 418
dormir, como un lirón /
una piedra / un tronco / un
leño 204

dormir(se) 433
dormitorio 39, 127
dorso 141
dos
cada – por tres 202
como – y – son cuatro 202
estar a – velas 202
estar entre – aguas 202
estar entre – fuegos 202
dotar 128
dote 167, 287
duda 414
dudar 340, 353, 357, 365, 403
dudoso 403
duelo 39
dueño/a 149
dulzón 194
duro
más – que un mendrugo / una
piedra 203

echado 418
echar 137, 176, 357
– de menos 185
– en falta 185
– la culpa 184
– mano 359
echarse 137, 176, 341
– (de cabeza) 176
– a perder 188
–selas 190
eclipse 293
económicas 264
edad, tercera 268
edil 288
editar 27
editor/-ora 27
editorial 292
efectivamente 39
efectivo 64
–s 298
pagar en – 249
efecto, en 64, 239
eficaz 64
eficiente 64
ejecución 275
ejecutar 275
ejecutivo/a 253
ejemplar 37
ejemplo 29, 155
ejercer 65
ejercitar 65
ejercitarse 352
elaborados 18
elaborar 50
elefante 170
elegir 50

elemento clave 232
elevado 50
elevar 151
elevarse 126, 172, 255
eliminatoria 287
élite 293
e-mail 280
embarazada 27
embarazar 27
embarazarse 27
embarcación 116
embarcar 254
embarcarse 24
embarcarse 352
embargar 254
embargo 276
   sin – 240
embriagar 29
emilio 280
emisor 97
emisora 97
emitir 50
emoción 39
emocionante 65
emotivo 65
empate 309
empellones, a 310
empeñarse 352
empero 239
empezar 136, 137, 341, 350, 357
emplazar 165, 273, 342
empleado/a 247
empleo 178
empollón 194
emprender 19, 137
empresariales 287
   (estudios) – 253
empresario/a 253
empréstito 250
empujar 342
empujones, a 310
empuñar 121
en 324–7
enaguas 298
enamorarse 348
encajar 65
encajonar 65
encantador 147
encantar 337, 400
encapuchado 53
encaramarse 171, 365
encarapitarse 171
encarar(se) 139
encararse 366
encarcelado 53
encargado/a 53, 149
   – de prensa 53

encargar 348
encausar 272
enchufe 293
encima de 327
encina 284
enclave 293
enclenque 130
encontrar 137
encontrar(se) 137, 367, 434
encuesta 27, 271
   – judicial 27
encuestado 53
enderezar 56
energético 65
enérgico 65
enfadar(se) 138, 431
énfasis 286
enfermar(se) 432
enfermedad 261, 268
enfrentar(se) 138, 367
enfrente
   – de 323, 327
   estar – de 138
enfurecerse 138
enfurecido 27
enganche 255
engañar 139
engaño 26, 139
engastar 91
engatusar 139
engrandecerse 126
engreído 159
engrosar 27
enhorabuena 286
enjuagar 86
enjugar 86
enjuiciar 65, 272
enjuto 130
enojarse 138
enredador/-ora 154
enrollar
   ¡como enrolla! 236
ensayar 148
ensayarse 365
enseñante 165
enseñar 140, 342
ensueño 78
entablar 137, 273
entender 358, 403
   a mi – 310, 326
enterarse 365
entonces 237, 238
entrañable 112
entrar 352, 358, 368
entredicho, poner en 185
entregar 128
entregarse 342

entrenar(se) 432
entretenerse 136, 352
entretenido 418
entrevista 345, 365
entrevistarse 186, 365
entusiasmar 187, 337
entusiasmarse 350
entusiasmo 350
envejecimiento 267
enviar 141
enzarzarse 270
época, hacer 196
equidad 273
equipar 65
equiparar 65
equipo 39, 146
equivocar 363
equivocarse 363
erario 266
ermita 27
ermitaño/a 27, 31
esbelto 130
esbozo 133
escacharrarse 5
escala 97
   a – internacional 312
escalada 255
escalamiento 261
escalar 171
escalera(s) 299
escalo 97
escamotear 344
escandalizarse 348
escándalo 26
   armarse un – 195
escanear 280
escáner 280
escapar(se) 272, 434
escaparate 181
escarceos 298
escasear 189
escasez 267
escena 65
escenario 39, 65
esclarecer 56
escoger 90, 338
escolar 39
escolta 291
escombros 298
esconder 344
escondidas, a 310
escopeta 114
escrito, por 331
escrutar 148
escuálido 28
escuchar 363
escuchimizado 130

escudriñar 148
esdrújula, palabra 233
esencial 393
esfera 162
esforzarse 148, 350
esfuerzo 350
esmerarse 148, 350
esmero 350
esmirriado 130
espabilado 152
espabilarse 114
espaciador 278
espacio 39
espada 291
espalda(s) 141
   a –s de 311
español, a lo 310
española, a la 310
espantarse 348
esparadrapo 6
espárragos, mandar a uno a freír 196
especia 66
especial, en 326
especie 66
espécimen 297
espectáculos 263
espectadores 34
espectro 39
especulaciones 253
especular 253
espejo, al 312
esperanza 414
esperar 352, 358, 363, 400, 402, 412
espina 97
espino 97
espiral 293
esquelético 130
esquema 133
esquina 167
esquinazo, dar el 196
establecer 393, 395
estaca 160
estación 39
estadio 40
estadística 299
estafa 140
estafar 139
estampado 156
estanque 120
estar 358, 415–22
   – al + inf 422
   – + gerund 381
   sala de – 127
esto 237
   en – 326
estock 231, 253
estorbar 156

estrafalario 24
estratagema 24, 140, 285
estrella 283
   tener buena/mala 197
estremecer(se) 431
estrenar 186
estreñido 26
estribillo 31
estropear 142
estudio 40
estudioso 39
estufa 143
estupendamente 8
estupendo 142
¡estupendo! 235
estúpido 177
etapa reina 232
evadido 53
evaluar 89
evasión 263
evasivas, recurrir a 31
eventual 28
evidencia 274
evitar 338, 393
evolucionar 40
examinar 148, 274
examinarse 367
excederse 365
excepto que 409
exclamación 234
excluído 53
excursión 182
excusarse 347
exento 266
exhibir 140
exhortar 342
exigir 37, 161, 344, 393
exiliado/a 54, 263
exilio 276
eximir 266
exitazo 194
éxito 28, 32, 46
expansión 254
expectación 66
expectativa 66
expediente 264
expedir 141
expensas
   a – de 298
   a mis – 298
experimentar 40
explotación 345
explotar 40
exponer 140
exportación 254
   de – 18
exposición estrella 232

expresar 86
expresarse 129
exprimir 86
expropriación 276
expulsar 276
éxtasis 286
extenderse 126
extenso 29
extenuar 28
exteriores 287
extinción 262
extrañar 185, 337, 400
   ser de – 400
extrañarse 348, 400
extraño 24, 400
¡extraordinario! 235

fábrica 28
fabuloso 142
facha 113, 291
facilidad 351
facilitar 40, 128
factor sorpresa 232
factura 255
facturar 11
facultado 351
faena 140, 178
fajo 247
falda 150
falla 98
fallar 275, 277
fallecimiento 260
fallo 40, 98, 275
falsear 265
falso 26
falta 40, 131
   echar en – 185
   hace – 393
faltar 189, 352, 358
fama, de mala 30
famélico 130
familiar 40, 265, 268
familiares 45
fan 229
fanega 246
fanfarrón 159
fantasma 292
farolero 159
fascinar 337
fastidiar 142, 156, 337
fastidioso 28
fatigarse 348, 358
fatuo 159
favor
   a – de 313
   a – de 275
   por – 11

fax 229
faxear 280
faz 119, 120, 294
fe, de buena 321
fecha 26
   – límite 232
   – tope 232
felicidad 66
felicitación 66
felicitar 349
feliz 123
femenino 233
feo
   más – que Picio 203
feraz 86
feroz 86, 170
festividad 179
festivo, día 179
fianza 273
   bajo – 250, 316
fiarse 365
fichero 279
fiera
   estar hecho una – 197
   ponerse hecho una – 138
fiesta 28, 179
fiestón 194
figurarse 162, 404, 407
fijarse 353
fila 67, 142
filantrópico 112
filial 287, 293
filo 118
fin
   a – de que 398
   al – y al cabo 237
   en – 237
final 28, 111, 292
   a –es de 309
financiar 266, 269
financiero 255
finanzas 269
fingir 31, 337
firma 40
fiscal 40, 263, 265, 266, 270
fiscales 251, 262
fiscalía 270
fiscalidad 262
física 289, 299
   persona – 263
fisio 226
fisonomía 50
flaca 6
flaco 130
flagrante
   en – delito 272
flas(h) 229

floppy 278
flor 294
   ser la – y nata 197
fluctuación 252
fluctuar 252
flujograma 280
foca 104
foco 104
follón, armarse un 195
fomentar 50, 257
fonazo 6
fonda 104
fondo 104, 141
   al – de 312
   en el – 312
fondos 134, 256, 257
   cheque sin – 248
footing 229
foráneo 19
forense 272
forma 40, 156
   de – que 239, 398
   de una – 310
   en baja – 179
formación 41
formal 41
formalizar 259
formas, de todas 321
formatear 280
fornido 143
fortuna 134, 174
   buena – 174
   por – 331
forzar 342, 399
forzudo 143
fosa 98
foso 98
foto 285
fotografía 41
fracaso 28
fraccionamiento 266
fracturar 169
fraganti, in 272
frailuco 194
francote 194
frasco 118
frase 41, 46, 233
fraude 263, 293
frecuencia 28
fregar 156
freidora 295
frenarse 258
frente 292
   – a 327
   hacer – a 139
fresquito 193
frigo 226

frío
   más – que el hielo / un tempano 203
frito
   me tiene – 8
   traer – 188
fruta 98
fruto 98
fuego 143
   estar entre dos –s 197
fuera
   estar – de sí 197
fuerte 143
   – como un roble 203
   pisar – 199
fuertecilla 193
fuerza
   a – de 313
   a la – 311
fuerzas 298
fuga 276
fulgurar 119
fumar como un carretero 204
función
   en – de 326
   en –es 326
fundación 66
fundamento 66
fundar 86
fundir 86
fundir(se) 431
funeral(es) 298
funerarios 259
furibundo 13
furioso 29
fusil 114
fusilar 134, 275
fusión 257
futuro 234
   – perfecto 234

gabán 109
gabardina 109
gafas 144
gala 28
galería 272
galgo, correr como un 204
gallina 170
   ponérsele a uno la carne de – 196
   ser la – de los huevos de oro 197
gallo 170
gama 104
gamberro/a 154
gamo 104
gana
   de buena – 321
   tener –(s) 349

ganar 131, 344
gandul 163
gángster 297
garantizar 262
garrote 160, 275
gas
　– ciudad 232
　a todo – 311
gasolina 30
gastar 91
gastos 265, 274
gatas, a 311
gatear 369
gato 170
　buscar tres pies al – 197
　Estaban/había cuatro –s 202
　hay – encerrado 197
gema 285
gemelos 144
general, por lo 332
género 233
generoso 112
génesis 291
genial 28
gente(s) 299
gerente 230
gerundio 234
gesta 98
Gestapo 285
gestar 66
gestionar 66, 249, 252, 253
gesto 98
gimnasia 98
gimnasio 98
gira 98, 182
giro 98, 249
glamour 229
global 260
globalización 277
globo 162
gloriarse 348, 431
gobernador(a) 66
gobernante 66
golear 186
golpe
　asestar un – a 144
　dar el – de gracia a uno 197
　dar un – a 144
　de – 321
　pegar un –a 144
golpear 144
gordezuelo 145
gordinflón 145
gordo 6, 26, 145
gorra 98
gorrión 286
gorro 98

gozar 136, 348
　–la 136
grabadora 86
gracia 41, 274
　(dar las) –s 349
　muchísimas –s 11
gracioso 41, 146
grada 99
grado 99
　de buen – 321
gráfica 280
　– de estadísticas 252
gráfico 280
grana 99
grande 29, 303
　a lo – 311
　más – 440
　menos – 440
　pasarlo en – 136
granel, a 309
granizada 177
grano 99
　ir al – 197
granuja 155, 292
grapadora 86
grava 164
gravable 264
gravados 266
gravamen 263, 265, 266
gravar 263, 264
grave, palabra 233
graznar 170, 171
graznido 170, 171
gresca 28
　armarse una – 195
gripe 293
grosero 46, 117
grueso 145
grupa 104
grupo 56, 104, 146
guapo 147
guarda 66
guardabosque 66
guardapolvo 109
guardar 279
guardarse 186, 347
guardería 268
guardia 66, 285, 291
guardián/guardiana 66
guarro 173
guerrilla 28
guerrillero 28
guía 291
guiar 153
guijarro 164
guión 234

guisa
　a – de 313
gustar 11, 337
gusto 359
　a – 311
　tener – 346

haberes pasivos 266
habérselas 190
hábil 28, 351
habilidad 351
habitación 39, 126
habituar(se) 342
habla 150
hablar 129
　– como un loro 204
　Ni – 197
　¡ni –! 236
hacer 339, 350, 359, 393, 399
　– bien 352
　– caso 355
　– falta 337
hacerse 124
　– con 114
hache 283
hacia 328
Hacienda
　Delegación de – 263
　Inspección de la – Pública 263
　Ministro/a de – 35
hado 174
halar 17
hallar 137
hallarse 19
hambre 283
haragán 163
harina
　ser – de otro costal 197
hartarse 348
harto 152, 348
hasta 328, 412
hay
　¿qué –? 5
haya 284
helada 99, 261
helado 99
helar(se) 431
hélice 293
hembra 283
henchido 153
henchirse 348
hender 86, 125
hender(se) 431
heredados 263
hereje 288
herida 29
herido 54

herir 29, 134
hermoso 147
herramienta 278, 295
higiene 293
higuera 284
    está en la − 8
hijo/a 157
¡híjole! 235
hilandero/a 67
hilera 67, 142
hilo 67, 127
hincapié, hacer 184
hincha 292
hinojos, de 320
hipermercado 175
hipoteca 265
hipotecario, crédito 250
historia 41, 67
historial 67
historieta 67
hito
    de − en − 321
hobby 229
hogar 268
hojear 279
holgazán 163
hombre 237
¡hombre! 235, 236
hombrecillo 193
hombretón 194
hombro
    al − 312
    a −s 312
honesto 41, 67
honor 67
    en − de 326
honorable 67
honorarios 173, 262, 298
honra 67
honradez 67
honrado 67
honroso 67
hora
    − punta 17, 232
    −s pico 17
    a (las) primeras/altas −s de la
        noche 308
    a última − 308
    por − 331
    ser − 349
    ser − de que 414
horario pico 17
hormigón 25
horrible 30
hosco 29
hospedar 24
hospedarse 24

hostal 28
¡hostia(s)! 235, 236
hoyo 111
hoyuelo 192
hoz 294
hueco 111
huérfano/a 267, 268
huerta 99
huerto 99
huesos, estar calado/mojado
        hasta los 197
huésped 286
huesudo 130
hule, cheque de 248
hundimiento 256
hundir 86
huracán 183
hurtadillas, a 311
hurtar 168, 344
¡huy! 8, 236

icono 278
idear 163
idioma 150
idiota 177
ignorar 41, 403
ijada 150
ilegal 270
ilusión 41, 350
ilusionar 187
ilustración 42
imagen 285
imaginar 163
imaginar(se) 162, 404, 407, 432
imagino 405
imbécil 177
impactar 363
imparcial 275
impedir 339, 398
imperativo 234, 393
imperfecto 234
impermeable 109
implantado 19
implicado 54
imponer 344
imponible 264
importador 18
importante 42, 393
importar 189, 337, 396
importunar 29
imposibilitar 351
imposible 235, 372
impositivo 264
impotencia 351
impresión, producir una 344
impresora 278
imprimir 278

improviso, de 321
impuestos 257
impulsar 342
imputados 54
inasequible 254
inaudito 403
incapacidad 260, 267, 351
incautación 276
incautarse 276, 348
incendiar 186, 363
incendio 143, 261, 262
incentivar 19
incidencia 28
incidir 352
    − en 19
incitar 342
incivilizado 117
inclinación 342
inclinado 418
inclinar 342
inclinarse 342
incluido 67
inclusive 67
incluso 67
incomodar 156
incomodarse 138
inconsciente 42
incordiar 156
incorporar 365
increíble 142, 236, 403
incrementarse 126
incremento 254, 255
increpar 85
inculcar 344
inculpado/a 271
inculpar 272
inculto 117
incumbir 337
incumplir 186
incurrir 353
indagar 149
indemnización 260, 267
indemnizar 50, 275
independiente de que 409
independizarse 186
indicar 115, 140, 396, 397
indicativo 234
índice 252, 255
indígena 157
indigencia 26
indigente 164
indignación 349
indignarse 349, 359
índole 293
indolente 163
inducir 342
indultar 275

indulto 275
inevitable 401
infantil 50
infectado 54
inferior 50
infiltrado 54
infinitivo 234
inflación 258
influir 353
info 226
información 68
informar 115, 367
informarse 367
informática 68, 277
informático 277
informe 68, 260, 274, 298
infracción 131, 264, 271
infundir 344
ingeniosidad 29
ingenuidad 28
ingresar 266, 353
  – un cheque 248
ingreso(s) 18, 262, 264, 265, 267,
  269, 298
inicial 293
iniciar 50, 137, 277
iniciativa 295
injuria 29
injuriar 29, 33
injusto 275
inmediaciones 116
inmediato, a 323
inmediato, de 320
inmobiliaria 251, 287
inmobiliarios, valores 251
inmuebles, bienes 256
inmundo 173
inocente 273, 274
inquirir 42, 367
inscrito 54
insinuar 396, 397
insistencia 353
insistir 353
insolvencia 256
inspección 271
inspeccionar 148
inspirar 359
instancia(s) 29, 270
  a –s de 311
instantáneo 256
instar 342
instrucción 273
instruir 42, 272
insultar 33
integrar 42
íntegro 270
inteligente 151

intemperie, a la 312
intentar 147, 148, 338
intento 338
interés 249, 251
  tener – 353
  tipo de – 250
  tipos de – 256
interesado 54, 353
interesar 337
interesarse 349, 353
intereses 249, 256, 298
interior 287
interlocutor 50
intermediario 257
Internacional 287
Internet, en 279
interno/a 276
interrogación 68, 234
interrogante 288
interrogar 272
interrogatorio 68, 272, 345
intervenciones 267, 269
intervenir 42, 363
intoxicar 29
intransigente 175
intrépido 180
introducir 165
inútil 401
invalidar 260
invalidez 260, 268
invención 68
inventar 27, 163, 265
invento 68
inversa, a la 310
inversión 251
inversionista 251
invertir 42, 68, 251, 252
investigación 271, 298
investigar 149
investir 68
invitación 342
invitado 54
invitar 342, 396
inyección 275
ir 343, 359
  + gerund 381
  + pp 383
  a + inf 380
  en lo que va de – 327
  ¡vamos, hombre! 236
  ¡vaya! 8
ir(se) 434
ironizar 186
irracional 42
irritarse 138, 349
irrumpir 369
irse 130

ítem 297
izar 151
izquierda, a la 312

¡ja! 236
jactancioso 159
jactarse 348, 431
jalar 17
jamás 371
jarra 180
jefe/a 27, 149, 289
jerga 150
jerigonza 150
jesuita 285
jeta 119
jet –set 229
jilguero, cantar como un – 204
jilí, ser un(a) – 177
jilipolla(s), ser un(a) – 177
¡jo! 5, 235
joder 5, 142, 156, 235,
  236
jodido 179
¡jolín(es)! 235
jornal 173
jorobar 156
joven 157
  de – 320
jovial 123
jubilación 29, 262
jubilado 54
júbilo 29
judicial 68, 287
juego, entrar/poner en 197
juez/a 270
jugar 86, 365
jugarreta 140
juicio 273
  a mi – 310, 326
  poner en tela de – 26
junto a 313, 323
jurado/a 271
juramento 274
jurar 274, 338
jurídico 68, 259
jurisdicción 273
jurisprudencia 270
jurista 270
justicia 270
  – gratuita 268
justificante 260, 265
justificar 280
justo 275, 401
juzgado 272
juzgar 23, 65, 86, 275

kit 230

labia 99
labio 99
labor 178, 285
ladera 122, 150
lado 150
    al – de 313
    al (otro) – de 313
    al otro – 312
    de un – 321
    por otro – 240, 332
    por un – 240, 332
    tirar/irse cada uno por su – 197
ladrar 171
ladrido 171
lágrimas, estar hecho un mar de 197
laguna 42
lamentable 179
lamentar 50, 338, 401
lancha 116
lanzamiento 254
lanzar 176
lanzarse 6, 176, 341
lápiz 294
    a – 313
laptop 230, 277
larga, a la 310
largarse 130
largo 29
    a lo – de 313
lástima 401
lata
    dar la – 156, 197
    ser una – 197
laúd 286
laureles, dormirse en/sobre los 197
lavadora 295
leche
    de una mala – 5
    ¡me cago en la – ! 235
    tener mala – 197
lectura 29
leer(se) 434
legal 270
legar 81
legislativas 287
legua 246
leguleyo/a 270
lejano 416
lejos 416
    a lo – 312
    de – 321
lelo, quedar 196
lengua 150
    – madre 232
lenguaje 150, 273
lente 144, 288
lento 353

leña 99
leño 99
    dormir como un – 204
león 170
lerdo 177
lesión 29, 50
lesionar 29
letrado/a 270
letrero 151
levantar 151, 273
levantar(se) 431
liar(se) 81
liberar 69
libertad 351
libertar 69
líbido 285
libra 104, 243
librar 69
librarse 347
libre 359
librería 29
librero 29
libreta 104
libreto 104
libro 104
librote 194
licencia 42
licenciado/a 54, 270
líder 149, 230
liebre, levantar la 197
lifting 230
ligar 81
ligera, a la 310
light 230
lima 43
    comer como una – 204
limitarse 186
límite 117, 293
limpiar 168
lindar 24, 367
linde 117, 288
lindo 147
línea, en 279
lío
    meterse en –s 198
    tener –s 197
    tener un – 197
liquidación 254
liquidar 266
lirón, dormir como un
    204
listo 151, 342
listón 256
litigioso 274
lívido 29
living 127
llama 69, 143

llamada 69
llamamiento 69
llamarada 69
llana, palabra 233
llanta 105
llanto 105
llavero 112
llegar 124, 341
    – a ser 124
lleno 152
llevar 91, 153, 186, 188, 318, 342,
    434
    + gerund 382
    + pp 382
    – tiempo 354
llevarse 153, 188, 434
llorar 363
    – como un niño / una Magdalena
    204
llorón 194
lluvia, bajo la 316
lobo, negro como la boca del 201
localidad 43
    – dormitorio 232
localización 262
locas, a tontas y a 311
loco 29
    estar – de atar 197
    estar – de remate 197
lógico 401
logo 226
lograr 338, 393
loma 104, 122
lombriz 294
lomo 104, 141
loncha 168
lonja 168
look 230
loro
    ¡al – ! 236
    hablar como un – 204
luces, entre dos – 197
lucha 135, 350
luchar 350
lucido 69
lúcido 69, 152
lucir 13, 118
lucirse 119
luego
    – de 412
    – que 412
lugar
    en – de 326
    tener – 158
lugarete 193
lujo 69, 263
lujoso 69

lujuria 69
lujurioso 69
lumbre 143
luminoso 51
luna, estar en la 197
lupa 144
luz
   – piloto 232
   a la – de 312
   dar a – 197
   salir/sacar a – 197

machacar 169
macho 5, 283
macroeconómicos 251
madera 99
   ¡toca -! 197
madero 99
madre 30
   ¡ – mía! 235
   – patria 232
   de puta – 142
   ¡de puta – ! 235
madreselva 286
maestro/a 166
Magdalena, llorar como una
    204
magistrado/a 270
magistratura 270
majo 147
mal 416
¡maldición! 235
maldito
   ¡ – sea! 235
maleante 154
maletero 47
malgastar 91, 154
malhechor/-ora 154
malhumor 30
malhumorado 29, 32
malicia 43
maliciar 10
malísimo 30
malla(s) 299
malo 164
maltratar 141
maltrato 345
malvado/a 154
manager 230
manchado 172
mandamiento 273
mandar 141, 339, 394
mandato 277
mando 25
   bajo el – de 316
manera
   a la – de 310

a mi – 310
de cierta – 321
de cualquier – 239
de – que 239, 398
de todas –s 321
de una – 310
sobre – 333
manga 105
mangar 168
mangas
   estar en – de camisa 197
mango 105
maníaco 29
maniático 29
manifestación 43
manifestar 115, 340
maniobra 286
mano 285
   a – 313
   a – armada 311
   echar – 121, 197, 359
   echar una – 115, 197
   irse/venir/llegar a las –s 198
   de segunda – 198
   tener buena/mala – para algo
    197
manta 99
mantener 51, 91
mantenimiento 69
manto 99
manutención 69
mañana 291
   a la – 308
   a la – siguiente 308
   a media – 309
   de – 320
mapa 285
máquina, a 313
marasmo 258
maratón 288
maravilla
   ¡qué – ! 235
maravillarse 348
maravilloso 147
marca 105
marcar 280
marcha 43
   ¡qué – ! 236
marcharse 26, 130, 434
marco 105
marea 100
   contra viento y – 200
mareo 100
margen 117, 285, 287
marginado 54
marketing 230, 254
marrano 173

marrón 29
mártir 288
más
   – . . . que 372
   – que 409
   como el que – 198
   estar de – a 198
   sin – ni – 198
masa, en 326
masacre 287
masculino 233
matar 91
matarse 341, 350
materia 69
material 69
materias primas 253
materno 158
matiz 294
maullar 170, 171
maullido 170
máximo, al 259
mayor 183, 440
   al por – 309
mayúsculas 234
mazmorra 276
moderar 254
¡mecachis! 235, 236
media 70
mediados
   a – de 309
medianoche, a (la) 308
medias, a 311
médica 289
medicación 70
medicamento 70
medicina 70, 272
médico 261, 289
medida 258
medio 70
medio 303
mediodía, a(l) 308
meditar 163
medrar 126
mejor, a lo 311, 407
mejor 394, 401
mejora 155
mejoramiento 19
mejoría 155
melancólico 178
melena 161
mella
   hacer – en/a uno 198
memoria 277
   de – 321
menesteroso 164
menor 440
   al por – 309

menos
  a – que 409
  echar de – 185
  no poder – 188
mentalizar 348
mentalizarse 87, 342
mentar 87
mente 294
mentir 87
menú 278
menudear 190
mercado 18, 254
mercancía 25
mercantiles, estudios 253
merdoso 173
merecer la pena 337
mesa 32
  a/en la – 312
meta 291
metálico 43, 134
  pagar en – 249
metamorfearse 124
meter 165
  a todo – 311
meterse 156, 186, 341, 359
  – en donde no le llaman 198
metralleta 57
metrópoli 294
mezquino 30
micro-ordenador 277
miedo, tener 360, 401
miel 294
miembro 271, 284
¡mierda! 235
  ¡(a)1a – ¡
migas, hacer (buenas) 198
mil
  – gracias 203
  a las – y quinientas 203
mili 226
milla 242
millares, a 309
millón
  un – de gracias 203
minimizar 278
ministro/a 289
minúsculas 234
mira
  ser de –me y no me toques 198
mirada, echar una 182
mirar 138, 182, 360, 364
  ¡mira! 8
  mira/mire 237
miras
  con – a 317

mirlo
  ser un – blanco 198
mis 230
miseria 26, 29
misiva 295
mismo 304
  así – 239
míster 230
mitad
  a – de 309
mobiliario 261, 264
moche, a troche y 311
moco
  a – tendido 311
moda 100
  a la – 310
  de – 310, 321
modalidad 259
modelo 155, 284
módem 278
modista 289
modisto 289
modo 100
  a mi – de ver 310
  de – que 239, 398
  de cierto – 321
  de tal – que 239
  de todos –s 321
  de un – 310
  en – 326
  en cierto – 321
mofarse 347
mofletudo 145
mojado
  estar – hasta los huesos 197
mojar(se) 431
mole 293
molesta 401
molestar 29, 156, 337
molestarse 138
momento, de 320
monarca 288
moneda 134
  ser – corriente 198
monetaria 257
monetario 255
monitor 278
monoparental 267
monopolio 257
monta, ser de poca 198
montaña 71, 122
montañero 70
montañés 70
montañoso 70
montar 253
montaraz 70
monte 43, 71, 122

montés 70
montículo 122
monzón 288
moradas, pasarlas 201
morado
  ponerse – de comer 201
moral 71, 292
moraleja 71
morir(se) 350, 434
moro
  Hay –s en la costa 198
moroso 29
mosca, picarle a uno la 198
mosquito 170
mostrador 247
mostrar 140
mote 158
motejar 365
motivar 394
motivo 51, 360
  con – de 317
moto 285
motorista 30
movedizo 71
mover 92, 342
moverse 92
movible 71
móvil 71, 287
mozo/a 157
muchacho/a 157
mudar 349
muebles, bienes 256
muela 133
muerte 274
muestra 156
muestrario 156
mugido 171
mugir 171
mugriento 172
mujer 8, 236
mujeruca 194
multa 276
multimedia 277
multinacional 287, 293
multirriesgo 261
mundial 287
mundo
  desde que el – es el – 198
  valer un – 200
municiones 298
municipales 287
muñeca 100
muñeco 100
muralla 160
muro 160
músculo 30
muslo 30

nacional 287
nacionalizado 54
nacionalizar 258
nada 371
   ¡ – de eso! 198
   ¡ –, –! 236
   como si – 198
   no saber – de – 198
   ¡para – ! 236
nadar como un pez 204
nadie 371
nafta 30
naipe 35
nalgas 128
narices
   ¡de – ! 235
   hinchársele a uno las – 198
   meter las – en algo 198
nariz
   meter la – en algo 198
natal 157
natalidad 268
nativo 157, 158
natural 43, 157, 401
naufragado 54
nave 116
Navidad(es) 298
   ¡Felices – ! 298
navío 116
necesario 394
necesidad 338, 365, 414
necesitado 54, 164
necesitar 17, 338, 365, 394
necio 177
negar 26, 87, 92, 273, 340,
   404
negarse 347, 365
negativa 100, 295, 347, 365
negativo 100
negocio 175
negra
   pasarlas –s 201
   tener la – 201
   tocarle a uno la – 201
negrita 280
negro 174
   – como la boca del lobo 201
   ponerse – 138
   ponerse – de comer 201
   tan – como boca de lobo 203
   trabajar como un – 201
   verlo todo – 200
   verse uno – para hacer algo 201
nena 8
nene/nena 157
neto 257
nevada 177

ni 371
   – ... – 371
   – que 409
   – siquiera 371
nieves 298
ninguno 371
niño, de 320
niño, llorar como un 204
niño/a 157
nivel
   – de vida 257
   a – de 313
   a – literario 312
no 370–2, 412, 439
   ¡ – no! 236
   ¡por qué – ! 235
noche
   a la – 308
   de – 320
   en toda la – 372
   pasar las –s en blanco 198
nombrar 71
nombre 158, 233
   – de pila 158
   de – 321
   en – de 326
   llamar las cosas por su – 198
nómina 173
nominar 71
norma 51
notar 181
notario/a 270
notificar 115
notorio 30
novedoso 71
novelón 192
nube
   estar en las –s 198
nublado, verlo todo 200
núcleo 51
nuevo 71, 304
   de – 321
nunca 371

o 250
   (–) ... o bien ... 240
   – ... – ... 240
oasis 286
obertura 55
obeso 145
objetar 25
objetivo 295
objeto
   con – de 317
obligación 342
obligaciones 252
obligar 342, 399

obra 178
   – cumbre 232
obsceno 46
obsequiar 365
obsequio 166
obsequioso 30
observar 181
obsesión 349
obstante, no 240
obstinación 353
obstinado 175
obstinarse 353
ocasión
   con – de 317
ocioso 163
octeto 277
ocular, testigo 271
ocultar 344
ocupación 178
ocupar 43, 114, 344
ocuparse 360
ocurrir 32, 158, 434
ocurrirse 337, 434
odio 345, 346
ofensiva 295
oferta 71
   – pública de adquisición 253,
     257
   – pública hostil 253
   – y demanda 254
oficial 72
oficina 40, 72
oficio 72
oficioso 72
ofrecer 6
ofrecerse 342
ofrecimiento 71
ofrenda 71, 166
oídas, de 322
oído
   de – 322
   hacer –s sordos 198
   ser todos –s 198
oír 339
   ¡oye! 8
ojalá 407
ojeada, echar una 182
ojeriza
   tener – a algo 198
ojo
   a los –s de 311
ojo
   andar con – 198
   en un abrir y cerrar de –s 198
   ¡(Mucho) – (con algo)! 198
   no pegar los –s en toda la noche
     198

saltar a los −s 199
ser el − derecho de uno 198
valer un − 200
¡ojo! 236
¡OK! 235
ola 72
¡olé! 235
oleada 72
oleaje 72
óleo 43
al − 313
oler 346
olvidado 54
olvidarse 365
once
meterse en camisa de − varas 202
onza 243
operación 345
operar 345, 364
opinar 51, 163
opinión, en mi 310, 326
oponerse 398
oposición 43, 123
opresión 345
optar 350
ora
− ... − 240
oración 233
orden 25, 270, 292
− del día 23
fuerzas del − 271
ordenación 265
ordenador 276, 277
ordenanza 266, 292
ordenar 339, 394
órdenes, bajo sus 316
ordinario 117
de − 322
oreja
con las −s gachas (R1) 199
enseñar la − 199
orfanato/orfelinato 268
orgulloso 159
orilla 117
−s 312
a −s de 312
oriundo 157
ortografía 233
osado 180, 418
osar 340
oscuras, a 311
oscuro
tan − como boca de lobo 203
ostentar 140
ostra
aburrirse como una − 204
¡ −s! 235, 236

otear 181
otero 122
otorgar 19, 128
oveja 170
ovillo 162

pachucho 8
paciente 294
pacificar 57
pack 230
padecer 364
padre 30
−s 30
paga 100, 173
pagar 364
pagaré 250
pago 100, 173, 250, 254, 259, 260
− automático 249
paisano/a 10, 30
pájaro 171
a vista de − 311
matar dos −s de un tiro 199
pala 105
palabra 372
bajo − 316
tener − / no tener − 199
tener/tomar la − 129, 199
palabrota 194
palma 105
palmo 105
palo 105, 160
pan
estar/vivir a − y agua 199
llamar al − − y al vino vino 198
ser − comido 199
venderse como − bendito 204
pana 87
panal 87
pancarta 151
pancita 192
panda 146, 292
pandilla 146
panel 277
pánico, tener 401
pantalla 278
pantalón/pantalones 299
perder hasta los −es 199
pantano 120
panzudo 145
pañal 87
paño 87
Papa 31
papa 72
papá 72
papel moneda 232
papelera 100

papelero 100
par
a la − que 309
de − en − 322
para 329−32
− que 398, 399
estar − 422
estar (como) − 422
parada 72, 262
paradero 72
parado 54, 72, 267
paradoja 295
parador 72
paraguas 286
paraíso 263
paralización 262
parangón 30
parar 346
parar(se) 432
pararrayos 25
parche 6
parcial, a tiempo 269
parecer 113, 162, 338, 404, 405
a mi − 310
parecerse 365
pared 160
pareja 291
sin − 267
paréntesis 234, 286
pariente/a 30, 45, 288
paro 72
parqué 251
párrafo 234
parrilla 192
párroco 73
parroquia 73
parroquiano 73
parsimonioso 30
parte 73, 292
de − de 323
en − 326
ponerse de − 188
por otra − 240, 332
por una − 240, 332
participar 353, 360
participio 233
− pasado 234
particular 43
partida 100, 146
partidario 399
partido 100
partir 43, 125, 130, 169
a − de 313
parto 73
pasa 105

pasada
  mala − 140
  ¡qué − ! 236
pasar 158, 341, 367, 368, 434
  − de 8
  −la bien 136
  −lo bien 136
  −lo bomba 136
  −lo cojonudo 136
  −lo de puta madre 136
  −lo en grande 136
  ¡qué pasa! 236
pasarse 188, 360, 434
pasear 369
pasear(se) 431, 432
paseo, mandar a uno a 196
pasión 349
pasivo
  − circulante 265
  − corriente 265
  − diferido 265
pasmoso 142
paso 105
  − a − 309
  palabra de − 279
  salir al − 188
pasta 5, 105, 134
pasto 105
pata 105
  mala − 174
  meter la − 199
patadas, a 311
patas, con 6
patente 294
patera 116
patético 30
patíbulo 275
pato 105, 171
patrimonio 51
patrón 149, 156
patrona 149
patronal 253, 287
patrono 149
pauta 156
pavimento 30
pecado 131
pecho, a 311
pedazos, hacer 169
pedir 161, 338, 344, 364,
    394
  − prestado 184, 250, 344
Pedro
  como − por su casa 199
pegar 144
  − un golpe a 144
  −sela 190
  cortar y − 279

peine 293
¡pélale! 6
pelas 106
pelea 135
peli 226
película, ser de 199
peligro 414
pellizcar 87
pelo 87, 106, 161
  −s 161
  no vérsele el − 199
  tomar el − 199
pelota 162
pelotas
  ¡de − ! 235
pelotera 135
pena 29, 87, 275, 401
  − capital 275
  a duras −s 311
  bajo − de muerte 316
  estar hecho una − 197
pendencia 135
pendiente 113, 122, 292
penetrante 152
penetrar 353
penitenciario 276
pensar 162, 340, 360, 404
pensión 44
pensionistas 268
peña 87, 164
peñasco 164
peonza, bailar como una 204
pepino, no importar un 196
pequeñuelo 193
percance 109
percatarse 365
percepción 263
perceptor/-ora 266, 267
percibir 44, 181, 255
perder 154
  echarse a − 188
pérdida 256, 260
perdiz 294
perezoso 163
perfección, a la 310
¡perfecto! 235
periferia 116
perillas, de 322
periplo 182
perito 260, 262
perjudicado 54
perjuicio 73
  daños y −s 274
permiso 179, 351
permitir 339, 398
pero 240
  poner −s a 25

perro 171
  ¡A otro − con ese hueso! 199
  llevarse como el − y el gato 199
perseguir 93, 272
perseverar 353
persistencia 353
persistente 175
persistir 353
persona − física y jurídica
    271
personaje 35
personal, cuenta 248
personarse 11
perspicaz 152
persuadir 342, 360, 396
pertinaz 175
pertinencia 32
pertinente 32
pertrecharse 348
pertrechos 298
pesa 100
pesado 418
pesar
  a − de 239, 313
  a − de que 408, 410
pesca 73
pescado 73
pese a que 409, 410
pesero/a 17
pesimista 178
peso 100
pesticida 285
petición 44
petróleo 30
petulancia 30
pez 73, 292, 294
  estar/moverse/sentirse como − en
    el agua 199
  nadar como un − 204
peces gordos 199
pezonera 118
pialador 10
piar 171
picacho 194
picado, caer en 199
picapleitos 270
picar 87
pícaro/a 155
pico 44, 111, 167
  cerrar el − 199
  horas/horario − 17
picota 275
pie 242
  a − 311
  de − 320, 321
  en − de 326
  No se tiene de − 199

no tener ni –s ni cabeza 199
piedad 44
piedra 164
  dormir como una – 204
  no dejar – por mover 199
piel 87
  – roja 283
  no caber en su – 196
pierna
  a – suelta 311
  dormir a – suelta 199
pieza 44
pijama 285, 299
pila, nombre de – 158
píldora
  dorar la – 199
  tragarse la – 199
pileta 120
pillar 121
pillín/-ina 155
pillo/a 155
piloto 289
pimienta 101
pimiento 101
pinchar 87
pinta 31, 113
Pinto
  estar entre – y Valdemoro 199
pintura 31
pinza(s) 299
¡pipudo! 236
pique, irse a 199
pirámide 293
pirárse(las) 130, 190
pirata 279
pisar 73, 364
piscina 120
piscolabis 286
piso, piloto 232
pisotear 73, 364
pistola 114
plan 73
  en – de 326
  tener – 5
plana 101
planeamiento 74
planear 74, 338
planeta 285
planificación 74, 262
planificar 74
plano 73, 101
plantado, dejar 184
plantar 74
plantear 74
plantilla 156, 280
plaqueta 277

plata 106, 134
platicar 129
plato 74, 106
plató 74
plausible 44
plaza 106
plazo 106, 255
  – de amortización 250
  – de carencia 260
  a corto/largo/medio – 256, 309
  a –s 255
plazuela 193
pleitear 272
pleito 270
plenaria 287
pleno 153, 287
plomo, ser (un) 5
pluma, a 313
pluscuamperfecto, (pretérito) 234
plusvalía 252, 263
población 74, 276
poblado 74
pobre 164, 304
  más – que una rata 203
pobrecito 193
pobretón 194
poco 371
podar 125
poder 74
  puede ser 406
poderío 74
poema 74
poesía 74
poli 226
policía 289, 291
  mujer – 289
policíaca 270
policíaco 75
policial 75
política 269, 299
póliza 258, 259, 261
pollera 10
polvareda 75
polvera 75
polvero 75
polvo 75
  estar hecho – 197
pólvora 75
pompis 128
ponderar 23
poner 92, 165, 361
ponerse 124, 137, 341
  – de cara a 138
  – hecho una fiera 138
  – negro 138
pope 31

populacho 194
por 329–32, 413
  – lo cual 240
  – lo que 240
  estar – 422
porfiado 175
porno
porque 240
porra 160
  ¡ –s! 236
  ¡a la – ! 235
porrón 118
portador 252
  cheque al – 248
portátil 287
portavoz 289
porte 113
portentoso 142
posaderas 128
pose 293
posesionarse 365
  – de 114
posesivo 233
posibilidad 414
  ante la – 316
posibilitar 187
posible 406
  hacer lo – 148, 351
posiblemente 406
postal 293
póster 151, 297
posterior, parte 141
postre 293
potencia 74
Potosí, valer un 200
poza 120
practicar 125
preciarse 348
precio 254, 255
precioso 44, 147
precipitaciones 298
precipitarse 177, 341
precisa 394
precisar 365, 394
preciso 394
precoz 44
predicamento 31
predicar en el desierto 199
preferir 338, 399
preguntar 42, 367
prejubilación 267
prejubilado/a 267
prejuicio 73
prenda, no soltar 199
preocupar 51
preocuparse 348, 349
preparación 75

preparado 342, 351
prepararse 342, 351
preparativos 75, 295
prescindir 367
presencia 113
    en – de 327
presenciar 75, 181
presentar 75, 140, 318
presente 166, 234
    tener – 188
preservativo 31
presidenciales 287
presidente/a 35, 289
presidir 364
presionar 394
preso/a 271
prestaciones 260, 267, 268
prestado
    pedir – 184, 250, 344
préstamo 250
prestar 250
prestarse 343
prestigiar 187
presto 351
presumido 159
presumir 365, 407
    ser de – 407
presunción 273
presunto 273
presuntuoso 159
presupuestaria, cuenta 248
presupuestario 256
presupuesto 259, 262, 266
pretender 31, 338, 394, 396
pretérito
    – anterior 234
    – (indefinido) 234
pretexto, bajo ningún – 316
prevaricar 31
prevenir 115
prever 32, 338, 406
previsto 406
    tener – 338
prima 259
primeras, de buenas a 321
primero 353
    el – en 327
primitivo 44
principiar 136, 137, 341
principio 111
    a –s de 309
prisa, darse/tener 114, 351,
    353
prisma 285
prismáticos 144
privar(se) 347
privatizar 269

privilegiado 54
privilegio 265
pro
    en – de 327
probable 406
probar 93, 147, 148,
    338
problema 285
procedente de 322
proceder 343
procedimiento 272
procesado 54
procesamiento 272
    – de textos 280
procesar 273, 280
proceso 44, 273, 277
procurador/-ora 270
procurar 44, 148, 338
prodigio 75
prodigioso 142
pródigo 75
producirse 159
profe 165, 226
profesor/-ora 165
profundizar 186, 364
programa 75
programación 75
programador/-ora 279
progresos 155, 298
prohibir 339, 398
prole 293
prolongarse 126
promedio 70
prometer 338
promoción 44
promocionar 254
pronombre 233
pronóstico 51, 269
pronto 351
    de – 322
prontuariar 272
pronunciar 129
pronunciarse 129
propaganda 45, 254
propiciar 398
propicio 51
propiedad 263, 279
propio 304
proponer 396
proponerse 338, 397
proporcionar 128
proposición 76
propósito 76
proseguir 93
prosperar 126
protección 267
    bajo la – de 316

proteccionista 258
protesta 349
protestar 349, 361, 365
proveedor 279
provisional 274
proyectar 176, 338
proyecto 338
    – de ley 276
prudencia 24
prueba 34
público 34
pudiente 167
pueblecito 192
pueblo 74
puénting 230
puerco 173
puerta 106
    a – cerrada 273
puerto 106
pues 11, 238
    – entonces 237
puesta 106
puesto 106, 178
pugnar 351
pulgada 242
pulpa 106
pulpo 106
pulsar 278
puñetazos, a 311
punible 271
punición 275
punir 275
puño
    irse/venir/llegar a los –s
    198
punta 101
    hora – 17
puntapiés, a 311
puntilloso 28
punto 101, 234
    – y coma 234
    –s suspensivos 234
    a – fijo 311
    de – 278
    dos –s 234
    estar a – de 422
    poner los –s sobre las íes
    199
puntual 45
pupilo/a 31, 106
purasangre 286
puro 304
puta
    ¡de – madre! 236
    ¡hijo de – ! 235
    ¡me cago en la – ! 235
    pasarlo de – madre 136

qué
  por el – dirán 199
¡qué va! 236
quebrantar 169
quebrar 169
quedar 110
quedar 124, 190, 337, 361, 434
quedarse 124, 361, 434
quejarse 347, 431
quemarropa, a 311
querella 31, 135, 273
querellado 54
querellante 271
querer 338, 389, 395
querido
  seres –s 261
quicio, sacar de 200
quiebra 256
quienquiera 413
quintal 246
Quintín, armarse la de San 195
quinto
  estar en el – coño 202
quisquilloso 28
quitar 31, 344
quizá(s) 406

rabiar 351
rabillo 167
radicación 263
radio 285, 292
  – receptor 232
  en la – 327
  por la – 331
ráfaga 183
raíz
  a – de 313
raja 168
rajatabla, a 311
rallar 88
rama 101
  andarse por las –s 200
ramo 101
rancio 45
ránking 230
raro 401
rasgar 169
raso, al 312
rastrillo 6
rata 106
rato 106
  al poco – 309
ratón 278
raya 106, 234
  mantener a – 200
rayar 88
rayo 106

razón
  a – de 309
  dar la – 200
  en – de 327
  entrar en – 188, 189
  meter en – 189
  poner en – 189
  tener – 361
reactivar 258
reactor 45
real 23, 45
realidad, en 239
realizar 13, 31, 51
realizarse 159
reanudar 32
reata 143
rebaja 58
rebajarse 341, 361
rebanada 168
rebasar 76, 367
rebelarse 166
rebeldía 274
rebenque 10
rebenqueada 10
rebosante 153
rebotado, cheque 248
rebuznar 170
rebuzno 170
recaer 90
recalentarse 258
recámara 127
recargo 259
recaudación 263
recelar 347
recepción 76
recesión 258
rechazar 404
rechazo 345
rechinar 121
rechoncho 145
recibimiento 76
recibo 76, 255
recio 143
reclamaciones 259
reclamar 161, 260, 268, 344, 361,
  395
reclusión 276
recluso/a 31, 276
recluta 291
recoger 90
recolección 31
recomendación
  bajo la – de 316
recomendar 395
recomponer 92
reconciliar(se) 63
reconocer 110, 149, 340

reconocimiento 345
reconvenir 31
récord 230, 297
recordar 364, 365
recordar(se) 432
recorrer 17, 90, 364
recorrido 182
recortar 91, 125
recrearse 136, 353
rector(a) 35
recuerdo 31
  en – de 327
recuperación 258
recuperar 51, 279
recuperarse 45
recurrir 270, 273
red 254, 279
redactar 27
redactor(a) 27
redonda, a la 312
reducción 265
reducir 125
reembolso 260, 265
reemplazo 262
referirse 11, 45
reflexionar 163
reforma 270
refrán 31
refugio 263
refulgir 119
regalar 128
regaliz 294
regalo 166
  de – 322
regañadientes, a 311
regatear 186, 257, 344
régimen 266, 297
regir 93
registrar 45, 148
reglamentar 93
reglar 93
regocijado 123
regordete 145
regresar(se) 433
regulador 266
regular 45, 93
rehabilitación 276
rehuir 340
rehusar 340
reinado 32
reincidencia 131
reiniciar 277
reino 32
reinserción 276
reír(se) 348, 433
reivindicar 275
rejas, entre 276

relación
  con – a 317, 327
  en – a 327
  en – con 317
relacionado 32
relaciones 45
relativo 233
relevancia 32
relevante 32
relinchar 170
relincho 170
rellenar 259
relleno 152
relucir 118, 119
relumbrar 118, 119
rematar 91
remate 111
remedar 88
remediar 88
remendar 88
remitir 141, 273
remolino 183
remordimiento(s) 298
remover 92
rencilla(s) 135
rendimiento 254, 265
renegar 92, 347
renovar 259
renta 32, 251, 263, 264
  – variable 251
rentabilidad 256
rentable 256
renuncia 345, 347, 366
renunciar 347, 366
reñir 34
reo 288
repantigado 418
reparación 262
reparar 181, 353, 361
repasar 46, 76
repaso 345
repecho 122
repente, de 322
repercutir 186
repleto 152
reporte 260
reportera 289
reposición 262
reposo
  casa de – 268
  clínica de – 268
repreguntar 274
reprobar 93
reprochar 344, 401
repugnado 27
repugnar 27
repulsa 345

repunte 258
requerimiento 273
requerir 17, 161
requisito 259
resarcirse 347
rescatado 54
rescindir 259
reseco 77
reserva 279, 291
reservar 279
resetear 277
residencia 28, 268
resistencia 45
resistirse 347, 366
resolver 338, 395
resolverse 338
respaldar 279
respaldo 141, 279, 291
respecto 76
  – de 313
  (con) – a 313, 317
respeto 76, 345
resplandecer 118, 119
responder 362
responsabilidad 261
responsabilizar 187
responsabilizarse 367
responsable 149, 367
respuesta
  en – a 326
resta 101
restar 46, 344
resto 101, 298
resuelto 338
resumen, en 240, 327
resumir 32
retahíla 143
retención 264
reticulado 280
retirada 76
retirar 249
retiro 76
retrato, robot 232
retroceder 280
reuma 285
revalorizar 269
revaluación 250
revaluar 269
reventar 351
reventón 262
revés 141
  al – 310
revestir 68
revisar 46
revisor(a) 25
revista, pasar 189
revolucionario 263

revolver 94
revólver 114
reyerta 135
rezagado 54
ría 101
riachuelo 193
ricacho 167, 194
ricachón 167
rico 46, 147, 167
rielar 119
rienda
  dar – suelta 200
riesgo 402
rifle 114
rigor 275
rincón 167
riña 28, 31, 135
riñón, costar un 200
río 101
Rioja 284
riqueza 264
ristra 127
ritmo 28
rivalidad 36
rivalizar 366
robar 168, 344
robo 260, 261, 262, 345
robusto 143
roca 164
rodado, canto 164
rodaja 168
rodar 76
rodear 76
rodilla 106
  de –s 320
rodillo 106
rogar 161, 395, 396
rojo
  – de ira 201
    estar al – vivo 201
    estar en números –s 201, 249
rollizo 145
Roma
  remover – con Santiago 199
romance 77, 293
románico 77
romanista 77
romano 77
romántico 77
rompecabezas 286
romper 169, 341
ronco 83
ropa 299
rosa, verlo todo color de 200
rosca 107
rosco 107
rostro 119

rotura 77, 262
rudo 46, 117
rugido 170
rugir 170
ruido, armarse un 195
ruin 32
ruina 32
rumano 77
rumbo
   (con) – a 317
ruptura 77
rutilar 119

sabana 88
sábana 88
   pegársele a uno las –s 200
saber 169, 338, 346
   –selas 191
   no sé 238
sabiendas, a 311
sacar 344
   – en claro / en limpio 200
saciarse 348
saco 108
sacudir 144
sagaz 152
sal 293
sala 126
salado 146, 255
salario 173, 257
saldo 249, 251
salida 28, 279
salir 26, 31, 130, 279, 343, 368
   –se con la suya 200
   a lo que salga 200
salir(se) 435
salón 127
saltar 176
salvaje 170
salvamento 262
salvar 46, 279
salvo que 409
sanción 275
sándwich 231
saneamiento 258
sangre 293
   calentársele/encendérsele la – a
      uno 200
santa
toda la – noche 8
santo
   no saber a qué – encomendarse
      200
sarampión 286
sarta 127, 143
sartén 285, 287
sastra 289

satisfecho 402
sauce 88
saúco 88
sea, o 238
secador 295
secadora 295
secar(se) 431
seccionar 125
seco 77
   en – 327
secretaria 77
secretaría 77
secuestrado 54
sede 293
seguida, en 327
seguidita, en 192
seguir 93, 354, 369
segundo
   el – en 327
seguridad 276
seguro 258, 259, 261, 262, 267, 349
   no ser – 404
seleccionar 280
sello 112
semáforo 46
semana, a media 309
semanario 88
semblante 113, 119, 120
semilla 77
semillero 77
seminario 88
senadora 289
sensato 32, 77
sensible 32, 77
sentado 418
sentar(se) 343, 431
sentencia 46, 274, 275
sentir 338, 402
seña 78
señal 78, 293
señalar 140
señor(a) 11, 149
señorita 166
separado 266
   por – 332
séptimo
   estar en el – cielo 202
ser 403, 415–22
   – de 124
   a no – que 408
   es que 237
   venir a – 124
serie 143
   en – 326
serio
   en – 327
   tomar en – 200

servicios 257, 268
servidor 278
servil 30
servilletero 113
servir 362
servirse 366
sesión 272
seso
   saltarse los –s 200
seta 107
seto 107
seudónimo 158
sexy 231
shock 231
show 231
si 410–11
sibarita 51
siempre que 409
sien 294
siete
   andar/recorrer las – partidas 202
   hacerse un – en la ropa 202
   pícaro de – suelas 202
   tener – vidas 202
sigla 107
siglo 107
significación 78
significado 78
sílaba 233, 295
silla eléctrica 275
sillón 194
silvestre 170
sima 85
simiente 294
simpático 32
simple 304
   tiempo – 234
sin 332, 371, 372
   – que 404
sincerarse 187
síndrome 293
siniestro 109, 260
sino 174, 240
sinrazón 286
síntoma 285
sinvergüenza 154
siquiera, ni 371
sirvienta 289
sisar 168
sisear 170
siseo 170
sitio 279
situación 178
situar 165
slip 297
slogan 297
soberbio 159

sobra
 de – 322
  estar de – 198
sobrar 190, 337
sobre 333
sobrecalentarse 258
sobrellevar 91
sobrenombre 158
sobresalir 119
sobretodo 109
sobrevenir 159
sobrevivir 366
sociedades 263
socio/a 253
socorrer 115
software 277
soga
 estar con la – al cuello 195
sojuzgar 131
solamente 78
solas, a 311
soler 187
solicitar 51, 161, 338, 344
solicitud 33, 46
solito 192
soliviantar 88
solo 78
sólo 78
soltero 266
solterón/ona 194
solucionar 14
solvencia 256
solventar 88
solvente 46, 250, 256
sombra, a la 312
someter 131
sondeado 54
sonreír(se) 348, 433
sonsacar 344
soñar 367
sopa, estar hecho una 197
soprano 284
sórdido 173
sordo
 más – que una tapia 203
sorprendente 142
sorprenderse 348
sortija 112
sospecha 272
sostener 78, 91
sotana 88
sótano 88
spot publicitario 231
stand 231, 297
star 231
stock 231
subasta 254

súbdito 46
subida 252, 255
subinvertir 251
subir 24, 151, 171, 172, 369
subir(se) 433
subjuntivo 234
sublevado 54
sublevarse 166
subrayar 280
subsidio 267, 268
suburbios 32
subvención 268, 269
subvencionar 269
subvenir 268
subyugar 131
suceder 32, 46, 158
sucesiones 263
suceso 32
sucio 28, 172
sucursal 248, 293
suela 101
sueldo 173
suelo 101
sueño 78
suerte 174
 – negra 174
 buena – 174
 mala – 174
suficiente 397
sufijo 233
sufrido 418
sufrimiento 29
sugerencia 78
sugerir 339, 397
sugestión 78
suicida 289
sujetadatos 277
sujeto 46, 266
sumario 272
sumergirse 176
suministrar 128
superávit 254, 297
superficie 111, 120
 gran – 175
superior 51
 la parte – 111
superioridad 46
superlativo 234
supermercado 175
suplicar 161, 395
suplicio 23, 275
suponer 404, 407
suprimir 125
supuesto
 – que 409, 410
 en el – de que 409
 por – 332

surfear 279
surgir 113, 159
susceptible 47, 349
suscribir 259, 364
suscribirse 364
suscriptor/-ora 251
suspender 47
suspendido 418
suspense 231
suspirar 351
sustantivo 233
sustentar 78
sustitución 261
sustituir 366, 367
sustraer 168, 344
suya
 hacer de las –s 197
 hacer de las –s 200
 ir a la – 200
 salirse con la – 200
suyo
 ir a lo – 200

tabacalera 287
tabique 160
tabla 32, 79
tablado 79
tablero 79
tablón 251
tabulación 280
tacaño 30
tachar 125
tacón 174
táctica 299
tajada 168
tajo 178
tal
 como si – 198
 con – (de) que 408
tal vez 406
talante 88
talar 125, 132
talento 88, 167
tallar 125
talón 174, 248
talonario 248
tampoco 371
tanto 440
 – ... como ... 240
 por lo – 240, 332
tapado 109
tapar 79
tapia 160
tapiar 79
tardar 7, 187, 367
tardar(se) 433
tarde

a la – 308
a media – 309
tarea 178
tarjeta
– de crédito 248, 261
– de débito 248
tarta 79
tasa 263
– real 251
tasador/-ora 34, 259, 263
tasajo 10
tasar 260
¡tate! 236
taxi
–s de sitio 17
tecla 278
teclado 278
teclear 278
técnico 47
tejido 28
tela 28
poner en – de juicio 185
tele 226
telefonazo, pegar un 5
teléfono
al – 312, 331
por – 312, 331
televisión
en la – 327, 331
por la – 327, 331
telón 192
tema 32, 52
temer 11, 338, 402
temer(se) 402
temor 345, 362
tempestad 79, 177
temporada 79
temporal 47, 79, 177, 267
tenaz 175
tender 341
tendido 418
tener + pp 382
tensión 47
tentar 343, 362
tercera
a la – va la vencida 202
terco 175
terminal 288
terminar 52, 346, 350, 362
terminar(se) 433
término 47
terremoto 286
terreno 79
sobre el – 200
territorial 263
terruño 79
tesoro 266

testarudo 175
testigo 271, 284, 288
testimoniar 271
tez 294
tía 5
tiempo 234
– récord 232
a – 309
a – completo/parcial 309
al mismo – 309
andando el – 200
El – es oro 253
tienda 175
tientas, a 311
tierra 79
tilde 234, 293
timar 139
timbre 263, 293
timo 255
tina 88
tinieblas 298
tinta 278
tiña 88
tío 5
tipo
– impositivo 264
–(s) de interés 250, 256
tira 107
– magnética 247
tirado, está 196
tirando
(voy) – 5
ir – 200
tirao, me voy 5
tirar 17, 132, 134, 154, 176, 367
tirarse (de cabeza) 176
tirita 6
tiro 107
a –s 311
Le salió el – por la culata 200
matar de un 134
pegar un – a 134
tirón, de un 322
titular 259
título 252
a – de 313
tiznado 172
tocante
en lo – a 313
tocar 337
todo
ante – 316
sobre – 333
togado 270
tomar 121
– prestado 184
tomar(se) 435

Tomás
una y no más, Santo – 202
tomate 293
tonelada 243
tóner 278
tónico 233
tonillo 193
tonto 177
a tontas y a locas 311
topar 137
toparse 367
tope 89
tópico 32
top-less 231
top-model 231
topo 89
torbellino 183
tormenta 101, 177
tormento 101
tornado 183
tornarse 124
tornillo, faltarle a uno un 200
torno
en – a 327
toro 10
torpe 177
torta 79
tortilla 79
tos 294
tostador/-ora 295
tra(n)scendencia 47
trabajo 178
– en serie 277
–s forzados 276
trabar 137
traducir 367
traer 153
traer(se) 435
traérselas 191
tragar
¡no trago! 236
trago, de un 322
trama 107, 285
tramitación 264
trámite 260
tramo 107, 252
trampa 140
tramposo 26
tranca 160
trancas
a – y barrancas 311
trance
en – de 327
transacción 18
transferencia 249
transformarse 124
transgresión 131

tránsito 52
transpirar 32
transportar 153
transportes 299
tranvía 285
trapicheos 299
tras 333–4
trasero 128
trasladar 153
traste
    dar al – con 200
    irse al – 200
trata 102
tratado 80
tratamiento 80
    – de textos 280
tratar 147, 362, 399
tratarse 187
trato 80, 102
traumático 260
través
    a – (de) 334, 369
trayecto 182
traza 107
trazo 107
trece
    mantenerse en sus – 203
    martes y – 203
trecho
    a –s 311
    de – en – 322
tremendo 142
tren ligero 17
trenca 109
trepar 171
tres
    – cuartos 108
    buscar – pies al gato 202
    dar – cuartos al pregonero 202
    donde Cristo dio las – voces 202
    ni a la de – 202
    no ver – en un burro 202
treta 139
tribu 294
tribunal 272
tributar 262
tributario 262, 263, 264, 265
trifulca 135
trinar 171
trino 171
triña 34
tripón 145
triquiñuela 140
triste 178, 402
tristón 178
triunfar 131
troche

a – y moche 311
trompa 47
trompicones, a 311
tronco 47
    dormir como un – 204
tropa(s) 299
tropel, en 327
tropezar 367
    – con 137
trozo 168
truco 139, 140
truculento 32
truncar 125
tú 14
tumbado 418
tuna 107
tunante 155
túnica, rasgarse la 200
tuno/a 107, 155
turbar 27
turco, cabeza de 200
turismo 47

ubicar 165
ufanarse 348
últimas, estar en las 200
ultimátum 297
último 353
    el – en 327
    por – 332
ultranza, a 311
unánime 353
underground 231
UNESCO 285
único 48, 304
unidad 278
unirse 366
uno
    – a – 309
urgente 395
urgir 190, 395
usado 183
usted 11
    a – 11, 13, 14
usurpar 114

vaca 83, 171
vacaciones 179, 266
vacante 294
vacilación 353
vacilar 353
vados 264
vago 48, 163
Valdemoro, estar entre Pinto y 199
vale 257
¡vale! 235
valer 190, 395

– la pena 337
valeroso 80, 180
valido 80
válido 80
valiente 52, 80, 180
valioso 80
valla 89
valle 89
valor 251, 252, 258
    – añadido 264
valorar 89
vanagloriarse 431
vanidoso 159
vano, en 327
vapulear 145
vaquero 299
vara 160, 246
variable 293
variar 349
varios 304
varita 160
vaso 180
vecino 367
    – de/a 323
vehículo 261
    – todo terreno 232
vejez 261, 268
vela 107
velar 364
vello 161
velo 107
vencer 131
vendaval 183
vender 27
    – se como churros / pan bendito
        204
vengarse 347
venir 343
    – a ser 124
    + ger 19
    + gerund 381
    ¡venga (venga)! 236
    ¡venga! 8
venir(se) 435
venta 254, 263
ventana 181, 278
ventanilla 181, 193, 247
ventrudo 145
ventura 174
    mala – 174
ver 181, 339, 362
    vamos a – 238
veras, de 322
verbena 28
verbo 234
verdad
    de – 322

no ser – 404
verdadero 23
verde 173
   a buenas horas mangas –s 201
   ponerle a uno – 201
   un chiste – 201
verdugo 275
veredicto 275
vergüenza 26
verificar 48
vérselas 191
verter 68
vertiente 122, 294
vestido de 321
vestiduras, rasgarse las 200
vestir 348
vestir(se) 68
veto 345
vetusto 183
vez
   a la – 309
   en – de 326
   una – que 411
viaje, de 182, 261, 322
víctima 283
vida, en mi 372
videojuegos 279
vidriera 181
vidrio 182
viejo 183
   – como el mundo 203
vientecillo 193
viento 183
   contra – y marea 200
vigía 291
vigoroso 143
vino
   llamar al pan pan y al – – 198

violento 48
virtud
   en – de 327
visionar 32
visita, de 322
vislumbrar 89, 181
vísperas
   en – de 299
vista 273
   a – de pájaro 311
   a primera – 309
   con –s a 317
   de – 321
   fijar la – (en) 182
   la – gorda 200
   saltar a la – 199
   testigo de – 271
vistazo, echar un 182
visto, por lo 332
visualización 278
visualizar 278
vitrina 181
vivienda 261, 267, 268, 269
   crédito – 250
   cuenta – 248
vivir 348
vivo, en 327
vizcachera 10
vocal 233, 284, 292
voluntad 349
   hacer su santa 200
voluntad
   tener 351
volver 94, 187, 369
   – en sí 200
   – la cara 138
volverse 124
votación 80

votar 350, 364
voto 80
voz
   a – en cuello/grito 311
   en – alta/baja 327
¡vuélale! 6
vuelta 182, 255
   dar la – 189, 201
   dar la – a 368
   dar –s a algo 201
   dar una – 200
vuelto 255
vulgar 117

web 231

ya, que 240
yacimientos 254
yarda 242
yema 285

zafarse 347
zafio 117
zaga, ir/quedar a la 201
zagal(a) 157
zambullirse (de cabeza) 176
zancadillas
   ponerle – a uno 201
zarpar 130
zarzal 293
zona 52
   – euro 232
zoom 231
zorro 10
zumbar 170
zumbido 170
zurrar 144